Hoche · Anthropological Complementarism

D1731439

Hans-Ulrich Hoche

Anthropological Complementarism

Linguistic, Logical, and Phenomenological
Studies in Support of A Third Way
Beyond Dualism and Monism

mentis
PADERBORN

Gedruckt mit Unterstützung des Förderungs- und Beihilfefonds Wissenschaft der VG Wort.

Bibliografische Information Der Deutschen Nationalbibliothek

Die Deutsche Nationalbibliothek verzeichnet diese Publikation
in der Deutschen Nationalbibliografie; detaillierte
bibliografische Daten sind im Internet über
http://dnb.d-nb.de abrufbar.

Gedruckt auf umweltfreundlichem, chlorfrei gebleichtem
und alterungsbeständigem Papier ⊚ ISO 9706

© 2008 mentis Verlag GmbH
Schulze-Delitzsch-Straße 19, D-33100 Paderborn
www.mentis.de

Printed in Germany
Einbandgestaltung: Anna Braungart, Tübingen
Satz: Rhema – Tim Doherty, Münster [ChH] (www.rhema-verlag.de)
Druck: AZ Druck und Datentechnik GmbH, Kempten
ISBN 978-3-89785-612-7

CONTENTS

PREFACE

There are some *subjective* reasons for my submitting the following essays in English rather than in my mother-tongue, German; but these are certainly of no interest to the reader. However, the following three *objective* reasons can and should be substantiated.[1]

First, as compared with the single-minded but in my view often somewhat shallow root positions of contemporary 'neurophilosophy',[2] there is a recent consciousness theory, put forward by the London psychologist Max Velmans, which seemed to me to be highly promising when I came across it in the nineties. It took me some time to find out that Velmans's use of several crucial terms of his theory is not only different from, but downright incompatible with, my own use of these technical terms. Hence to a great extent the following considerations are tacitly directed towards, and even against, Max Velmans; and the fifth of my essays is a frontal discussion of his 'reflexive theory' of perception in particular and of consciousness at large. So it was certainly advisable for me to use the language of Velmans's numerous publications, and the more so as they have received much attention.

Of course I am well aware that philosophical thoughts are sometimes so fine-grained and subtle that one may rightly doubt whether it is possible to render them, in the full wealth of all their nuances, in a language other than one's native vernacular. This is particularly notorious from the writings of such 'deep', 'dark', and 'pensive' German thinkers as Hegel and Heidegger, whose translations into, say, English or Japanese have driven a lot of translators and readers alike to despair.

However, it is precisely this observation which supplied me with a second cogent reason for thinking and writing in the foreign language I have the best command of, which happens to be English. For I have found out that trying to express philosophical thoughts in a foreign language naturally has a very wholesome effect. The *conceptual content* of an abstract discourse or argument certainly tends to gain a much greater clarity, even to its author himself, if it is given more than only a single *linguistic realisation*. Of course this may also be done within

---

[1] Let me pass over the well-known fact that English has taken the role of *the* international language of science that, in the Middle Ages, was played by Latin and, from the 19th century up to the rise of National Socialism, by German. Of course, the habit of publishing scientific and philosophical texts in English *indiscriminately* does not go undisputed. A well-considered plea for using one's own native tongue has recently been presented by Ralph Mocikat: 'Ein Plädoyer für die Vielfalt. Die Wissenschaftssprache am Beispiel der Biomedizin' ['A plea for diversity. The language of science, exemplified by the biomedical sciences'], in the monthly *Forschung & Lehre* (Bonn, Germany), February 2007, 90–92.

[2] Far from being intended to be abusive, this term has been brought into currency by some of the *defenders* of this fashionable style of doing philosophy.

one and the same language; but using two, or more, different languages has the additional clarifying effect that the author is compelled to look upon the same conceptual content from a much more unfamiliar, and possibly 'outlandish', linguistic angle. Perhaps one may even go as far as saying that a philosopher morally owes it to his readers not to submit to them any expositions he couldn't likewise express in another language he sufficiently masters.

Third, I cannot deny that I should like to submit the following essays to as many philosophical specialists as possible, notably in the fields commonly known today as 'linguistic philosophy' and 'the philosophy of mind and action'. But doubtless the great majority of these specialists are either English native speakers or philosophers working in, or coming from, non-anglophone countries who themselves prefer to publish in English. So I am confident that I have chosen the language best suited for my purpose, even though I and my readers have to put up with the fact that the idiomatic shortcomings of my personal use of English can hardly remain hidden from the critical eyes of a native 'speaker-reader' – a fact which nonetheless, I hope, is more than compensated by my having been constantly forced to render in a foreign language, and thus to make more lucid to myself, what I formerly used to think and say in German. This is particularly true of the considerations in the fourth and fifth of the following essays, which in part have to do with Husserl's 'transcendental phenomenology' – a subtle, not easily accessible, often somewhat idiosyncratically phrased, and hence frequently misinterpreted and misrepresented form of consciousness theory, which, in the last decades, many philosophers of mind and psychologists have simply ignored, if not considered outdated.

In view of the fact that I have chosen to publish the following essays in English, some readers may find it inconsistent that in my bibliographical notes I refer not only to English but also to German (and in a couple of cases: French) sources. But, apart from my hope that this booklet will also find a few readers sufficiently conversant with German, it ought to be noted that I endeavoured to make each of the following essays as much self-contained as possible so the reader need not follow the bibliographical references in order to simply understand what is being said. Rather, these references are supposed to acknowledge the relevant contributions of others or to hint at convenient ways of deepening the issues at hand. The latter is especially true in the case of self-references, of which I had to make ample use as I have been long since in considered opposition to contemporary mainstream philosophy, many of whose silent or rarely challenged *presuppositions* I cannot share, from which it follows that I often had to draw on the results of my own former research, which, of course, I couldn't include at full length in the present essays.[3]

---

[3] Let me add that I, unlike many others, am a strong believer in cross-referencing; for apart from parsimony, I often find it extremely illuminating to compare an author's different wordings relating to the same topic.

Let me add a note on the subtitle of this book. I chose to speak of a third way, not between, but *beyond* the alternatives of monistic and dualistic positions with respect to the mind-body problem in particular and philosophical anthropology, or the philosophy of man, at large. The reason is that a third way *between* two extreme positions might be easily taken to be a compromise, or a 'synthesis' mediating dialectically between a 'thesis' and an 'antithesis'. But I attach great importance to stating in advance that such a connotation would be highly misleading in the present case.

I take the opportunity to thank Professor Max Velmans, University of London, for having been kind enough to comment upon the fifth of the following essays and to reply in print to a shortened and considerably altered successor version thereof, which has been published together with Velmans's paper.[4] Likewise, I have to thank a number of other experts in different fields, among them, in alphabetical order, Professor Dr. Jochen Fahrenberg (psychology), University of Freiburg, Germany; Dr. Øystein Linnebo (philosophy), University of Bristol, England; Dr. Dr. Heiner Schwenke (philosophy and theoretical botany), Basel, Switzerland; and Dr. Jane F. Utting (physics), RWTH Aachen, Germany. Furthermore, I am grateful to the participants – mostly colleagues or pupils of mine – of the *Logisch-sprachanalytisches Kolloquium* (Logico-Linguistic Colloquy) held, since many years, at the Institute of Philosophy, Ruhr-Universität Bochum, Germany. Earlier versions of most of the essays incorporated in the present book have been thoroughly debated in this discussion circle, and I owe a lot of valuable commentaries and hints to all of its members, notably (again in alphabetical order) to Privatdozent Dr. Friedrich Dudda; Dr. Tania Eden; Professor Dr. Alexander Kleinlogel; Tobias Knobloch; Michael Knoop; and Professor Dr. Ulrich Pardey. To my daughter Dr. Susanne Hoche, University of Bristol, I am indebted for encouragement and some valuable remarks concerning matters logical and linguistic; to my new publisher, Dr. Michael Kienecker, Paderborn, for having willingly accepted this booklet for publication, and for a publication in English at that; to the VG WORT, Munich, for having awarded me a printing cost grant; and, once again, to my colleague Ulrich Pardey for having essentially contributed to this outcome by carefully reading the complete manuscript and commenting on it in writing. Last, not least in love, I should like to express my deep gratitude to my wife, who has shared my life with me for already more than half a century, and 'sine qua non'.

Hattingen (Ruhr), Germany,
May 10, 2008   Hans-Ulrich Hoche

---

[4] See Velmans 2007; Hoche 2007.

ANALYTICAL TABLE OF CONTENTS

INTRODUCTION

1. The aims of this book in a nutshell

The present collection of essays,[1] most of which have been written within the very last years, aims at founding a novel stance concerning that aspect of the time-honoured 'mind-body' problem which has to do with the relationship between *subjectively experienced consciousness* and *objectively observable occurrences in the central nervous system* ('consciousness-brain' problem). Although, from the times of ancient Greek philosophy up to the fashionable though dubious 'neurophilosophical' approaches of our days, this problem has found innumerable answers, *most* of them – and, as far as I can see, *all* of them that are presently being discussed by mainstream philosophers, psychologists, physiologists, neurobiologists, and other empirical scientists – may be roughly subsumed under the well-known generic labels of either *'dualism'* or *'monism'*.

Objecting at the same time to *both* of these overall positions – all variants of which, I think, may gain whatever little appearance of acceptability they own at all mostly in the light of the obvious shortcomings of their respective opposites –, I am going to suggest trying out a *'third way' beyond monism and dualism*, which I propose to call *'complementaristic'* in much the sense of Niels Bohr's.[2]

---

[1] Let me stress from the very beginning that the present booklet is intended to be, not a homogeneous monograph subdivided into a series of consecutive 'chapters', but a mere collection of 'essays' concerning related problems. This is to say, *inter alia*, that the single essays are as self-sufficient as possible, from which it follows that a small handful of passages will have to be repeated. In my eyes, this disadvantage is clearly outweighed by the advantage that they may be read in an arbitrary order. Cross-references will make it plain on every relevant occasion where to look for pertinent details and further information.

[2] In point of historical fact it ought to be noted that Niels Bohr and Werner Heisenberg seem to have elaborated the conception of complementarity in close co-operation. Let me summarise a passage, and translate a few sentences, from Heisenberg's reminiscences of Bohr in the years 1922 to 1927. Near the end of February, 1927, after one of his frequent late evening discussions with Bohr, Heisenberg went for a lonely walk in the Fälledpark behind Bohr's institute in Copenhagen. 'On this walk under the starry sky of the night it occurred to me, plausibly enough, that perhaps one might simply postulate that nature admits of only such experimental situations that can also be described within the mathematical scheme of quantum mechanics. As one could infer from the mathematical formalism, this means that apparently *one cannot accurately know the position and the velocity of a particle at the same time*.' But before Heisenberg could communicate this *indeterminacy principle* of his to Bohr, the latter left for a longer ski holiday to Norway, where he 'seems to have sketched the *concept of complementarity*, which was to make it possible to *render the dualism between the wave and the particle images the point of departure of the interpretation*. This concept of complementarity agreed exactly with the basic philosophical attitude he had practically always adopted and in which

2. Against a watered-down conception of complementarity

To be sure, current *'two-aspect theories'*, notably the one recently worked out by the London psychologist Max Velmans,[3] often claim to be of a 'complementaristic' character, too. However, to the best of my knowledge all contemporary consciousness-brain theories posing as 'complementaristic' more or less silently assume the existence of some entity, say a 'psychophysical mind',[4] which, being *one and the same* 'Je-ne-sais-quoi' or, speaking more down-to-earth, 'I dunno what', can be accessed in *two* 'complementary' modes which, though being in a way mutually exclusive, have to complement each other in order for there to be a comprehensive or all-around view of the matter in hand. So I take it that they are but variants or combinations of monistic and dualistic positions. This is testified conspicuously enough by Max Velmans himself, who characterises his 'complementaristic' two-aspect theory of consciousness as 'a form of nonreductionist monism (ontological monism combined with epistemological dualism)'.[5]

In the following essays, I am going to try and show, not only why I am loath to speak of *one and the same* psychophysical entity which is alleged to be accessible in *two* complementary ways, but also that we are not justified in believing that, with respect to any given subjective conscious experience and any seemingly 'corresponding' or 'correlated' neural event, we have but the choice of taking them to be either *one and the same* entity or else *two numerically different* ones.

3. Linguistic and logical problems of identity and non-identity

Now at first sight this may seem strange indeed. For if we have an entity *a* and an entity *b*, and if *a* and *b* are not *one and the same* entity, mustn't they needs be *two different* ones? But a closer look easily shows us that this is by no means

---

the shortcomings of our means of expression are considered a central philosophical problem. So he was disturbed by the fact that I did not want to start from the dualism between waves and particles. But after some weeks of discussion, which were not altogether free from tensions, we soon realised, in particular also thanks to the co-operation of Oskar Klein, that *basically we meant the same thing* and that also *the indeterminacy relation was but a special case of that more general complementarity*' (translated from Heisenberg 1964: pp. 66f.; all italics mine). – It should be added that most of the important literature concerning Bohr's concept of complementarity, as far as I have become acquainted with it, is of practically no relevance to the development of my conception of *psychophysical complementarity* in particular and *anthropological complementarity* in general. Hence I will abstain from quoting this or that well-known book or article from the fields of the history and the philosophy of science which some readers might miss.

[3] See esp. Velmans 1990, 2000.

[4] Velmans 2000: p. 251.

[5] Ibid.: p. 281 n. 5; cf. pp. 233, 249, 254.

invariably the case. For although it has been made evident by prominent possible-worlds theorists that we have to assume an 'intermundane' or 'trans-word' numerical identity or else numerical non-identity between any two 'inhabitants' of two *counterfactually possible worlds*' (variants of the real world, or of any world considered in a certain context to be real),[6] this is certainly not true of the 'inhabitants' of any two disconnected *'fictionally possible worlds*' (isolated worlds of fiction, say of novels or fairy tales). It is considerably less easy, however, to see that this somewhat trivial case is not the only example in which the supposedly exclusive alternative of being either *one and the same* thing or else *two different* things breaks down. Rather, in order to convince ourselves of the logical or 'depth-grammatical' fact that there are a great many other cases exemplifying this consequential phenomenon – for instance, that a person and a natural number, or a neural event and a conscious experience, cannot properly be said to coincide or differ *numerically* –, we have to unearth the hidden logical structure of ordinary-language identity statements and their denegations.

So the logico-linguistic propaedeutic offered in the first three of the following papers, written in 2005–2006, should be considered an integral part of the studies on consciousness presented in the present book. In the first essay – *Hare's Two Definitions of 'Entailment' and the Generic Relation of 'Linguistic Implication'* – I will gradually work out a fundamental relation which I take to be the basis of a sound and sober research into the multifarious 'linguistic implications' obtaining between fully interpreted sentences (or, in precisely this sense: 'propositions') of ordinary language. In the second essay – *Five Kinds of Linguistic Implication* – I will develop criteria for splitting up this highly generic relation into three subrelations ('semantic implication', 'pragmatic implication', and 'catapragmatic implication') and two sub-subrelations ('semantic presupposition' and 'catapragmatic presupposition'). The application of some of these criteria I take to be highly effective tools for doing what has been called 'linguistic analysis', i.e., conceptual analysis carried out in a linguistic key. Whereas the concepts of semantic and pragmatic implication, and the criteria necessary for telling them apart, play a major role in, say, the development of analytical metaethics in the wake of Richard M. Hare's 'universal prescriptivism',[7] in our present context it is mainly *semantic presupposition* that we have to focus our interest upon. For in the third essay – *Identity Statements and Nonsense* – I will have to draw, inter alia, on Bertrand Russell's analysis of 'definite descriptions' and identity statements containing such individual constants; and since Peter F. Strawson's early writings it has been a frequently repeated objection against this analysis that it fails to do justice to the difference between entailment ('logical implication') and the intricate and multiform linguistic phenomenon commonly called 'presupposition'. In fact I think we are justified

---

[6] *Loci classici* are Kripke 1971, 1972.

[7] See esp. Hare 1952, 1963, 1981; Hoche 1992, 1995d, 1995e, 2001, 2004; Dudda 1999.

in accepting Russell's analysis only on condition we can prove that the relevant form of presupposition, which I suggest to call *semantic* presupposition, is but a special case – or a subrelation – of that particular form of entailment which I will call, not just *logical*, but *semantic* implication; and the first two of the following essays serve precisely the purpose of making this as plain as possible.

4. A 'noematic' approach to consciousness

Whereas the first three of the following essays, though admitting of an illuminating *application* to the consciousness-brain problem, in themselves are of a much wider philosophical interest, the fourth one – *Consciousness*, the first draft of which dates back to 1998 – addresses the central topic of the present book, 'anthropological complementarism', in a most straightforward way. Prompted by my having become acquainted with Max Velmans's 'reflexive model' of consciousness, which at first sight looks highly promising indeed but on closer inspection looses its attractiveness rapidly, this paper tries to clarify the salient features of *subjectively experienced* consciousness – that is, of *my own* consciousness as it presents itself *to myself* in what nowadays is usually called the 'first-person perspective' – in a direct (though largely exemplary) way. For intrinsic reasons, the favourite among my examples is sense perception, especially *visual perception* or *seeing*. I will suggest that the alleged 'psychical *event*' of my seeing a given material object (say, a dog approaching me) should be considered to be, not some 'process' or 'happening' being performed on either a physiological or else a psychical 'inner stage',[8] but what, for the sake of accuracy (though doubtless a bit circumstantially), might be called 'the object (say, the dog) *as*, *qua*, or *in its capacity of*, being seen by me at the given moment of time and in the given mode of visually appearing to me'.

At first sight, this replacement may certainly seem to be a revealing specimen of a philosophical hair-splitting in general and an *obscurum per obscurius* in particular. I am confident, however, that at least the more benevolent among my readers will convince themselves in due course that it would be philosophically short-sighted to suppose so. Not the least advantage of this replacement seems to me to be the fact that attending to physical objects out in the world and attending to psychical events allegedly going on, in one way or another, 'within' myself cannot be shown once for all to be mutually exclusive. After all, if we can easily see a visual object and hear an auditory object at the same time, or can both see and hear a blackbird on the top of the roof simultaneously, why in the world shouldn't we be able to perceive a bodily object and to experience a mental event at the same time, too? If we keep in mind, however, that we cannot simultaneously *perform* the abstraction

---

[8] Cf. Ryle 1949: *passim*.

leading us to physical objects *themselves* and *undo* this very same abstraction, which leads us to the objects *qua being given* to each of us[9], the incompatibility between the physical world and my own consciousness as experienced by myself can hardly escape our attention.

Furthermore, suggesting a substitution of noematic phenomena for noetic ones may at first sight seem to be strikingly similar to Velmans's claim that there is no 'phenomenological difference' between, say, 'seeing the cat' and 'the cat seen [as seen; as-seen]'. In fact it was for precisely this reason that I found it worth while scrutinising the most pertinent of Velmans's publications, and working out a detailed evaluation and criticism of his position.[10] But in so doing I couldn't fail to realise that Velmans's 'object (as) perceived' in a way may be well compared to *Kant*'s notion of a '(transcendental) phenomenon' – Velmans repeatedly points to this fact himself –, whereas my 'object *as [qua]* perceived by me' should be rather compared to a '(noematic) phenomenon' in very much the *Husserlian* sense – which is something completely different (though much less known, and hence much less esteemed, in contemporary philosophy).

5. A plea for a pure noematics

It should be noted, however, that Husserl's concept of a noematic phenomenon, which is embedded in the complicated framework of his 'transcendental phenomenology', is just as little the point of *departure* of my considerations as is Kant's concept of transcendental phenomena for Velmans's theory. Rather, it is the point of a remarkable *convergence*. Besides, there are at least the following two major differences between Husserl's noematic phenomenon and my object *as [qua; in its capacity of being]* perceived by, or otherwise given to, me.

First, whereas Husserl's conception of a noematic phenomenon is intimately connected with his fundamental and exacting method of 'transcendental reduction', the conception of an 'object *as [qua]* perceived by myself', which I will take pains to work out and defend in the fourth essay, is based on a set of relatively simple considerations. This is not to say, however, that I want to belittle transcendental reduction; on the contrary, unlike most contemporary philosophers, including many phenomenologists, I consider it one of the most important achievements of 20th century philosophical thinking. However, I take it that it is by far not as dark and enigmatic as it is mostly thought to be, but rather appears

---

[9] See esp. sections 6 and 8, below.

[10] See Essay V of the present collection, and Hoche 2007. The latter is a considerably shortened and modified version of the former – in fact: a somewhat unsatisfying compromise between my intentions and the editor's idiosyncratic wishes – and has been commented upon in Velmans 2007.

to be a matter of course if only we adopt an unbiased attitude towards what we use to call 'consciousness'.

Second, whereas for Husserl – arguably with the only exception of his latest work[11] – the 'noematic' phenomena are strictly paralleled with 'noetic' phenomena, I think we ought to be tough-minded enough to radically dispose of the latter once the former have been discovered, or brought into view. This discovery will, I think, always remain Husserl's greatest achievement. But, with the reservation just mentioned, he seems to have hesitated to decidedly give up the 'noetic' or, if you will, the *strictly 'processual'* side of my own conscious experiences. Methodologically, however, doing away with the latter would simply be an obvious application of the basic parsimony principle of shunning 'distinctions without a difference' ('Occam's Razor'), or of Frege's noteworthy admonition to *make* distinctions wherever there *are* differences and to be careful to *make none* where there *are none*.[12] To be sure, a dyed-in-the-wool phenomenologist may find it repugnant if not illogical to speak of a 'noema' unless it is thought to be the counterpart of a 'noesis'. But even if this were a cogent objection (which I think it is not) we would be free to give up the words 'noema' and 'noematical phenomenon' as technical terms. In any case these expressions seem to me to be useful by way of a Wittgensteinian 'ladder', which can and must be thrown away after it has served its heuristic purpose.[13] Hence, in characterising *my own* conscious experiences, insofar as they present themselves to *myself*, as being through and through 'noematic', what I intend to convey is no more and no less than the idea that conscious 'events' in the 'first-person perspective' should be considered to be, not mysterious or hidden 'goings-on', 'events', or 'processes' taking place on an 'inner stage', but incessantly changing and transient objects *qua being perceived* (or feared, desired, despised, acted upon, etc., as the case may be) *by myself* – objects which in a way are 'out in the world', though certainly not in the much better known, if not familiar, way *physical* objects are 'out in the world'.

6. My own consciousness as experienced by myself is not a part of nature

Conscious phenomena in this sense cannot come into view unless we deliberately cancel or undo an involuntary abstraction which, since our earliest childhood, has become our second nature. There are compelling reasons for performing this abstraction; for unless we exclusively attended to the physical objects *themselves*,

---

[11] Husserl 1934–1937; see Hoche 1973a: Part I.

[12] See Frege 1897: p. 154; 1899: pp. VI, 17.

[13] See Wittgenstein 1922: 6.54.

irrespective of their constantly varying modes of appearing or being given to myself and (I daresay) each of us, we couldn't help being downright drowned in a chaos of ever-changing 'phenomena' which are not even capable of being neatly separated from one another, not to speak of being given discriminative names. The cancellation of that vital and most natural abstraction, which in my eyes is one of the main conditions for being able to cope with the world at all, has usually been interpreted as a 'reflection' – although the word 'deflection' might have been a better term for this change of attitude, which is a deviation from our normal way of looking on the world without, however, being something like a 'bending *back*'. Nonetheless I think we may safely call it a 'reflexive' attitude provided we see to it that what we and our hearers have in mind is neither the 'introspection' or 'inspection' of many classical philosophers and psychologists nor Husserl's 'noetic reflection' but rather something closely akin to what Husserl sometimes called 'noematic reflection'.

In its capacity of being the deliberate cancellation of an habitual abstraction, this reflective or 'deflective' attitude may be aptly considered to be the uphill restitution of the full concreteness of what is originally given to each of us. So while adopting this attitude I cannot help loosing sight of the physical *objects themselves* out in the world. Furthermore, whereas these *objects themselves* are given to me through the mediation of suitable continua of *objects qua being experienced* by myself, the latter are given to me in the most immediate way possible at all; for the existence of an object qua being experienced by myself may, and should, be taken to be nothing over and above its being experienced by myself.[14] As these two ways of being 'get-at-able' not only *differ* from each other in the most profound way to be conceived of but, what is more, are strictly *incompatible* with each other, it would be a misguided and misguiding though doubtless deeply ingrained and widespread prejudice to regard (the contents of) *my own* consciousness[15] as part(s) of the 'world', or of 'nature'. With much more justification, we may downright consider them the very 'negative' of nature.[16]

By the way: If consciousness as it is experienced by the conscious subject herself or himself were really a part of nature, then, I take it, we would be confronted with grave ontological and epistemological questions apt to open the floodgates to obscurantism. For instance, in this case we could hardly avoid asking ourselves at what moment in time during the development of the individual embryo or foetus

---

[14] In this restricted and well-defined sense we may exhume the slogan, dating from Berkeley, 'esse est percipi'.

[15] Unless otherwise indicated, by 'consciousness' I always understand, not the *objectified* consciousness of others as it presents itself to me, but *truly subjective* consciousness, i.e., *my* consciousness as it presents itself to *myself*, or as it is *experienced by myself* ('consciousness in the first-person perspective').

[16] See Hoche 1986: esp. 1.3, 3.6, and Essay IV: esp. 3.11, 3.18, of the present collection.

subjective consciousness becomes part of the living organism – provided it is not part and parcel of organic, or even inorganic, matter from the outset; and suchlike questions have in fact been raised in discussions of the moral problems of abortion, pre-implantation diagnostics, or stem cell research. Furthermore, if subjective experience as such were also an appropriate topic of objective science, i.e., of research carried out in the third-person perspective, then not only biologists but even chemists and physicists engaged in basic research would be compelled either to take it into account explicitly or else to consciously and methodically suppress it. Hence I think we may conclude that, if contemporary mainstream philosophers of mind tend to consider 'conscious events' as properties of something material, preferably the brain (which in fact they do), and if they do not face the foregoing questions (which they do not even think of doing), then, unwittingly or not, as a matter of fact they ignore the central feature of subjective conscious experience, which amounts to denying, or at least gravely distorting, it. The same is true when ethologists and others assure us that, 'with the utmost probability', not only humans but also non-human primates, dogs, etc. are endued with subjective experiences. For outside the field of what can be investigated from the third-person point of view, the conception of 'probability' (and the related conception of an empirical 'hypothesis') is certainly out of place.

7. The major ontological tenets of mine

To be sure, this view crucially depends on my personal ontological tenets, which therefore I ought to render as explicit as it is possible in a few words.

First, I cannot help following Kant and those post-Kantian philosophers who firmly believe that human philosophising – which is the only sort of philosophising we know of – must be done, not from some God's point of view, but from a human point of view.

Second, I cannot help following Husserl who counts the essential mode of an object's being *cognitively* accessible to us among the basic *ontological* features of an object of the sort in question; for simply abstracting from, or making light of, this inalienable way of coming to know an object of a given sort would surely amount to falling back behind Kantian standards. So I should like to suggest to follow Husserl in adopting a thoroughgoing parallelism between *types of objects* and *types of coming to know, or experiencing, objects.*[17]

Third, it should be added that, in the last resort, the cognitive access to an object is not some *human* access at large but *my own* particular access. For any mediated knowledge, useful and indispensable though it certainly is, would be

---

[17] Cf. esp. Husserl 1913, tr. 1931: §§ 3, 138, 142.

null and void if I were *principally* deprived of the possibility of obtaining it myself in a direct way.

Hence I think it reasonable to believe that an object I can *possibly speak about* is *eo ipso* an object I can *in principle know about*, and that *the way I could possibly obtain immediate knowledge of an object of a given type belongs to the essential ontological properties of an object of this type, or to the essential characteristics of the corresponding concept.*

8. Complementarism proper

So I take it that there is an unbridgeable gulf between *my own* conscious experience as it is given to *myself* on the one hand and everything else on the other, including the consciousness of my fellow-men (and other higher animals) as it is given to *me*, or my consciousness as it is given to *them*, or my body as it is given to *others*, or *someone else's* body as it is given to *me*; and since it is impossible to occupy both sides of this gulf at the same time, a specific form of an anthropological *complementarism* is the inevitable result of this view.

However, as either side of this unbridgeable gulf disappears as soon as the other one comes into view, we ought not to speak of *one and the same* object which is alleged to be given partly in the first-person and partly in the third-person perspective and which, in precisely this sense, has two sides or aspects. Remarkably enough, even such a keen thinker as Max Planck turned out to be quite inconsistent in this respect. On the one hand, he sharp-sightedly anticipated what I take to be the basic creed of *complementarism proper*: '[…] it is not possible to immediately overlook both the bodily and the mental occurrences from a unified point of view; and as we cannot come to a clear result unless we cling to the point of view we have chosen, which, however, is incompatible with the other one, *the question of how bodily and mental occurrences are connected to each other becomes meaningless. If so, there are either bodily occurrences or mental occurrences, but never both of them at the same time.*[18] For this reason' – and here, I think, Planck fell a victim to a consequential inconsistency; he seems to simply have been backsliding to an old-fashioned dual-aspect theory à la Spinoza – 'there is nothing in the way to saying: *Bodily and mental occurrences* do not at all differ from each other. They *are the very same occurrences, only looked at from two opposing sides.*'[19]

---

[18] Perhaps, this wording reminds the reader, as it reminds me, of a famous dictum of Epicurus which in a way may be taken to foreshadow the fundamental conception of complementarism: 'Death is nothing to us, since *when we are, death has not come, and when death has come, we are not*' (Letter to Menoikeus, in: Diogenes Laertius, 2nd vol., X.125).

[19] Translated from Planck 1946: sect. II, p. 357; my italics.

If we are intent on avoiding this inconsistency, we must be alive to the fact that, at any given moment in time, any conscious person whatsoever has to do with *either this side or that side* of the gulf that separates the 'objective' and the 'subjective' – i.e., with either 'objective' *objects themselves* or 'subjective' *objects qua being experienced* by the given cognitive subject in the given cognitive situation. Hence assuming a 'unity', a 'connection', or any other *real* (that is, neither intentional nor conceptual) relation between what belongs to nature and what belongs to consciousness presupposes adopting the – in my view: outdated and in fact untenable – position of philosophising, not from a *human* and, what is more, from *my own* point of view, but from a point of view allegedly outside the phenomenal world accessible to us, namely, from the point of view of an omniscient God. So I think it simply doesn't become a post-Kantian and post-Husserlian philosopher to assume a *real* relation between the subjective and the objective, between consciousness and the physical world. Some such real relation, however (say, 'connection', 'unity', 'identity', 'numerical difference', and so on), is required for all monistic as well as dualistic solutions to the mind-body problem – and likewise to the problem of how my consciousness *for myself* and my consciousness *for my fellow-men* are conceptually related to one another. Therefore I cannot see a truly respectable alternative for defending a *complementaristic solution* to these problems which – far from being a 'dual-aspect' theory in the sense of, say, Spinoza's or Velmans's, which would require the assumption of one and the same entity presenting two numerically different sides, faces, or aspects – assumes the existence of two perspectives which nonetheless are perspectives on neither one and the same entity nor two numerically different entities.[20]

9. Suitable and unsuitable methods in philosophy

Let me finally turn to the *methods* which I have tried to apply to the problems dealt with in the following essays. Since most of these problems are *genuine philosophical problems*, I have mostly used *genuine philosophical methods*. This might seem to be a matter of course, and my remark to be 'not remarkable' (Searle) and hence a speech-act theoretical 'infelicity' (Austin). However, a closer look at the contemporary mainstream research work on consciousness theory and the mind-body problem teaches us that this is by no means the case. For we may surely say that the bulk of what has been done by the leading research workers in these fields is characterised by the marked tendency to shy away from *genuine philosophical methods* and to adopt, adapt, and even imitate instead those

---

[20] It is precisely because the latter claim is likely to seem most unintelligible at first sight that I thought it advisable to include in this booklet the logico-linguistic propaedeutic worked out in detail in the first three essays.

methods they believe to have proven decisive for the striking success of modern science, which is concerned with the *objective world*.

In taking up this stance, however, they often seem to lose sight of the fact that the methods which, in the early 20th century, led to the development of the relativity theories, quantum and wave mechanics, etc., may in a way be taken to have given proper heed to the role of *subjectivity* in coming to know *objectivity*. Similarly, Jakob von Uexküll's (1909) research into the *subjective* spatio-temporal worlds (German: 'Umwelten') of non-human animals, though it surely failed to bring about as much as a 'paradigm shift' in theoretical biology, at least opened up a rewarding pathway for novel research. Furthermore, in spite of the fact that modern science is doubtless a science of *objectivity* and that its methods are, and have to be, basically *objective*, i.e., adequate for research work done from the *third*-person perspective, this is not the whole story. As Heiner Schwenke, who formerly was himself engaged in biological research, convincingly worked out, 'acceptance of some methodological principles which seem to be generally acknowledged among scientists is irreconcilable with naturalism, i.e. the view that science can in principle investigate all facts. [...] On the basis of these principles, [he argues] *ex suppositione* that both the scientific discourse and the testing of theories by data would be blocked if one tried to investigate all facts scientifically. [...] non-scientific knowledge is not only a precondition of gaining scientific knowledge but [...] also the building material of which scientific knowledge is constructed.'[21] So in more than one respect subjective traits seem to me to make themselves felt within the objective sciences themselves; only they often go unheeded.

For these reasons we should not find it surprising that a methodologically reflected inquiry into consciousness has to be largely[22] a study of *subjectivity* and hence as a rule must be carried out by means of methods suitable, not for the third-person, but for the *first*-person perspective. I think we cannot take seriously enough what Thomas Nagel once said in a slightly different connection: 'It happens again and again that the methods of one subject are taken as a model of intellectual respectability or objective rationality, and are then applied to a quite different subject for which they were not developed and for which they are unsuited. The results are shallow questions, nonexplanatory theories, and the anathematization of important questions as meaningless.'[23]

It is true that inquiries into what is given to us from each one's personal *first*-person perspective, and hence also the methods pertaining to such inquiries, have lately fallen into deep disrepute. Not for the least part, I think, this has happened

---

[21] Schwenke 2005, from the English 'Summary'; see also Schwenke 1992.

[22] Only research into the consciousness of *others* has to be carried out in the *third*-person perspective and hence requires *objective* methods which can, and indeed should, heavily draw on the methods successful in modern science.

[23] Nagel 1978: p. 145.

on the ground of what seems to me to be a misinterpretation of highly influential passages from Wittgenstein's and Ryle's.[24] Ironically, however, precisely the latter two philosophers have been leading figures in the development of quite novel and, if properly applied,[25] efficacious methods which in my eyes may be considered *genuine philosophical ones*. What I have in mind are, of course, the specific methods of *analytic* or *linguistic philosophy*.[26]

10. How to determine the methods suitable for philosophical inquiries

That these methods are not particularistic or provincial but relevant to philosophy as such may be recognised if we ask ourselves what the defining characteristics of philosophy at bottom are. To be sure, the search for a state-of-the-art *definition* of philosophy has proven hopeless. However, I think we may safely say that in point of fact we tend to use the concept of philosophy as a mere 'residual concept', i.e., to regard as 'philosophical' all and only those problems which, in more than two millennia, haven't succeeded yet in being dealt with by one or other of the more or less well-defined humanities and sciences which have, as it were, successively crystallised out from the mother lye of what in Greek antiquity was called 'philosophía' in the very broad sense of a striving, not just for 'wisdom', but for knowledge of whatever kind.[27]

---

[24] See my criticism of this misinterpretation in Hoche & Strube 1985: A.V–VI.

[25] In fact, it strikes me that such methods, if used by present-day philosophers at all, are often applied suboptimally or worse. Obviously, putting them to philosophical work in an adequate and fruitful way is a skill that requires not only a fine linguistic sensitiveness but also intensive training.

[26] I am well aware of the fact that, in the presence of 'leading' younger consciousness theorists, analytic philosophers of my generation are expected to apologise for not having been able yet to overcome the 'linguistic phase' of 'analytic philosophy' (see, e.g., Bieri 1981: pp. 13, 17). I should like to counter the charge of such inability by essentially two arguments. First, if we are to consider philosophy done 'in a linguistic key' to be but an early and immature phase of 'analytic philosophy' proper, it is not at all evident to me how to characterise the latter methodologically in a way that would justify the label 'analytic' (cf. Hoche & Strube 1985: pp. 15, 99f., 199f.; Hoche 1990: passim). Second, it is a widespread tendency to measure the history of philosophical 'movements' rather in years than in decades or centuries. This tendency seems to me to be dictated by focussing one's interest on subtle differences rather than on basic common features. Furthermore, I think it is characteristic not so much of those interested in *themselves doing* – in a 'systematic' or, to be more precise, in a 'problem-oriented' way – philosophy proper as of those who prefer the attitude of the historically-minded *onlooker*. In fact, for the philosophical *actor* or *doer* 'linguistic philosophy' has a very long history, dating back to Plato and Aristotle; however, it has succeeded in ripening to a systematically elaborated shape and a keen awareness of its essential methods only within the last hundred and something years, and this process has, I do hope, by far not yet reached its end.

[27] For details, see Hoche 1990: ch. 1.

With the remarkable exception of mathematics,[28] these departmentalised and by now well-established branches of human learning as a rule concern themselves (1) with 'factual', 'material-related', or 'matter of fact' questions rather than 'linguistic' ones – to wit, with the multifarious 'things themselves' we encounter in the world rather than the way each of us uses to speak about these things in his or her personal idiolect –, (2) with 'real' rather than 'possible', 'impossible', and 'necessary' states of affairs, and (3) with 'objectivity', including what we may call the 'objectified subjectivities' of others as they are perceived by me, rather than 'subjectivity proper'.

Some readers may miss here a fourth point, to wit, the contradistinction between research into what *is* and research into what *ought to be*. However, I think it is at least debatable, first, whether the uncontroversial 'ought to *do*' may be paralleled with an 'ought to *be*', and second, whether the research into what each of us ought to do – in the face of a given situation – is the domain of the philosopher as such or rather a task each of us, in his capacity of a human being, has to cope with. Without question *metaethics* (for instance, research into such questions as what exactly we want to convey to our hearers (and to ourselves) when we use propositions of the form, say, 'So-and-so ought to perform such and such an action') is a basic domain of philosophy. In the field of *normative ethics*, however, the philosopher seems to me at best to function, as it were, as the deputy of the man in the street – and this only in default of another methodologically skilled expert (provided we are not prepared to completely leave the field to priests, theologians, jurists, politicians, and the like).

From what I just said in the last but one paragraph we may conclude that the second members of those three pairs of concepts – that is, *idiolectal language usage* (with respect to highly general and other pivotal terms), *modalities*, and *subjectivity* – may be taken to be the central and genuine domain of philosophy.[29] If so, the *genuine philosophical methods* may be subdivided into *methods of linguistic analysis*, *methods of modal analysis*, and *methods of the analysis of subjectivity proper*.

11. Linguistic and phenomenological methods

By 'subjectivity proper' I understand my own consciousness as it presents itself in my own first-person perspective, that is, what Husserl made the central topic of his so-called 'transcendental phenomenology' and what contemporary psychologists and philosophers of mind increasingly use to designate by the distinctive term

---

[28] It has often and, I think, rightly been claimed that, in the systematic or theoretical arrangement of the branches of human learning, mathematics, logic, and philosophy closely belong together and make up a third group besides the groups of the humanities and the sciences.

[29] See Hoche 2002: sect. 4.

'phenomenal consciousness'.[30] Hence the *methods of the analysis of subjectivity proper* may also, and more conveniently, be called *phenomenological methods*.

Likewise *modal analysis* – in the form of a systematic research into the necessary and general structures which, as a limiting framework, govern whatever is real and hence possible – is an integral part of what has been done by phenomenologists. Such research into the pre-empirical or 'a priori' features of reality seems to me to be best carried out by means of the method of 'free variation', that is, the unrestricted variation of purely imagined examples. This method may aptly be characterised as a systematic probing of the *limits* of what I can possibly conceive of in a specific form of imagination, to wit, 'pure' or 'eidetic' imagination.[31] Husserl always – that is to say: already in the years before what has been called his 'transcendental turn' in 1907 – insisted that phenomenological analysis ought to be 'eidetic analysis', that is, an analysis of whatever phenomenon in respect of its 'essence', and hence a form of modal analysis.[32] But the same methodological attitude has been adopted, at least programmatically, by other members, 'transcendentally'-minded or not, of the so-called 'phenomenological movement'.[33] In this spirit, the editors of Volume 1 of *Jahrbuch für Philosophie und phänomenologische Forschung* (1913) – Edmund Husserl, Moritz Geiger, Alexander Pfänder, Adolf Reinach, and Max Scheler – in their common *Announcement* stated that what united the contributors to this new journal was not a school or system but 'the shared conviction that the concepts and problems of the great traditions of philosophy can only be evaluated by *going back to the originary sources of intuition [Anschauung] and the insight into essences [Wesenseinsichten] which is drawn from this intuition*'.[34] – For these reasons we may also count the *methods of modal analysis*, insofar as they are not strictly logical methods,[35] among the *phenomenological methods*.

---

[30] See, for instance, Velmans 2000: passim; Windmann & Durstewitz 2000: pp. 76 f.; Metzinger 2006.

[31] See esp. Husserl 1925: pp. 72–87 (§ 9: 'Die Wesensschau als genuine Methode der Erfassung des Apriori [The intuition of essences as the genuine method of grasping apriority]'; 1948: §§ 86–93 (i.e., Part [Abschnitt] III, ch. II: 'Die Gewinnung der reinen Allgemeinheiten durch die Methode der Wesenserschauung [The acquisition of pure generalities by means of the method of intuiting essences]'). This method of 'phenomenological variation' may be compared to, and at the same time contrasted with, a method of 'linguistic variation' and the method of 'combination tests' often (if seldom satisfyingly) applied in ordinary language philosophy; see Hoche 1983; 1990: ch. 10.

[32] See esp. Husserl 1913, tr. 1931: §§ 1–26.

[33] For a survey, see Sepp 1988: esp. pp. 61–75 (Eberhard Avé-Lallemant) and p. 458 (Bibliographie, III).

[34] Translated from the facsimile in Sepp 1988: pp. 258 f. (citation: p. 259); my italics. Cf. ibid.: p. 71.

[35] Nowadays, modal analysis mostly takes the shape of 'possible worlds' theories. A *locus classicus* is Kripke 1972. As far as I know, no one has ever tried to systematically discuss the intriguing question of whether this logical approach and Husserl's (non-transcendental) phenomenological approach to modalities admit of some unification or mutual fecundating. See, however, Hoche 1990: chs. 9–10, where I discuss some basic problems of possibility, necessity, conceivability, and inconceivability.

If we do so, *genuine philosophical methods*, or at least the bulk of them, are partly *methods of phenomenology* (in a broader sense) and partly *methods of linguistic philosophy* (again in a broader sense, comprising 'ordinary language philosophy' or 'informal logic' on the one hand and 'ideal language philosophy' with its ramifications and formal foundations on the other).[36] Most of these methods are marked by a theoretical *egocentricity*. Whereas the phenomenologist has to research into his own consciousness as it is experienced – not really: perceived – by himself in his own first-person perspective, and to draw upon his personal imaginative competence when he inquires into problems of modality, the ordinary language philosopher – provided he is intent on reaching palpable and consequential results – in the last resort cannot but rely upon his own idiolect, and then leave it to his fellow-philosophers whether or not they think they can subscribe to the results he has reached in his 'idiolectal loneliness', that is to say, without resorting to an empirical, and perhaps statistical, inquiry into the pertinent linguistic habits of other native speakers.[37] It ought to be noted, however, that each of us from infancy has developed his or her personal idiolect in an incessant linguistic intercourse with his or her fellow-speakers, which sufficiently guarantees a far-reaching agreement among the idiolects of all members of a linguistic community with respect to all questions of practical life, especially of biological and social 'survival' – but not necessarily so with respect to subtle philosophical questions, which, most fortunately, do not have such a down-to-earth relevance.

As to linguistic or idiolectal methods, some readers would like to know why on earth we don't content ourselves with 'material' or 'matter of fact' problems in the first place. In the present context I think it suffices to reply as follows. There are time-honoured and at least in this sense genuine philosophical questions which lack a 'fact of the matter'[38] simply because they do not immediately relate to, and hence can be neither posed nor answered by inquiring into, any entities we can possibly encounter in the (objective) physical universe, or the (subjective) 'universe' of consciousness proper, or one of the (formal) 'universes' of mathematics and logic. Prominent examples seem to me to be such questions as 'What is knowledge?', 'What is causation?', or 'What is a moral obligation?'. As far as I can see, there

---

[36] In Hoche & Strube 1985: Part A, I tried to work out a systematic taxonomy of some of the multifarious methods of linguistic philosophy.

[37] See Hoche & Strube 1985: A.IV.1.f, where I try to make it plain why conceptual analysis can be philosophically fertile only on condition that it is carried out, not as linguistic analysis performed in a philological key, but as strictly idiolectal analysis. It is imperative, however, not to mistake one's personal idiolect for a 'private language' in the sense which Wittgenstein (1953: passim) has rightly discredited.

[38] Here I take the liberty of *adopting* Quine's frequently used phrase 'there is no fact of the matter' – for sources and a discussion see Hoche & Strube 1985: pp. 83f., 92, 94; Hoche 1990: 72–74, 76, 78f., 80 – and at the same time *adapting* it to the problem at hand, which I think is rather foreign to Quine.

is no other way of seriously coping with such questions besides asking ourselves
– and, in the last resort, asking myself in 'idiolectal loneliness' – how I, for one, *use
linguistic expressions to the point*. For instance, I may ask myself in what situations
I would normally say that somebody *knows*, or *does not know*, or *only believes
he knows*, that something is the case; or in what situations I would normally
say that an event *a* has been *caused* by an event *b* (or, more down-to-earth: '*a
because b.*'); or in what situations I would normally say that a given person has a
moral obligation (or again, more down-to-earth: [morally] *ought*) to act in such
and such a way.[39]

12. 'Linguistic phenomenology'

All of these examples are apt to show, furthermore, that linguistic (idiolectal) analyses often – if not always – have to take into account, and to vary in imagination,
non-linguistic situations, too. Hence we may be well-advised if we count the linguistic methods among the phenomenological methods rather than juxtaposing
them. In fact, John L. Austin had a perfectly good reason for recommending the
term *'linguistic phenomenology'* as a preferable alternative for the terms ' "linguistic" or "analytic" philosophy or "the analysis of language" '. Let me quote:

> When we examine what we should say when, what words we should use in what
> situations, we are looking […] not *merely* at words (or 'meanings', whatever they may
> be) but also at the realities we use the words to talk about: we are using a sharpened
> awareness of words to sharpen our perception of, though not as the final arbiter of, the
> phenomena.[40]

This insight has been impressively confirmed by Richard M. Hare in an essay
which in my view is truly worth reading:

> Philosophers are concerned with words as having meanings or uses; and these at any
> rate cannot be studied without seeing how words are used, in concrete situations, to say
> various things; and, of course, this involves (as is evident from our practice) a careful
> study of the situations, in order to find out what is being said. […] A full philosophical
> examination of language would involve a full examination of everything that can be

---

[39] These three questions have been dealt with, respectively, in Dudda 2007; Hoche 1977; and Hoche
1992; 1995d; 2001; cf. 2004. – Having finished this section, I came across a recent essay which, in
my eyes, deserves criticism in many respects (see Hoche 2008). For instance, in striking opposition
to what I just said, the author – a renowned academic philosopher and novelist – of all philosophical
problems chooses just 'mental causation', 'our will to morally restrict our freedom of action',
'rationality', and 'justice' as cases exemplifying 'questions in dealing with which you won't get far
by doing linguistic analysis' (translated from Bieri 2007: 340).

[40] Austin 1956: p. 130; cf. p. 129.

talked about – and if there are things that cannot be talked about, they cannot in any case become the subject of a philosophical enquiry.[41]

In precisely this spirit I have insisted since many years that the linguistic philosopher's basic tool should be what I call *his or her quite personal* 'combined imaginative and linguistic (idiolectal) competence' ('sprachgefühl'),[42] and in the following essays I will constantly have to draw upon *mine* – in the hope, of course, that my readers, after having carefully considered what is at issue in each particular case, will finally see themselves in a position to share the linguistico-phenomenological results I have reached in my 'idiolectal loneliness'.[43]

13. A note on philosophical truth

In the last paragraph of section 11, above, I touched upon the question of how to deal with philosophical 'what is'-questions. One such question is, of course, the question 'What is truth?', which Austin enjoined us to replace with the question '[…] how does the phrase "is true" occur in English sentences?'.[44] To this I fully subscribe; for substituting, to the greatest possible extent, finite verb forms for non-finite verb forms and noun-phrases is in general, I take it, a simple and yet often highly effective means for enhancing philosophical clarity.[45] However, as ought to be obvious by now, I think it crucial to tighten Austin's postulation and to ask the reader how he or she, *for one*, uses the phrase in question – in this case: the phrase 'is true' – *in his or her personal idiolect.* Let me try and briefly outline the answer I myself tend to consider appropriate. In my view this is very much to the point; for my readers may justly ask themselves whether I take my complementaristic approach to the mind-body problem and related anthropological problems to be 'true', and especially so in contrast with its countless dualistic, monistic, and dual-aspect competitors.

Leaving aside the often discussed speech-act theoretical aspects of using the simple predicate 'is true', which include, for instance, the important part it plays in assenting to someone or something, I think that I am wont to apply it[46] in by far

---

[41] Hare 1959: p. 51; cf. pp. 50–52. For a discussion and further sources, see Hoche & Strube 1985: A.VI, esp. A.VI.1.

[42] See, for instance, Hoche 1990: pp. 141, 146, 148, and Index of Subjects, entry 'competence, imaginative and linguistic', of the present collection.

[43] See the third paragraph of section 11, above.

[44] Austin 1950: p. 19.

[45] The same is true, by the way, of substituting the active voice for the passive voice, which is likewise apt to suppress conceptual structure.

[46] Note that I am speaking of the *simple predicate* 'is true' and not, for instance, of *expanded predicates* such as 'true to nature' or the *attribute* 'true' as it occurs, for instance, in 'a true friend' or 'true love'.

the most cases to verbally expressed, or at least expressible, propositions (beliefs, statements, assertions, etc.) insofar as I take them to be in accord with those experiences, perceptions, proofs, linguistic or emotional intuitions, etc., which I have learnt to consider the appropriate 'verifying evidence', or 'legal ground', for making an assertive use of these very propositions in the first place. At first sight, this may perhaps look like an exhumation of the time-honoured but nowadays disreputable 'correspondence theory of truth', which Frege, for one, claimed to have refuted.[47] But what I have in mind is solely the *correspondence of a given verbally expressed or expressible proposition with whatever experiences, perceptions, proofs, intuitions, etc., are acknowledged to give us the speech-act theoretical right to utter, use, or maintain that proposition with the illocutionary force of assertion ('assertive force').*[48]

Of course, as always the devil is in the details, into most of which this is not the place to delve. But let me say at least that much. According to the conception of truth just outlined, obviously a verbally expressed or expressible proposition – or a fully interpreted declarative sentence of, say, the English language – is *'true'* or *'false'* only on condition it is essentially related to an (at least potential) cognition of the relevant type. In this sense, my conception of truth is an 'epistemic' one. Since the 'redundancy theory of truth' is, of course, not touched by my stance on the problem of truth, the same holds true for my conception of a proposition. In other words: If a supposed proposition, be it of the simple form 'p' or the redundant form 'p is true.', *on principle* defies both a *preceding or simultaneous* speech-act theoretical justification and a verifying or falsifying check *ex post*[49] of the proper cognitive sort, then we should not hesitate to regard it, not as a ('principally' or 'as yet') indeterminate or undecidable proposition, but as a mere would-be or pseudo-proposition, which is strictly void of sound meaning, or 'nonsensical'.[50]

Now each of the statements I am going to make in the present collection of essays will hopefully meet the conditions of falling under the concept of a *genuine*, i.e., *true-or-false* proposition, and moreover, I do of course hope, more often than not even the conditions of being *true*. Predictably, this will not always be the

---

[47] Frege 1918: pp. 59f. It has often been said that Frege's attempt was a flop, and even beginners' mistakes have in effect been imputed to him; but Pardey (2004; 2006: ch. 8; 2007) took pains to rehabilitate Frege's arguments at great length. However, I am afraid I can follow neither Frege nor Pardey in all respects.

[48] For the systematic and historical relation between Frege's conception of 'assertive force' ('behauptende Kraft') and Austin's conception of 'illocutionary force' see Hoche 1990: 6.2.

[49] For this difference, see Hoche 1990: 7.4.

[50] Hence among such pseudo-propositions I count, for instance, predictions *as such*, i.e., as taken to relate, not to relevant indications presently existing or having already existed (as is the case, e.g., in a professional weather-forecast), but to contingent states of affairs in the future (Aristotle's 'contingentia futura', such as tomorrow's naval battle). Other sorts of pseudo-propositions will come up, as the cases arise, in the following essays.

case; for I don't know of any work of philosophy that is free from flaws, errors, and other shortcomings. Nonetheless, what I am after is decidedly *philosophical truth* and not just the deliberation of more or less plausible genuine or even spurious possibilities, which in philosophy, as elsewhere, all-too often tend to be surreptitiously taken for probabilities, facts, or even necessities. Rather, in the following essays I will be intent on founding whatever I am going to state on the experiential and/or linguistic 'evidence' which, in each case at hand, seems to me to be appropriate. So I hope I will be able to make a few 'steps in the right direction' which, however, must doubtless be followed by a great many others and probably also adjusted in more than one respect. From this it follows that I should like to urge my readers to critically examine these essays in a productive and constructive rather than a merely receptive and historically-minded attitude, that is, in the spirit of issue-related collegiality, which is keen on improving, exploiting, and 'exhausting' rather than merely filing or rashly discarding what others have to say.

Let me conclude this introduction by quoting a dictum of Hare's which seems to me to be utterly worth heeding:

> I shall be less disturbed if my readers disagree with me than if they fail to understand me. [...] I have therefore tried to adopt throughout as definite a standpoint as possible, in the belief that it is more important that there should be discussion of the points herein raised, than that I should survive it unscathed.[51]

---

[51] Hare 1952: Preface, p. III.

I

HARE'S TWO DEFINITIONS OF 'ENTAILMENT' AND THE GENERIC RELATION OF 'LINGUISTIC IMPLICATION'

Summary

In effect, Richard M. Hare proposes *two different* definitions of what he takes to be 'entailment' (sects. 1–2). If properly applied, both of them are promising indeed (sects. 3–5). At the same time, however, they capture on the one hand *less* and on the other hand *more* than ought to be expected of an entailment-relation (sects. 6–7). Moreover, either one fails to do justice to one or other formal criterion of adequacy to be postulated for a definition of entailment (sect. 8). The latter shortcoming can be overcome by merging Hare's two definitions into one by way of stipulating a restriction of the domain on which to define the relation (sect. 9). Still, this relation is not yet entailment proper but a highly generic relation of 'linguistic (or: idiolectal) implication' (sect. 10). But it can be naturally split up into a number of philosophically fertile subrelations and sub-subrelations, which I will discuss in the following essay (opening sect. 0).

0. The philosophical import of defining a generic relation of linguistic, or idiolectal, implication

0.1.   What I am going to do in the present essay may at first sight appear to be an exemplary case of futile philosophical hair-splitting. So who comes across it might be willing to know in advance whether *reading* it would be worth while in the first place. Hence let me assure that I found its *writing* paying for at least the following two basic philosophical reasons.

0.2.   First, I think that exhausting the rich possibilities of *metaethics* along the lines of Richard M. Hare's 'Universal Prescriptivism' (see 1.1 and 3.3, below) requires, in the last resort, a foundation of some such sort as the one to be offered in the present essay and its continuation in the following Essay II of this collection.

0.3.   Second, to my mind the philosophical, psychological, and neurobiological discussions of the so-called *'mind-body problem'* have long since reached a dead-lock in that there seems to be no chance of overcoming the seeming alternative of *dualistic* and *monistic* (or reductionist) positions, both of which I think to be not only unpromising but also *untenable*. A possible (and, as far as I can see, the *only* possible) way out seems to me to be a *complementaristic* position in somewhat the sense of Niels Bohr's (see Essays IV–VI of the present collection; Hoche 2007).

This position takes subjective conscious experiences and objective neurological events to be *neither numerically the same nor numerically different* occurrences, and one way of establishing it has to include a logical analysis of identity-statements on the basis of Russell's 'theory of definite descriptions' (see Essay III of the present collection). Hence it is imperative to make sure that, contrary appearances notwithstanding, existential presupposition can be accepted as a subcase of what I will call 'semantic implication' (see 0.4, below).

0.4.   In the common interest of these two quite divergent philosophical aims, in the present essay I am going to work out a satisfying definition of the highly generic relation of a 'linguistic (or: idiolectal) implication' which, as I will try to show in the following Essay II, may be naturally split up into three subrelations, namely, 'semantic (or: analytical) implication', 'pragmatic implication', and 'catapragmatic implication', and two sub-subrelations, namely, 'semantic presupposition' and 'catapragmatic presupposition'.

1. Hare's weaker definition of 'entailment'

1.1.   In order to be able to develop his metaethical theory of 'Universal Prescriptivism', Richard M. Hare had to start by devising a definition of the relation of entailment which, contrary to what is customary in logic, does not resort to the concepts of truth and falsehood. For he thought it appropriate to define the 'prescriptivity' of a given moral 'ought'-sentence – or its being used, on a certain occasion, as a full-blown 'value-judgement' – as the judgement's 'entailing' the corresponding imperative.[1] Imperatives, however, do not of course belong to the type of entities which can sensibly be said to be true or false. Hare was confident that for this metaethical purposes the relation of informal entailment, i.e., entailment as a relation between (fully interpreted) ordinary-language sentences, 'may be defined accurately enough' by what I shall dub 'Hare's weaker definition of entailment' ('HWDE'):

---

[1] 'I do not wish to claim that all "ought"-sentences entail imperatives, but only that they do so when they are being used evaluatively. [...] I am making this true by definition; for I should not say that an "ought"-sentence *was* being used evaluatively, unless imperatives were held to follow from it': Hare 1952: 11.1, p. 164. This is specified as follows: 'I propose to say that the test, whether someone is using the judgement "I ought to do X" as a value-judgement or not is, "Does he or does he not recognise that if he assents to the judgement, he must also assent to the command 'Let me do X'?" ': ibid.: 11.2, pp. 168/9, and repeated as a self-quotation in Hare 1963: 5.7, p. 79. It should be noted that, in this crucial passage of Hare's, the stronger phrase 'he must also assent to' takes the place of the weaker phrase 'he cannot dissent from', which we have to expect if we attend to the literal wording of Hare's 'weaker' definition of entailment (HWDE) to be discussed in what follows in section 1.

HWDE: A sentence P entails a sentence Q if and only if the fact that a person assents to P but dissents from Q is a sufficient criterion for saying that he has misunderstood one or other of the sentences.[2]

1.2.   This definition stands in need of some clarifications; for plausible though it certainly seems to be, it is much less clear than one might think at first sight. I take it that its substantial content is intended to be tantamount to

HWDE$_1$:   A sentence P entails a sentence Q $=_{\text{def}}$ If a person assents to P but dissents from Q he must have misunderstood one or other of the sentences

or, if we disambiguate the position of the modal operator, introduce some familiar logical symbols,[3] choose a tenseless version (as is usually done in formal logic), and speak of respectively myself, to

HWDE$_2$:   A sentence P entails a sentence Q $=_{\text{def}}$ $\square$ ((I assent to P & I dissent from Q) $\rightarrow$ (I misunderstand P $\vee$ I misunderstand Q)).[4]

1.3.   I don't think we run the risk of a substantial loss of contents if we formulate HWDE$_2$ in terms of 'not understanding' rather than 'misunderstanding'. For 'misunderstanding' can safely be taken to mean 'not understanding *plus believing of oneself that one understands*',[5] and the italicised 'doxastic surplus' over and above the simple failure of understanding seems to me to be quite irrelevant to our present purpose. I think it is irrelevant to Hare's purpose, too. Nonetheless, speaking in terms of misunderstanding is doubtless very plausible in this connection; for whoever assents to, or dissents from, a sentence must at least *believe* that he

---

[2] Hare 1952: 2.4, p. 25. Why I call this definition 'weaker' can be seen from note 1, above, and especially from subsect. 1.4, sect. 2, and subsect. 8.10, below. – In what way the refinement which Hare adds to this definition in a footnote may be relevant to our present purposes will be briefly discussed in 4.1, note 15, and 5.2, note 22, below.

[3] I shall use the symbols '¬', '&', '∨', '→', '↔', '◊', and '□' in order to regiment the ordinary-language phrases 'it is not the case that', 'and', 'and/or', 'if ..., then __', 'if and only if ..., then __', 'it is (counterfactually, or: objectively) possible that', and 'it is (objectively) necessary that', respectively.

[4] This interpretation of HWDE is, I think, sufficiently confirmed by the following variant of HWDE given in Hare 1952: 11.3, p. 172: 'to say that one judgement entails another is simply to say that you cannot assent to the first and dissent from the second unless you have misunderstood one or the other'. For if we substitute 'I' for 'you', the formalisation of this citation can be given a logically equivalent form which virtually coincides with HWDE$_2$.

[5] This claim can be systematically justified by a two-way application of HWDE or an improved successor definition; see 3.2 with sentences (3.2.1) and (3.2.2), below. This fact, however, does by no means preclude our making use of the result already in the *formulation* of such a definition; for doing so is not a vicious 'circle in definition' but rather a specimen of the methodological 'zigzagging' which generally cannot be dispensed with in the course of producing a finer (material or linguistic) tool by means of a grosser one.

understands it. Or, to put it differently: Since the element of my believing that I (properly) understand a given sentence must be taken to be already contained in the concepts of my assenting to and dissenting from this sentence, it need not be stated over again by means of speaking in terms of misunderstanding instead of simply not understanding. So I suggest to replace HWDE$_2$ with any one of the following three definitions, logically equivalent among themselves (and with many others):

HWDE$_3$: A sentence P entails a sentence Q $=_{def}$ □ ((I assent to P
       & I dissent from Q) → (¬I understand P ∨ ¬I understand Q));

HWDE$_4$: A sentence P entails a sentence Q $=_{def}$ □ (I understand P
       & I understand Q & I assent to P → ¬I dissent from Q);

HWDE$_5$: A sentence P entails a sentence Q $=_{def}$ ¬◊ (I understand P
       & I understand Q & I assent to P & I dissent from Q).

If this interpretation of Hare's definition is acceptable, HWDE can be given, for instance, the following everyday-language formulation as well:

HWDE′: A sentence P entails a sentence Q if and only if it is not possible that I
       understand P, understand Q, assent to P, and [but] dissent from Q.

1.4.   Next, let me say a word about the relation between 'dissenting from' and '(not) assenting to' a given sentence. I think it is obvious that, as a rule, we have to distinguish between my *dissenting* from a given indicative sentence (because I know or strongly believe that its negation is true) and my simply *not assenting* to it (because I have no idea whether it is true or false), and similarly between my *dissenting* from an imperative sentence (because I intend, or intend somebody else, not to do what I, or they, have been told) and my simply *not assenting* to it (because I still want to leave it open what to do, or because I think it inappropriate that I have been asked to do such and such a thing, or because I don't care which course of action somebody else is going to take, etc.). By so saying I imply, of course, that *dissenting from* Q amounts to *assenting to non-Q* whereas *not assenting to* Q need not include assenting to non-Q; for it is always possible that, because of lack of evidence or lack of determination, I can neither assent to Q nor assent to non-Q. So HWDE′ can be changed into

HWDE″: A sentence P entails a sentence Q if and only if it is not possible that
       I understand P, understand Q, assent to P, and assent to non-Q.

1.5.   Finally, since we may safely assume that here we have to do with what may be called 'objective' or 'counterfactual' possibility, I should like to suggest that, for the purposes of ascertaining actual cases of informal entailment, HWDE″ is to be 'operationalised' as follows:

HWDE''':   A sentence P entails a sentence Q if and only if I cannot conceive, in the mode of counterfactual imagination,[6] a counterfactually possible world with respect to which I am prepared to say here and now that I understand P, understand Q, assent to P, and assent to non-Q.[7]

2. Hare's stronger definition of 'entailment'

2.1.   As I have indicated in subsection 1.1, above, there is a second, and *stronger*, definition of 'entailment' which Hare also, if not predominantly, had in mind. As far as I can see, he never did as much as expressly formulate it; but if he had done so, certainly it ought to have run more or less like this:

HSDE: A sentence P entails a sentence Q if and only if the fact that a person assents to P but does not assent to Q is a sufficient criterion for saying that he has misunderstood one or other of the sentences.

2.2.   At first sight, HSDE might seem to be, not the stronger, but the weaker of the two definitions in question. For if we subjected HSDE step by step to all the considerations applied to HWDE in section 1, above – which, of course, we need not do here anew –, it would surely wind up as follows:

HSDE''':   A sentence P entails a sentence Q if and only if I cannot conceive, in the mode of counterfactual imagination, a counterfactually possible world with respect to which I am prepared to say here and now that I understand P, understand Q, assent to P, and do not assent to Q.

If we compare HSDE''' with its counterpart HWDE''' put down in section 1.5, above, we cannot possibly fail to state that *not assenting to Q* is less, or something weaker, than *assenting to non-Q*. None the less I think there are at least two good reasons for accepting my suggestion to regard HSDE as the stronger and HWDE as the weaker of Hare's two divergent definitions.

---

[6]   Cf. Hoche 1990: ch. 9 ('Möglichkeit und Vorstellbarkeit' ['Possibility and conceivability']), esp. 9.3, 9.5.

[7]   Frequently, the clumsy phrase 'with respect to which I am prepared to say here and now that' can be replaced with the simple words 'in which'. However, there are cases in which the simplified version will not do (see the following Essay II: 5.3–5.5). Furthermore, I think it important to make it as clear as possible that the wording chosen belongs to my real language (the language I speak in the real world) and not to the language I (would) happen to speak in the counterfactually possible world in question, which *need not* but of course *can* differ from the one I speak here and now.

2.3.   The first of these reasons is this. If we compare the variant

HWDE$_4$:   A sentence P entails a sentence Q $=_{def}$ $\square$ (I understand P
            & I understand Q & I assent to P $\rightarrow$ $\neg$I dissent from Q)

to be found in 1.3, above, with its counterpart

HSDE$_4$:   A sentence P entails a sentence Q $=_{def}$ $\square$ (I understand P
            & I understand Q & I assent to P $\rightarrow$ I assent to Q)

– in which the phrase 'I assent to Q' results from cancelling the double negation in the phrase '$\neg$I do not assent to Q', which we would get purely mechanically –, then HSDE$_4$ clearly turns out to be stronger than HWDE$_4$. For *assenting to Q* on a given condition is certainly more than *not dissenting from it, or not assenting to its negation non-Q*, on the selfsame condition.

2.4.   There is a second, and perhaps more cogent, reason for regarding HSDE as stronger than HWDE: If Q is 'entailed' by P according to HSDE, then Q is 'entailed' by P also according to HWDE, whereas the reverse is not true. But before turning to prove this claim (see subsection 8.10, below), let us first make ourselves a bit more familiar with Hare's two definitions (section 3), clarify a couple of related methodological questions (sections 4–5), and convince ourselves of the fact that neither one is truly qualified for defining a concept which we are prepared to accept as a concept of *entailment* or *logical implication* proper (sections 6–8).

3. Some exemplary applications of Hare's definitions

3.1.   Both of Hare's definitions of what he calls 'entailment' are likely to look plausible at first sight. For it may easily appear that each of us can find out without much ado whether or not an exemplary definiens is true. Replace, for instance, the sentences P and Q by the sentences

(3.1.1)   Tim is a brother of mine.

(3.1.2)   Tim and I have the same parents.,

respectively. Provided I take the terms 'brother' and 'parents' in their strict biological and/or legal senses, thus excluding such readings as 'half-brother', 'blood-brother', 'foster-parents', and the like,[8] I plainly cannot imagine a counterfactually possible world with respect to which I am prepared to say here and now that I understand (3.1.1), understand (3.1.2), assent to (3.1.1), and *do not assent to* (3.1.2) – or even *dissent from* it, i.e., assent to its sentential negation

---

[8] For this *caveat*, see sect. 8.7, note 38, below.

(¬3.1.2) It is not the case that Tim and I have the same parents
          [Tim and I haven't got the same parents].

So according to HSDE‴ as well as to HWDE‴, (3.1.2) is entailed in (3.1.1), which indeed looks plausible enough. There is a notorious lot of similar examples, having to do with the inevitable bachelors, unmarried men, brothers, and male siblings, for the clear-cut character and indubitability of which we have to pay the price of their utmost triviality.

3.2. Let us now take somewhat more interesting pairs of sentences such as the following two:

(3.2.1)   I misunderstood her remark.

(3.2.2)   I didn't understand her remark (properly) but I thought [believed] I did [Though I thought I understood her remark in fact I did not].[9]

(3.2.3)   I hope [am hoping] he will come.

(3.2.4)   I am looking forward to his coming, and I am not sure [do not believe] he will not come.

Although these examples may be in need of some minor refinements, I take it that, according to HSDE‴ as well as to HWDE‴, the first sentences of these ordered pairs entail the second sentences, and arguably also *vice versa*. Cases like these are certainly somewhat less uncontroversial than the ones just mentioned in subsection 3.1; but this drawback, if in fact it is one, seems to me to be outweighed by their enhanced utility in doing conceptual analysis.

3.3. This seems to me to be especially true of such highly non-trivial examples as

(3.3.1)   I (strongly) believe that (according to my personal normative standards) I morally ought to help her.

(3.3.2)   I intend to help her.

At first sight one might be inclined to doubt that, according to HWDE‴ or HSDE‴, there is any entailment-relation between (3.3.1) and (3.3.2); but, as I know from my teaching experience in metaethics, a certain amount of 'maieutic' explication is likely to change things considerably. Basically, in a Harean key we can try and explain to the sceptic that the genuine moral 'ought' – in using which we refer to, and find vent for, our deepest personal convictions in matters

---

[9] Cf. 1.3 with note 5, above. – In my exemplary sentences I shall strictly distinguish between the uses of round and square brackets: What is put in *round brackets* may as well be omitted but is useful in that it hints to nuances of meaning or renders a reading unambiguous; what is put in *square brackets*, however, is to be understood as an *alternative* to the preceding expression(s).

of moral behaviour – can best be characterised as being not only 'prescriptive' and 'universalisable' but also *'overriding'* all other prescriptions and preferences of ours.[10] So a way may be opened up how to make use of Hare's metaethical insights without having to cope with what I take to be the formal disadvantages of imperative logic.[11]

4. Modes of assent, 'linguistic maieutics', and the role of respectively my own idiolect

4.1.   I just indicated in 3.3 that in the case of less trivial examples some amount of 'maieutic' explanation may be needed. By this I tried to imply that there are different modes of assent, and that sometimes on second or third looks we can well assent to a sentence which at first sight we are inclined to dissent from, or at least hesitate to assent to. As Hare rightly says, assenting to a given sentence should essentially be interpreted in terms of believing or intending something, depending on whether the sentence is of indicative or imperative mood;[12] and it is well-known that believing as well as intending can be a matter of more or less spontaneity or, if seen from the opposite point of view, consideration.

4.2.   As far as a strict and formalisable *logic* of believing and intending is concerned, if such a 'doxastico-theletic' logic is feasible at all it must doubtless be based on the concepts of a *non-spontaneous, well-considered*, and possibly *maieutically enlightened* – in a word: *'rational'* – conviction and intention. For otherwise the most elementary cases of absent-mindedness and similar phenomena all of us know from everyday life would be bound to frustrate the attempt to devise such a logic from the very beginning. For this reason, in my attempts to establish the groundwork of an integrated logic of conviction and intention I laid stress upon including, in a 'doxastically, theletically, and pragmatically' extended calculus of 'natural deduction', the following two derivation rules of 'deductive closedness':

(RB1)   If $\varphi \vdash \psi$ then (Bi) $\varphi \Rightarrow$ (Bi) ψ;

(RW1)   If $\varphi \vdash \psi$ then (Wi) $\varphi \Rightarrow$ (Wi) ψ,

---

[10] Cf. Hare 1981: esp. pp. 24, 53, 65. 'To treat a principle as overriding [...] is to let it always override other principles when they conflict with it and, in the same way, let it override all other prescriptions, including non-universalisable ones (e. g. plain desires)': ibid.: p. 56, cf. 3.4–3.8.

[11] For details, see Hoche 1992: 2.2–2.3; 1995e; 2001: II.2–3, III.2–4; and the following Essay II: 3.8, 4.5.

[12] Cf. Hare 1952: 2.2. – I take it that not only assenting to an indicative sentence but also assenting to a sentence in the subjunctive mood, such as 'Had he been in time he wouldn't have missed me.', has to do with *believing*. However, this is not the place to discuss methodological problems of 'possible worlds history' at any more detail.

or in words: If a sentence ψ can be derived from a sentence φ by means of the classical rules of the predicate calculus (including the propositional calculus), then if the sentence 'I believe [want] φ to be the case.' has been entered on an earlier derivation line then the sentence 'I believe [want] ψ to be the case.' may be entered on a later derivation line (with premise-numbers unaltered).[13]

4.3.   Hence we should ask ourselves whether the concept of assenting used in HWDE''' and HSDE''' ought likewise to be based on the concepts of *non-spontaneous, well-considered*, and possibly *maieutically enlightened* believing and intending, i.e., whether to think of a spontaneous or rather a 'rational', well considered mode of assenting. It seems to me preferable to decide this question in favour of the second option: The concept of assenting, if it is used in the definition of such a basic logical concept as informal entailment, should certainly be interpreted in terms of 'rational' – i.e., non-spontaneous, well-considered, and possibly maieutically enlightened – conviction and intention.[14] There is some indication that this is the course which also Hare took. For had he admitted also of the spontaneous, rash, and ill-considered mode of assenting he could hardly have spoken, as in fact he did in HWDE, of 'a sufficient criterion for saying that he has misunderstood one or other of the sentences'; rather, in this case he should have spoken of a criterion for *either* having misunderstood one or other of the sentences *or else* having overlooked some essential interrelation of theirs.[15]

4.4.   In speaking of 'maieutics' I adopt, of course, a term of Plato's. But whereas doing 'maieutics' in the Platonic dialogues has often to do also with problems of mathematical or scientific matters of fact, what I have in mind in the present connection is strictly confined to what may be called 'linguistic maieutics' or, more frequently, 'linguistic analysis', i.e., helping ourselves or somebody else remem-

---

[13] Hoche 2001: IV.3; 2004: V.2–3; VIII.4, IX.1. – In these publications, instead of 'theletic' I used the term 'buletic'; but my colleague Prof. Dr. Alexander Kleinlogel, Bochum, was so kind as to point out to me that 'theletic' is by far the better choice, and the more so as an ancient Greek adjective 'buletikós', unlike 'theletikós' (θελητικός), has not been handed down to us.

[14] One might be tempted to opt for the opposite decision because a criterion is 'something that settles a question with certainty' (Malcolm 1959: 60), or because 'the application of a criterion must be able to yield either an affirmative or a negative result' (ibid.: 24). But I don't think that this important requirement is in the way of careful consideration and the taking of 'second looks'.

[15] On the other hand, Hare added a footnote to his definition of entailment in 1952: 2.4, p. 25, which may be taken to point in the opposite direction: 'More complicated entailments, such as those in mathematics, might be covered by extending this definition as follows: the definition given [i.e., HWDE] would be treated as a definition of *direct* entailment, and *indirect* entailment would be defined as holding between two sentences P and R when there is a series of sentences $Q_1, Q_2 \ldots Q_n$ such that P directly entails Q_1, Q_1 directly entails Q_2, &c., and Q_n directly entails R. But even this may not be sufficiently exact.' See, however, 5.2 with note 22, below.

ber how exactly we 'use to use' our basic vocabulary of everyday language, or appealing to our personal and individual linguistic competence. This competence of ours has developed within the shared language of our linguistic community, and *must* have done so, as we know at the latest since Wittgenstein's (1953) cogent arguments against what he calls a 'private language'. For all that I take it that our common language has its 'idiolectal edges' in that there are, or principally might be, some minor interpersonal deviations in the use of a number of expressions, mostly words the accurate usage of which is, as it were, not crucial for our 'social survival'. So, strictly speaking, each of us commands their own 'idiolect' within the framework of our common language. But, to repeat this important point, this 'idiolect' is not, and cannot possibly be, a 'private language' in the sense of Wittgenstein's. Hence by doing 'linguistic analysis' ('linguistic maieutics') we can step by step try and assimilate to each other our slightly diverging personal idiolects. None the less I think that the primary task of doing linguistic analysis is to remind respectively *myself* of how exactly I 'use to use' my own idiolect, and thus, for instance, to enhance the consistency of my way of speaking by weeding out unnoticed discrepancies in my using one and the same term on different occasions, or to make myself aware also of the more indirect and remote 'implications' of what I say and take to be true. Doing so has proved to be extremely useful for tackling philosophical problems, and as it is hard enough toil by itself I think we should not overburden it with the additional attempt to look for refined ways of convincing our fellow-philosophers of our personal way of using language – an attempt which is always extremely time-consuming and mostly without a chance of success. For this reason I have suggested to run linguistic analysis as an *idiolectal* analysis and strictly leave it to others whether or not to accept those parts of my personal idiolect which are relevant to the specific problems at hand.[16]

5. Grammatical intricacies and the import of formal logic

5.1.   In section 4, above, I argued that in applying Hare's definitions HWDE and HSDE we are well advised if we think of the *non-spontaneous, well-considered*, and possibly *maieutically enlightened* mode of assent. Hence we might perhaps presume that also examples like the following couple of sentences, which has repeatedly been used in logic and the computer sciences, should be accessible to an application of those definitions:

---

[16] Cf. Hoche & Strube 1985: A.IV.1.f.

(5.1.1)   The guard searched all who entered the building except those who were
           accompanied by members of the firm, and some of Fiorecchio's men
           entered the building unaccompanied by anyone else, and the guard
           searched none of Fiorecchio's men.

(5.1.2)   Some of Fiorecchio's men were members of the firm.[17]

Let us ask ourselves whether we can imagine a counterfactually possible world
with respect to which we are prepared to say here and now that we understand
(5.1.1), understand (5.1.2), assent to (5.1.1), and do not assent to (5.1.2) – or even
dissent from it, i.e., assent to its negation

(¬5.1.2) None of Fiorecchio's men were members of the firm.

I think it is obvious that this question would have to be answered in the *positive*
if we had to think of the *spontaneous* mode of assent. In section 4, however, this
mode of assent has been declared to be irrelevant to our present task. But what
about the *non-spontaneous* mode of assent? It seems to me that in this case the
appeal to some linguistic maieutics, which, I take it, is really helpful in the more
complicated cases considered in section 3, would be of little or no use. For what
makes it difficult to cope with the present example is not that we have to remind
ourselves of the way we 'use to use' one or other of the terms involved. Rather, the
problem seems to me to be that the complicated arrangement and unusual length
of sentence (5.1.1), which is a sentential conjunction of three sentences some
of which are highly intricate in themselves, simply overburdens our psychical
capability of putting our linguistic competence to work.

5.2.   So what is called for seems to be not some doing of maieutics but rather
a radical simplification of the grammatical structure of the sentences involved. To
analyse just *one* practicable way of tackling the problem, we could start by trying
to convince ourselves that the first conjunctive member of (5.1.1), i.e.,

(5.2.1)   The guard searched all who entered the building except those who were
           accompanied by members of the firm.,

'says in effect' (as Quine baldly puts it) the same as

(5.2.2)   Every person that entered the building and was not searched by the
           guard was accompanied by some member(s) of the firm.[18]

Here the simple words 'says in effect' can be replaced with the more sophisticated reading 'entails, and is entailed by, in the sense of some such definition as
HWDE or HSDE'. This, though clumsy, would have the advantage of making

---

[17] As far as I can see, this example has first been used in Quine 1950: § 30, pp. 167–169.

[18] Ibid.: § 30, p. 167.

it unmistakably clear that in preparing the translation of an ordinary-language sentence into a symbolised sentence of the predicate calculus (which is what Quine is after)[19] we cannot dispense with our linguistic – and, in the last resort: idiolectal – competence,[20] which is but systematically worked out and improved upon by HWDE, HSDE, and any of their follower definitions to be discussed in this paper. In the present case, the application of some such definition has to focus especially on the use of 'except'-constructions. Similarly, with respect to the second conjunctive member of (5.1.1), i. e., to

(5.2.3)   Some of Fiorecchio's men entered the building unaccompanied by any-
           one else.,

we can state, again repeating Quine's own bald words, that 'clearly the intended meaning'[21] of (5.2.3) is

(5.2.4)   Some of Fiorecchio's men entered the building, and anyone accompa-
           nying them was one of Fiorecchio's men.

Here, too, the statement can be made more precise by saying that, according to some such definition as HWDE or HSDE or any one of their follower definitions, (5.2.3) entails, and is entailed by, (5.2.4). Next, if we have some practice in, or are by nature good at, carrying out less trivial assenting tests, with a bit of luck and concentration we can convince ourselves that the conjunction of the second and third conjunctive members of (5.1.1), i. e.,

(5.2.5)   Some of Fiorecchio's men entered the building unaccompanied by any-
           one else,
           and the guard searched none of Fiorecchio's men.,

according to HWDE and HSDE entails

(5.2.6)   Some of Fiorecchio's men entered the building without having been
           searched by the guard or accompanied by anyone else.

Finally on the same set of psychological conditions we can find out that (5.2.2) – or, for that matter, (5.2.1) – and (5.2.6) together entail

(5.1.2)   Some of Fiorecchio's men were members of the firm.[22]

---

[19] Ibid.: § 30.

[20] This competence, or to be more precise: *respectively my own integrated imaginative and idiolectal competence*, seems to me to be of the utmost importance for doing linguistic analysis or maieutics; cf. Hoche & Strube 1985: A. IV.1.f (pp. 109–113) and 4.3 (pp. 145–147); Hoche 1990: 8.1 (pp. 141 f.).

[21] Quine 1950: p. 168.

[22] The possibility of proceeding in the way just sketched may be the rationale behind Hare's refinement of HWDE quoted in 4.3, note 15, above. If so, it becomes obvious that Hare was perfectly right in conceding that 'even this may not be sufficiently exact'.

5.3.   Certainly such a piece of reasoning, dependent as it is on a number of not altogether common psychological capabilities and exertions, is not truly satisfying. However, it can be made much more conspicuous if we lean on the formal tools of the predicate and the propositional calculi.[23] Then we can formalise (5.2.2), (5.2.5), (5.2.6), and (5.1.2) as, say,

(5.2.2') $(x) (Bx \ \& \ \neg Gx \rightarrow (\exists y) (Ayx \ \& \ My))$;

(5.2.5') $(\exists x) (Fx \ \& \ Bx \ \& \ (y) (Ayx \rightarrow Fy)) \ \& \ (x) (Fx \rightarrow \neg Gx)$;

(5.2.6') $(\exists x) (Fx \ \& \ Bx \ \& \ \neg Gx \ \& \ (y) (Ayx \rightarrow Fy))$;

(5.1.2') $(\exists x) (Fx \ \& \ Mx)$,

respectively, and convince ourselves more or less mechanically[24] that we can deduce (5.2.6') from (5.2.5'), and (5.1.2') from the conjunction of (5.2.2') and (5.2.6'). But it should be stressed once again that we cannot make these tools applicable in the first place unless we can rely on our non-formal competence to ascertain what we 'mean to say' or 'have in mind' when we are using such ordinary-language sentences as the ones here considered.

5.4.   Let me conclude this section by expressly pointing out that there is a remarkable difference between the examples considered in section 3 and the example just discussed in section 5. Whereas the latter – the Fiorecchio case –, once it is translated into a symbolic logical notation, can be handled by an application of the predicate calculus, the former cases can't; for in those pairs of sentences each member contains at least one predicate which does not show up in the other one. For this reason, those examples are useful in doing conceptual analysis, whereas in this respect cases like the Fiorecchio example are totally barren – at least as long as one silently passes over the non-formal problems, briefly touched upon in subsections 5.2–5.3, of translating them into a formal idiom.

6. Arguably, Hare's definitions capture *not all* cases of entailment

6.1.   In spite of the promising prospects outlined so far, and especially in section 3, above, neither HWDE nor HSDE proves to be qualified for defining a relation we would be ready to consider to be *entailment* proper. This verdict can be

---

[23] I take it that the axioms, laws, or derivation rules of these calculi can themselves be justified in the last resort by using some such method as the ones represented by HWDE or HSDE and their successor definitions. However, the tendency to make light of these methods, which we just encountered in the Quine citations in subsection 5.2, above, seems to me to abound also in the soundness proofs usually offered by formal logicians.

[24] *More* mechanically if we choose a 'reductive' procedure on the basis of the so-called Polish notation; *less* mechanically if we choose, for instance, an 'axiomatic' method or a calculus of 'natural deduction'.

based on two or three grounds. First, *arguably* HWDE and HSDE capture *too little*, i.e., not all cases of implications we are inclined to regard as entailments (subsections 6.2–6.4). Second, at the same time there can be no doubt that both of them capture *too much*, i.e., also cases of implications which are certainly something different from entailments (section 7). Third, either one fails to satisfy one or other *formal criterion of adequacy*: HWDE defines a relation which is not transitive, and HSDE defines a relation which is not subject to the law of so-called transposition (section 8).

6.2.   In so saying I have to lean, of course, on a 'preconceived' idea of entailment; but obviously this is no different from what Hare does. In fact, what Hare has in mind is not a 'stipulative' but an 'explicative' definition, to wit, an explication of the precise use of a technical term which has long since been employed by logicians; only he tries to extend the possible use of this term so as to permit its application also to cases in which truth and falsity cannot come into play, especially to imperatives. Nonetheless in all cases in which truth and falsify *can* come into play he should have seen to it that that his definitions do not diverge too much from the customary use of the term 'entailment'. It is true that in this case 'clear and agreed definitions are not available';[25] however, we are certainly on the safe side if we say that 'at the very least, strict implication is a concept closely related to that of entailment; and if it is not identical with it (though it may well be), it is both the clearer of the two and the one which is easier to express in a logical system'.[26] Hence according to my 'preconceived' idea in all cases in which we have to do with true or false sentences the definition of 'entailment' should square with the definition usually given for strict implication or entailment, to wit: 'φ entails χ if and only if it is necessary that if φ then χ' ('$\varphi \vDash \chi =_{def} \Box\,(\varphi \rightarrow \chi)$') or, logically equivalent, 'φ entails χ if and only if it is not possible that φ and [but] not χ' ('$\varphi \vDash \chi =_{def} \neg\Diamond\,(\varphi\ \&\ \neg\chi)$').

6.3.   According to this traditional and ubiquitous definition of entailment, the first sentence of the following couple surely *does* entail the second:

(6.3.1)   This (Euclidean) polygon is a hexagon.

(6.3.2)   The sum of the angles of this (Euclidean) polygon equals eight right angles.

However, can I imagine a counterfactually possible world with respect to which I am prepared to say here and now that I understand (6.3.1), understand (6.3.2), assent to (6.3.1), and *dissent from* (6.3.2), i.e., *assent to its negation*? And can I imagine a counterfactually possible world with respect to which I am prepared to say here and now that I understand (6.3.1), understand (6.3.2), assent to (6.3.1),

---

[25] Flew 1979: 153, entry 'implication and entailment'.
[26] Hughes & Cresswell 1968: 27; see also Flew: ibid.

and simply do *not assent to* (6.3.2)?[27] To my mind, *both* of these questions have to be answered in the *positive*: First, I may have simply *miscounted* the number of the triangles into which I have split the hexagon; and second, I may have *not the slightest idea* of how to find out the sum of the angles of a triangle and/or how to proceed in the general case of a polygon having more than three angles. So according to Hare's definitions, (6.3.1) *does not* 'entail' (6.3.2).

6.4.   I don't think that these answers should be objected to by the reminder that we have admitted, in 4.3, above, only a *rational* – i.e., *non-spontaneous, well-considered*, and possibly *maieutically enlightened* – mode of assent. For as I hasted to add in 4.4, above, I am only thinking of *linguistic* rationality and maieutics, of a *linguistic* consistency in the way I use my terms –, and so mishaps due to carelessness in non-linguistic matters have been as little ruled out as mathematical ignorance. Furthermore, in view of what I said about the two 'closedness rules' in 4.2, above, we would hardly be prepared to say that a geometrical sentence like (6.3.2) can be 'derived' from a geometrical sentence like (6.3.1) *'by means of the classical rules of the predicate calculus (including the propositional calculus)'*. Rather, I think, we would prefer the view that explicating 'mathematically' the methods of proceeding from (6.3.1) to (6.3.2) is not fish from the same kettle as explicating 'semantically' what is the intended meaning of a more or less complicated sentence of a non-symbolised language. However, I am well aware that the different branches of mathematics require a differential and much deeper treatment, for which here there is not the space – and the less so because what is at stake includes such delicate issues as Kant's 'synthetic a priori', Frege's 'geometrical source of knowledge' ('geometrische Erkenntnisquelle'), and the controversial distinctions between purely linguistic, purely intuitive, and purely factual knowledge.

7. In any case, Hare's definitions capture *not only* cases of entailment

7.1.   As we just saw, taken *as definitions of entailment* HWDE nor HSDE capture *to little*. At the same time, however, taken in the same way they capture *too much*. This can be seen, for instance, from the following example. Suppose I assent (say, in answering questions by making my choices in a psychotherapeutic questionnaire) to the sentence

(7.1.1) My wife deceives me.

but *dissent from*, or simply *do not assent to*, the sentence

---

[27] Cf. the discussion of a related example – the pair of sentences 'This is a cube.' and 'This has twelve edges.' – between Langford 1942: 327f., and Moore 1942: 663.

(7.1.2) I (strongly) believe [am convinced] that my wife deceives me.

If I do so, I may justly be taken to have 'misunderstood one or other of the sentences'. Hence, according to both of the definitions considered so far (7.1.1) ought to *entail* (7.1.2).

7.2.   If this were in fact the case, however, the combination of (7.1.1) with the negation of (7.1.2), to wit, the sentence

(7.2.1) My wife deceives me, and [but] I don't believe that my wife deceives me.,

would have to be self-contradictory, which it is clearly not; for 'it may quite well be true',[28] as can be gathered from the fact that the modalised sentence

(7.2.2) It is possible that my wife deceives me but that I don't believe so
         [that I don't believe that my wife deceives me].

obviously *is* true. Or in simpler words: It is possible that (7.1.1) is true and (7.1.2) is false; so according to the traditional definition of entailment quoted at the end of 6.2, above, the former does *not* entail the latter. Furthermore, (7.2.1) is a clear-cut case of 'Moore's paradox', on which there is wide agreement that it should not be mistaken for a self-contradiction of the garden variety. So, both HWDE and HSDE seem to capture, not just logical implication or entailment proper, but something *more*.[29]

8. Furthermore, Hare's definitions of 'entailment' violate one or other formal criterion of adequacy

8.1.   There is a third and perhaps more fundamental reason which disqualifies HWDE and HSDE for being acceptable as definitions of entailment proper. For I think there are at least three uncontroversial properties we require of any relation we are willing to accept as an entailment-relation: its 'reflexivity', its 'transitivity', and its being subject to what logicians often call the 'law of transposition'. However, the relation defined by HWDE, though being *reflexive and transposable*, is *not transitive*, and the relation defined by HSDE, though being *reflexive and transitive*, is *not transposable*. So each of Hare's definitions of what he calls 'entailment' fails to satisfy one or other formal criterion of adequacy. For this reason (and, of course, for the reasons indicated in sections 6 and 7), from now on I will avoid referring to what is defined by HWDE and HSDE as – weaker and stronger –

---

[28] Cf. Moore 1944: p. 175.

[29] In this exemplary case, I will suggest to speak of 'pragmatic implication'; see the following Essay II: section 3.

'entailment'; instead, I will simply call these relations 'W-implication' ('weak[er] implication') and 'S-implication' ('strong[er] implication').

8.2.   Let me first oppose to each other, in a more conspicuous way, the two seeming alternatives of defining what Hare mistakes for (informal) entailment; I will call them the definitions of 'W-implication' (DWI) and 'S-implication' (DSI):[30]

DWI: Given two interpreted sentences of a natural language, φ and χ, let us say that φ *W-implies* χ if and only if it is not possible that I understand φ, understand χ, assent to φ, and [but] *dissent from χ*.

DSI: Given two interpreted sentences of a natural language, φ and χ, let us say that φ *S-implies* χ if and only if it is not possible that I understand φ, understand χ, assent to φ, and [but] *do not assent to χ*.

8.3.   On behalf of a greater simplicity in the *formal treatment of the definientia*, let us make the requirement of understanding once for all and hence rewrite DWI and DSI as follows:

DWI*:   On condition that φ and χ are completely interpreted sentences of my personal idiolect[31] within the framework of our common natural language and that I understand the actual use of φ and χ,[32] let us say that φ

---

[30] As I will be going to use Latin capital letters as predicate signs, I replace Hare's letters 'P' and 'Q' with the Greek lower case letters 'φ' and 'χ'; however, I will go on using schematic letters also *autonymously*, i.e., as standing also for themselves. Hence, even where I will be using 'φ', 'χ', etc., and likewise their sentential negations '$\neg\varphi$', '$\neg\chi$', etc., as *names* for sentences (as opposed to *abbreviations* of sentences) – as will be the case in the following definitions –, for reasons of simplicity and conspicuousness I will dispense with inverted commas.

[31] Cf. 4.4, above.

[32] By this stipulation it is required that I understand 'φ' and 'χ' not only as *sentences of (say) the English language*, which is already guaranteed by the stipulation that they belong to my personal idiolect, but also as *sentences used by the given speaker in the given speech-act theoretical situation*; or, in other words, that I grasp, not only the *'linguistic sense'* or meaning which belongs already to an *English sentence as such* and permits, *inter alia*, its translation into a foreign language, but also the *'Fregean sense'*, notably the thought (proposition) expressed by the sentence *on the occasion given*. For these distinctions see esp. Künne 1983: 196–200; Strube 1985; Hoche 1990: ch. 6 ('Sprechakt, Satz und Sinn' ['Speech-act, sentence, and meaning']), esp. 6.3–4. – Let me add to this two remarks. (1) I take it that the first part of our stipulation, i.e., the requirement that I grasp the *'linguistic sense'* of the idiolectal sentences involved, is naturally embedded in the requirement that I have at least a basic command of my idiolect as a whole, including, e.g., the sentential negator 'it is not the case that'. (2) It should be noted that within the framework of 'assenting tests', i.e., in applying DWI, DSI, or DLI (see 10.1, below), more often than not we refer to 'inhabitants', not of the real world, but of a simple fictional quasi-world (artificial mini-world) constructed *ad hoc* – which has the consequence that the *'Fregean senses'* of the sentences involved are not genuine, i.e., true-or-false, *thoughts* but only quasi-true or quasi-false *quasi-thoughts* (Frege: 'Scheingedanken'); for details, see Hoche 1992: 2.4.

W-implies χ if and only if it is not possible that I assent to φ and [but] *dissent from* χ.

DSI*:   On condition that φ and χ are completely interpreted sentences of my personal idiolect within the framework of our common natural language and that I understand the actual use of φ and χ, let us say that φ *S-implies* χ if and only if it is not possible that I assent to φ and [but] *do not assent to* χ.

If we take the complex condition just specified to be understood and confine ourselves to formalising only the 'logically operative' parts of the two definitions, DWI* may be given the following symbolised form:

DWI*′: $\varphi^{W} \Rightarrow \chi =_{\text{def}} \neg \Diamond (A\varphi \ \& \ A\neg\chi),$[33]

which, in virtue of some uncontroversial rules of the propositional calculus and of modal logic, is logically equivalent to

DWI*″: $\varphi^{W} \Rightarrow \chi =_{\text{def}} \Box \neg (A\varphi \ \& \ A\neg\chi);$

DWI*‴: $\varphi^{W} \Rightarrow \chi =_{\text{def}} \Box (A\varphi \rightarrow \neg A\neg\chi).$

In contradistinction, the 'logically operative' part of DSI* may be symbolised as follows:

DSI*′: $\varphi^{S} \Rightarrow \chi =_{\text{def}} \neg \Diamond (A\varphi \ \& \ \neg A\chi),$

which is logically equivalent to

DSI*″: $\varphi^{S} \Rightarrow \chi =_{\text{def}} \Box \neg (A\varphi \ \& \ \neg A\chi);$

DSI*‴: $\varphi^{S} \Rightarrow \chi =_{\text{def}} \Box (A\varphi \rightarrow A\chi).$

8.4.   Now we must certainly accept it as a necessary truth that I assent to the conjunction 'φ & ¬χ' if and only if I assent to φ and likewise assent to ¬χ; hence we have

(8.4.1) $\Box (A(\varphi \ \& \ \neg\chi) \leftrightarrow A\varphi \ \& \ A\neg\chi).$

So instead of DWI*″ we may likewise write

(8.4.2) $\varphi^{W} \Rightarrow \chi =_{\text{def}} \Box \neg A(\varphi \ \& \ \neg\chi).$[34]

---

[33] As I did before, I will take the phrase 'to dissent from a given sentence' to mean the same thing as 'to assent to the negation of this sentence'; cf. 1.4, above.

[34] In English philosophy, especially since the beginnings of the 20th century, in trying to ascertain the existence or non-existence of certain supposed semantic relations it was use and wont to pose oneself the question of whether or not, by uttering, or otherwise assenting to, a propositional combination of the form 'φ, and [but] not χ' one would offend against linguistic usage. (At least from Moore 1903 up to Searle 1983 there are a lot of publications which bear witness to this; for some examples, see

If we follow the propositional calculus and consider conjunction a commutative relation, that is, free of any temporal or causal connotations, the definiens of (8.4.2) is logically equivalent to

(8.4.3) $\Box \neg A(\neg \chi \,\&\, \varphi)$

and hence, because of (8.4.1), to

(8.4.4) $\Box \neg (A \neg \chi \,\&\, A \varphi)$,

which, according to DWI*'', is the definiens for

(8.4.5) $\neg \chi^{W} \Rightarrow \neg \varphi$.

Hence, *W-implication* is shown to be subject to the law of *transposition*.

8.5.   No less easily we can convince ourselves that *S-implication* is a *transitive* relation. For that '$\varphi^{S} \Rightarrow \psi$' follows from '$(\varphi^{S} \Rightarrow \chi) \,\&\, (\chi^{S} \Rightarrow \psi)$' can be immediately seen if we take a look at the related definientia:

(8.5.1) $\Box (A\varphi \to A\chi) \,\&\, \Box (A\chi \to A\psi)$

is logically equivalent to

(8.5.2) $\Box ((A\varphi \to A\chi) \,\&\, (A\chi \to A\psi))$,[35]

which entails

(8.5.3) $\Box (A\varphi \to A\psi)$.

8.6.   But what about the transitivity of W-implication? Let us suppose that '$\varphi^{W} \Rightarrow \psi$' follows from '$(\varphi^{W} \Rightarrow \chi) \,\&\, (\chi^{W} \Rightarrow \psi)$'; then we would have to expect that

(8.6.1) $\Box (A\varphi \to \neg A\neg \chi) \,\&\, \Box (A\chi \to \neg A\neg \psi)$

entails

(8.6.2) $\Box (A\varphi \to \neg A\neg \psi)$.

However, far from being able to prove this we can find counterexamples which show that *W-implication is not transitive*. Let us replace, for instance, the triple of symbols φ, χ and ψ with the triple of sentences, interpreted in accordance with each other,

---

Hoche 1981: sect. 1.) So the use of definition DWI, and hence of Hare's HWDE, virtually coincides with an analytical method that has frequently been used in the English philosophical tradition. However, one can easily see that the application of definition DSI does not fully agree with this analytical method.

[35] See, e.g., Hughes & Cresswell 1968: p. 34, Theorem T3.

(8.6.3)   I don't believe it is raining.

(8.6.4)   It is not raining.

(8.6.5)   I believe it is not raining.

We can easily see that this triple fulfils (8.6.1) without fulfilling (8.6.2). For if I assent to the statement that I don't believe it is raining then I cannot assent to the statement that it is raining, and if I assent to the statement that it is not raining then I cannot assent to the statement that I don't believe it is not raining; but if I assent to the statement that I don't believe it is raining then I can, of course, likewise assent to the statement that I don't believe it is *not* raining – for I may be in a position in which I have not the slightest idea of whether or not it might be raining at the present moment.[36] The same is true for the triple

(8.6.6)   I have no son who lives in London.

(8.6.7)   My son doesn't live in London.

(8.6.8)   I have a [at least one] son who doesn't live in London.

For if I assent to the statement that I have no son who lives in London then I cannot assent to the statement that my son lives in London, and if I assent to the statement that my son doesn't live in London then I cannot assent to the statement that I have no son who doesn't live in London; but if I assent to the statement that I have no son who lives in London then I can well assent to the statement that I have no son who doesn't live in London – for I may have no son at all.[37] Note that this triple does not yet exemplify a true specimen of what linguists use to call '(existential) presupposition'; but the following triple certainly does.

(8.6.9)   I have no son (at all).

(8.6.7)   My son doesn't live in London.

(¬8.6.9)   I have a [at least one] son.

That this triple, too, fulfils (8.6.1) without fulfilling (8.6.2) is easily to be seen: If I assent to the statement that I have no son then I cannot assent to the statement that my son lives in London, and if I assent to the statement that my son doesn't live in London then I cannot assent to the statement that I have no son; but if I assent to the statement that I have no son then I *can*, and even *must*, assent to the – very same – statement that I have no son. Principally the same can be said about

---

[36] Of course, here we have to make a strict difference between sentences of the forms 'I don't believe that p.' and 'I believe that not p.'. It is true that this difference, and similarly the difference between sentences of the forms 'I don't want you to do *a*.' and 'I want you not to do *a*.', is largely ignored in everyday English (and other languages I am acquainted with); but I think that this is due to the fact that in practical life, outside the humanities and sciences, people do not normally tend to show signs of being undetermined.

[37] I owe this example to Michael Knoop.

the following triple, which again exemplifies a clear-cut case of presupposition, though not of existential presupposition. As it is a bit tricky I think it should not be here omitted.

(8.6.10)   I didn't use to smoke [I was no smoker].

(8.6.11)   I haven't given up smoking.

(¬8.6.10) I used to smoke [I was a smoker].

It is clear that if I assent to the statement that I didn't use to smoke then I cannot assent to the statement that I have given up smoking. But I think it is less clear whether if I assent to the statement that I haven't given up smoking then I cannot assent to the statement that I didn't use to smoke; for it might be claimed, first, that if I didn't use to smoke then I had no opportunity to give up smoking, and second, that I cannot possibly have done what I had no opportunity to do. However, this is not the way we use to speak in everyday language; as a matter of linguistic fact, if we say of someone that they haven't given up smoking it is doubtless understood that they still use to smoke, nor would we think it appropriate to say of a baby (not to mention a dog, an elm-tree, etc.) that it hasn't given up smoking. From this we can see that the question of whether a non-smoker has given up smoking is not to be answered in the negative but to be treated as not arising at all, or as 'not applicable' (which is the characteristic mark of the linguistic phenomenon of presupposition). Therefore I take it that if I assent to the statement that I haven't given up smoking then I am certainly not in a position to assent to the statement that I didn't use to smoke. But finally, of course, if I assent to the statement that I didn't use to smoke then I *can*, and even *must*, assent to the – very same – statement that I didn't use to smoke. – From these four counterexamples, which can already be presumed to belong in only two comprehensive groups, we may safely conclude that *W-implication* is *not transitive*.

8.7.   This is not to say, of course, that W-implication is *intransitive*, which it is clearly *not*, as can be seen from the triples

(8.7.1)   Tom is a bachelor
           (in the modern non-academic and non-zoological sense of the word).[38]

(8.7.2)   Tom is an unmarried man.

(8.7.3)   Tom is unmarried.

and, unless we disown Hare's valuable insight mentioned in subsection 1.1, above,

---

[38] Hörmann 1976 called attention to the automatic (involuntary, subconscious) efficacy of the psycho-linguistic phenomenon of 'sense-constancy', which he paralleled with such well-known psychological phenomena as size-constancy, brightness-constancy, or colour-constancy. Sense-constancy induces us to make sense, to the utmost limits of what seems to be possible at all, of a sentence we are confronted with (even of a seemingly self-contradictory sentence such as 'Not all women are

(8.7.4.)   (According to my personal normative standards; or: in my eyes) you (morally) ought to do it.[39]

(8.7.5)   Do it.

(8.7.6)   I hereby ask you to do it.

Whereas the first of these triples is trivial to the point of being worn-out and hardly bearable any more, the second triple surely requires a comment. If we follow Hare, which I think we are well advised to do, then if I assent to the statement that in my eyes you morally ought to do it I cannot dissent from the imperative 'Do it.', i.e., assent to its negation 'Don't do it.'; and if I assent to the 'primary' imperative 'Do it.' I cannot dissent from the 'explicit' imperative[40] 'I hereby ask you to do it.', i.e., assent to its negation 'I hereby ask you not to do it.'.[41] Likewise, if I assent to the statement that in my eyes you morally ought to do it then I cannot assent to 'I hereby ask you not to do it.'. So both of the triples (8.7.1) through (8.7.3) and (8.7.4) through (8.7.6) can be seen to fulfil (8.6.2) as well as (8.6.1), which is sufficient to show that W-implication is *not intransitive*, either.

8.8.   Whereas *W-implication* is *not transitive* (without, however, being intransitive), *S-implication* is *not transposable*. If it were, the propositional equivalence '$(\varphi \overset{S}{\Rightarrow} \chi) \leftrightarrow (\neg\chi \overset{S}{\Rightarrow} \neg\varphi)$' would be true, i.e., the following two formulae would have to entail each other:

(8.8.1) $\Box(A\varphi \rightarrow A\chi)$;

(8.8.2) $\Box(A\neg\chi \rightarrow A\neg\varphi)$.

But that this is not always true can be seen, for instance, from the following pairs of sentences, which I mechanically constructed on the basis of the triples used in subsection 8.6, above.[42]

---

female.'). The price of doing so is the automatic reinterpretation of one or more constituent parts of the sentence. An assenting test according to DWI*, DSI*, or DLI (see 10.1, below) cannot yield a significant result unless, in performing it, we systematically block the loop-holes opened, or left open, by sense-constancy, which can best be done by rendering the wording of the sentences in question as precise as possible; hence the clarifying parenthesis, in which my speaking of the 'non-zoological sense' alludes to the fact that, if I am right, (certain sorts of) baby seals are also called 'bachelors'. See also sect. 3.1 with n. 8, above.

[39] Again, the parentheses have the function to counter the efficacy of sense-constancy.

[40] For Austin's distinction between 'primary' (or 'implicit') and 'explicit performatives', see Austin 1962a: esp. pp. 32, 69, 83, 90 f., 149 and Lectures V–VII.

[41] That *this, and nothing else*, is the negation of the explicit imperative (8.7.6) I have pleaded in Hoche 1995c.

[42] Of course there is an *explanation* for the fact that the counterexamples against the transposability of S-implication are closely connected to the counterexamples against the transitivity of W-implication; see 9.5–6, below.

(¬8.6.4)   It is raining.
(¬8.6.3)   I believe it is raining.

(¬8.6.7)   My son lives in London.
(¬8.6.6)   I have at least one son who lives in London.

(¬8.6.7)   My son lives in London.
(¬8.6.9)   I have at least one son.

(¬8.6.11)   I have given up smoking.
(¬8.6.10)   I used to smoke.

For if I assent to the statement that it is raining then I must also assent to the statement that I believe it is raining; but if I assent to the statement that I don't believe it is raining then I need not, of course, assent to the statement that it is not raining.[43] Similarly, if I assent to the statement that my son lives in London then I must also assent to the statement that I have at least one son who lives in London; but if I assent to the statement that I have no son who lives in London then I need not assent to the statement that my son doesn't live in London – for I may have no son at all. Again, if I assent to the statement that my son lives in London [that I have given up smoking] I must assent to the statement that I have at least one son [that I used to smoke]; but if I assent to the statement that I have no son at all [that I never smoked] then I *need not*, and in fact *cannot*, assent to the statement that my son doesn't live in London [that I haven't given up smoking].

8.9.   The upshot of all this is that *W-implication is not transitive* and *S-implication is not transposable*. However, *both of them are reflexive*. For

(8.9.1) $\Box (A\chi \rightarrow A\chi)$

is an instance of the necessary truth '$\Box (\varphi \rightarrow \varphi)$', which is uncontroversial in all systems of modal logic. Likewise, the necessary sentence

(8.9.2) $\Box (A\chi \rightarrow \neg A\neg\chi)$

must be accepted as true; for given consistency or the principle *tertium non datur* (which, I think, ought not to be called into question at least in considerations of the present type), if I assent to a sentence χ then I cannot possibly at the same time also assent to its negation, i.e., to $\neg\chi$.

8.10.   From this it follows that if a sentence φ S-implies a sentence χ then φ also W-implies χ. For according to some basic rules of modal logic and the propositional calculus, the conjunction of (8.8.1) and (8.9.2), i.e.,

---

[43] Cf. 8.6 with n. 36, above.

(8.10.1) $\Box (A\varphi \rightarrow A\chi) \,\&\, \Box (A\chi \rightarrow \neg A\neg\chi),$

entails

(8.10.2) $\Box (A\varphi \rightarrow \neg A\neg\chi),$

which is to say that, because of the necessary truth (8.9.2), we have to acknowledge the necessary truth

(8.10.3) $\Box ((\varphi^S \Rightarrow \chi) \rightarrow (\varphi^W \Rightarrow \chi)).$

The reverse, however, is not true; for as not assenting to $\neg\chi$ does not, of course, commit me to assenting to χ (cf. 1.4, above), we have to accept the negations

(8.10.4) $\neg\Box (\neg A\neg\chi \rightarrow A\chi);$

(8.10.5) $\neg\Box ((\varphi^W \Rightarrow \chi) \rightarrow (\varphi^S \Rightarrow \chi)).$

In this sense, *S-implication* is indeed *'stronger' than W-implication* (see 2.4, above).

9. An attempt to merge Hare's two definitions into one by stipulating a restriction of the domain

9.1.   As we saw in sections 6 through 8, there is more than one reason why we can accept none of Hare's definitions HWDE and HSDE, or their slightly improved variants DWI and DSI (see 8.1–8.3, above), as a definition of a relation we would be willing to let pass for *logical implication* or *entailment*. So what can we do if we want to go on pursuing Hare's aim of developing such a definition? Certainly a first step – though in fact *only* a *first* step, as can be seen in the following Essay II – might consist in constructing, on the basis of the definitions of W-implication (DWI) and S-implication (DSI), the definition of a relation that is reflexive, transitive, and transposable. As we just saw in 8.9, both S-implication and W-implication satisfy the condition of reflexivity, and as we just saw in 8.10, if a sentence φ S-implies a sentence χ then φ must also W-imply χ whereas the reverse does not hold:

(8.10.3) $\Box ((\varphi^S \Rightarrow \chi) \rightarrow (\varphi^W \Rightarrow \chi));$

(8.10.5) $\neg\Box ((\varphi^W \Rightarrow \chi) \rightarrow (\varphi^S \Rightarrow \chi)).$

Hence at first sight we might perhaps be tempted to believe that S-implication is reflexive, transitive, and transposable. This is not the case, however; for in 8.8, above, S-implication turned out to be *not* transposable. A possible impression to the contrary would be due to the prejudice that a stronger (or subordinated) relation must needs share all the properties of any weaker (or superordinated) relation. That this prejudice is unwarranted and in fact untenable can be seen from a well-known counterexample. The relation of being an ancestor is weaker than, or superordinated to, the relation of being a father, and yet the former is transitive whereas the latter is not. Similarly, though W-implication is weaker than, or superordinated to, S-implication, the former is transposable and the latter not. As we can easily convince ourselves, '$\neg\chi^W \Rightarrow \neg\varphi$' follows from '$\varphi^S \Rightarrow \chi$' via '$\varphi^W \Rightarrow \chi$', but '$\neg\chi^S \Rightarrow \neg\varphi$' does by no means follow from '$\varphi^S \Rightarrow \chi$'.

9.2.   Hence, if we are intent on constructing, on the promising basis of the definitions of W-implication and S-implication, the definition of a relation which is reflexive, transitive, and transposable, I think there is no other way than merging the former two into one. To reach this aim, I suggest to *restrict* the domain on which to define the novel relation by stipulating that the 'linguistic (or: idiolectal) implication', as I will call it, is to be defined for *all and only those* pairs of interpreted sentences φ and χ which stand to each other in the 'W-S-relation'

$$(9.2.1) \qquad (\varphi^W \Rightarrow \chi) \leftrightarrow (\varphi^S \Rightarrow \chi),[44]$$

i.e., because of DWI$^{*'''}$ and DSI$^{*'''}$ (see 8.3, above),

$$(9.2.1') \qquad \Box(A\varphi \rightarrow \neg A\neg\chi) \leftrightarrow \Box(A\varphi \rightarrow A\chi).$$

According to the propositional calculus, (9.2.1) is logically equivalent to

$$(9.2.2) \qquad (\varphi^W \Rightarrow \chi) \,\&\, (\varphi^S \Rightarrow \chi) \vee \neg(\varphi^W \Rightarrow \chi) \,\&\, \neg(\varphi^S \Rightarrow \chi).$$

---

[44] Because of the truth of (8.10.3), i.e., '$\Box((\varphi^S \Rightarrow \chi) \rightarrow (\varphi^W \Rightarrow \chi))$', of which we could convince ourselves in subsection 8.10, above, it would of course suffice to require only '$(\varphi^W \Rightarrow \chi) \rightarrow (\varphi^S \Rightarrow \chi)$'. In view of Dudda 1999: 40f., Definitions 2.3.1 and 2.3.2, we could perhaps think of reading the latter requirement as 'χ is not stronger than φ'; but for the following two reasons I suggest not to do so: First, speaking of the 'strength' of an interpreted sentence is hardly illuminating; and second, my definiens for the definiendum 'χ is stronger than φ' would in this case have to be '$\neg((\varphi^W \Rightarrow \chi) \rightarrow (\varphi^S \Rightarrow \chi))$' or, logically equivalent, '$(\varphi^W \Rightarrow \chi) \,\&\, \neg(\varphi^S \Rightarrow \chi)$', whereas according to Dudda's Definition 2.3.1, in which either the first or else the third condition for being 'stronger than' seems to me to be superfluous, the definiens would be either '$(\chi^S \Rightarrow \varphi) \,\&\, \neg(\varphi^S \Rightarrow \varphi)$' or else '$(\chi^W \Rightarrow \varphi) \,\&\, \neg(\varphi^S \Rightarrow \chi)$'. It should be added, moreover, that Dudda's and my own restrictions have quite divergent aims, which is partly due to the fact that Dudda makes use of what may be called 'combination tests' proper, which can only yield W-implication (cf. 8.4 with note 34, above), whereas I recently learnt to prefer what may be called 'assenting tests' (see, however, 10.1, note 54, below), which primarily yield S-implication, of which W-implication is but an attenuation. As we can see from the context of Dudda's Definitions 2.3.1 and 2.3.2, and as he expressly confirmed in a personal communication, our attitudes towards cases in which φ W-implies but does not S-imply χ are downright unreconcilable: Whereas in such cases Dudda seems to be intent on *answering* the question 'Does φ imply χ linguistically?' *in the negative*, I propose *to ignore, not to admit*, or to *repudiate the question as 'not applicable'*. From this it follows that in my interpretation linguistic (or: idiolectal) implication is subject to the law of transposition (see 10.3, below), whereas in Dudda's it is *not*.

So this restriction brings it about that φ *implies* χ linguistically (idiolectally) if and only if φ *both* W-implies *and* S-implies χ, that φ *does not imply* χ linguistically (idiolectally) if and only if φ *neither* W-implies *nor* S-implies χ, and that in case that φ W-implies χ without S-implying χ[45] the question of whether φ implies χ purely linguistically or idiolectally can be answered neither in the positive nor in the negative but has to be ruled out, or repudiated, as 'not arising' or, as it is often called in everyday-life questionnaires, *'not applicable'*.

9.3.   This ruling out might perhaps be thought to be intolerably *ad hoc*, or a mere trick done with intent to exclude undesirable counterexamples. In fact, this *is* what I am aiming at with my manoeuvre; but I don't see why this trick shouldn't be allowed. Rather, I think it is a legitimate move in philosophy and science to restrict a given domain so that it displays a maximum of interesting and scientifically fertile properties. A precedent has been set, for instance, in as old and noble a branch of mathematics as number theory, where the concepts of being 'prime' and being 'composite' are only defined for natural numbers (positive integers) *greater than 1*. That is, although nobody doubts, of course, that the number 1, too, belongs to the natural numbers, it is counted to be neither prime nor composite. For this number, the question of whether it is prime is not negated in the straightforward way (as it is the case with the composite numbers) but simply left out of consideration, or regarded as not arising in the first place. As all powers of 1 equal each other ($1^1 = 1^2 = 1^3$ etc.), its exclusion from the domain on which to define the concept of primes has the great advantage of permitting to state for the rest of the natural numbers what is sometimes called 'the fundamental theorem of arithmetic', namely, that every positive integer greater than 1 can be expressed as the product of its prime factors *in a unique fashion*.

9.4.   That the equivalence (9.2.1) or, for that matter, (9.2.1′) is not true by itself, i.e., not a necessary truth, and that therefore we have to *explicitly postulate* it whenever we think we have a reason to do so, ought by now to be clear. Nonetheless we may feel it surprising that cases of weak implication and cases of strong implication do not always and necessarily coincide. For I think one is likely to expect at first sight that if my judgement on χ depends *solely* on my *understanding* φ and χ and my *assenting* to φ, and thus leaves no room for the efficacy of any *extra-linguistic* information, then there should be no 'cognitive cleavage' between my not dissenting from χ and my assenting to χ, and hence between weak and strong implication. For what on earth, over and above my understanding the two sentences and my assenting to the first of them, should justify my proceeding from my negative attitude of not dissenting from χ to my positive attitude of assenting to it? But although the plausible expectation that

---

[45] Because of the truth of (8.10.3), i.e., '$\Box((\varphi \stackrel{S}{\Rightarrow} \chi) \rightarrow (\varphi \stackrel{W}{\Rightarrow} \chi))$', the reverse can never be the case.

weak and strong implications must needs fall together is fulfilled in the bulk of the cases we can conceive of, there *is* such a 'cognitive cleavage' in two well-defined sorts of cases, representatives of which we have already become acquainted with in subsections 8.6 and 8.8, above. Let me now try and *explain* this phenomenon.

9.5. As to the first sort of such cases, my assenting to a sentence of the form

(9.5.1)   p.

commits me not only to *not dissenting from* the corresponding sentence of the form

(9.5.2)   I believe that p.

but also to positively *assenting to* it (see sect. 7, above). This 'non-empirical' or at best 'quasi-empirical'[46] linguistic *finding* can be given a plausible *explanation*. My assenting to (9.5.1), if it is not downright taken to be identical with my believing that this sentence is true, is at least based upon, and hence includes, my so believing (cf. 4.1, above), and so it is *not some detail of the contents* of (9.5.1) and (9.5.2) but, as it were, *the very act of assenting* to (9.5.1) which commits me to assenting to (9.5.2), too. This explains at the same time why, as we could see in 8.8, above, the 'transposed' case behaves quite differently. My assenting to

(¬9.5.2)   I don't believe that p.

commits me to the negative attitude of *not dissenting from*

(¬9.5.1)   Not p.

– that is, of not assenting to (9.5.1) – but *not at all* to the positive attitude of *assenting to* (¬9.5.1); so here we have a case in which the 'W-S-relation' (9.2.1) does not hold. Again, this 'non-' or 'quasi-empirical' linguistic *finding* can be *explained* – in this case by the fact that here we have *neither a detail of the contents* of (¬9.5.2) and (¬9.5.1) *nor the efficacy of the very act of assenting* to (¬9.5.2) that can lead us from assenting to (¬9.5.2) to assenting to (¬9.5.1); for from believing

---

[46] The method of assenting tests is certainly *experimental*; but it is *not empirical*. For my personal imaginative and idiolectal competence on which it is based (cf. 5.2 with note 20, above), i.e., which serves as the falsifying or verifying *evidential basis* in the application of such tests, is *not an empirical evidence*. At best, it is an empirical evidence *sui generis*; but I prefer to regard it as a *non-empirical evidence*. My reason for this assessment is that my competence of '*what* to say *when*', although genetically it refers back to an interplay of former empirical perceptions of mine and my former empirical acquisition of our common language, has long since been uncoupled from what I *presently* perceive and from the way my linguistic community *presently* speaks. This, and this alone, makes it possible that we *can*, and *should*, do 'arm-chair philosophy' – a term which, I think, has been quite unrightfully discredited. See Hare 1960; 1981: 80; Hoche 1981: 5.3; Hoche & Strube 1985: A.IV.1.

that I *don't* believe that p there is, of course, no linguistic bridge opening up the way to believing that not p.

9.6.   The second sort of cases in which we find a 'cognitive cleavage' of the type indicated in 9.4, above, has to do with the tricky problem of *presupposition*. On the one hand, my assenting to, say,

(¬8.6.11) I have given up smoking.

commits me to *assenting to*, and *a fortiori* to *not dissenting from*,

(¬8.6.10) I used to smoke.

This linguistic *finding* can be easily *explained* as follows. What is explicitly *asserted* by uttering (¬8.6.10) in the ordinary way, to wit, with 'assertive force',[47] is already *presupposed* in (¬8.6.11), that is, *contained in it in an implicit and, as it were, capsulate form*. On the other hand, my assenting to

(8.6.10)   I didn't use to smoke.,

though it *does not* commit me to *assenting to* – and even commits me to *not assenting* to –

(8.6.11)   I haven't given up smoking.,

does commit me to *not dissenting from* (8.6.11), i.e., to not assenting to (¬8.6.11), so that my assenting to (8.6.10) commits me to assenting to *neither* (8.6.11) *nor* (¬8.6.11). Again, this linguistic *finding* can be easily *explained*. Because of the fact that what is, or would be, explicitly asserted by uttering (¬8.6.10) is contained in (¬8.6.11) *in an implicit or capsulate form*, this part of the content of (¬8.6.11) is *immune against*, or *not reached* by, the negation operating on (¬8.6.11), and so what would be explicitly asserted by uttering (¬8.6.10) – that is, the contradictory of what would be explicitly asserted by uttering (8.6.10) – is still contained, in an implicit and capsulate form, in (8.6.11). *Mutatis mutandis*, the same is true of the sentences

(¬8.6.7)   My son lives in London.
(¬8.6.9)   I have a [at least one] son.
(8.6.9)   I have no son (at all).
(8.6.7)   My son doesn't live in London.

---

[47] Frege's technical term 'assertive force' ('behauptende Kraft'), which he used time and again, has been generalised by John L. Austin (who, by the way, translated Frege 1884, tr. 1950 into English) to the term 'illocutionary force'; see esp. Austin 1962a: 33, 72f., 100, 108, 114f. note, 116, 120, 144, 147f.

What is explicitly asserted by uttering (¬8.6.9), scil., that there exists a son of mine, is already contained, though in an implicit and capsulate form, in (¬8.6.7); this *capsulate* form, however, is responsible for the fact that the presupposition that I have at least one son *survives*, as it were, the passage from (¬8.6.7) to its negation (8.6.7) *wholly untouched*,[48] and so my assenting to (8.6.9) commits me to assenting to *neither* (8.6.7) *nor* (¬8.6.7).[49] Things are slightly different in the related but not strictly presuppositional 'quadruple' of sentences

(¬8.6.7)   My son lives in London.

(¬8.6.6)   I have a [at least one] son who lives in London.

(8.6.6)   I have no son who lives in London.

(8.6.7)   My son doesn't live in London.

What is asserted by (¬8.6.6) is partly presupposed and partly asserted by (¬8.6.7), and for this reason my assenting to (¬8.6.7) commits me to assenting to, and hence, *a fortiori*, to not dissenting from, (¬8.6.6). However, neither the capsulate content of both (¬8.6.7) and (8.6.7), scil., the existential presupposition that I have at least one son, nor its negation (i.e., that I have no son at all) is already contained, explicitly or implicitly, in (8.6.6). Therefore, assenting to (8.6.6) does not commit me to assenting to either (8.6.7) or (¬8.6.7); but it commits me to not dissenting from (8.6.7), i.e., to not assenting to (¬8.6.7).

10. Definition of a generic relation of linguistic, or idiolectal, implication

10.1.   In view of these considerations, perhaps one might think it useful to define the relation of a purely linguistic or idiolectal implication in a way that completely excludes such '*quadruples*' of sentences as the ones just considered in 9.5 and 9.6, above. This would amount to excluding, not only such (ordered)

---

[48] In this case, and arguably also in the preceding one, this can be explained by the well-known linguistic phenomenon that *sentential* negation, which is symbolised by the sentential negator '¬' and is the only one which is considered in standard systems of formal logic, usually coincides with the negation, not of the subject (or, more generally speaking, the Fregean 'argument'), but of the predicate (or Fregean 'function') of the sentence.

[49] In the case of *existential* presupposition, there is a *second* (and more conspicuous) reason why we cannot say that such sentences as (8.6.9) linguistically imply such sentences – or rather strings of words – as (8.6.7): If (8.6.9) is *true*, then (8.6.7) is *not an interpreted sentence at all*; for if I have no son(s), the individual constant 'my son' simply lacks an interpretation. So in this case, not only the 'W-S'-requirement indicated by (9.2.1), but also the – I take it, more fundamental – requirement that φ and χ have to be *interpreted* sentences is not met (see the following Essay II: sect. 7).

pairs of sentences as $\{\,(\neg 9.5.2), (\neg 9.5.1)\,\}$, $\{\,(8.6.6), (8.6.7)\,\}$, $\{\,(8.6.9), (8.6.7)\,\}$, and $\{\,(8.6.10), (8.6.11)\,\}$, but also the corresponding 'transposed' pairs such as $\{\,(9.5.1),$ $(9.5.2)\,\}$, $\{\,(\neg 8.6.7), (\neg 8.6.6)\,\}$, $\{\,(\neg 8.6.7), (\neg 8.6.9)\,\}$, and $\{\,(\neg 8.6.11), (\neg 8.6.10)\,\}$. This option has in fact been *taken into consideration*; but what in my opinion speaks against *accepting* it is, first, the difficulty of a nontrivial conceptual delimitation[50] and, second, the fact that this option would deprive us of interesting and important philosophical issues.[51] For this reason I prefer to stick to the alternative indicated in 9.2, above, i.e., to the alternative of banning, or ruling out, only such (ordered) *pairs* of sentences as $\{\,(\neg 9.5.2), (\neg 9.5.1)\,\}$, $\{\,(8.6.6), (8.6.7)\,\}$, $\{\,(8.6.9), (8.6.7)\,\}$, and $\{\,(8.6.10), (8.6.11)\,\}$. So I would like to suggest the following definition of the generic relation of a purely linguistic (idiolectal) implication:

DLI: On condition, first, that φ and χ are completely interpreted sentences of my personal idiolect within the framework of our common natural language, second, that I understand the actual use of φ and χ, and, third, that φ and χ stand to each other in the 'W-S-relation' $'(\varphi \overset{W}{\Rightarrow} \chi) \leftrightarrow (\varphi \overset{S}{\Rightarrow} \chi)'$,[52] let us say that φ *implies* χ *linguistically (idiolectally)* if and only if it is not (counterfactually or objectively) possible[53] that I assent to φ and [but] do not assent to χ.[54]

---

[50] If all 'neuralgic quadruples' were cases of *believing* (see 9.5, above) and of *existential presupposition* (see the second example discussed in 9.6, above), in view of Frege's insight that 'existence is a property of *concepts*' and not a property 'of the *things* which fall under the concept' (Frege 1884, tr. 1950: § 53; my italics) one could be tempted to think of defining the relation of a purely linguistic or idiolectal implication only for such pairs of sentences which are, as it were, related to each other by a suitable *property of a thing* which is referred to in both of them. But as we saw, things are not that simple.

[51] On the one hand, Dudda (1999: 39f.) discusses the feasibility of postulating a special kind of 'doxastic implication' disjunct from 'pragmatic implication' but decides *against* this option, which is *fortunate* in that otherwise an integrated logic of conviction and intention (see Hoche 2001; 2004) and hence a formal approach to metaethics (see esp. Hoche 1992; 1995d) would be doomed to failure. On the other hand, Strawson (1952), who has been very influential in this respect, has been generally (though arguably not altogether correctly: see Knoop 2003) understood to completely separate 'presupposition' from 'entailment', which would be *unfortunate* in that, strictly speaking, this decision would circumvent us from adopting Russell's theory of definite descriptions and hence from analysing identity-statements in a way that could be applied to assessing the logical justifiability of psychophysical 'monisms' as well as 'dualisms' (see 0.3, above, and Essay III of the present collection).

[52] See 9.2, above.

[53] How this phrase ought to be 'operationalised' may be seen from 1.5, above.

[54] Because of the requirement that φ and χ are to stand to each other in the relation $'(\varphi \overset{W}{\Rightarrow} \chi) \leftrightarrow (\varphi \overset{S}{\Rightarrow} \chi)'$ we are free to replace the concluding words 'that I assent to φ and [but] do not assent to χ' with the words 'that I assent to φ and [but] dissent from χ' and also with the

The 'logically operative' part of DLI may be reformulated more briefly and conspicuously like this:

DLI′: φ implies χ *linguistically (idiolectally)* if and only if it is not possible that I assent to φ and [but] do not assent to χ.

In symbols, we may write this in either one of the following logically equivalent ways:[55]

DLI$_1$: $\varphi \stackrel{L}{\Rightarrow} \chi =_{\text{def}} \neg \Diamond\, (A\varphi\ \&\ \neg A\chi)$;

DLI$_2$: $\varphi \stackrel{L}{\Rightarrow} \chi =_{\text{def}} \Box\, (A\varphi \to A\chi)$.

Because of DLI$_2$, if we like to do so we can replace DLI′ with

DLI″: φ implies χ *linguistically (idiolectally)* if and only if it is necessary that if I assent to φ then I assent (also) to χ.

10.2.   I think it imperative to add to this definition a number of further clarifications. (1) The idiolectal sentences φ and χ are to be interpreted *in accordance with each other*, or as used on *one and the same* occasion. (2) If they are of indicative form (without, however, being 'explicit performatives': see the following Essay II: 4.2, 4.4), then instead of speaking of an 'interpreted sentence' we may simply speak of a *'proposition'* as long as by this extraordinarily ambiguous technical term we understand a 'sentence as used [not necessarily: uttered] by a particular speaker on a particular occasion'.[56] (3) By the stipulation that I understand the *actual use* of φ and χ it is required that I grasp, not only their 'linguistic' sense, but also their full, or 'Fregean', sense (for details, see 8.3, note 32, above). (4) It is to be understood that φ and χ are *not self-contradictory*. (That they might be meaningless pseudo-sentences or other nonsensical 'strings of words' is already excluded by the wording of DLI.) (5) The requirement that φ and χ are to stand to each other in the 'W-S-relation' '$(\varphi \stackrel{W}{\Rightarrow} \chi) \leftrightarrow (\varphi \stackrel{S}{\Rightarrow} \chi)$' seems to commit us to making a 'test before the test'. However, the procedure may also be described like this. Suppose we have convinced ourselves that the 'W-S-relation' *holds*, i.e., that either φ S-implies χ or else that φ does not W-imply χ. Then we know that φ *L-implies* χ or that φ *does not L-imply* χ, as the case may be, and so there is

---

words 'that I assent to the combination "φ and [but] non-χ"' (see 8.4, above). So applications of DLI may be called *'assenting tests'* or *'combination tests'* with *precisely the same right* (cf. 9.2, note 44, above).

[55] That the definientia of DLI$_1$ and DLI$_2$ do not at all differ from those of DSI*′ and DSI*‴ (see 8.3, above) is neither surprising nor to be considered a disadvantage; for as far as their 'logically operative' parts are concerned, these definitions completely coincide: They differ from each other *only*, though of course *crucially*, in the conditions on which they are supposed to hold.

[56] Hare 1952: 2.4, p. 25; cf. Strawson 1950: sect. II.

nothing left to be done. Suppose, on the other hand, that we have convinced ourselves that the 'W-S-relation' *does not hold*, i.e., that φ W-implies χ *without* S-implying it (the reverse is not possible because of the truth of (8.10.3), i.e., '$\Box((\varphi \stackrel{S}{\Rightarrow} \chi) \rightarrow (\varphi \stackrel{W}{\Rightarrow} \chi))$'; see 8.10, above). In this case, the question of whether or not φ L-implies χ simply does not come up, and so the test has to be broken off. Therefore we have to *dismiss the preliminary tests without making any use of their results*. In particular, this includes that we are not allowed to use their results as counterexamples against the transposability of linguistic implication (see 9.2, note 44, above; 10.3, below). (6) Whoever is conversant with Grice's (1961: sect. III; 1975) 'conversational implicatures' ought to see from my definition that what I call 'linguistic (idiolectal) implication' is fish from a different kettle. Very roughly speaking, and making use of Morris's (1938: esp. chs. IV and V) terminology, which widely differs from the one I employ in the present paper, we may perhaps say that *all* sub-kinds of linguistic or *idiolectal* implication – including what I will call, in the following Essay II (sections 3–4), 'pragmatic' and 'catapragmatic' implications – have to do with 'semantics' whereas 'conversational implicatures', which make up 'a certain subclass of *nonconventional* implicatures' (Grice 1975: 45; cf. 47; my italics), have to do with 'pragmatics'.[57]

10.3. Let me finally add that, because of the requirement inserted in DLI that φ and χ stand to each other in the relation '$(\varphi \stackrel{W}{\Rightarrow} \chi) \leftrightarrow (\varphi \stackrel{S}{\Rightarrow} \chi)$', *linguistic (idiolectal) implication* can be safely expected to share with W-implication the property of being subject to the *law of transposition*, with S-implication the property of being a *transitive* relation, and with both W- and S-implication the property of being a *reflexive* relation – which was the reason why I decided in favour of DLI in the first place. That linguistic (idiolectal) implication is in fact *transitive* and *reflexive* can be formally proved in precisely the ways shown in 8.5 and 8.9, above; and that it is *transposable*, i.e., that '$\varphi \stackrel{L}{\Rightarrow} \chi$' and '$\neg\chi \stackrel{L}{\Rightarrow} \neg\varphi$' or, according to DLI$_2$,

(10.3.1) $\Box(A\varphi \rightarrow A\chi)$;

(10.3.2) $\Box(A\neg\chi \rightarrow A\neg\varphi)$

are logically equivalent to each other can be shown as follows. Thanks to the stipulation that any two sentences φ and χ for which the relation of linguistic or idiolectal implication is to be defined *at all* have to fulfil the condition '$(\varphi \stackrel{W}{\Rightarrow} \chi) \leftrightarrow (\varphi \stackrel{S}{\Rightarrow} \chi)$', we can make use of the premises, equivalent to each other,

---

[57] As a matter of fact, *linguistic (idiolectal) implication* shares with *conversational implicature* just one out of five 'features' of the latter listed by Grice (1975: 57 f.): In view of the subrelation of pragmatic implication (see the following Essay II: sect. 3) we can also say of linguistic implication what Grice says of conversational implicature: 'what is said may be true – what is implicated [implied] may be false' (ibid.: 58).

(9.2.1) $(\varphi \overset{W}{\Rightarrow} \chi) \leftrightarrow (\varphi \overset{S}{\Rightarrow} \chi)$;

(9.2.1′) $\Box(A\varphi \rightarrow \neg A\neg\chi) \leftrightarrow \Box(A\varphi \rightarrow A\chi)$;

(9.2.1″) $\Box(A\neg\chi \rightarrow \neg A\varphi) \leftrightarrow \Box(A\varphi \rightarrow A\chi)$

and, of course, likewise of the premises, again equivalent to each other,

(10.3.3) $(\neg\chi \overset{W}{\Rightarrow} \neg\varphi) \leftrightarrow (\neg\chi \overset{S}{\Rightarrow} \neg\varphi)$;

(10.3.3′) $\Box(A\neg\chi \rightarrow \neg A\varphi) \leftrightarrow \Box(A\neg\chi \rightarrow A\neg\varphi)$.[58]

By comparing (9.2.1″) with (10.3.3′) we can see that (10.3.1) and (10.3.2) are both of them equivalent to '$\Box(A\neg\chi \rightarrow \neg A\varphi)$' and hence equivalent to each other.

---

[58] If we had replaced the concluding words of DLI, to wit, 'that I assent to φ and [but] do not assent to χ', with the words 'that I assent to φ and [but] dissent from χ' or, equivalently, with the words 'that I assent to the combination "φ and [but] non-χ"', which we have been free to do (see 10.1, n. 54, above), we would now need the premise (9.2.1) for proving that linguistic implication is *transitive* (cf. 8.6, above). This shows once again the importance of the requirement (9.2.1). – Let me add that (9.2.1′) has the simplest form '$\Box\varphi \leftrightarrow \Box\chi$', which in basic systems of modal logic would follow from '$\Box(\varphi \leftrightarrow \chi)$' (see, for instance, Hughes & Cresswell 1968: p. 31, Axiom A6, and p. 34, Theorem T3), whereas the reverse is not always true. In fact, from (9.2.1′) we must by no means conclude '$\Box((A\varphi \rightarrow \neg A\neg\chi) \leftrightarrow (A\varphi \rightarrow A\chi))$', which is false (see 8.6 and 8.10, above).

II
FIVE KINDS OF LINGUISTIC IMPLICATION

Summary

By means of a two-level criterion for assenting or combination tests, a highly generic relation in the field of interpreted ordinary-language sentences which I suggest to call 'linguistic (or: idiolectal) implication' may be naturally split up into three sub-relations, scil., 'semantic (or: analytical) implication', 'pragmatic implication', and 'catapragmatic implication', and two sub-subrelations, scil., 'semantic presupposition' and 'catapragmatic presupposition'. *Semantic implication* is defined as the set-theoretical intersection of linguistic implication and strict implication or entailment and helps explicate the traditional concept of analyticity. *Pragmatic implication* comes very close to being a correlate of 'Moore's paradox' and can serve as the basis for an integrated logic of believing and intending, which is useful for a further development of metaethics. *Catapragmatic implication* is less important but will none the less be mentioned for historical as well as systematic reasons. *Semantic presupposition* will be defined as a subcase of semantic implication. Choosing such a definition is, I take it, a prerequisite for vindicating Russell's theory of definite descriptions, the philosophical fertility of which can hardly be overestimated. *Catapragmatic presupposition* neatly mirrors semantic presupposition but is of minor philosophical interest; hence it will only be touched in passing.

1. A criterion for distinguishing between five kinds of linguistic implication

1.1.   On the basis of the motivations offered in the preceding Essay I ('Hare's Two Definitions of "Entailment" and the Generic Relation of "Linguistic Implication"'),[1] I should like to propose the following criterion for distinguishing between three kinds and two subkinds of linguistic or idiolectal implication. In former publications,[2] I used to call this criterion the 'criterion for combination tests' (C-CT), and I will stick to this established name although it might as well be called a 'criterion for assenting tests'.

---

[1] Though I think that also the present essay stands on its own, I seriously advise the reader, especially the critically minded one, to treat it as the *continuation* of Essay I, which offers a wealth of background information.

[2] For more or less slightly deviating predecessor formulations see Hoche 2004: sect. 2; 2001: II.1; 1995d: 1.3; Dudda 1999: 2.3. Similar criteria, in which, however, the case of presupposition was still omitted, have been proposed in Hoche 1981; 1990: 8.2–8.5; 1992: 1.5–1.12; 1995e: sect. II; Hoche & Strube 1985: A.IV.3–4.

C-CT: On condition, first, that φ and χ are completely interpreted sentences of my personal idiolect within the framework of our common natural language, second, that I understand the actual use of φ and χ, and, third, that φ and χ stand to each other in the relation '$\Box\,(A\varphi \to \neg A\neg\chi) \leftrightarrow \Box\,(A\varphi \to A\chi)$',[3] let us say that φ *implies* χ *linguistically (idiolectally)* – or, for short: that φ *L-implies* χ – if and only if it is not (counterfactually or objectively) possible that I assent to φ and [but] do not assent to χ – or, which is to say the same thing: if and only if I cannot conceive, in the mode of counterfactual imagination, a counterfactually possible world with respect to which I am prepared to say here and now that I assent to φ and [but] do not assent to χ.[4]

If we make out a linguistic implication of this generic type, let us take a second step and test the modalized combination 'It is (counterfactually or objectively) possible that φ and [but] that not χ.'.[5] As far as this modalization or 'possibilisation' is concerned, there are exactly three possibilities: it can be *false*, *true*, or *nonsensical* (in the way of being *ungrammatical*, i.e., violating at least one rule of the 'surface grammar' or the 'depth grammar'[6] of the natural language in question).

[1] If this possibilisation is *false*, then let us say that φ *implies* χ *semantically* (or: *analytically*).

[2] If the possibilisation is *true*, then let us say that φ *implies* χ *pragmatically*.

---

[3] In words: 'It is necessary that if I assent to φ then I do not assent to non-χ if and only if it is necessary that if I assent to φ then I assent to χ.', or simply: 'I cannot assent to non-χ if I assent to φ if and only if I must assent to χ if I assent to φ.'. As I worked out in the preceding Essay I (esp. sections 8–10), this rather clumsy stipulation cannot be dispensed with if we are intent on rendering linguistic implication a relation which is transitive, reflexive, and subject to the so-called law of transposition.

[4] Cf. Hoche 1990: ch. 9 ('Möglichkeit und Vorstellbarkeit' ['Possibility and conceivability']), esp. 9.3, 9.5. That we cannot always do without this admittedly somewhat bulky 'operationalisation' may be seen, for instance, from the case discussed in 5.3 and 5.5, below; but see also 4.1, below. – As in the preceding Essay I (see ibid.: 8.2 with note 30) I will use schematic letters also *autonymously*, i.e., as standing also for themselves. Hence, even where I will be using 'φ', 'χ', etc. – and likewise their sentential negations '$\neg\varphi$', '$\neg\chi$', etc. – as *names* for sentences (as opposed to *abbreviations* of sentences), for reasons of simplicity and conspicuity I will dispense with inverted commas.

[5] If necessary, this sentence is to be 'operationalised', *mutatis mutandis*, along the lines presented in the preceding (first) paragraph of C-CT. – It should be noted that I strictly distinguish between the uses of round and square brackets: What is put in *round brackets* may as well be omitted but is useful in that it hints to nuances of meaning or renders a reading unambiguous; what is put in *square brackets*, however, is to be understood as an *alternative* to the preceding expression(s).

[6] Cf. Wittgenstein 1953: § 664.

[3] If the possibilisation is neither true nor false but *ungrammatical*, then let us say, in default of a better term, that φ *implies* χ *catapragmatically*.

Finally, if [a] either both φ and non-φ imply χ *semantically* according to [1] or else both φ and non-φ imply χ *catapragmatically* according to [3], and if [b] χ is *'purely contingent'* in the sense of being either a contingent (i.e., neither logically true nor logically false) atomic sentence or else a molecular sentence having only contingent constituents,[7] then let us say that χ *is semantically or catapragmatically presupposed by* φ *and also by non-φ.*

1.2.   The opening paragraph of this criterion stands in need of some clarifications. (1) As C-CT is a *criterion* for deciding whether φ implies χ linguistically at large and, if so, in what specific way it does, and as a criterion is supposed to be applicable without much ado in real situations, in using C-CT – and likewise in other forms of doing conceptual analysis – we cannot normally wait until an intersubjective linguistic agreement has been brought about; therefore the relation of linguistic implication has to be defined on the domain of sentences of my personal *idiolect*.[8] (2) The idiolectal sentences φ and χ are to be interpreted *in accordance with each other*, or as used on *one and the same* occasion. (3) If they are of indicative form (without, however, being 'explicit performatives': see subsections 4.2 and 4.4, below), then instead of speaking of an 'interpreted sentence' we may simply speak of a *'proposition'* as long as by this extraordinarily ambiguous technical term we understand a 'sentence as used [not necessarily: uttered] by a particular speaker on a particular occasion'.[9] (4) By the stipulation that I understand the *actual use* of φ and χ it is required that I grasp, not only their 'linguistic' sense, but also their full, or 'Fregean', sense.[10] (5) It is to be understood that φ and

---

[7] The details of condition [b] I owe to Knoop 2001.

[8] Cf. Hoche & Strube 1985: A. IV.1.f. – Of course, such a 'personal language' must not be mistaken for a 'private language', for the impossibility of which Wittgenstein (1953), to my mind, has indicated good grounds.

[9] Hare 1952: 2.4, p. 25; cf. Strawson 1950: sect. II.

[10] By this stipulation it is required that I understand φ and χ not only as *sentences of* (say) *the English language*, which is already guaranteed by the stipulation that they belong to my personal idiolect, but also as *sentences used by the given speaker in the given speech-act theoretical situation*; or, in other words, that I grasp, not only the *'linguistic sense'* or meaning which belongs already to an *English sentence as such* and permits, *inter alia*, its translation into another language, but also the *'Fregean sense'*, notably the thought (proposition) expressed by the sentence *on the given occasion*. For these distinctions see esp. Künne 1983: 196–200; Strube 1985; Hoche 1990: ch. 6 ('Sprechakt, Satz und Sinn' ['Speech-act, sentence, and meaning']), esp. 6.3–6.4. It should be noted that within the framework of C-CT, more often than not we refer to 'inhabitants', not of the real world, but of a simple fictional quasi-world (artificial mini-world) constructed *ad hoc* – which has the consequence that the *'Fregean senses'* of the sentences involved are not genuine, i.e., true-or-false, *thoughts* but only quasi-true or quasi-false *quasi-thoughts* (Frege: 'Scheingedanken'); cf. Hoche 1992: 2.4.

χ are *not self-contradictory*. (That they might be meaningless pseudo-sentences or other nonsensical 'strings of words' is already excluded by the wording of C-CT.) (6) The requirement that φ and χ are to stand to each other in the relation '$\Box\,(A\varphi \rightarrow \neg A\neg\chi) \leftrightarrow \Box\,(A\varphi \rightarrow A\chi)$' seems to commit us to making a 'test before the test'. However, the procedure may also be described like this. Suppose we have convinced ourselves that that relation *holds*. Then we know that φ *L-implies* χ or that φ *does not L-imply* χ, as the case may be, and so there is nothing left to be done. Suppose, on the other hand, that we have convinced ourselves that that relation *does not hold*. In this case, the question whether or not φ L-implies χ simply does not arise, or is simply 'not applicable'. *Hence we have to break off the test and to dismiss, or forget about, the results so far obtained.* In particular, we have to refrain from using these results as alleged counterexamples against the transposability of linguistic implication in general and semantic implication and semantic presupposition in particular (see 2.4 and 6.4–6.5, below, and the preceding Essay I: 9.2, note 44; 10.2, no. (5); 10.3).

1.3.   As for the sub-criteria [1] and [2], we can easily convince ourselves that [1] virtually coincides with the definition usually given in modal logics for strict, necessary, or logical implication, to wit: '$\varphi \vDash \chi =_{\text{def}} \neg\Diamond\,(\varphi\ \&\ \neg\chi)$', and that [2] has been tailored in accordance with Moore's remark that the paradoxes called after him are not self-contradictory but 'may quite well be true'.[11] What is less easily seen is how the concept of [3] catapragmatic implication fits in. I trust, however, that this will become sufficiently clear once we differentially scrutinise some examples for each of the cases [1] through [3].

1.4.   From the concluding paragraph of C-CT the reader can see that the relation of semantic (catapragmatic) *presupposition* is defined as a subrelation of semantic (catapragmatic) *implication* and hence has only to do with the *meanings, to the exclusion of any other speech-act theoretical aspects*, of the sentences concerned. So semantic, and likewise catapragmatic, presupposition in the sense of the present paper differs from what is called 'presupposition' in the full sense of linguistics and the philosophy of language,[12] the discussion of which is not a concern of mine. The reader should keep this in mind in order to avoid irrelevant criticism.

---

[11] Moore 1944: p. 175.

[12] In the philosophy of language, in which the concept of presupposition originates, some *loci classici* are Frege 1892a, tr. 1952: pp. 39–41; Strawson 1950: sect. III; 1952: ch. 6 sect. 7; 1959: ch. 6 sect. [3]; Austin 1962a: Lecture IV.

2. Semantic implication

2.1.   The 'operative' part of the definition of semantic implication given in C-CT may be briefly reformulated like this:

DSI: φ implies χ *semantically* if and only if it is not possible that I assent to φ and [but] do not assent to χ, and the modalized combination 'It is possible that φ and [but] that not χ.' is false.

We may write this more conspicuously in either of the following logically equivalent ways:

DSI$_1$: $\varphi \overset{\sigma}{\Rightarrow} \chi$ iff $\neg\Diamond(A\varphi \ \& \ \neg A\chi) \ \& \ \neg\Diamond(\varphi \ \& \ \neg\chi);$[13]

DSI$_2$: $\varphi \overset{\sigma}{\Rightarrow} \chi$ iff $\Box(A\varphi \rightarrow A\chi) \ \& \ \Box(\varphi \rightarrow \chi).$

Because of DSI$_2$, we can replace DSI with

DSI': φ implies χ *semantically* if and only if it is necessary that if I assent to φ then I assent (also) to χ, and also necessary that if φ then (also) χ.

That the two conjuncts of DSI and its variants are logically independent of each other, so that none of them can be simply omitted, is easily seen, for instance,[14] from the sentences

(2.1.1) This (geometrical body) is a cube.

(2.1.2) This (geometrical body) has twelve edges.

For if we substitute them for φ and χ, respectively, the second conjunct of DSI$_2$ becomes true and the first one false. In the case of the sentences

---

[13] On behalf of a better logical tractability of the definiens of DSI$_1$, instead of ' "$\Diamond(\varphi \ \& \ \neg\chi)$" is false.' I write '$\neg\Diamond(\varphi \ \& \ \neg\chi)$'. This is justified by the so-called redundancy theory of truth, which can be corroborated by an application of C-CT and according to which the sentence 'φ is true [a true sentence].' has the same truth-value as the sentence φ, and consequently the sentence 'φ is false [a false sentence].' – i.e., '$\neg\varphi$ is true [a true sentence].' – the same truth-value as the sentence '$\neg\varphi$'. Mind, however, that, as has been stated in C-CT, a string of words (symbols) of the form 'It is possible that φ but that not χ.' or, for that matter, '$\Diamond(\varphi \ \& \ \neg\chi)$' need not be a (true or false) sentence but can well be ungrammatical and hence *meaningless* (see also 4.5, below). In this case, the (apparent) sentential negation '$\neg\Diamond(\varphi \ \& \ \neg\chi)$' is, of course, likewise a *meaningless* string of symbols. For this reason some readers might find it illegitimate that I here incorporate '$\neg\Diamond(\varphi \ \& \ \neg\chi)$' into a sentential conjunction; but I think it is not. Of course it is true that if the sentence ' "$\Diamond(\varphi \ \& \ \neg\chi)$" is false [a false sentence].' is *false* then '$\neg\Diamond(\varphi \ \& \ \neg\chi)$' can be either a false sentence or no sentence at all; but if the sentence ' "$\Diamond(\varphi \ \& \ \neg\chi)$" is false [a false sentence].' is *true*, as is implied by DSI, then '$\neg\Diamond(\varphi \ \& \ \neg\chi)$' is true, hence a sentence, and hence admissible as a constituent of a logical formula.

[14] For a detailed discussion of the following examples, see the preceding Essay I: sections 3, 6, and 7.

(2.1.3) My wife deceives me.

(2.1.4) I (strongly) believe [am convinced] that my wife deceives me.

it is just the other way round: By a substitution of them, the first conjunct of DSI_2 turns out to be true and the second false.[15] However, in the case of the sentences

(2.1.5) Tim is a brother of mine.

(2.1.6) Tim and I have the same parents.

both conjuncts of DSI_2 become true. So it is obvious that both of the conjuncts of DSI_2 are needed and that this definition of semantic or 'analytical' implication precisely picks out the non-empty set-theoretical intersection of logical implications, which may be either 'analytical' or else 'synthetic a priori' in the traditional sense, and linguistic implications at large.[16]

2.2. Now suppose that $\varphi \stackrel{\sigma}{\Rightarrow} \chi$ and that also $\chi \stackrel{\sigma}{\Rightarrow} \psi$; then we have, according to DSI_2:

(2.2.1) $\Box(A\varphi \rightarrow A\chi) \ \& \ \Box(\varphi \rightarrow \chi)$;

(2.2.2) $\Box(A\chi \rightarrow A\psi) \ \& \ \Box(\chi \rightarrow \psi)$

and hence also the conjunction of (2.2.1) and (2.2.2), i.e.,

(2.2.3) $\Box(A\varphi \rightarrow A\chi) \ \& \ \Box(\varphi \rightarrow \chi) \ \& \ \Box(A\chi \rightarrow A\psi) \ \& \ \Box(\chi \rightarrow \psi)$,

which is logically equivalent to

(2.2.4) $\Box(A\varphi \rightarrow A\chi) \ \& \ \Box(A\chi \rightarrow A\psi) \ \& \ \Box(\varphi \rightarrow \chi) \ \& \ \Box(\chi \rightarrow \psi)$;

(2.2.4') $\Box((A\varphi \rightarrow A\chi) \ \& \ (A\chi \rightarrow A\psi)) \ \& \ \Box((\varphi \rightarrow \chi) \ \& \ (\chi \rightarrow \psi))$,

the latter of which is immediately seen to entail

(2.2.5) $\Box(A\varphi \rightarrow A\psi) \ \& \ \Box(\varphi \rightarrow \psi)$,

i.e., the definiens of '$\varphi \stackrel{\sigma}{\Rightarrow} \psi$'. So '$\varphi \stackrel{\sigma}{\Rightarrow} \psi$' is logically entailed by '$(\varphi \stackrel{\sigma}{\Rightarrow} \chi) \ \&$ $(\chi \stackrel{\sigma}{\Rightarrow} \psi)$', and hence semantic implication is a *transitive relation*.

2.3. It may seem to be still easier to convince ourselves that semantic implication is a *reflexive relation*, too; but mind that there is a problem. According to DSI_2, we have

(2.3.1) $\varphi \stackrel{\sigma}{\Rightarrow} \varphi$ iff $\Box(A\varphi \rightarrow A\varphi) \ \& \ \Box(\varphi \rightarrow \varphi)$.

---

[15] Although (2.1.3) implies (2.1.4) not semantically but pragmatically this remark is certainly worth making also in the present context.

[16] So DSI_2 or DSI' may be regarded as a redefinition of the traditional concept of *analyticity*, which, in my eyes, can and should be rehabilitated, if only in respectively my own personal idiolect.

Certainly the first conjunct of the definiens of (2.3.1) is a basic truth of modal logic; but first appearances notwithstanding, the second need not be. For if φ is, say, an imperative then the second conjunct of the definiens (2.3.1) is ungrammatical and hence not a true sentence, and so it would be wrong to believe that any interpreted sentence whatsoever implies itself semantically. From this we can, and must, conclude, however, that if φ does not imply itself semantically then it implies itself catapragmatically (cf. 3.4 and 4.5, below).

2.4.   So semantic implication has been shown to be a reflexive and transitive relation. Let us next ask ourselves whether semantic implication is also subject to the law of *transposition,* i.e., whether '$\varphi\,^\sigma\!\Rightarrow\chi$' and '$\neg\chi\,^\sigma\!\Rightarrow\neg\varphi$' and hence, according to DSI_2,

(2.4.1) $\Box\,(A\varphi \rightarrow A\chi)\ \&\ \Box\,(\varphi \rightarrow \chi);$

(2.4.2) $\Box\,(A\neg\chi \rightarrow A\neg\varphi)\ \&\ \Box\,(\neg\chi \rightarrow \neg\varphi)$

are logically equivalent to each other. Now we stipulated in C-CT that any two sentences φ and χ for which the relation of linguistic or idiolectal implication shall be defined *at all* have to fulfil the condition '$\Box\,(A\varphi \rightarrow \neg A\neg\chi) \leftrightarrow \Box\,(A\varphi \rightarrow A\chi)$'. So in the present case we can make use of the premises, equivalent to each other,

(2.4.3) $\Box\,(A\varphi \rightarrow \neg A\neg\chi) \leftrightarrow \Box\,(A\varphi \rightarrow A\chi);$

(2.4.3′) $\Box\,(A\neg\chi \rightarrow \neg A\varphi) \leftrightarrow \Box\,(A\varphi \rightarrow A\chi)$

and, of course, likewise of the premise

(2.4.4) $\Box\,(A\neg\chi \rightarrow \neg A\varphi) \leftrightarrow \Box\,(A\neg\chi \rightarrow A\neg\varphi).$

By comparing (2.4.3′) and (2.4.4) with each other we see that the first members of the conjunctions (2.4.1) and (2.4.2), i.e.,

(2.4.5) $\Box\,(A\varphi \rightarrow A\chi);$

(2.4.6) $\Box\,(A\neg\chi \rightarrow A\neg\varphi),$

are equivalent to '$\Box\,(A\neg\chi \rightarrow \neg A\varphi)$' and hence equivalent to each other. Clearly, the second conjuncts of (2.4.1) and (2.4.2) are equivalent to each other, too. So the whole of (2.4.1) is equivalent to the whole of (2.4.2), that is, semantic implication is *transposable.* This was, of course, to be expected; for the class of semantic implications is, as I tried to make clear in 2.1, above, nothing but the non-empty intersection of the classes of linguistic implications at large and logical implications, both of which are characterised by transitivity, reflexivity, and transposability.

2.5.   As for *examples* of semantic implication in the strict sense of C-CT, a first one I have already presented in subsection 2.1, above, to wit, the pair of sentences

(2.1.5)   Tim is a brother of mine.

(2.1.6)   Tim and I have the same parents.

If I assent to (2.1.5) then I must also assent to (2.1.6) and, *a fortiori*, cannot dissent from it – provided, of course, that I am not taking, for instance, the word 'brother' in one of its extended or deviant senses of 'half brother', 'stepbrother', 'brother-in-law', 'blood brother', 'really good friend', etc.[17] So according to C-CT, (2.1.5) implies (2.1.6) linguistically. Our second step according to C-CT has to consist in testing the modalization

(2.5.1)   It is (counterfactually or objectively) possible that Tim is a brother of mine and that Tim and I do not have the same parents.

If again we consciously take account of, and systematically 'neutralise', the efficacy of sense-constancy, we have to admit that (2.5.1) is *false*, and so to conclude that (2.1.5) implies (2.1.6) *semantically*. Admittedly, this is a simple, trivial, utterly outworn, and philosophically useless example; but at least it has the advantage of being relatively uncontroversial.

2.6.   Now let us consider the following, less trivial pair of sentences:

(2.6.1)   I intend to arrest all the suspects, and I am convinced that Tom is one of the suspects.

(2.6.2)   I intend to arrest Tom.

Judging on the basis of my personal linguistic competence (or rather my integrated 'imaginative and idiolectal competence'),[18] I cannot help saying that whoever assents to (2.6.1) but in the same breath refuses to assent to (2.6.2) – and stubbornly abides by this position after having been pointed out the awkwardness of his linguistic behaviour – may be considered to show a remarkable lack of their command of English, especially of the vocabulary of intention and conviction. Or, in simpler words: Whoever assents to (2.6.1) must also assent to (2.6.2) – and hence cannot dissent from it –, and so (2.6.1) implies (2.6.2) linguistically. In the next step we have to ask ourselves what to say about the possibilisation

---

[17] Hörmann 1976 called attention to the automatic (involuntary, subconscious) efficacy of the psycho-linguistic phenomenon of 'sense-constancy', which he paralleled with such well-known psychological phenomena as size-constancy, brightness-constancy, or colour-constancy. Sense-constancy induces us to make sense, to the utmost limits of what seems to be possible at all, of a sentence we are confronted with (even of a seemingly self-contradictory sentence such as 'Not all women are female.'). The price of doing so is the automatic reinterpretation of one or more constituent parts of the sentence. An assenting test according to C-CT cannot yield a significant result unless, in performing it, we systematically block the loop-holes opened, or left open, by sense-constancy, which can best be done by rendering the wording of the sentences in question as precise as possible.

[18] Side by side with one's capability of coping with the efficacy of sense-constancy, this personal imaginative and linguistic (idiolectal) competence seems to me to be of the utmost importance for one's doing linguistic philosophy in general and performing assenting tests according to C-CT (or combination tests according to its predecessor criteria) in particular; cf. Hoche & Strube 1985: A. IV.1.f (pp. 109–113); Hoche 1990: 8.1 (pp. 141 f.).

(2.6.3) It is (counterfactually or objectively) possible that I intend to arrest all the suspects and that I am convinced that Tom is one of the suspects but that I do not intend to arrest Tom.

Now this is certainly *false*, and so, according to C-CT, sentence (2.6.1) implies sentence (2.6.2) *semantically*.

2.7.   As a still less trivial example, already immunised against the efficacy of sense-constancy by means of two round-bracket parentheses, let us consider the pair of sentences

(2.7.1) I strongly believe that (according to my personal normative standards) I (morally) ought to look after Jane.

(2.7.2) I want [intend] to look after Jane.

If I assent to the first one then I must also assent to the second – and hence cannot dissent from it –, and so (2.7.1) implies (2.7.2) linguistically. Next take the pertinent modalization

(2.7.3) It is (counterfactually or objectively) possible that I strongly believe that (according to my personal normative standards) I (morally) ought to look after Jane but that I do not want [intend] to look after Jane [that I do not even think of looking after Jane].

As I, for one, cannot conceive of a situation with respect to which I am prepared to say here and now that I strongly believe to be under the moral obligation in question and nonetheless do not even think of doing what I believe I morally ought to do, I cannot help regarding (2.7.3) as *false*. So, according to C-CT, the linguistic implication of (2.7.2) in (2.7.1) is again a *semantic* one. Naturally, this diagnosis will hardly go wholly undisputed. But if we succeed in making a case for it, it may be expected to be highly relevant to the linguistic analysis of the concept of moral obligation, and of the moral principle of the Golden Rule as well.[19]

3. Pragmatic implication

3.1.   Before scrutinising the logical properties of pragmatic implication, let us first consider two examples which are closely related to the ones just deliberated in subsections 2.6 and 2.7. Take, instead of the pair of sentences (2.6.1) and (2.6.2), the similar couple

---

[19] For a detailed elaboration of this question and the related question raised in subsect. 3.2, below, see esp. Hoche 1992; 2001; 2004.

(3.1.1)   I intend to arrest all the suspects, and Tom is one of the suspects.

(2.6.2)   I intend to arrest Tom.

It ought to be clear that not only (2.6.1) but also (3.1.1) implies (2.6.2) linguistically at large; for if I assent to (3.1.1) without also assenting to (2.6.2)[20] I will justly be taken as having a poor command of current English, especially that part of it which has to do with the vocabulary of willing, wanting, and/or intending. However, in contradistinction to (2.6.3), the modalization

(3.1.2)   It is possible that I intend to arrest all the suspects and that Tom is one of the suspects but that I (nonetheless) do not intend to arrest Tom.

is certainly *true*; for it is by no means necessarily the case that I also *know*, or at least *believe*, that Tom is one of the suspects. So, according to C-CT, (3.1.1) implies (2.6.2) *pragmatically*.

3.2.   Similar results are yielded by testing the pair of sentences

(3.2.1)   (According to my personal normative standards) John (morally) ought to help Richard.

(3.2.2)   I want [intend] John to help Richard.

If I assent to (3.2.1) but refuse to assent to (3.2.2), I will rightly be suspected to use the expression 'ought' without its full prescriptive force, i.e., in a purely descriptive manner, which, however, is incompatible with my prefixing to the 'ought'-judgement the words 'according to my personal normative standards'. So I think we cannot but conclude that (3.2.1) implies (3.2.2) linguistically. Taking the next step prescribed by C-CT, we find out that the possibilisation

(3.2.3)   It is possible that (according to my personal normative standards) John (morally) ought to help Richard but that I do not want John to do so.,

in contradistinction to (2.7.3), is obviously *true*. For I can easily imagine a situation with respect to which I am prepared to say here and now that John, according to my personal normative standards, morally ought to help Richard without my being aware of this fact (i.e., without my knowing that a constellation of morally relevant facts of the kind in question has come up, or without my having the slightest idea that Richard needs help, or help of the sort understood); so I need

---

[20] Note that this is all I need to say. For it is obvious that if I assent to an arbitrary sentence χ then I cannot at the same time assent to its negation, i.e., to $\neg\chi$, or that '$\Box(A\chi \rightarrow \neg A\neg\chi)$'; and from this it follows, in virtue of some basic rules of the propositional calculus and modal logic, that '$\Box(A\varphi \rightarrow A\chi) \rightarrow \Box(A\varphi \rightarrow \neg A\neg\chi)$' is true. – Mind, however, that the reverse, i.e., '$\Box(A\varphi \rightarrow \neg A\neg\chi) \rightarrow \Box(A\varphi \rightarrow A\chi)$', need not be true. This is the reason why, for the specific purposes of our criterion C-CT, in 1.1, above, we had to *explicitly stipulate* that the requirement '$\Box(A\varphi \rightarrow \neg A\neg\chi) \leftrightarrow \Box(A\varphi \rightarrow A\chi)$' be fulfilled.

not want John to help Richard. From this it is clear that, according to C-CT, (3.2.1) implies (3.2.2) not semantically but *pragmatically*. This, too, should be carefully taken into consideration if we are engaged in the linguistic analysis of the concept of moral obligation. Again, at first sight my diagnosis is likely to meet with scepticism, if not grave objections; but this is the price one always has to pay for choosing examples of some philosophical interest and potential fertility.[21]

3.3.   Let us now try and find out whether also pragmatic implication is a reflexive and transitive relation, and whether the law of transposition holds of this specific kind of linguistic implication, too. According to the 'operative' part of C-CT, we have

DPI: φ implies χ *pragmatically* if and only if it is necessary that if I assent to φ then I (also) assent to χ, and the modalized combination 'It is possible that φ and [but] that not χ.' is true.

We may write this more conspicuously in either of the following two logically equivalent ways:

DPI$_1$: $\varphi \overset{\pi}{\Rightarrow} \chi$ iff $\Box(A\varphi \to A\chi)$ & $\Diamond(\varphi$ & $\neg\chi)$;[22]

DPI$_2$: $\varphi \overset{\pi}{\Rightarrow} \chi$ iff $\Box(A\varphi \to A\chi)$ & $\neg\Box(\varphi \to \chi)$.

Because of DPI$_2$, we can replace DPI with

DPI': φ implies χ *pragmatically* if and only if it is necessary that if I assent to φ then I assent (also) to χ, but not necessary that if φ then (also) χ.

3.4.   Now suppose that pragmatic implication is a *reflexive* relation, i.e., that '$\varphi \overset{\pi}{\Rightarrow} \varphi$' is true. Then, according to DPI$_2$, also the conjunction

(3.4.1) $\Box(A\varphi \to A\varphi)$ & $\neg\Box(\varphi \to \varphi)$

has to be true. But this is obviously not the case; for although the first conjunct is, of course, true, the second conjunct – and with it the whole conjunction – is never true but either false or, if φ is an imperative or an 'explicit performative' of whatever kind,[23] ungrammatical and hence meaningless. So pragmatic implication is *not reflexive*, and even *irreflexive*. In fact, every sentence implies itself either semantically or catapragmatically (see 2.3, above, and 4.5, below), and hence no sentence can imply itself pragmatically.

---

[21] See also the preceding Essay I: section 3.

[22] According to DPI, '$\Diamond(\varphi$ & $\neg\chi)$' is true (i.e., a true sentence) and hence, *a fortiori*, a sentence and not just a meaningless string of symbols; therefore, it can be incorporated into a logical formula. Cf. 2.1 with note 13, above.

[23] See 4.1, 4.2, and 4.4, below.

3.5.   Let us further suppose that pragmatic implication is a *transitive* relation, i. e., that '$(\varphi \overset{\pi}{\Rightarrow} \chi)$ & $(\chi \overset{\pi}{\Rightarrow} \psi)$' logically entails '$(\varphi \overset{\pi}{\Rightarrow} \psi)$'. Then the same must be true of the pertinent definientia. Therefore we have to ask ourselves whether or not the sentences, logically equivalent to each other,

(3.5.1) $\Box(A\varphi \rightarrow A\chi)$ & $\neg\Box(\varphi \rightarrow \chi)$ & $\Box(A\chi \rightarrow A\psi)$ & $\neg\Box(\chi \rightarrow \psi)$;

(3.5.1′) $\Box((A\varphi \rightarrow A\chi)$ & $(A\chi \rightarrow A\psi))$ & $(\neg\Box(\chi \rightarrow \psi)$ & $\neg\Box(\varphi \rightarrow \chi))$

logically entail

(3.5.2) $\Box(A\varphi \rightarrow A\psi)$ & $\neg\Box(\varphi \rightarrow \psi)$.

It is easy to see that the first conjunct of (3.5.1′) entails the first conjunct of (3.5.2) but is utterly irrelevant to the second conjunct of (3.5.2); however, I, for one, am unable to conceive of any way of proving that the second conjunct of (3.5.1′), or (3.5.1′) as a whole, should entail the second conjunct of (3.5.2). So I take it that pragmatic implication *cannot* be shown to share, with semantic implication and with linguistic implication at large, the property of being a *transitive* relation.

3.6.   Now the results of subsections 3.4 and 3.5 may perhaps appear to be strange, if not paradoxical; for one might expect that the sub-relation of pragmatic implication has to share all its properties with its super-relation of linguistic (idiolectal) implication at large. But such an expectation would be unwarranted. For no implication of the kinds here considered can possibly be taken to be a purely linguistic one. As it were, linguistic implication never occurs 'chemically pure' or, to use another simile taken from chemistry, purely 'atomically'; it is necessarily found in a 'molecular' form. The reason may be explained as follows: For two interpreted sentences φ and χ, the string of words 'It is necessary that χ if φ.' is necessarily either a true proposition or a false proposition or no proposition at all but nonsensical in the sense of being ungrammatical, and there is no fourth possibility. Hence, whenever φ linguistically (idiolectally) implies χ the conjunction

(3.6.1)   It is necessary that if I assent to φ then I assent (also) to χ, and the string of words 'It is necessary that χ if φ.' is a true sentence or a false sentence or no sentence at all.

is true. From this it follows logically that in this case also the following disjunction holds true:

(3.6.2)   It is necessary that if I assent to φ then I assent (also) to χ, and the string of words 'It is necessary that χ if φ.' is a true sentence, or it is necessary that if I assent to φ then I assent (also) to χ, and the string of words 'It is necessary that χ if φ.' is a false sentence, or it is necessary that if I assent to φ then I assent (also) to χ, and the string of words 'It is necessary that χ if φ.' is no sentence at all.

This is to say that there is always a second conjunct which makes its influence felt, and it is due to this influence that some sorts of linguistic implication have logical properties which others lack. We have not the slightest reason, except perhaps a psychological one,[24] to surmise that pragmatic implication, as a sub-case (sub-relation, subordinated relation) of linguistic implication, must share with the latter all of its logical properties. The simplest way to convince ourselves of this fact seems to me to be a comparison with a well-known everyday relation. I take it that with respect to the logical property of *transitivity* the relation of linguistic implication is completely analogous with the well-known and unproblematic relation of being an ancestor. If person *a* is an ancestor of person *b* and person *b* is an ancestor of person *c*, *a* is doubtless an ancestor also of *c*. Now being a parent is certainly a sub-case of being an ancestor, and yet it would be strange to expect that if *a* is a parent of *b* and *b* a parent of *c* then *a* must needs be a parent of *c*; on the very contrary, this is extremely rarely the case, and is always incestuous. Nor is this difference between being an ancestor and being a parent surprising; as compared with being an ancestor, being a parent involves an additional defining element, to wit, immediacy, and it is obvious that it is precisely this additional element of immediacy that prevents transitivity of parentage.[25] Similarly, the additional 'specific difference' in the definiens of DPI written down in section 3.3, above, is responsible for the fact that pragmatic implication, in contradistinction to its more generic 'super-relation' of linguistic implication, can be shown to be neither reflexive nor transitive.

3.7.   However, pragmatic implication shares with linguistic implication at large the property of being subject to the law of *transposition*. For in 2.4, above, we could convince ourselves that the sentences

(2.4.5) $\Box (A\varphi \to A\chi)$;

(2.4.6) $\Box (A\neg\chi \to A\neg\varphi)$

are logically equivalent to each other, and it is obvious that

(3.7.1) $\neg\Box (\varphi \to \chi)$;

(3.7.2) $\neg\Box (\neg\chi \to \neg\varphi)$

---

[24] What I have in mind is the tendency to confuse the *properties* and the *component characteristics* of a concept; the 'latter are properties of the things which fall under a concept, not of the concept' (Frege 1884, tr. 1950: § 53). Whereas the set of *component characteristics* of a concept devolves upon all of its sub-concepts (and is at the same time enriched by additional 'specific differences'), its logical *properties* need not be hereditary; for instance, it is often the case that a ('super-'-)concept can be fulfilled whereas one or other of its sub-concepts is empty. As I am going to show in the text, the same is true of the logical *properties* of (at least: dyadic) relations.

[25] An analogous but possibly even more conspicuous example may be taken from arithmetic: Being an immediate predecessor of a natural number is doubtless a sub-case of being a predecessor of it, and yet only the latter relation is a transitive one.

are logically equivalent to each other, too. – Now the reader might perhaps be tempted to think that this cannot be possibly true and refer, for instance, to the set of sentences

(2.1.3)   My wife deceives me.

(2.1.4)   I (strongly) believe [am convinced] that my wife deceives me.

(¬2.1.4)   I don't believe that my wife deceives me.

(¬2.1.3)   My wife doesn't deceive me.

For whereas (2.1.3) certainly implies (2.1.4) pragmatically, it appears that (¬2.1.4) implies (¬2.1.3) not even linguistically at large. It should be noted, however, that the pair of sentences $\{(¬2.1.4), (¬2.1.3)\}$ has once for all been excluded from the domain of sentences for which the generic relation of linguistic implication, and hence the subrelation of pragmatic implication, has been defined in the first place. For this pair does not meet the condition '$\Box(A\varphi \rightarrow \neg A\neg\chi) \leftrightarrow \Box(A\varphi \rightarrow A\chi)$' stipulated in C-CT: If I assent to (¬2.1.4) I cannot assent to the negation of (¬2.1.3), that is, to (2.1.3), but I need not assent to (¬2.1.3), and so for this instantiation '$\Box(A\varphi \rightarrow \neg A\neg\chi)$' comes out true and '$\Box(A\varphi \rightarrow A\chi)$' false.[26]

3.8.   Let me finally call your attention to a property of *pragmatic* implication which ought to make this kind of linguistic implication nearly as attractive for logicians as *semantic* implication has always been. Since the utterance of a pragmatic implicatum, such as (2.6.2) or (3.2.2), amounts to expressly stating that a speech-act theoretical 'sincerity condition' of uttering the corresponding pragmatic implicans, say (3.1.1) or (3.2.1), is fulfilled,[27] a pragmatic implicatum *always* contains a 'doxastic' or 'theletic' verb, i.e., a verb of believing or willing[28] in a wide sense including such verbs as 'to know', 'to approve', and the like. Because of this fact and the intimate relation between the so-called propositional attitudes of believing and willing, especially the fact that willing is parasitic upon believing,[29] any pragmatic implication can be converted into a semantic implication if we add to the pragmatic implicans a doxastic or epistemic operator in the first grammatical person, such as 'I believe that', 'I am convinced that', or 'I know that'.[30] This, in turn, makes it possible to envisage an integrated logic of believing and willing,

---

[26] For details, see the preceding Essay I: 8.6, 8.8, 9.4.

[27] The *locus classicus* is Searle 1969: ch. 3.

[28] In publications prior to 2005, instead of 'theletic' I used the term 'buletic'; but my colleague Prof. Dr. Alexander Kleinlogel, Bochum, was so kind as to point out to me that 'theletic' is by far the better choice, and the more so as an ancient Greek adjective 'buletikós', unlike 'theletikós' (θελητικός), has not been handed down to us.

[29] See Hoche 2004.

[30] An example can be found by comparing the pair of sentences (3.1.1) and (2.6.2) considered in subsect. 3.1, above, with the pair of sentences (2.6.1) and (2.6.2) considered in subsect. 2.6, above.

especially to devise 'doxastico-theletic' calculi of truth and 'pragmatico-doxastico-theletic' calculi of warranted assertibility which prove to be useful in the logical analysis of moral 'ought'-judgements.[31]

4. Catapragmatic implication

4.1.   Now let us scrutinise the pair of sentences, interpreted in accordance with each other,

(4.1.1)   Answer her letter.

(4.1.2)   I want [intend] you to answer her letter.

Certainly we cannot, without absurdity or being suspected to have misunderstood at least one of these sentences, assent to the interpreted imperative sentence (4.1.1) and, at the same time, refuse to assent to the interpreted indicative sentence (4.1.2). For this reason (4.1.1), according to C-CT, implies (4.1.2) linguistically (idiolectally) in the generic sense. So again we have to form the relevant modalized combination or 'possibilisation', scil.,

(4.1.3)   It is possible that answer her letter
            and [but] that I don't want [intend] you to answer her letter.

This, however, is neither true nor false but clearly nonsensical or *ungrammatical* in that it violates a well-known rule of English surface grammar, the rule, i. e., that the conjunction 'that' has to be followed by an indicative and not an imperative construction. In order to take no risk, let us convince ourselves that the same grammatical rule is quite doubtless violated in the operationalised version, provided for by C-CT:

(4.1.3′)   I can conceive, in the mode of counterfactual imagination, a counterfac-
            tually possible world with respect to which I am prepared to say here and
            now that answer her letter and [but] that I don't want [intend] you to
            answer her letter.

So, according to C-CT, (4.1.1) implies (4.1.2) *catapragmatically*. By the way, I take it that the reverse is equally true. In this sense we may say that (4.1.1) und (4.1.2) are 'catapragmatically equivalent' to each other.

4.2.   Now suppose we replace the 'primary performative'[32] (4.1.1) with its 'explicit' counterpart

---

[31] See esp. Hoche 1992; 2001; 2004.

[32] For Austin's distinction between 'primary' (or 'implicit') and 'explicit performatives', see Austin 1962a: esp. pp. 32, 69, 83, 90f., 149 and Lectures V–VII.

(4.2.1)   I hereby ask [beg; command; advise; recommend; etc.] you to answer
          her letter.

Again, if someone assents to (4.2.1), he cannot in the same breath refuse to assent
also to (4.1.2).[33] If we proceed to the pertinent possibilisation

(4.2.2)   It is possible that I hereby ask you to answer her letter
          and [but] that I don't want [intend] you to answer her letter.,

the trickiest question we have to answer is whether it is *true* (which *at first sight* it
certainly seems to be) or rather *ungrammatical* in the sense of offending against
English 'depth grammar', and hence nonsensical. In fact, I think that (4.2.2)
violates a pretty recondite rule of the depth grammar – not only of English
but, I take it, of all languages admitting of the linguistic institution of explicit
performative speech acts. By prefixing to a statement (interpreted sentence) a
negating or modalizing phrase like 'it is not the case that' or 'it is possible that', we
regularly deprive this statement of its 'assertive' or, more generally speaking, of its
'illocutionary force', and so, if the 'explicit performative' particle 'hereby' happens
to occur in it, this particle gets rid of its performative character and undergoes
a subtle change of meaning.[34] So (4.2.2) in its most natural reading is not the
possibilisation now needed and looked for, and if we refuse this straightforward
reading and forcefully try instead to understand (4.2.2) otherwise, namely, in the
sense prescribed by C-CT, we subtly but definitely violate depth grammar. So
irrespective of our choosing the 'primary' form (4.1.1) or its 'explicit' counterpart
(4.2.1), the speech-act theoretical sincerity condition of these imperatives, i.e.,
(4.1.2), is implied by them *catapragmatically*.

4.3.   Furthermore, let us consider the relation between (4.1.1) and

(4.3.1)   (According to my personal normative standards)
          you (morally) ought to answer her letter.

Provided my readers share my personal linguistic intuitions (or, to be more precise: my combined imaginative and idiolectal competence),[35] by applying the
method just used in sections 4.1 and 4.2, i.e., the criterion C-CT, they ought
to convince themselves that (4.3.1) implies (4.1.1) *catapragmatically*. This seems
to me to be the true core of Hare's allegation that a moral 'ought-to-do'-judge-

---

[33] Note, however, that no implication whatsoever is yielded if we replace (4.2.1) with, say, 'I am asking
[I am going to ask; I will ask] you to answer her letter.'. For of course I can ask you to do something
without intending you to do it; for instance, by such an insincere request I may rather intend you to
publicly confess that you are not skilful, not strong, or not brave enough to perform a certain feat.

[34] For details, see Hoche 1990: 8.4; 1995c.

[35] See section 2.6 with note 18, above.

ment, if it is endowed with truly 'prescriptive force', 'entails' the corresponding imperative.[36]

4.4.   By now, the reader may perhaps be tempted to believe that catapragmatic implication has needs to do with (primary or explicit) *imperatives*; but assuming this would be wrong. Consider, for instance, the non-imperative sentences

(4.4.1)   I hereby state that all members are present.

(4.4.2)   I (strongly) believe that all members are present.

If I assent to (4.4.1) I cannot help assenting to (4.4.2), too. Moreover, the modalization

(4.4.3)   It is possible that I hereby state that all members are present but that I don't (strongly) believe that all members are present.,

if it *is* in fact the modalization required by the explicit performative (4.4.1) and its sincerity condition (4.4.2), i. e., if the meaning of the explicitly performative particle 'hereby' is not being unawares replaced with quite a different one, is *ungrammatical* for the reasons already specified in subsection 4.2, above. So, according to C-CT, (4.4.1) implies (4.4.2) *catapragmatically*.

4.5.   As to the logical properties of catapragmatic implication, I take it that the question whether this special kind of implication is transitive or reflexive or subject to the law of transposition does not admit of a formal treatment. It is not even possible to formally define this relation along the lines of DSI_2 or DPI_2; for the best that could be done this way would be something like

DCI*: $\varphi \overset{x}{\Rightarrow} \chi$ iff $\square\,(A\varphi \rightarrow A\chi)$ & the expression '$\square\,(\varphi \rightarrow \chi)$' is neither true nor false but a meaningless string of symbols.

However, by scrutinising appropriate examples we can easily convince ourselves that catapragmatic implication is not a transitive relation; for instance, the 'ought'-sentence (4.3.1) implies the imperative (4.1.1) catapragmatically, and the imperative (4.1.1) implies the 'I intend'-sentence (4.1.2) also catapragmatically, but (4.3.1) implies (4.1.2) not catapragmatically but – as we could see in 3.2, above – pragmatically. But as long as we confine ourselves to the field of *imperatives*, it is plausible to

---

[36] 'I do not wish to claim that all "ought"-sentences entail imperatives, but only that they do so when they are being used evaluatively. [...] I am making this true by definition; for I should not say that an "ought"-sentence *was* being used evaluatively, unless imperatives were held to follow from it': Hare 1952: 11.1, p. 164. 'I propose to say that the test, whether someone is using the judgement "I ought to do X" as a value-judgement or not is, "Does he or does he not recognise that if he assents to the judgement, he must also assent to the command 'Let me do X'?"': ibid.: 11.2, pp. 168/9; cf. Hare 1963: 5.7, p. 79.

believe that catapragmatic implication is the exact counterpart of semantic implication in the field of indicatives: Between imperatives only, catapragmatic implication
seems to be reflexive, transitive and subject to the law of transposition – a fact
(or perhaps rather an impression) which may have contributed to Hare's mixing
up catapragmatic implication with (informal) entailment. Because of the rather
restricted importance of catapragmatic implication for the purposes of philosophical analysis,[37] at least in this respect dwelling upon this issue at more length would
hardly pay off. But there is a second, and more cogent, reason for not doing so in
the present context. We cannot treat these questions properly without studying
in detail Hare's fourfold distinction between what he called 'some sub-atomic
particles of logic', to wit: 'phrastic', 'tropic', 'neustic', and 'clistic';[38] and certainly
the present collection of essays on Anthropological Complementarism is not the
proper place to do so.

5. Some examples of semantic presupposition

5.1.   The definition of semantic presupposition given in C-CT (see 1.1, above)
may be reformulated in the following, more conspicuous way:

DSP: On condition, first, that φ and χ are completely interpreted sentences of
        my personal idiolect within the framework of our common natural lan-
        guage, second, that I understand the actual use of φ and χ, third, that φ and
        χ stand to each other in the relation '$\Box (A\varphi \rightarrow \neg A\neg\chi) \leftrightarrow \Box (A\varphi \rightarrow A\chi)$',
        and fourth, that χ is purely contingent, let us say that φ semantically pre-
        supposes χ if and only if and the following four conditions are fulfilled:

   (1) It is not possible that I assent to φ and [but] do not assent to χ.

   (2) It is not possible that φ and (that) not χ.

   (3) It is not possible that I assent to non-φ and [but] do not assent to χ.

   (4) It is not possible that non-φ and (that) not χ.

Taking the prerequisite conditions listed in the first paragraph of DSP as being
understood, and focussing our attention on conditions (1) through (4), we may
write DSP more conspicuously in either one of the following logically equivalent
ways:

---

[37] Although, as we could see, moral 'ought'-judgements imply *'I want [intend]'-sentences pragmatically*
    and *imperatives catapragmatically*, I tried to show that for metaethical purposes it is incomparably
    more rewarding to study the former relation (see esp. Hoche 1992; 1995d; 1995e; 2001).

[38] See Hare 1966; 1971; 1989.

DSP_1: $\varphi \overset{\sigma\text{P}}{\Rightarrow} \chi$ iff $\neg\Diamond\,(\text{A}\varphi \,\&\, \neg\text{A}\chi) \,\&\, \neg\Diamond\,(\varphi \,\&\, \neg\chi) \,\&$
$\qquad\qquad\quad \neg\Diamond\,(\text{A}\neg\varphi \,\&\, \neg\text{A}\chi) \,\&\, \neg\Diamond\,(\neg\,\varphi \,\&\, \neg\chi);$[39]

DSP_2: $\varphi \overset{\sigma\text{P}}{\Rightarrow} \chi$ iff $\Box\,(\text{A}\varphi \rightarrow \text{A}\chi) \,\&\, \Box\,(\varphi \rightarrow \chi) \,\&\, \Box\,(\text{A}\neg\varphi \rightarrow \text{A}\chi)$
$\qquad\qquad \,\&\, \Box\,(\neg\varphi \rightarrow \chi).$

Because of DSP_2, we can replace the second ('operative') paragraph of DSP with

DSP′: (1) It is necessary that if I assent to φ then I assent to χ.

$\qquad$ (2) It is necessary that if φ then χ.

$\qquad$ (3) It is necessary that if I assent to non-φ then I assent to χ.

$\qquad$ (4) It is necessary that if non-φ then χ.

5.2. The following (ordered) pair of English sentences, if taken to be completely interpreted in accordance with each other, can be seen to fulfil the conditions of DSP and DSP′:

(5.2.1) My son lives in London.

(5.2.2) I have at least one son.

To begin with, that (5.2.1) and (5.2.2) belong to the domain of objects for which the relation of semantic presupposition is to be defined in the first place can be seen from the fact that both of them are supposed to be completely interpreted sentences of the English language, that (5.2.2) is contingent, i.e., neither logically true nor logically false, and that (5.2.1) and (5.2.2) stand to each other in the relation '$\Box\,(\text{A}\varphi \rightarrow \neg\text{A}\neg\chi) \leftrightarrow \Box\,(\text{A}\varphi \rightarrow \text{A}\chi)$'. For if I fully understand both of them, then if I assent to the first I cannot *dissent from* the second and must, furthermore, positively *assent to* it, and so '$\Box\,(\text{A}(5.2.1) \rightarrow \neg\text{A}\neg(5.2.2)) \,\&\, \Box\,(\text{A}(5.2.1) \rightarrow \text{A}(5.2.2))$' and, *a fortiori*, '$\Box\,(\text{A}(5.2.1) \rightarrow \neg\text{A}\neg(5.2.2)) \leftrightarrow \Box\,(\text{A}(5.2.1) \rightarrow \text{A}(5.2.2))$' are true.

5.3. Next, let us ask ourselves whether conditions (1) through (4) are fulfilled. For condition (1), the question has already been answered in the positive. If I assent to (5.2.1) I must also assent to, and *a fortiori* cannot dissent from, (5.2.2). Similarly, condition (3) is obviously fulfilled. If I assent to the sentential negation of (5.2.1), i.e., '*It is not the case that* my son lives in London.' or, in precisely this sense,[40]

(¬5.2.1) My son doesn't live in London.,

then I must also assent to (5.2.2). So both (5.2.1) and (¬5.2.1) imply (5.2.2) at least linguistically at large. However, it is much more difficult to decide whether

---

[39] At least in the present context there is no reason to make a distinction between 'non-φ' and 'not φ'.

[40] This caveat is important because of the manifold possible uses of negation in natural language, into which here there is not the space to delve.

conditions (2) and (4) are fulfilled. If we apply DSP′ it certainly seems to be necessary that, if my son lives in London – and likewise if my son does *not* live in London – then I have at least one son; but if we apply DSP we may hesitate to say that it is not possible that my son lives in London – or that my son dos *not* live in London – and that I have no son. Of course there can be no doubt that the modalized combination ('possibilisation')

(5.3.1)   It is possible that my son lives in London and [but] that I have no son.

is *not true*. But should we say that it is *false*, or rather that it is *ungrammatical*? The answer is, I think, not at all easy. But before turning to the operationalised version of (5.3.1) which I suggested in C-CT, and which is to decide this question above doubt, let us dwell for a moment upon the simple form (5.3.1) itself; for doing so seems to me to be the best way of showing that in doubtful cases an operationalised version cannot be dispensed with.

5.4.   To make things at least a little bit easier, we should replace this example, which is freely invented and belongs to a fragmentary fictional world,[41] by two examples adopted from the real world concerning which the reader may be taken to know what is, and what is not, the case. So let us ask ourselves what we are prone to say about the two possibilisations

(5.4.1)   It is possible that the founder of special relativity was born in Germany
          and [but] that there is not exactly one founder of special relativity.[42]

(5.4.2)   It is possible that the (present) king of France is bald
          and [but] that (at present) there is not exactly one king of France.

At least at first sight and outside the biasing context of the present discussion, one might be easily tempted to regard (5.4.1) as being rather false than nonsensical but (5.4.2) as being rather nonsensical than false. The reason for tending to judge these two cases differently can be seen if we compare with each other the *unmodalized* conjunctions which are at the bottom of these possibilisations, scil.

(5.4.3)   The founder of special relativity was born in Germany
          and [but] there is not exactly one founder of special relativity.

---

[41] I think it imperative that we should strictly discriminate, by means of whatever technical terms, between counterfactually possible words ('*objectively* possible worlds') and fictional worlds ('*absolutely* possible worlds'); see Hoche 1990: 9.5–9.6, cf. 10.7.

[42] To be sure, Hendrik A. Lorentz, Mileva Marić (Albert Einstein's first wife), Michele Besso, and many others influenced the formation of Einstein's theory of special relativity to various and partly high degrees (see, for instance, Neffe 2005: chs. 7–8); but certainly none of them can be called a 'founder' of this theory in the very same sense as Einstein himself can and must be. But even if novel researches into the history of physics should come to quite a diverging judgement this would not, of course, impair the use I make of my example.

(5.4.4)   The (present) king of France is bald
          and [but] (at present) there is not exactly one king of France.

Since I know that the second member of the conjunction (5.4.3) is *false*, I know
that its first member is not void of reference and hence either true or false, and
that therefore (5.4.3) as a whole is false. Moreover, one feels inclined to believe
that a true or false indicative sentence cannot be changed into nonsense by simply
modalizing it. Although this need not invariably be true,[43] in the present case
there seems to be no room for a reasonable doubt. Hence it is plausible to regard
(5.4.1) as at least meaningful, i.e., as a true or false statement. Finally, I take it that
(5.4.1) cannot be true. So what is left is the *falsity* of (5.4.1). But the case of (5.4.2)
presents itself as being remarkably different. I know that the second member of the
pertinent conjunction (5.4.4) is *true*, and from this I gather that its first member, and
therefore the whole conjunction, lacks reference and hence may be taken to be a
mere pseudo-statement. Finally, I am doubtless justified in believing that a pseudo-
statement cannot be changed into a true or false statement by simply prefixing to it
the operator 'it is possible that'. So in the case of (5.4.2) both truth and falsity have
to be excluded, and what is left is a pseudo-statement, or something *nonsensical*.
Instead, we may perhaps speak of something 'ungrammatical'; for arguably it is
a rule of 'universal grammar' that we must use a sentence only if it has reference.
In the freely invented example (5.3.1), however, we have not the slightest idea of
whether, in this fragment of a fictional world, the speaker is to be taken as having
a son and, what is more, as having exactly one son in question. So our linguistic
competence in cases such as (5.3.1) simply lets us down.

5.5.   For this reason we are well advised if we stick to the operationalised form
indicated in the formulation of C-CT, i.e., in the case of the sentences (5.2.1),
(5.2.2) and (5.3.1), to the form

(5.5.1)   I can conceive, in the mode of counterfactual imagination, a counterfac-
          tually possible world with respect to which I am prepared to say here and
          now that my son lives in London and [but] that I have no son.

According to my personal imaginative and linguistic (idiolectal) competence I
cannot but say that this is *false*. Of course the question remains why I have chosen
this relatively complicated and clumsy form instead of the considerably simpler
version

(5.5.2)   I can conceive, in the mode of counterfactual imagination, a counterfac-
          tually possible world in which my son lives in London and [but] I have
          no son.

---

[43] See 4.2, above.

There are at least two reasons for this choice. First, in view of this version my linguistic competence – or, to be more precise, my combined imaginative and idiolectal competence – fails again in the way just described in 5.4, above. Second, I think it important to make it as clear as possible that the wording chosen belongs to my real language (the language I speak in the real world) and not to a merely possible language (the language I happen to speak in the counterfactually possible world in question, which *need not* but of course *may* differ from the one I speak here and now).[44]

5.6   From our last findings we have to conclude that (5.2.1) implies (5.2.2) semantically in the precise sense of C-CT. Now we have to find out whether (¬5.2.1) implies (5.2.2) semantically as well. I take it that my readers are in a position to repeat the considerations of subsection 5.5 – only with 'lives' replaced by 'doesn't live' – by themselves, and that they will convince themselves, first, that also (¬5.2.1) implies (5.2.2) semantically, and hence, second, that both (5.2.1) and (¬5.2.1) semantically presuppose (5.2.2) in precisely the sense of C-CT, DSP, or DSP'.[45]

6. Some logical properties of semantic presupposition

6.1.   Let us now ask whether semantic presupposition is a *transitive relation*. Suppose that this is the case, i.e., that '$(\varphi \overset{\sigma P}{\Rightarrow} \chi)$ & $(\chi \overset{\sigma P}{\Rightarrow} \psi)$' entails '$(\varphi \overset{\sigma P}{\Rightarrow} \psi)$'. Then according to DSP$_2$ (see 5.1, above) we have to expect that

$$(6.1.1) \quad \Box(A\varphi \rightarrow A\chi) \ \& \ \Box(\varphi \rightarrow \chi) \ \& \ \Box(A\neg\varphi \rightarrow A\chi) \ \& \ \Box(\neg\varphi \rightarrow \chi) \ \&$$
$$\Box(A\chi \rightarrow A\psi) \ \& \ \Box(\chi \rightarrow \psi) \ \& \ \Box(A\neg\chi \rightarrow A\psi) \ \& \ \Box(\neg\chi \rightarrow \psi)$$

---

[44] See also Hoche & Strube 1985: A.I.4, p. 34.

[45] In the case of non-indicative sentences, there is a catapragmatic counterpart to semantic presupposition, which, in the concluding paragraph of C-CT, I called 'catapragmatic presupposition'. Take, e.g., the imperative 'Please tell my son that I tried to call him up.' and its negation 'Please don't tell my son that I tried to call him up.'. If I assent to either one of these sentences and at the same refuse to assent to the sentence 'I have at least one son.', I will be taken to be confused, or to have a poor command of English, or something else of that ilk, and so we have to diagnose a linguistic implication in the generic sense. If we go on to scrutinise the modalized combinations prescribed by our criterion C-CT, we cannot help pleading the specification 'catapragmatic', which at first sight looks rather strange. But there is a parallel case with ordinary semantic implication: On the condition that the term 'bachelor' is taken in its modern non-academic and non-zoological sense, the imperative 'Pretend to be a bachelor.' seems to imply the imperative 'Pretend to be unmarried.' *semantically*, and yet according to C-CT the verdict 'catapragmatic' cannot be avoided. However, this ought not to surprise us; for catapragmatic implication seems to be in the field of imperatives what semantic implication is in the field of standard indicative sentences (excluding 'explicit performatives'); see sect. 4, above.

entails

(6.1.2) $\Box(A\varphi \rightarrow A\psi)$ & $\Box(\varphi \rightarrow \psi)$ & $\Box(A\neg\varphi \rightarrow A\psi)$ & $\Box(\neg\varphi \rightarrow \psi)$.

This turns out to be in fact the case.[46] To make this more conspicuous, let us arrange the conjuncts of (6.1.1) somewhat differently, repeat two of them, and introduce an additional bracketing:

(6.1.1') $\{\Box(A\varphi \rightarrow A\chi)$ & $\Box(A\chi \rightarrow A\psi)\}$ &
$\qquad\quad \{\Box(\varphi \rightarrow \chi)$ & $\Box(\chi \rightarrow \psi)\}$ &
$\qquad\quad \{\Box(A\neg\varphi \rightarrow A\chi)$ & $\Box(A\chi \rightarrow A\psi)\}$ &
$\qquad\quad \{\Box(\neg\varphi \rightarrow \chi)$ & $\Box(\chi \rightarrow \psi)\}$ &
$\qquad\quad \{\Box(A\neg\chi \rightarrow A\psi)$ & $\Box(\neg\chi \rightarrow \psi)\}$.

The *first line* (or first { }-expression) of (6.1.1') entails the *first conjunct* of (6.1.2); for

(6.1.3) $\Box(A\varphi \rightarrow A\chi)$ & $\Box(A\chi \rightarrow A\psi)$

is logically equivalent to

(6.1.4) $\Box((A\varphi \rightarrow A\chi)$ & $(A\chi \rightarrow A\psi))$,

which logically entails

(6.1.5) $\Box(A\varphi \rightarrow A\psi)$.

If in this derivation of (6.1.5) from (6.1.3) we substitute $\neg\varphi$ for φ then we see that the *third line* (or third { }-expression) of (6.1.1') entails the *third conjunct* of (6.1.2). Furthermore, the *second line* (or second { }-expression) of (6.1.1') is immediately seen to entail the *second conjunct* of (6.1.2), and likewise the *fourth line* (or fourth { }-expression) of (6.1.1') is immediately seen to entail the *fourth conjunct* of (6.1.2).

6.2.   So semantic presupposition is a *transitive* relation. However, it is *not reflexive*. For if it were, '$\varphi \ {}^{\sigma P}\!\!\Rightarrow \varphi$' or its definiens

(6.2.1) $\Box(A\varphi \rightarrow A\varphi)$ & $\Box(\varphi \rightarrow \varphi)$ & $\Box(A\neg\varphi \rightarrow A\varphi)$ & $\Box(\neg\varphi \rightarrow \varphi)$

would be true; but because of the falsity of the last two conjuncts (6.2.1) as a whole is *false*.[47] Now, if presupposition is transitive but not reflexive, it follows as a corollary that it is *not symmetrical* either; for taken together, '$\varphi \ {}^{\sigma P}\!\!\Rightarrow \chi$' and '$\chi \ {}^{\sigma P}\!\!\Rightarrow \varphi$' would entail the falsity '$\varphi \ {}^{\sigma P}\!\!\Rightarrow \varphi$'. In sum: Presupposition is *transitive*, *not reflexive* (and, as we can easily see, even *irreflexive*), and *not symmetrical* (and

---

[46] I am grateful to Michael Knoop for having called my attention to this proof.

[47] Note that, because of the accepted truth of '$\Box(\varphi \rightarrow \varphi)$', φ is of a form which cannot render '$\Box(\neg\varphi \rightarrow \varphi)$' nonsensical.

even *asymmetrical*); and this is exactly what we would expect on the basis of our normal understanding of presupposition – though, of course, we may find it surprising if we think of presupposition as a subcase of semantic (analytical) implication.

6.3.   In view of the fact that we have defined semantic presupposition as a subcase of semantic implication, we may be likewise surprised to see that it cannot be proved to be subject to the law of *transposition*, i.e., that '$\varphi \;^{\sigma P}\!\!\Rightarrow \chi$' and '$\neg\chi \;^{\sigma P}\!\!\Rightarrow \neg\varphi$' cannot be shown to be logically equivalent to each other. According to DSP$_2$, the definiens for the definiendum '$\varphi \;^{\sigma P}\!\!\Rightarrow \chi$' is

(6.3.1) $\Box\,(A\varphi \to A\chi)\ \&\ \Box\,(\varphi \to \chi)\ \&\ \Box\,(A\neg\varphi \to A\chi)\ \&\ \Box\,(\neg\varphi \to \chi),$

and the definiens for the definiendum '$\neg\chi \;^{\sigma P}\!\!\Rightarrow \neg\varphi$' is

(6.3.2) $\Box\,(A\neg\chi \to A\neg\varphi)\ \&\ \Box\,(\neg\chi \to \neg\varphi)\ \&\ \Box\,(A\chi \to A\neg\varphi)\ \&\ \Box\,(\chi \to \neg\varphi).$

Although the first two conjuncts of (6.3.1) are logically equivalent to the first two conjuncts of (6.3.2), as we could see in 2.4, above, the complete conjunctions (6.3.1) and (6.3.2) show not the slightest traces of being logically equivalent to each other. So there is no reason to believe that semantic presupposition is subject to the law of transposition; but as we saw in 3.6, above, this is nothing to worry about.

6.4.   It should be kept in mind, however, that semantic presupposition, *as long as we only take it as a case of semantic implication*, could be shown, in 2.4, above, to *be* subject to the law of transposition. Precisely *this*, however, might be doubted; for at least *existential* presupposition, to which we confined ourselves so far, seems to defy this law. Take, for instance, the set of sentences, interpreted in accordance with each other,

(5.2.1)   My son lives in London.

(5.2.2)   I have at least one son.

($\neg$5.2.2) I have no son(s) (at all).

($\neg$5.2.1) My son doesn't live in London.

Although in section 5, above, we found out that (5.2.1) semantically presupposes (5.2.2), it might seem as if we must *deny* that ($\neg$5.2.2) implies ($\neg$5.2.1) even linguistically at large. It should be noted, however, that for no less than *two reasons* the pair of sentences $\{\,(\neg5.2.2), (\neg5.2.1)\,\}$ falls outside the scope for which linguistic implication, and hence its 'subsubrelation' of semantic presupposition, has been defined at all: *First*, this pair of sentences does not fulfil the third requirement stipulated in the opening paragraph of C-CT, to wit, '$\Box\,(A\varphi \to \neg A\neg\chi) \leftrightarrow \Box\,(A\varphi \to A\chi)$'; for if I assent to ($\neg$5.2.2) I can neither assent to the negation of ($\neg$5.2.1), that is, to (5.2.1), nor to ($\neg$5.2.1), and so for this instantiation '$\Box\,(A\varphi \to \neg A\neg\chi)$' proves to be true and '$\Box\,(A\varphi \rightarrow A\chi)$' proves to be false.[48] *Second*, and this may be taken to be even more fundamental: If I assent to (¬5.2.2) I cannot accept (¬5.2.1) as a fully interpreted sentence; for if I have no son(s) at all then the individual constant 'my son', and hence (¬5.2.1) as a whole, are void of reference. So not only the third but also the first two stipulations listed in the opening paragraph of C-CT are violated.

6.5.   Linguists know, of course, that there are other kinds of semantic presupposition besides existential presupposition. However, *philosophically* they are certainly much less important, and hence in the present context – which is only intended to lay a solid logical foundation for the conception of what I call 'Anthropological Complementarism' – we need not, and should not, bother about their taxonomy. Nonetheless, let us look at least at an example, say, the set of sentences, interpreted in accordance with each other,

(6.5.1)   I have given up smoking.

(6.5.2)   I used to smoke.

(¬6.5.2)   I didn't use to smoke.

(¬6.5.1)   I haven't given up smoking.

I think my readers will be able to convince themselves, along the lines of the arguments given in the foregoing subsection 6.4, that (6.5.1) semantically presupposes (6.5.2) but that the relation of linguistic implication and, hence, the subsubrelation of semantic presupposition has not been defined for the pair of sentences $\{(\neg6.5.2), (\neg6.5.1)\}$. Therefore the question of whether (¬6.5.2) semantically presupposes (¬6.5.1) must not be *answered in the negative* but *refuted as 'not arising'* or *'not applicable'* in the first place, and so the string of symbols '(¬6.5.2) semantically presupposes (¬6.5.1)' is not a false sentence but no sentence at all. In this case, however, in contradistinction to the case discussed in 6.4, above, only the third stipulation inserted in the opening paragraph of C-CT is violated whereas the first two stipulations are fulfilled.

7. The paradox of existential presupposition and its solution

7.1.   Because of its great philosophical significance I should like to return once more to the problem of *existential* presupposition. As we have seen in 6.4, above, if the string of words

(¬5.2.2)   I have no son(s) (at all).

is a *true sentence* then the string of words

---

[48] Cf. 3.7, above, and the preceding Essay I: 8.6, 8.8, 9.4–9.6.

(¬5.2.1)   My son doesn't live in London.

is *not a fully interpreted sentence at all*. So an assenting test or combination test in accordance with C-CT cannot even be started; it is blocked from the very beginning. Disregarding this is tantamount to believing that informal logic, as it is represented, for instance, by the carrying through of combination tests, has to do not only with propositions[49] but also with mere would-be propositions or pseudo-propositions. It is true that proponents of many-valued logics are inclined to speak, in the case in question, of a proposition (or sentence) having a third truth-value,[50] and some other logicians prefer to speak of a proposition (or statement, or sentence, respectively) having no truth-value at all,[51] or having a 'truth-value gap'.[52] However, I think it more correct to speak in this case of *no proposition at all*; for the formal as well as the informal semantic approach of this paper has certainly been designed, from the very beginning, to be a *bivalent* one.[53] Consider the situation in formal logic, which, I think, is in many respects very similar. In doing sentential or propositional logic we take it for granted, and rightly so, that we are *free or unrestricted* in our assignment of truth-values to the elementary sentences involved. In the case in question, however, this necessary condition is not fulfilled. For if we assign one of the truth-values True or False to our proposition (¬5.2.1), or to its formalised counterpart, we *needs must* assign the truth-value False to the proposition (¬5.2.2), or to its formalised counterpart, and so are *not free or unrestricted* in our truth-value assignment, and hence violate a rule of the 'logic-

---

[49] Cf. clarification (3) in subsect. 1.2, above.

[50] See, for instance, Blau 1978: I.2.3, pp. 50–64.

[51] It is true that Strawson, for one, admits of 'statements' that are neither true nor false. However, as Knoop is driving home to us in his illuminating 2003 paper, it is imperative that we should note that, *in the study of logical relations, he invariably and expressly excludes them*. See, for example, Strawson 1952: ch. 6 sect. 7, pp. 176f.: 'We are to imagine that every logical rule of the system, when expressed in terms of truth and falsity, is preceded by the phrase "Assuming that the statements concerned are either true or false, then …" Thus the [syllogistic] rule that A is the contradictory of O states that, *if corresponding statements of the A and O forms both have truth-values*, then they must have opposite truth-values; the [syllogistic] rule that A entails I states that, *if corresponding statements of these forms have truth-values*, then if the statement of the A form is true, the statement of the I form must be true; and so on' (Strawson's italics).

[52] See, for instance, Quine 1960: 'Failing objects of reference for their definite singular terms, such sentences [as 'Pegasus flies'] are likely to be looked upon as neither true nor false but simply as uncalled-for': § 23, p. 113; in this case, they contain 'truth-value gaps, as we may call them': § 37, p. 177.

[53] I do not intend to speculate, in this paper, on the respective merits and demerits of two-valued and three- or n-valued logics; however, I take it that as long as we are determined to do *two-valued* logic we silently commit ourselves to allow for *true-or-false* propositions (or: *completely* interpreted sentences) *only*, and hence to regard proposition-like strings of words which are neither true nor false as mere pseudo-propositions.

game' which is so basic and so much a matter of course that it is hardly ever paid explicit attention to and expressly mentioned. Or to put it another way: In doing logics, either formal or informal ones, we take it for granted that we study the relationships between *propositions*, and as soon as a move in our 'logic-game' is bound to result in the degeneration of one of the propositions involved into a mere *pseudo-proposition*, this move ceases to be a legitimate one and hence has to be retracted.

7.2.   It seems to me that what I have just tried to set forth in subsection 7.1 has been utterly neglected by quite a number of critics who find fault with Russell's analysis of sentences containing a definite description.[54] Russell's suggestion to analyse his well-known example

(7.2.1)   The (present) king of France is bald.

as meaning the same as, say,

(7.2.2)   There is exactly one (present) king of France,
            and there is no (present) king of France who is not bald.

has often been criticised by calling attention to the (alleged) fact that (7.2.1) is an interpreted sentence (proposition, statement) lacking a truth-value whereas (7.2.2) is an interpreted sentence having the truth-value of the False, which, so the story goes, violates the basic and sacrosanct principle that linguistic analysis, in elaborating an analysans, must never tamper with the truth-value of the sentence to be analysed (i.e., the analysandum). Against this garden variety of criticising Russell's theory of description I should like to object, first, that (7.2.1) is not a proposition lacking a truth-value but a mere would-be proposition, and second, that it is not the task of linguistic or conceptual analysis to work out logical analysantia for *propositions* and *would-be propositions* indiscriminately. It cannot be denied that Russell himself has provoked that criticism by choosing, and dwelling upon, his king-of-France example. But if we replace the merely apparent or fake proposition (7.2.1) with a real proposition such as the analysandum

(7.2.3)   The (present) queen of the United Kingdom is bald.

and compare the latter with its Russell analysans

(7.2.4)   There is exactly one (present) queen of the United Kingdom, and there
            is no (present) queen of the United Kingdom who is not bald.,

we see at once that these two sentences share with each other the feature of being (I take it) *false*. Similarly, the analysandum

---

[54] See esp. Russell 1905: pp. 51, 55; 1911: p. 159; Whitehead & Russell 1910: Introduction, pp. 23, 30 f., 66–71, and *14.

(7.2.5)   The (present) queen of the United Kingdom has already reigned for half a century.

and its Russell analysans, which I think I need not write out, share with each other the feature of being *true*. So if applied to genuine propositions, Russell's analysis is truth-value preserving; and if applied to mere would-be propositions, his analysis replaces a would-be proposition by a genuine but false proposition. *Historically*, of course, Russell's motivation to deal with definite descriptions and other sorts of 'incomplete symbols' has been quite a different one – but for my present aim, which is purely *systematic*, I think it legitimate to rationally reconstruct his feat in the following succinct way. From a systematic point of view, it seems to me to be philosophically fertile to regard Russell's theory of descriptions as an attempt, not at all to analyse propositions and pseudo-propositions indiscriminately, but to *analyse propositions* and to *eliminate a certain sort of mere would-be propositions* by replacing them by genuine though false propositions. By the way, from reading Frege Russell must have been acquainted with a purely formal analogue of such a procedure: In Frege's mature theory of what, since 1891, tr. 1952 (p. 21), he simply called the 'horizontal one' (scil., the 'horizontal stroke'), he interpreted the sign '—x'[55] as virtually meaning 'that x is the True', i.e., as a first-order function transforming every name of the truth-value of the True into a related name of the truth-value of the True, every name of the truth-value of the False into a related name of the truth-value of the False, and also every other object name whatsoever into a name of the truth-value of the False.[56] Similarly, by his analysis of sentences containing definite descriptions Russell may be taken to substitute a true proposition for a true proposition and a false proposition for a false proposition as well as for a mere pseudo-proposition. Since, of course, a pseudo-proposition need not always be *known* to be such a fake, this procedure has the advantage of making it impossible to inadvertently violate the boundaries of logic, which in its formal as well as informal variants is restricted to genuine interpreted sentences, true or false, and has to see to it that it does not mistake for such a sentence what in fact *only looks* like one. But at the same time this procedure is neither gratuitous nor *ad hoc*; for Russell's theory of definite descriptions can be fully justified by assenting tests (combination tests) according to C-CT,[57] not

---

[55] Before 1891, tr. 1952, Frege had interpreted this sign in a subtly *different* way. Instead of merely speaking of the 'horizontal stroke' he had then used the more suggestive term 'content-stroke' ('Inhaltsstrich').

[56] Cf. Hoche 1976: sect. 2. Roughly speaking, and using a simple example, we may say: 'that "2 + 2 = 4" is true' is *true*, 'that "2 + 2 = 5" is true' is *false*, and 'that 2 is true', according to Frege – whose demarcation line between falsity and meaninglessness did not at all coincide with the one favoured by contemporary linguistic philosophers – is likewise *false*.

[57] I take it that my readers by now are in a position to carry out the necessary combination tests by themselves.

to mention the well-known linguistic fact that a definite description of the form 'the so-and-so' genetically refers to a complete existential proposition of the form 'There is exactly one so-and-so (in question).'.

8. Another application of this solution: A paradox alleged to be deducible from my definitions exposed as a merely apparent one

8.1.   The solution of the paradox of existential presupposition just offered in section 7 can also be applied to a tricky problem which resembles the one exposed in subsection 6.4, above, but is somewhat more complicated.[58] In section 5, above, we could convince ourselves that

(5.2.1)   My son lives in London.

semantically presupposes

(5.2.2)   I have at least one son.

In a similar way we can show that, according to C-CT, (5.2.1) semantically implies (but does *not*, of course, presuppose)

(8.1.1)   I have at least one son (who lives) in London.

Hence, as semantic implication has been shown to be subject to the law of *transposition*, we should expect the negation

(¬8.1.1) I have no son (who lives) in London.

to imply the negation

(¬5.2.1) My son doesn't live in London.

semantically. Furthermore, (¬5.2.1) certainly implies

(5.2.2)   I have at least one son.

semantically; hence, as semantic implication has also been shown to be a *transitive* relation, also (¬8.1.1) should be expected to imply (5.2.2) semantically. But at first blush this looks preposterous; for it certainly appears that if I assent to (¬8.1.1) I

---

[58] I am grateful to Michael Knoop for having called my attention to this problem. – It is true that this problem could be coped with in a much simpler manner, to wit, in the *first*, though not in the second, of the two ways presented in 6.4–6.5, above (see also the preceding Essay I: 8.6, 8.8, 9.5). However, I think it worth while pursuing also the following line of arguments.

need not at all assent to (5.2.2), and hence that (¬8.1.1) implies (5.2.2) not even linguistically at large. Let me call this 'Knoop's paradox'.

8.2.   However, I think that Knoop's paradox can be *dissolved* by means of a case distinction. This case distinction can be motivated in two different but converging ways. (a) Judging from our everyday linguistic competence, we can easily convince ourselves that I am prepared to assent to (¬8.1.1) only on condition that I can assent either [case 1a] to

(¬5.2.2)   I have no son(s) (at all).

or else [case 2a] to

(8.2.1)   (It is true that) I have at least one son, and [but] none of my sons lives in London.

(b) Using the roundabout of logical symbolisation, we come to a closely related distinction. (¬8.1.1) is likely to be rendered as, say,

(¬8.1.1')   ¬(∃x) (Sx & Lx),

and according to the classical first-order predicate calculus this is logically equivalent to

(¬8.1.1'')   (x) (Sx → ¬Lx),

which we are used to translating into ordinary English in one or other of the following two ways:

(8.2.2a)   All of my sons do not live in London.
(8.2.2b)   None of my sons live(s) in London.

But neither one of the ordinary-language sentences (8.2.2a) and (8.2.2b) is semantically equivalent to (¬8.1.1); for unlike the latter, they are understood to contain an existential presupposition: We would never use them unless we had at least one son (or, to be more correct: at least *two* sons; but I think in the present context this refinement may be safely neglected). The fact that (¬8.1.1') and (¬8.1.1'') are logically equivalent whereas their ordinary-language translations (¬8.1.1) and (8.2.2a,b) are not semantically equivalent is not really surprising; for it is due to the well-known fact that, with respect to existential presupposition, English and many (or most, if not all) other natural languages follow Aristotle's syllogistic rather than our contemporary predicate calculus. Now (¬8.1.1') is logically equivalent to

(8.2.3)   (¬(∃x) (Sx & Lx) & ¬(∃x) Sx) ∨ (¬(∃x) (Sx & Lx) & (∃x) (Sx));

therefore, if we assent to (8.2.3) – and hence to (¬8.1.1') – we have to assent either to the first [case 1b] or else to the second disjunct of (8.2.3) [case 2b].

8.3.   In cases [1a] and [1b], by claiming that I have no son at all I virtually declare ($\neg$5.2.1) to be a sentence which is not fully interpreted and which, for this very reason, I cannot, and hence do not, understand; for knowing the reference of the definite description 'my son' is certainly an integral part of understanding ($\neg$5.2.1). Because of this twofold violation of the explicit requirements of C-CT, the alleged combination test with the sentences ($\neg$8.1.1) and ($\neg$5.2.1) is null and void and hence has to stop short. For this reason, ($\neg$8.1.1) cannot be rightly claimed to imply ($\neg$5.2.1) even linguistically, not to mention semantically. In cases [2a] and [2b], however, I can and must also assent to (5.2.2), which is a conjunct of (8.2.1), and the formalisation of which is a conjunct of the second disjunct of (8.2.3). Or, in simpler words and using again the symbol '$^{\sigma}\!\Rightarrow$' for 'semantically implies': Either [cases 1a,b] there is *no* legitimate combination test which could show that ($\neg$8.1.1)$^{\sigma}\!\Rightarrow$($\neg$5.2.1), and then we *cannot* apply the transposability and transitivity of semantic implication and claim that, because of the uncontroversial ($\neg$5.2.1)$^{\sigma}\!\Rightarrow$(5.2.2), ($\neg$8.1.1)$^{\sigma}\!\Rightarrow$(5.2.2) holds true. Or else [cases 2a,b] there *is* a legitimate combination test showing that ($\neg$8.1.1)$^{\sigma}\!\Rightarrow$($\neg$5.2.1), and then of course we *can* apply the transposability and transitivity of semantic implication and claim that because of ($\neg$5.2.1)$^{\sigma}\!\Rightarrow$(5.2.2) also ($\neg$8.1.1)$^{\sigma}\!\Rightarrow$(5.2.2) is true. In these cases, however, ($\neg$8.1.1)$^{\sigma}\!\Rightarrow$(5.2.2) can be shown directly, i.e., without making use of the transposability and transitivity of semantic implication. Hence we may say that if and only if ($\neg$8.1.1)$^{\sigma}\!\Rightarrow$(5.2.2) can be proved *indirectly*, to wit, by using transposability and transitivity, it can also be proved *directly*. So Knoop's paradox has been exposed as being a merely apparent one.

(1.1.2)   *a* is a prime number

yields a false proposition if and only if *a* can be divided by a natural number which is neither *a* nor 1, and hence, he continues, it is 'obvious' ('offensichtlich') that '*a*' cannot be replaced with 'Caesar'.[2] In contradistinction to this, I have come by the impression that even nowadays a great many logicians and philosophers are far from finding this *obvious*; and in fact I think that Carnap's reasoning, as it stands, does not suffice yet.

1.2.   However, there are ways to make his argument more convincing. For a first attempt, let us start from the fact that the string of words (1.1.1), if it has a genuine sense at all, means neither more nor less than the string of words

(1.2.1)   There is (exactly) one prime number Caesar is identical to.[3]

Hence, if (1.2.1) can be shown to be strictly meaningless (i.e., senseless or non-sensical in the sense of 'void of a genuine meaning'), the same must be true of (1.1.1). Again, if (1.2.1) means anything at all, it certainly means as much as the (genuine or apparent) countably infinite disjunction

(1.2.2)   Either Caesar is identical to the number 2, or Caesar is identical to the number 3, or Caesar is identical to the number 5, or Caesar is identical to the number 7, or [...].

For this reason (1.1.1) is meaningless if and only if (1.2.2) is meaningless.[4] Again, according to the propositional calculus the disjunction (1.2.2) is meaningless if and only if it includes at least one disjunct which is meaningless. Furthermore, as none of the disjuncts differs from any one of the others in a logically relevant respect, by 'parity of reasoning' we may conclude that (1.2.2) contains *at least one* meaningless disjunct if and only if *all* of its disjuncts lack a genuine meaning, among them, say, the string of words

(1.2.3)   Caesar is identical to the number 3.

From this it follows that Carnap is right in insisting on the meaninglessness of (1.1.1) *if and only if* the exemplary string of words (1.2.3), which at first sight

---

[2] Carnap 1931, tr. 1959: §§ 1, 4. – For Carnap's choice of the example, cf. Frege 1884, tr. 1950: § 56.

[3] Cf. Wiggins 1980: 4, 9, 30f. – In the case of *genuine propositions* having the same grammatical forms as (1.1.1) and (1.2.1), this can be shown by means of 'assenting tests' carried out in both directions; see the preceding Essays I and II.

[4] It may be objected that (1.2.2), which is to be understood as an *infinite* disjunction, does not belong to a natural language at all and hence, *a fortiori*, cannot be a *meaningful* proposition of natural language, from which it would follow that my argument begs the question. However, this objection can be easily avoided by changing (1.1.1) into a string of words of the form 'Caesar is a prime number *smaller than n*'. I think it is obvious that such a change would not in the least touch the *rationale* of my argument.

looks like a false identity-statement, is in fact meaningless, i.e., a mere pseudo-proposition.[5] Hence, if we want to find out whether the two of them are in fact mere pseudo-propositions or not, we can work from either side. Whereas formal logicians and linguists, in their endeavour to brand such strings of words as syntactically ill-formed or as violating semantic selection-restrictions, respectively, would tend to work from the side of (1.1.1), in this paper I prefer to choose the opposite course and work from the side of (1.2.3). This takes us to the questions how to analyse identity-statements of ordinary language, and what (kinds of) criteria of identity and non-identity are at our disposal.

2. Definite descriptions and identity-statements

2.1   Unlike (1.2.3), such strings of words as

(2.1.1)   The author of *Principia Mathematica* is identical to the author of *Why I Am Not A Christian*.

(2.1.2)   The present king of France is identical to M. Nicolas Sarkozy.

(2.1.3)   The inventor of the bifocals is identical to the first US ambassador to Paris.

may be taken to be less likely to be suspected of being *nonsensical*; at first sight, in their cases the only question may seem to be whether they are *true* or *false* identity-statements. This is not correct, however. For as the logico-mathematical standard work *Principia Mathematica* happens to have been written by *two* authors, one of whom also wrote *Why I Am Not A Christian*, (2.1.1) can be called neither true nor false and so is in a way nonsensical, too. Similarly, (2.1.2) can be called neither true nor false and hence is in a way also nonsensical; for at present, i.e., in the year of 2007, there exists *no* king of France *at all*.[6] But the latter way(s)

---

[5] This ought to be kept in mind if we remember that most logicians would admit the union of the two unit sets { Caesar } and { 3 }, i.e., { Caesar } ∪ { 3 }, and define it as the set { x | x = Caesar ∨ x = 3 }. If we simply follow them, we can hardly deny that the expression purporting to name the latter is only meaningful if the expression 'Caesar = Caesar ∨ Caesar = 3', and hence also the expression 'Caesar = 3', is meaningful, too. If somebody feels like using this equivalence as an objection against what I say in this paper, certainly they must likewise use it as an objection against Carnap, whose logical competence should be deemed to be above any doubt – and, by the way, also as an objection against Husserl (1901a: 4th Investigation, §§ 12, 14; 1929a: §§ 89–90). But what counts more than this *argumentum ab auctoritate* is the fact that we can avoid the above-mentioned difficulty by devising a polysortal predicate calculus (see, e.g., Oberschelp 1992) for which we can expressly stipulate that expressions such as 'Caesar is a prime number' (see ibid., § 30, p. 175) are to count syntactically *ill-formed*.

[6] I am not sure whether we should say that (2.1.2) is nonsensical in the same way as (2.1.1); but certainly both of them are nonsensical in a way, or in ways, different from the meaninglessness of

of being nonsensical will prove to be much less virulent than the way in which (1.2.3) is nonsensical; for, as I am going to show in the next subsections, (2.1.1) and (2.1.2) can be easily converted into meaningful, though false, propositions whereas (1.2.3), as I will try to prove later on, can *not*. So far, only (2.1.3) is above suspicion; for if it is an historical fact, first, that Benjamin Franklin was really the *only* person who invented the bifocal eyeglasses (which, of course, might be called into question on the basis of novel historical findings), and second, that he was really the *leading* one among the three commissioners sent to France by the Continental Congress in 1776 (which, perhaps, might be called into question, too), then (2.1.3) is a true and, *a fortiori*, a meaningful identity-statement.

2.2.   According to Russell's theory of 'definite descriptions',[7] (2.1.3) can be analyzed, *inter alia*, as the 'three member conjunction', put in the historical present tense,

(2.1.3')   There is exactly one person who is an inventor of the bifocals, and there is exactly one person who is the first US ambassador to Paris, and there is at least one person who is an inventor of the bifocals and (also) a first US ambassador to Paris.

What seems to me to speak *in favour* of this analysis is the fact that completely elaborated assenting tests on the basis of those suggested, and richly exploited, by Richard M. Hare[8] make it clear that what I propose to call 'semantic presupposition' is a subcase of what I propose to call 'semantic implication',[9] which is absolutely required for (2.1.3) and (2.1.3') to be 'semantically equivalent' to each other. However, what is often taken to speak *against* the soundness of this analysis is the fact that if the semi-formalised analysans (2.1.3') is *false* then the ordinary-language analysandum (2.1.3) can be *either false or nonsensical* in the sense of lacking part of its reference, or of not being a completely interpreted sentence of the English language. The falsity of the conjunction (2.1.3') can be due to the falsity of the first, or the second, or the third of its members. If the third conjunctive member is the only false one, then (2.1.3) is clearly *false*; but if one or other of the first two members is false, or if both of them are false, then (2.1.3) is *nonsensical* in that it lacks reference. Now one might be tempted to think that this reflects upon the analysis in question; for certainly an analysis is inadequate unless

---

(1.1.1) and (1.2.1)–(1.2.3). Of course we can come across such strings of words as (2.1.1) and (2.1.2) in everyday speech; but in such cases we would hardly be prepared to say that their users *properly understand* what they say. So I would not admit that there are speech-act theoretical situations in which they are 'really used', and hence that they are meaningful.

[7] See esp. Russell 1905: 51, 55; 1911: 159; Whitehead & Russell 1910: Introduction, pp. 23, 30 f., 66–71; *14. Cf. also Wiggins 1965: sect. VII.

[8] See Essay I of the present collection.

[9] See Essay II: esp. sections 5–7, of the present collection.

the analysandum and the analysans share their truth-values. However, I take it that being nonsensical ought to be considered, not an additional truth-value, but the denegation of having a truth-value at all. A string of words which is neither true nor false because it lacks complete interpretation and reference should be taken to be, not a nonsensical proposition, but a mere would-be proposition or pseudo-proposition; and only genuine true-or-false propositions belong to the domain of objects for which truth-values, truth-value sharing, meaning, semantic equivalence, and other logical properties are defined in the first place.

2.3.   So a popular form of objection against a Russell style analysis of definite descriptions in general and identity-statements in particular seems to me to be unwarranted. Hence, the fact that a strictly analogous treatment of such examples as (2.1.1) and (2.1.2) would doubtless correlate *nonsensical strings* of words with *false* ones is utterly irrelevant to the basic idea of Russell's analysis. For as (2.1.1) and (2.1.2) are mere pseudo-propositions, which fall outside the scope of logical entities for which such concepts as 'logical analysis', 'analysandum', and 'analysans' make sense at all, we are not even justified in saying that (2.1.1) and (2.1.2) are nonsensical 'analysanda' which, contrary to an inviolable rule of adequacy, are to be replaced with false 'analysantia'. What counts is nothing but the fact that a Russell style analysis of definite descriptions, if applied to genuine propositions, is truth-value preserving, and that such a procedure, if applied to mere would-be propositions, replaces a would-be proposition with a genuine but false proposition. *Historically*, of course, Russell's motivation to deal with definite descriptions and other sorts of 'incomplete symbols' has been quite a different one – but for my present aim, which is purely *systematic*, I deem it legitimate to rationally reconstruct his feat in the following succinct way. From a systematic point of view, it seems to me to be philosophically fertile to regard Russell's theory of descriptions as an attempt, not at all to analyse propositions and pseudo-propositions indiscriminately, but to *analyse propositions* and to *eliminate a certain sort of mere would-be propositions* by replacing them with genuine though false propositions. From reading Frege, Russell must have been acquainted with a purely formal analogue of such a procedure: In Frege's mature theory of what, since 1891 (p. 21), he simply called the 'horizontal one' (scil., the 'horizontal stroke'), he interpreted the sign '—x'[10] as virtually meaning 'that x is the True', i.e., as a first-order function transforming every name of the truth-value of the True into a related name of the truth-value of the True, every name of the truth-value of the False into a related name of the truth-value of the False, and also every other

---

[10] Before 1891, tr. 1952, Frege had interpreted this sign in a subtly *different* way. Instead of merely speaking of the 'horizontal stroke' he had then used the more suggestive term 'content-stroke' ('Inhaltsstrich').

object name whatsoever into a name of the truth-value of the False.[11] Similarly, by his analysis of sentences containing definite descriptions Russell may be taken to substitute a true proposition for a true proposition and a false proposition for a false proposition as well as for a mere pseudo-proposition. Since, of course, a pseudo-proposition need not always be *known* to be such a fake, this procedure has the great advantage of making it impossible to inadvertently violate the boundaries of logic, which in its formal as well as its informal variants is restricted to genuine interpreted sentences, true or false, and has to see to it that it does not mistake for such a sentence what in fact *only looks* like one.

3. A problem with Caesar and the number 3

3.1.   To make a long story short: I think we may conclude from what I said in section 2, above, that a Russell style analysis of ordinary-language identity-statements such as (2.1.3) by semi-formalised sentences such as (2.1.3′) is basically sound. So it seems natural enough to try out an analogous analysis of the string of words

(1.2.3)   Caesar is identical to the number 3.

by some such sentence as

(1.2.3′)   There is exactly one person to whom we refer, in non-subcultural historical English contexts of the beginning 21st century, by the name-radical 'Caesar',
and there is exactly one number to which we refer, in non-subcultural mathematical English contexts of the beginning 21st century, by the name-radical '(the) Three',
and there is at least one entity to which we refer, in non-subcultural historical English contexts of the beginning 21st century, by the name-radical 'Caesar' and (also), in non-subcultural mathematical English contexts of the beginning 21st century, by the name-radical '(the) Three'.

Readers who do not know, or are not ready to accept, the theory of grammatically proper names implicit[12] in (1.2.3′) are free, of course, to replace (1.2.3′) with a

---

[11] Roughly speaking, and using a simple example, we may say: 'that "2 + 2 = 4" is true' is *true*, 'that "2 + 2 = 5" is true' is *false*, and 'that 2 is true', according to Frege – whose demarcation line between falsity and meaninglessness did not at all coincide with the one favoured by contemporary linguistic philosophers – is likewise *false*. For details see Hoche 1976.

[12] For an explication of this name-theory, and especially for the consequential distinction between what I call a 'name-radical' and a 'name' (which is comparable to the distinction between a 'sentence of a given language' and a 'sentence [as] used on a certain speech-act theoretical occasion'), see Hoche

more familiar (and simpler, though, I take it, highly arbitrary and hence doubtful) version such as

(1.2.3″)   There is exactly one conqueror of Gaul,
          and there is exactly one positive square root of 9,
          and there is at least one entity that is a conqueror of Gaul and (also)
          a positive square root of 9.

Whichever version we choose: the sentences (1.2.3′) and (1.2.3″) have a common problem, to wit, the occurrence of the term 'entity' in the third conjuncts. Of course, there are no objections against substituting for this term some such term as 'thing' or 'object'; however, it cannot possibly be replaced with either 'person' or 'number'. For suppose we replace it with 'person', i. e., change the third conjunct of, say, (1.2.3″) into

(3.1.1)   There is at least one person
          who is a conqueror of Gaul and (also) a positive square root of 9.

By so saying, we would presuppose, or silently take it for granted, that it is meaningful to ascribe to a person the mathematical property of being a square root. But as what is at stake is the question of whether it is meaningful to ascribe to a person the mathematical property of being a prime number (see section 1, above), it would be difficult to reject the objection that we are begging the question. *Mutatis mutandis*, the same would be true in the case of (1.2.3′), and again if we replaced 'entity' with 'number' in either (1.2.3′) or (1.2.3″).

3.2.   Obviously, it would be no way out to change (1.2.3″) into the logically equivalent form

(1.2.3‴)   There is exactly one conqueror of Gaul,
          and all and only conquerors of Gaul are positive square roots of 9.

For here, the second (and last) conjunct may be abbreviated and formalised as

(3.2.1) $(x)\,(Cx \leftrightarrow Px)$,

which is logically equivalent to

(3.2.1′) $\neg(\exists x)\,(Cx \,\&\, \neg Px \lor Px \,\&\, \neg Cx)$.

1985. – It should be noted that a Russell style analysis inevitably requires the prior change of proper names into suitable definite descriptions *proper* (see (1.2.3″)) or – preferably, I think – *sui generis* (see (1.2.3′)). Apart from this requirement, the use of proper names in identity-statements provokes the noteworthy objection, raised in Pardey 1994: esp. 4.6, and 2006: pp. 309–315 ('Begriffskonflikte 4: Identität und Veränderung der Sprache') that, say, the grammatically proper names 'Hesperus' and 'Phosphorus' in 'Hesperus [Vesper] is the same planet as Phosphorus [Lucifer].' belong to *different* ('punctual') languages.

However, (3.2.1′) is meaningful if and only if its negation,

(¬3.2.1′) (∃x) (Cx & ¬Px ∨ Px & ¬Cx),

is meaningful, and the latter faces a similar problem as does (3.1.1).

3.3.   However, there might seem to be a simple way out; for why shouldn't we replace, in the third conjunct of (1.2.3′) or (1.2.3″), the term 'entity' with the adjunctive term 'person or [and/or] number'? I think the answer is simple. By this term – and similarly by such hybrid abbreviations as 'pember' or 'nurson' – we can only understand as much as by the term 'entity that is a person or a number'; that is,

(3.3.1)   There is at least one person or number
          that is a conqueror of Gaul and (also) a positive square root of 9.

means the same as

(3.3.2)   There is at least one entity that is a person or number (and)
          that is a conqueror of Gaul and (also) a positive square root of 9.

But if we compare (3.3.2) with the original third conjunct of (1.2.3″), i.e.,

(3.3.3)   There is at least one entity
          that is a conqueror of Gaul and (also) a positive square root of 9.,

we can easily convince ourselves that the additional phrase 'that is a person or a number' in (3.3.2) is redundant or, as it were, idling. For if the entity in question is a conqueror of Gaul then it is, *a fortiori*, a person, and if it is a positive square root of 9 then it is, *a fortiori*, a number. So in the case at hand, the term 'entity' – or, for that matter, 'object' or 'thing' – renders us the same services as the inflated term 'entity (object; thing) that is a person or a number'.

4. Sortal concepts and individual binding

4.1.   But now we have to ask ourselves whether the term 'entity', as it occurs in (3.3.3) and hence in (1.2.3″) – and similarly in (1.2.3′) – renders us any service *at all*. If Frege's analysis of a statement of number in his *Foundations of Arithmetic* (1884, tr. 1950) is convincing, then this question has to be answered in the negative. And I think that Frege's analysis *is* convincing. In fact, by now it seems to be generally accepted that not only the *counting* of objects but already the mere *identification* or *individuation* of them[13] is impossible unless we subsume them under what is nowadays mostly called a *sortal concept*.[14]

---

[13] See Hoche 1975, tr. 1983.

[14] The technical term 'sortal' seems to date back to Strawson 1959: 5.2 [8], p. 168, where he introduces 'the distinction between *sortal* and *characterising* universals' as follows: 'A sortal universal supplies a

4.2.   In *The Foundations of Arithmetic* (1884, tr. 1950), what Frege is most eager to find is an answer to the following question: '[W]hen we make a statement of number, what is that of which we assert something?' (§ 45); and his reply is

> that the content of a statement of number is an assertion about a concept [and not, for instance, as had been suggested by others, about an object or an agglomeration of objects]. This is perhaps clearest with the number 0. If I say "Venus has 0 moons", there simply does not exist any moon or agglomeration of moons for anything to be asserted of; but what happens is that a property is assigned to the *concept* "moon of Venus", namely that of including nothing under it. If I say "the King's carriage is drawn by four horses", then I assign the number four to the concept "horse that draws the King's carriage". (§ 46)

4.3.   This, though convincing, stands in need of two qualifications. First, what is understood is, of course, a temporal or spatial delimitation, or, as the case may be, some other kind of what I propose to call an 'individual binding' of the concept.

> It may be objected that a concept like "inhabitant of Germany" would then possess, in spite of there being no change in its defining characteristics, a property which varied from year to year, if statements of the number of inhabitants did really assert a property of it. […] The fact is that the concept "inhabitant of Germany" contains a time-reference as a variable element in it, or, to put it mathematically, is a function of the time. Instead of "*a* is an inhabitant of Germany" we can say "*a* inhabits Germany", and this refers to the current date at the time. Thus in the concept itself there is already something fluid. On the other hand, the number belonging to the concept "inhabitant of Germany at New Year 1883, Berlin time" is the same for all eternity.[15]

---

principle for distinguishing and counting individual particulars which it collects. It presupposes no antecedent principle, or method, of individuating the particulars it collects. Characterising universals, on the other hand, whilst they supply principles of grouping, even of counting, particulars, supply such principles only for particulars already distinguished, or distinguishable, in accordance with some antecedent principle or method.' Cf. ibid.: 6.2 [6], p. 202: A sortal universal 'of itself provides a principle for distinguishing, enumerating and reidentifying particulars of a sort'. I take it that, on the level of linguistic expressions, sortal universals have their counterparts in what Quine 1960: § 19, p. 92, calls 'general terms with divided reference'. But the origin of the conception, though not the name, of 'sortals' (sortal concepts, universals, or terms) is certainly Frege 1884, tr. 1950: § 54; see 4.2–4.4, below. The most recent definition of the concept of a 'sortal' I know of, and an interesting one at that, is to be found in Linnebo 2005: 217.

[15] Frege 1884, tr. 1950, § 46. – This passage of Frege's shows, I think, that Cantor's (1885: 440) criticism is out of place. – It has been suggested that Frege's words (quoted in the following subsect. 4.4) 'which isolates what falls under it in a definite manner' ('der das unter ihn Fallende bestimmt abgrenzt') may arguably be taken to refer, not once more to the prohibition of 'any arbitrary division […] into parts', but precisely to what I call the individual binding. However, in my opinion such an interpretation would be hardly compatible with the context; cf. esp. Frege 1884, tr. 1950, §§ 30–32, 54.

Similarly, there is no definite number belonging, for instance, to the concept '(*x* is a) pupil'; but, at least in principle and ignoring the problem of vagueness,[16] we can determine the numbers belonging to such individually bound concepts as '(*x* is a) pupil at any one boarding-school in UK in 2006' or '(*x* is a) pupil of Socrates', which can be interpreted as being partial saturations of the polyadic relations '*x* is a pupil of kind *k* at place *s* in time *t*' and '*x* is a pupil of *y*', respectively. The relevance of such individual bindings of concepts to the central issue of our present paper will become obvious very soon.

4.4.   The second qualification, likewise offered by Frege himself, will turn out to be equally important to our issue of nonsense as opposed to falsity. It is the introduction of the conception of what nowadays we are wont to call 'sortality':

> [...] the concept, to which the number is assigned, does in general isolate in a definite manner what falls under it. The concept "letters in the word three" isolates the *t* from the *h*, the *h* from the *r*, and so on. The concept "syllables in the word three" picks out the word as a whole, and as indivisible in the sense that no part of it falls any longer under that same concept. Not all concepts possess this quality. We can, for example, divide up something falling under the concept "red" into parts in a variety of ways, without the parts thereby ceasing to fall under the same concept "red". To a concept of this kind no finite number will belong. [...] Only a concept which isolates what falls under it in a definite manner, and which does not permit any arbitrary division of it into parts, can be a unit relative to a finite Number.[17]

4.5.   It should be noted, however, that, whereas the prerequisite of 'individual binding' is required in order for us to be able to *stop* counting and thus to reach a '*finite* number', the prerequisite of 'sortality' is required in order for us to be able to *start* counting in the first place. For if an object already counted could be arbitrarily and indefinitely divided into parts which fall under the same concept as does the whole, then it would be impossible to go on counting, and we could never leave the starting block.

---

[16] It should be noted that for Frege a vague concept is not a concept at all; for time and again he insists on a concept having precise boundaries, or a sharp delimitation, in the sense that for every object it must be determined once and for all whether or not it falls under it; see, e.g., Frege 1969: 133, 168, 194f., 212, 248, 260, 262f.

[17] Frege 1884, tr. 1950, § 54. – Whereas '*number*' stands for the German term 'Zahl', '*Number*' (with capital 'N') is Austin's translation of 'Anzahl', i.e., cardinal number or 'positive whole number' ('which give[s] the answer to the question "How many?"'): see ibid.: § 2, translator's note, and § 4, Frege's note.

5. Purely formal concepts neither sortal nor open to individual binding

5.1.   If we are prepared to accept Frege's foregoing arguments to the effect 'that the content of a statement of number is an assertion about a concept' which meets the two conditions of being, first, an *individually bound concept* and, second, a *sortal concept* (i.e., one 'which isolates what falls under it in a definite manner, and which does not permit any arbitrary division of it into parts'), then we will have to acknowledge that there cannot be 'statements of numbers' – to wit, statements 'as to *how many* of something there are'[18] – about purely formal concepts such as 'object', 'thing', or 'entity'.

5.2.   By an 'object' ('thing', 'entity') in the widest and purely formal sense, which is essential to formal logic, we may understand any 'subject of possibly true predications', or 'the subject of true and false predications'.[19] The concept of an 'object' in this sense is purely formal in that it issues from a given material concept, not *via* a mediating sequence of higher *species* and *genera*, i.e., by a *generalisation*, but by what is frequently called a pure *formalisation*. Take, for instance, the material concepts 'poodle' or 'triangle'. By way of a *generalisation* we can reach such higher *species* and *genera* as 'dog', 'mammal', 'vertebrate', 'animal', 'living organism' and 'material (concrete) object' in the one case and 'polygon', 'geometrical figure in the Euclidean plane', 'mathematical object' and 'abstract object' in the other. But we cannot simply go on in the same way and top either series with one of the concepts 'object', 'thing', 'entity', and the like. Rather, we reach the latter by a *formalisation*, i.e., a making empty of any contents whatsoever, which is well known from formal logics and mathematics. In this procedure we make, not a mediate transition to ever higher species and genera, but, by way of abstracting from all material contents, an immediate transition to mere empty forms; or, as Husserl put it, 'all material contents of the concepts are changed into indeterminates, i.e., into modes of the empty "anything-whatever" ["Etwas-überhaupt"]'.[20] In this sense the concept of an 'object' or 'anything-whatsoever' is not a genuine genus but a mere *pseudo-genus*. Wittgenstein goes even a step farther; for as a consequence of his remarkable distinction between 'saying' and 'showing (itself)' he brands the purely formal concept of an 'object' as being rather

---

[18] Translator's (i.e., J. L. Austin's) note to Frege 1884, tr. 1950: § 26, p. 34e.

[19] Husserl 1913, tr. 1931: § 3, p. 49; cf. § 22, p. 80. Virtually the same definition of the concept 'object' has been given by Carnap 1928: §§ 1, 18.

[20] Translated from Husserl 1929a: § 29 (cf. Cairns 1973: 49, entry 'Etwas[-]überhaupt'). See also Husserl 1900: §§ 67, 70; 1901a: 3rd Investigation, §§ 11, 24; 1901b: 6th Investigation, § 60; 1913, tr. 1931: §§ 12–13; 1929a: §§ 6, 12, 29, 82, 87; 1934–1937: § 9f).

a mere *'pseudo-concept'* and says that we cannot properly say such things as 'There are objects.', 'There are 100 objects.', or 'There are *x* objects.'.[21]

5.3.   Now we can easily convince ourselves that this concept (or pseudo-concept) of an 'object', 'thing', or 'entity' cannot 'be a unit relative to a finite Number', i.e., something a 'statement of number' can be made about. For it is *neither sortal nor open to individual binding*. First, it does not meet Frege's condition that it 'isolates what falls under it in a definite manner, and [...] does not permit any arbitrary division of it into parts'; for it is obvious that, at least in principle, any part of anything we can make a true or false assertion about is again something we can make a true or false assertion about. Second, it is not even conceivable how to subject the purely formal concept of an 'object' or 'thing' at large to an individual binding, namely, how to determine such a binding in detail. For suppose we try out the binding to the range of whatever is presently in this room. Then justice is done, *inter alia*, to all chairs, tables, cupboards, plants, animals, and persons that are now in this room, and likewise, of course, to all conceivable fragments or pieces of these artefacts and living organisms; but what then about, say, prime numbers? If, on the other hand, we choose a binding to the range of whatever is greater than 10 and smaller than 100, then justice is done, *inter alia*, to all natural numbers and prime numbers which lie within the open interval between 10 and 100; but what is necessarily left out in this case are not only material objects and persons but even a great many mathematical objects of different sorts, such as complex numbers, polygons, polyhedra, polynomials, and so forth.

5.4.   From this it follows in particular that the concept of an 'entity (object; thing) that is a person or a number' (see 3.3, above) admits of an individual binding to *neither* the range of whatever resides in a certain place at a certain moment in time *nor* the range of what lies within a given arithmetical interval; and I think it is obvious that we wouldn't fare better with any other attempt whatsoever to find a way of individual binding which suits persons as well as (natural or prime) numbers. Furthermore, it seems to me to be clear that this difficulty even increases if we cancel the qualification 'that is a person or a number' and speak of 'entities (objects; things)' at large. So we have to conclude that neither the simple and purely formal concept 'entity (object; thing)' nor the disjunctive and seemingly

---

[21] Wittgenstein 1922: 4.12–4.128, esp. 4.1212, 4.122, 4.126, 4.1272. – Cf. already Frege 1884, tr. 1950, § 29, where he says, although with respect to an alleged *property*-word 'one': 'The content of a concept diminishes as its extension increases; if its extension becomes all-embracing, its content must vanish altogether. It is not easy to imagine how language could have come to invent a word for a property which could not be of the slightest use for adding to the description of any object whatsoever.' This very quotation itself can serve us as a suitable example; for here, the (apparent) property-word 'object' plays the part of a mere syntactical dummy: the words 'any object whatsoever' say no more than the words 'anything whatsoever' (cf. 5.2 with note 20, above).

material concept 'entity (object; thing) that is a person or a number' can be used as a basis for a 'statement of number', i. e., as Austin put it, a statement 'as to *how many* of something there are' (see subsection 5.1, above).

6. An assessment of the import of the foregoing considerations

6.1.   From what has been said so far I think we have to conclude that the apparent statements (3.3.1) through (3.3.3) and the apparent statements (1.2.3′) and (1.2.3″), in which they occur as members – and hence the apparent proposition (1.2.3) which we intended to analyse by means of them – are only *would-be statements*, or *pseudo-propositions* – unless, of course, in some way not to be seen yet we finally succeed in replacing the virulent terms 'entity (object; thing)' or 'entity (object; thing) that is a person or a number' with an expression of a concept which is both *sortal* and *open to individual binding*.[22]

6.2.   However, it might be objected that this is too rash a conclusion; for the foregoing line of reasoning might appear to show *too much* and hence to be basically unsound. In fact, at first sight it looks as if not only the purely formal concept 'object' but also the non-formal genus 'material (real; physical; spatio-temporal; concrete) object' lacks the property of being sortal; for any fragment or piece of a material object is itself a material object, and so the concept of a material object, although it is clearly open to individual binding, seems not to fulfil the condition that it 'isolates what falls under it in a definite manner' and 'does not permit any arbitrary division of it into parts'. Hence it would seem, for example, that not only

(1.2.3)   Caesar is identical to the number 3

but, surprisingly enough, also

(6.2.1)   Caesar is identical to the Palatine Hill.

is a mere *pseudo-proposition*. For at first sight it looks as if we cannot help analysing it as, say,

---

[22] Let us suppose that Frege admired, *inter alia*, Julius Caesar and the number 3. If so, we can subsume both of these objects under the concept 'x is an object admired by Frege'. We need not take pains to decide the difficult question of whether this admittedly somewhat strange concept is *sortal*. However, although the predicate used to denote it contains the proper name 'Frege', surely it is *not open to individual binding* in the required sense of the word. For over and above Caesar and the 3, Frege might have admired *all* successful politicians or *all* prime numbers, etc., and then no definite number can be assigned to this concept. Similar considerations apply, I take it, to such strange concepts as '*called* (a) so-and-so', say, to '*called* green' or '*called* a conscious experience', the latter of which plays a crucial part in discussing the problem of 'other minds' (see the following Essay IV: 3.17).

(6.2.1′)   There is exactly one conqueror of Gaul,
         and there is exactly one hill on which the city of Rome was founded,
         and there is at least one (material) object which is a conqueror of Gaul
         and (also) a hill on which the city of Rome was founded.;

and at first sight, again, in the 'third conjunct' of this sentence it might well seem impossible to replace the expression '(material) object' with a predicate more suitable for counting. Nonetheless we are rightly inclined to count (6.2.1) a *false*, and hence a genuine, proposition. For it seems to be generally accepted that a material object *a* and a material object *b* numerically differ from each other if and only if they occupy two different places at one and the same moment in time;[23] and in the present example, we can easily convince ourselves that this sufficient and necessary condition for numerical non-identity is fulfilled.

6.3.   So it might look as if we have reached an impasse. But on second thoughts we can see a way out. For a decisive difference between our examples (1.2.3) and (6.2.1) can, I think, be produced along the following lines. *Any* material object whatsoever can be regarded as at least a *potential (distinguishable; separable) part*[24] of an all-embracing material object, to wit, the physical world, universe, or cosmos; and *any nameable (identifiable)* material object whatsoever can be regarded as an *actual (distinguished; distinct)*[25] *part* of it. Hence in *speaking* of physical objects we

---

[23] A *locus classicus* is Locke 1690: Bk. II, Ch. 27, §§ 1–3: 'For we never finding, nor conceiving it possible, that two things of the same kind should exist in the same place at the same time, we rightly conclude that whatever exists anywhere at any time, excludes all of the same kind, and is there itself alone' (§ 1); 'though these three sorts of substances [to wit, God, finite intelligences, and bodies] do not exclude one another out of the same place ['A spirit and a body … may occupy the same place, and God is omnipresent': footnote], yet we cannot conceive but that they must necessarily each of them exclude any of the same kind out of the same place' (§ 2). For some qualifications, see Leibniz 1704: Bk. II, Ch. 27, § 1.

[24] For my present purposes, I am going to use the term 'part' in more or less the everyday sense. By a 'part', I understand, first, something less than the whole, i.e., a *proper part* of the whole, and, second, an *independent part*, i.e., a *piece, fragment,* or *segment* of the whole. In terms of Husserl 1901a: 3rd Investigation, the latter would be called a 'Stück', as opposed to a 'Moment' or dependent part such as the colour, extension, or shape of a given thing, each of which requires specific supplementation. If we follow this way of speaking, by a part of the *material* (real; physical; spatio-temporal) world we cannot help understanding a *material* (real; physical; spatio-temporal) fragment of it, i.e., for its part a *material* object.

[25] Here, we should by no means substitute 'separated' or 'separate' for 'distinguished' or 'distinct'; for the connotations of lacking (spatial) connection, or being (spatially) apart or isolated, should be strictly avoided. For instance, in spite of an obvious element of vagueness in determining its boundaries, the Palatine Hill is certainly a *distinct* but not a *separate or isolated* part of the site of Rome. Had we spoken, in the exemplary proposition (6.2.1), not of Caesar and the Palatine Hill, but, say, of the five-pound note in my wallet and the chestnut on my desk, then of course we would have been concerned with objects that are not only *distinct* but also clearly *separate*.

invariably refer to *actual* or *distinct parts* of the physical world. So in the context of *speaking* of a material (real; physical; spatio-temporal; concrete) object we can safely replace the term '*material (real; physical; spatio-temporal; concrete) object*' with the term '*actual (distinct) part of the physical world*'; and this substitution turns out to be consequential. For whereas any potential part of a physical object is a physical object, too, obviously it is *not at all* the case that any potential part of an actual (distinct) part of the physical world is again an actual (distinct) part of the physical world. In this sense, the concept of an *actual* or *distinct part of the physical world*, unlike the concept of a *physical object*, 'does not permit any arbitrary division of it into parts' and hence can serve as a suitable basis for counting. Thinking this way seems to me to be the attitude we silently and unhesitatingly adopt in everyday life. For although, except of course for chemical and microphysical considerations, we take any actual or potential part of, say, a diamond to be itself a diamond, we would not even dream of regarding the task of counting the diamonds in the queen's crown or in a given jewellery bag as being a bogus or nonsensical one. Likewise, in a kindergarten nobody should scruple to ask the children to count 'the red things on the table'.[26]

6.4.   Finally, it should be noted that a comparable line of reasoning is not possible if we take as our 'universe of discourse', not the physical universe, but the pseudo-universe of entities or objects *tout court*. For the concept of an *actual* or *distinct part of the (pseudo-)universe of objects tout court* is not a clear-cut or well-defined concept at all. This is due to the fact that in this case the concept of 'a part' is utterly ambiguous; for the *kind of parts* which an object has, or can have, depends on the *kind of object* it is. For instance, the parts of a natural number can naturally be taken to be, say, its factors, or its prime factors, or its summands; and the parts of a five-pound note, if the latter is taken, not as a material object made of paper etc., but as a monetary value, are not what we get by tearing the note into pieces but rather the change – coins or notes – we would get for it (taken again, of course, as monetary values).

---

[26] If this is acceptable, Frege's (1884, tr. 1950, § 54) paradigmatic example of 'the concept "red"[,] [to which] no finite number will belong', should be taken to be highly controversial. (Such a striking degradation of an apparent 'paradigm-case' need not give us qualms; after all, astronomically the most famous moon, to wit, the Moon, may be rightly regarded as being no moon at all but rather a co-planet of the Earth.) For the same reason, I take it that clearly distinct conscious experiences of mine, such as my being afraid that my present arguments are not convincing and my being afraid of an undesirable development of the present Iranian crisis, can be regarded as *actual parts* of my consciousness as a whole, and similarly, that clearly distinct neuronal patterns in different regions of my cortex can be regarded as *actual parts* of my present overall brain activity. If so, a potential objection against treating the relation between a given neuronal activity of mine and a given conscious experience of mine along the lines of the relation between Caesar and the number 3 can be disposed of (see sect. 0, above).

6.5.   Hence I am confident that the foregoing considerations, which draw on important and well-known, though certainly controversial, claims of Frege's and Russell's, have to be accepted at least as a promising point of departure for a deeper and more detailed research into the tricky problem of how to determine the boundaries between sense and nonsense. Nonetheless, let me add, in the following section 7, the outlines of an *alternative* strategy.

7.   There is no universal criterion for numerical (non-)identity

7.1.   In subsection 6.2, above, I made use of the following sufficient and necessary condition for a material object *a* and a material object *b* to be numerically different from each other: *a* and *b* numerically differ from each other if and only if they occupy two different places at one and the same moment in time.[27] Obviously, this condition is not applicable in the domain (or pseudo-domain) of objects *tout court*; for objects in the purely formal sense of anything a true or false predication can be made about *need not* have the property of existing in space and time, and in the case of abstract objects, such as numbers, they *cannot* exist that way. Instead, philosophers often refer to what they call 'Leibniz's law', which states that 'if *a* is identical with *b*, then any property of *a* is a property of *b*, or whatever is true of *a* is true of *b*. Formally, this would be $a = b \rightarrow (\Phi)(\Phi a \leftrightarrow \Phi b)$.'[28] Although a number of *caveats* have to be added to this principle,[29] at least in formal logics it has proved to be useful. On the face of it, the *conversion* of this principle is nothing but Leibniz's famous 'principle of the identity of indiscernibles', to wit, '$(\Phi)(\Phi a \leftrightarrow \Phi b) \rightarrow a = b$', which in the history of philosophy has rightly been regarded as highly controversial.[30] However, it can certainly be defended if

---

[27] It should be noted that primarily I make use of a sufficient and necessary condition, not of *identity*, but of *non-identity* in the domain of material objects. As we are interested, not just in a *sufficient and necessary condition*, but, what is more, in a *criterion* in the strict sense of the word to be outlined near the end of the present sect. 7.1, this seems to me to be the only strictly satisfying option open to us; but in the present context it would be not to the point to enter into a discussion of this tricky issue.

[28] Flew 1979: 150, entry 'identity'. Cf., however, Norman Kretzmann in Edwards 1967: Vol. 7 p. 382: '[Leibniz's] various versions may be accurately synthesised as follows: Those entities are the same, one of which may be everywhere substituted for the other, preserving the truth(-value) […]. [T]he context generally makes it plain that [the] principal intended application [of the principle] was to terms in propositions actually expressed in some notation.'

[29] Some of them are mentioned in Flew 1979: 187, entry 'Leibniz's law', and in Edwards 1967: Vol 7 p. 382 (see the preceding note 21). As I will reject the principle as a useful criterion of identity, I need not delve into details.

[30] For instance, Kant (*inter alia* in his *First Critique* [1781]: A 263f., 271f., 281) has convincingly argued that this principle holds, not for 'phenomena', but only for 'things in themselves' (in his

only we admit, unlike Leibniz himself,[31] not only 'purely qualitative' properties, but also 'purely positional' and 'mixed' properties (difficult though it may be to carry out a truly satisfying demarcation).[32] Hence in principle I am not at all averse to proceeding to the resulting *equivalence* '$a = b \leftrightarrow (\Phi)\ (\Phi a \leftrightarrow \Phi b)$', which renders the combination of 'Leibniz's law' with Leibniz's 'principle of the identity of indiscernibles' a *sufficient and necessary* condition for identity. Note, however, that the right side of this equivalence is in effect an empirical all-proposition, which opposes strict verification.[33] So the combined principle cannot in fact serve as a *criterion* for identity; for a criterion is generally taken to be 'something that settles a question with certainty'.[34] But as the equivalence '$a = b \leftrightarrow (\Phi)(\Phi a \leftrightarrow \Phi b)$' can be transposed to '$\neg(\Phi)\ (\Phi a \leftrightarrow \Phi b) \leftrightarrow \neg a = b$' or '$a \neq b \leftrightarrow (\exists \Phi)\ (\Phi a\ \&\ \neg \Phi b \lor \Phi b\ \&\ \neg \Phi a)$', it looks at first sight as if it could serve as a universal *criterion for non-identity*. For it says that any old object a and any old object b are numerically different from each other if and only if there exists at least one property such that only (exactly) one of them has it – and this question is in principle verifiable.

7.2.   So, after all, at first sight the combination of 'Leibniz's law' with Leibniz's 'principle of the identity of indiscernibles' appears to be precisely as effective as the special criterion for non-identity in the domain of material objects touched upon in 6.2 and 7.1, above. But a closer look is apt to show us that this is not the case. The difference seems to me to be as follows. If we can spot a moment in time at which a and b can be seen, or otherwise immediately *perceived*, at two different places, then as a rule this fact admits of no rational doubt; and for the most part this is even true if, from undisputed premises, we can only indirectly *conclude* that a and b 'must'[35] occupy two different spatial positions at one and the same given moment in time. But once we have convinced ourselves that we are justified

---

'*transcendental*' sense of the word). Of course, this holds only for Leibniz's own interpretation of the principle.

[31] See, e.g., Leibniz 1704: Bk. II, Ch. 27, § 3.

[32] The terminological distinction between 'purely qualitative', 'purely positional', and 'mixed' predicates seems to date back to Carnap 1947: 138, 146f. Goodman (1954: sect. 3.4) has criticised this distinction, but on grounds which I take to be doubtful; see Hoche 1977: sect. XVIII; 1979b. In the present context, however, it seems to me to be unnecessary and hence inadvisable to enter into a discussion of the related problems.

[33] The *locus classicus* is Popper 1934, tr. 1959: esp. §§ 13–15.

[34] Malcolm 1959: 60; cf. 44: 'establish with certainty'; 56: 'settle the question'; and esp. 24: 'The application of a criterion must be able to yield either an affirmative or a negative result'; see also Birnbacher 1974: 9f., 54. The intimate connection between 'verification' and 'criterion' is succinctly summarised in Hick 1960: 53f. For the distinction between 'criterion' and 'evidence' (or 'symptom'), see, e.g., Austin 1962b: 115f.; 141.

[35] This is the 'must' of what has often been called 'relative' (or: 'subjective') modality; see, e.g., Kneale 1962: esp. 626, 628; Hoche 1990: 9.1–9.2.

in ascribing a given property to an object *a*, then sometimes it may turn out to be difficult, or rather impossible, to decide whether or not an object *b lacks* this property. Take, for instance, the number 3 and Julius Caesar. We can easily find out that 3 is one of the square roots of 9; but how can we find out whether or not Julius Caesar, too, belongs to the set of square roots of 9? Strictly speaking, what we are confronted with is the (genuine or alleged) question 'Is Caesar a square root of 9?'; and, speaking strictly again, we can answer this question only by carrying out a well-defined operation, to wit, by multiplying Caesar by himself and looking whether or not the result of this operation equals 9. As of course we have not the slightest idea what the multiplication of Caesar and Caesar could possibly mean, it would be proper to say that we are not in a position to answer the above question – or that the apparent YES-NO-question is only a pseudo-question, and any direct answer to it a pseudo-proposition. Instead of following this line, however, we are normally inclined to accept the question without much ado and simply answer it in the negative. But in doing so, in fact we take it for granted that Julius Caesar is not identical to the number 3 – for if he *were* identical to the 3, then *of course* he would be a square root of 9. So what we are naturally inclined to do in this case amounts to a clear-cut case of begging the question. Now in the present case this may seem to be a venial sin; for certainly no man of sound mind is ever tempted to take the identity of Caesar and the 3 even into consideration. Nobody in his senses is likely to claim that Caesar and the 3 are, 'in actuality', one and the same 'topic-neutral' thing which presents itself partly as a number and partly as a human being and hence has mathematical as well as spatio-temporal and physical properties, although not all of them show themselves in both manners of appearing. On the other hand, however, it is a fact that many philosophers who, at least *prima facie*, have a right to be taken seriously, namely, proponents of 'mind-brain identity theories' and of 'dual-aspect theories', have indeed claimed, in a strictly parallel way, that, pending forthcoming empirical evidence, some given subjectively experienced conscious event and some given objectively observable neural event may be one and the same object which presents itself partly in the first-person perspective, in which, and in which alone, it displays phenomenal properties such as 'qualia', and partly in the third-person perspective, in which, and in which alone, it displays physical properties. So I take it that the combination of 'Leibniz's law' with Leibniz's 'principle of the identity of indiscernibles' is inapplicable just in those cases in which we would need it most badly, to wit, in cases of alleged 'cross-category identity'.[36]

---

[36] Some *loci classici* are Cornman 1962: 129; Rorty 1965: 190, 213. – As far as I can see, in all cases of 'intra-category identity' there are more or less complicated *special* criteria, for instance criteria for the identity or non-identity of (say, natural) numbers, of physical objects, of length, of size, of colour, of moments of time (even within different inertial systems), and so on. – I had only just finished a former version of this essay when I came across Linnebo 2005, who offers novel and, I think,

7.3.   As I cannot conceive of any other sufficient and necessary condition for numerical identity or non-identity in the alleged realm of objects *tout court*, in my eyes we are not in fact justified to make any use of such 'cross-category' or 'inter-category' relations at all. So I think we have to conclude that the alleged cross-category identity-statement

(1.2.3)   Caesar is identical to the number 3

– and, hence (see 1.2, above), Carnap's example

(1.1.1)   Caesar is a prime number

– have to be regarded, not as false propositions, but as nonsensical pseudo-propositions.[37]

8. Why nonetheless the string of words 'Caesar is identical to the number 3' could still seem to be meaningful though false

8.1.   For all that I cannot deny that we are very strongly tempted indeed to account the string of words

(¬1.2.3)   Caesar is not identical to the number 3

an obvious *truth*; and this temptation can be made perfectly understandable by the following consideration. The upshot of what we found out so far can be correctly summarised by means of the – in my opinion true – statement

(8.1.1.)   It would be improper to use the individual terms 'Caesar' and 'the number 3' to simultaneously flank the two sides of identity-predicates such as '$x = y$', 'x is identical to y', 'x is (one and) the same F as y', etc.

For this rather bulky statement we can aptly substitute the following abbreviation, which I also take to be true:

---

promising definitions of the concepts 'sortal', 'maximal sortal', 'category', 'intra-category identity statement', and 'cross-category identity statement' (sect. 5, esp. p. 217f.). As these definitions make use of Linnebo's newly introduced terms 'referential intermediary', 'unity relation', and 'referential attempt' (sect. 3, esp. p. 209f.), this is not the place to enlarge upon them. As far as (alleged) cross-category identity-statements such as (1.2.3) are concerned, Linnebo argues that they can be taken to be either 'false' or 'downright meaningless' (201f.), depending on whether or not '*all* grounds for the identity or non-identity of objects are taken into account' (202); but on the whole he prefers the falsity option (217, 218f.; for my somewhat divergent solution see sect. 9.5, below). All in all, I think that the differences between our positions are mainly due to our divergent viewpoints, philosophical backgrounds, and leading interests; in any case I think they are not substantial with respect to my overarching goals (see sect. 0, above).

[37] For an important qualification, see sects. 9.4–9.6, below.

(8.1.2)   We cannot say 'Caesar is identical to the number 3'.

However, as soon as we think we are justified in replacing the direct-speech sentence (8.1.2) with the seemingly equivalent and surely more elegant indirect-speech wording

(8.1.3)   We cannot say that Caesar is identical to the number 3

we begin to go astray. For in passing from (8.1.2) to (8.1.3), we do not simply change a true sentence of the 'formal mode of speech' into a likewise true sentence of the 'material mode of speech'.[38] Rather, we transform a genuine and true proposition into a meaningless would-be proposition; for whereas in (8.1.2) we merely, and legitimately, quote or *'mention'* the string of words 'Caesar is identical to the number 3', in (8.1.3) we squarely *'use'* it. In so doing, we make ourselves guilty of complicity, and possibly in a way also of a contradiction in terms; for in effect we are precisely doing what, in the same breath, we declare to be inadmissible. Or in short: The whole of (8.1.3) is senseless because it contains a senseless string of words, to wit, (1.2.3), as an integral part. If we do not realise this and, furthermore, make the transition from (8.1.3) to the apparently equipollent

(8.1.4)   It is not true [or: it is not the case] that Caesar is identical to the number 3

then the confusion reaches its climax; for of course we take (8.1.4) to be but a more complicated reading for the simple negation

($\neg$1.2.3)   Caesar is not identical to the number 3.

8.2.   Certainly we would hardly commit this error if only we realised that we are likewise justified to go on from (8.1.1) to

(8.2.1)   We cannot say 'It is not the case that Caesar is identical to the number 3'.

and hence to

(8.2.2)   We cannot say 'Caesar is not identical to the number 3'.

For by precisely the line of reasoning just displayed and shown to be illegitimate in 8.1, above, 'psycholinguistically' we would be forced to make the gradual transition from (8.2.2) to the increasingly less acceptable formulations

(8.2.3)   We cannot say that Caesar is not identical to the number 3;

(8.2.4)   It is not true [or: it is not the case] that Caesar is not identical to the number 3;

(8.2.5)   Caesar is identical to the number 3.

---

[38] Cf. Carnap 1934, tr. 1937: esp. sects. 64, 74.

8.3.   The upshot of all this is that the meaningful proposition

(8.1.2)   We cannot say 'Caesar is identical to the number 3'.

is true only on condition that it is interpreted as meaning as much as

(8.3.1)   The string of words 'Caesar is identical to the number 3' is a (mean-
            ingless) *pseudo-proposition*.

But in everyday life we rarely, if ever, think of *nonsense* as an alternative to *falsity*,
and so we are naturally inclined to read (8.1.2), not as (8.3.1), but as

(8.3.2)   The string of words 'Caesar is identical to the number 3' is a *false
            proposition*.

However, because of the truth of (8.3.1) the proposition (8.3.2) is itself a false
proposition.

9. The systematic ambiguity of cross-category non-identity statements: Numerical versus categorial non-identity

9.1.   So far, I have developed my argument against the meaningfulness of certain
alleged identity-statements by using the predicate 'x is identical to y'. However,
the expression 'identical to (or: with)' is a highly sophisticated and at the same
time historically young one; it certainly belongs to an extremely elaborated mode
of speech, and according to *Merriam Webster's Collegiate Dictionary* is has not
been found in English texts prior to 1599. If we look for a more primitive and
down-to-earth equivalent, doubtless our best choice is the expression '(one and)
the same as'. However, in, say,

(2.1.3)   The inventor of the bifocals is identical to the first US ambassador to
            Paris.

we cannot simply substitute this expression for 'identical to' without violating the
rules of English depth grammar, and a pedant might feel prompted to ask: 'The
same inventor, or the same ambassador, or the same what?'. In this unproblematic
case, it is easy to answer this question by saying, for instance,

(9.1.1)   The inventor of the bifocals is *(one and) the same person* as
            the first US ambassador to Paris.

But in the case of the string of words (1.2.3), it is obvious that neither 'person'
nor '(natural) number' nor any other material predicate would do, and so we
would have to take recourse to a purely formal predicate such as 'entity', 'thing',
or 'object', and say, for instance,

(9.1.2)   Caesar is *(one and) the same object* as the number three.

But now we remember that even this way-out is blocked. For if (9.1.2) were a meaningful sentence at all, Harean assenting tests (or rather the two-stage procedure of 'pragmatico-semantic combination tests' developed on their basis)[39] would certainly show that it could be replaced, without any change of meaning, with

(9.1.3)   Caesar and the number 3 are not two (or more) different objects[40]
          but one and the same object;

and hence in so saying we would squarely ignore the outcome of sections 4 and 5, above, to wit, the fact that objects *tout court*, i.e., objects in the purely formal sense of the word, *as such* do not admit of being counted.

9.2.   Let me add in passing that this consideration shows that we are in a position to argue in favour of the meaninglessness of such strings of words as (1.2.3) or (9.1.2) without making use of a Russellian analysis of identity-statements, and of definite descriptions in general. This may be found useful; for although I believe that such an analysis can be defended against garden-variety objections (see section 2, above), one could think of a quite different objection, which in the present context may be of some interest. On the basis a Russell style analysis of identity-statements, it can be proved that an appropriate logical formalisation of a sentence of the form

(9.2.1)   The F is identical with the G

entails an appropriate logical formalisation of a sentence of the correlative form

(9.2.2)   The F is identical with the F [i.e., with itself].

If so – and if it is in fact apposite to characterise identity as 'a relation that holds only between an object and itself'; or to say that '[i]dentity is really nothing but self-identity'; or even to say that, 'if one thing is certain in this life, it is that everything is identical with itself'[41] –, then we may be easily lead (or arguably: lured) to the conclusion that 'we cannot avoid having the universe [of discourse] as the extension of the predicate of self-identity'.[42] Now this conclusion would not

---

[39] See the preceding Essays I and II.

[40] As '[a]ffirmation of existence is in fact nothing but denial of the number nought', and hence 'existence is analogous to number' (Frege 1884, tr. 1950: § 53), we may perhaps likewise say that affirmation of identity is in fact nothing but denial of any number greater than one, and that therefore not only existence but also identity is 'analogous to number'.

[41] B. A. Brody in Edwards 1967: Vol. 5, p. 66; Castañeda 1975: 122; Forster 1992: 1; cf. also Frege 1893: § 4. – However, as I tried to drive home in Hoche 2006, I doubt that this interpretation is sound. See also Frege 1879, tr. 1952: § 8; 1892a, tr. 1952: 25–27; and the interpretation of these passages in Hoche 1982: 170–177.

[42] Forster 1992: 1.

be detrimental to the arguments developed in this essay; for although I consider the idea of an 'object' in the widest and purely formal sense a pseudo-*genus*, for my present purposes I need not go as far as Wittgenstein, who downright takes it to be a pseudo-*concept* (see 5.2, above). Nonetheless that conclusion might be thought dubious for type-theoretical reasons, into a discussion of which, however, this is not the occasion to enter.

9.3.   Returning to 9.1, above, we should attend to the fact that what I said there makes it quite plain that so far we have invariably and silently been reading the string of words

(1.2.3)   Caesar is identical to the number 3

in a way which we could make more explicit by using the even *more* elaborated and artificially sounding formulation

(9.3.1)   Caesar is numerically identical to the number 3,

by means of which we allude to the fundamental though in everyday language frequently blurred distinction between *numerical identity* (selfsameness) and *qualitative identity* (absolute agreement in all respects or details – think, for instance, of 'identical (i.e., monozygotic) twins' or 'two identical cars'). In this numerical interpretation, which is certainly by far the most plausible one, (1.2.3) has been shown to be a mere pseudo-statement, and so has what might appear[43] to be its propositional denegation, scil.,

(¬1.2.3)   Caesar is not identical to the number 3

or, for that matter,

(¬9.3.1)   Caesar is not numerically identical to the number 3.

Now, just as we are prone to read (1.2.3) as saying as much as (9.1.3),[44] we are likewise quite naturally tempted to read (¬1.2.3) or (¬9.3.1) as saying as much as

(¬9.1.3)   Caesar and the number 3 are not one and the same object
              but two (or more) different objects

and, hence, as

(¬9.1.3′) Caesar is numerically different from the number 3.

---

[43] As I take it that (1.2.3) is not a genuine proposition but a nonsensical string of words, the string of words (¬1.2.3) cannot *be* the propositional denegation of (1.2.3), nor a propositional denegation in the first place.

[44] See 9.1, above.

9.4. This, though unwarranted, at first sight seems to be plausible enough. For it is, I think, a linguistic fact that we are strongly inclined to treat examples like these – to wit, strings of words which have to do with identity – in a way which characteristically differs from the way we treat examples containing predicates the application of which is *quite obviously* restricted to individuals of more or less well-defined sorts, such as integers ('even'/'odd') or adult humans ('married/ unmarried' ['single']). For instance, in everyday life we would hardly hesitate to acknowledge the difference between, say,

(9.4.1)   She is not married (*but* unmarried).,

which might be used as a genuine though false proposition about Queen Elizabeth II, the present monarch of the United Kingdom, and

(9.4.2)   She is not married (*nor* unmarried).,

which might be used as a genuine and true (though possibly strange-sounding) proposition about the 'Queen Mary II', the recent flagship of the maritime jet set. In accordance with (9.4.2), in everyday life we are well aware of the fact that, from *a*'s not being married, we cannot always conclude that *a* is unmarried, or single. In patent contradistinction to this, we are not normally prepared to admit, alongside the alleged proposition

(9.4.3)   Caesar and the number 3 are not one and the same object
          (*but* two different objects)

– which, for whatever reasons, we tend to regard as exhausting the totality of alternatives to be conceived of –, also a proposition

(9.4.4)   Caesar and the number 3 are not one and the same object
          (*nor* two different objects).

Accordingly, we normally feel we are justified in concluding, from *a* and *b* not being one and the same entity, that *a* and *b* must be two different entities.[45]

9.5.   Instead, I propose to say that even in case the divergent parentheses are only implied or silently understood (which is often the case) – that is, when (9.4.3) and (4.4.4) are both of them reduced to the simple string of words

(9.5.1)   Caesar and the number 3 are not one and the same object

or to the still shorter

(¬1.2.3) Caesar is not identical to the number 3

---

[45] Of course, what makes itself felt in such cases is, *inter alia*, the difference between 'contradictory' and 'contrary' oppositions, of which the latter cannot be true together but can well be false together.

–, then in each case we have to do with a *systematically ambiguous* wording, or, strictly speaking, not with *one* string of words but with *two* of them, which, however, run completely alike,[46] and of which one is *nonsensical* and the other one *true*. Spelled out, the nonsensical string of words amounts, of course, to (9.4.3), which says that Caesar and the number 3 differ *numerically*, and the true one to (9.4.4), which, though in the suspect and misleading material mode of speech,[47] says in effect that Caesar and the number 3 differ, as we may say, *categorially*.[48] However, from this we should not conclude that also the positive counterpart

(1.2.3)   Caesar is identical to the number 3

must be ambiguous in an analogous way, i.e., that in one of its possible readings it is a *nonsensical* would-be proposition purporting to state *numerical* identity, and in the other one a genuine though *false* proposition erroneously stating what might perhaps be called '*categorial* identity'; for the systematic ambiguity of (¬1.2.3) seems to rest, not on an ambiguity of (1.2.3), but on the ambiguity of the propositional negator.[49] In any case, the systematic ambiguity of non-identity statements seems to me to be remarkable. For I think that what they who take cross-category identity-statements to be 'just *false*' really have in mind is not numerical but *categorial* non-identity. They subscribe to the perfectly adequate view that, say, Caesar and the number 3 differ from each other categorially, or that

---

[46] There are parallel though frequently overlooked examples in psycholinguistics, linguistics, and linguistic philosophy. For instance, the sentence 'Not all women are female.' can be taken to be either an *analytically false* proposition or, due to the efficacy of the psycholinguistic (though philosophically highly consequential) principle of 'sense constancy', an *empirically true* proposition; see Hörmann 1976: esp. 278 f.; Hoche 1995c: sects. 8–9. Similarly, the perfectly acceptable negation 'It is not the case that I hereby promise to come.' does by no means testify the alleged existence of 'neustic' or 'illocutionary (de)negations', in which, among others, Hare (1952: 21; 1971: 15; 1989: 35) and Searle (1969: 32f.) believe. For whenever we prefix a sentential negator (or a modal operator such as 'it is possible that') to a so-called explicit performative such as 'I hereby promise to come.', the explicitly performative particle 'hereby' of necessity undergoes a systematic change of meaning; see Hoche 1990: 8.4; 1995c; and Essay I: 8.7 with fn. 38, and Essay II: 2.5 with fn. 17, 4.2, 4.4, of the present collection.

[47] See section 8.1 with note 38, above.

[48] For the concept of a 'categorial difference', see also the following section 9.6, below. – Intra-category non-identity statements such as 'The murderer is not identical to the gardener.' are, of course, systematically ambiguous in basically the same way. But in these cases the difference is unspectacular; for in their categorial reading they are, by hypothesis, false propositions, and in their numerical reading they are either true or false, as the case may be. So here the question of nonsensical would-be propositions does not turn up.

[49] Hence, abiding by using the symbol '¬' in the sentence-name '(¬1.2.3)' would be inadvisable; for it would tend to blur the ambiguity of the negator. This ambiguity has to do, *inter alia*, with the distinction between contradictories and contraries (see sect. 9.4 with note 45, above), and can perhaps be counted to be another one among the many ambiguities of negation. But this is not the place to fully discuss these intriguing questions.

they do not belong to one and the same category or logical type. I take it that this accords well with one of the reasons which Linnebo explicitly adduces in favour of his position that cross-category identity-statements such as (1.2.3) should be taken to be 'just false': 'Natural numbers and persons are not the sorts of objects that *can* be identical, as their identity is governed by completely different considerations. [...] Since [natural numbers and physical bodies have] *incompatible* properties, no natural number *can* be identical with a physical body.'[50]

9.6.   As I just indicated in section 9.5, (9.4.4) can be taken to be an example of the material mode of speech and might hence be thought to be offensive or, strictly speaking, even a nonsensical would-be proposition. But in applying Hörmann's psycholinguistic 'charity' principle of 'sense constancy',[51] we can read it benevolently as meaning neither more nor less than the innocuous and true 'formal mode of speech' sentence

(9.6.1)   We cannot (properly) say 'Caesar and the number 3 are one and the same object', nor can we (properly) say 'Caesar and the number 3 are two different objects'.,

which for its part may be taken to be a variant of the propositional conjunction of (8.1.2) and (8.2.2). If we want to make use of the fruitful contemporary conceptions of 'categories' and 'category-mistakes',[52] (9.6.1) can be aptly replaced with

(9.6.2)   Caesar and the number 3 do not belong to the *category* (or: type) of things that can be numerically identical to, or numerically different from, each other.

or with

(9.6.3)   If we say 'Caesar and the number 3 are numerically identical to, or numerically different from, each other' then we commit a *category-mistake*.

Instead, I propose to use the simpler formulation

(9.6.4)   Caesar is *categorially* different from the number 3.

---

[50] Linnebo 2005: 219; second and third italics mine. – Arguably, also the fact that Oberschelp 1992: § 30, p. 175f., believes that *it depends on our free decision* whether we prefer to consider strings of words such as (1.1.1) to be syntactically ill-formed and hence meaningless, or to be meaningful but 'quite simply false', may be due to the systematic ambiguity of strings of words such as (1.1.1) and (1.2.3).

[51] Hörmann 1976.

[52] *Loci classici* are esp. Ryle 1938; 1945; 1949; 1954; see also Hoche & Strube 1985: Part A, ch. V, and note 36, above.

However, if for (9.6.4) we substitute the still shorter (¬1.2.3), then we run the risk of entering a slippery slope; for as (9.6.1) through (9.6.4) are *true* statements, the string of words

(1.2.3)   Caesar is identical to the number 3

is then liable to take on the appearance of a genuine but *false* statement. But (1.2.3) would be *false*, rather than *nonsensical*, only if we silently understand it as meaning something like

(9.6.5)   Caesar is *categorially* identical to the number 3.,

which would be but an exotic variant of the false statement

(9.6.6)   Caesar belongs to the *category* (or: type) of things that can be numerically identical to, or numerically different from, the number 3.

But I don't think it worth while to introduce, alongside the useful concepts of *numerical* and *qualitative identity*, an artificial concept of *categorial identity*.[53] However, its negative counterpart, the concept of being *categorially different*, is certainly required; for sometimes we urgently feel the need of having a shorter and more convenient alternative for saying, circumstantially enough, that an object a and an object b cannot be subsumed under a common generic concept which would be qualified as the basis of a statement 'as to *how many* of something there are' (see 5.1 and 6, above), and hence that they are neither one and the same object nor two numerically different objects[54] – and precisely this purpose is succinctly served by saying that a and b are *categorially different*.[55,56]

---

[53] At the most, I think, we could use it for stating that *categorial identity* is a prerequisite for both *qualitative* and *numerical identity*. By the way: It stands to reason that also *qualitative identity* is a prerequisite for *numerical identity*; for if we say, e.g., that young Tom and old Tom are one and the same person then, I take it, what we have in mind is the *person* Tom himself and not a couple of his *'personal time-slices'*, which are neither qualitatively nor numerically identical to each other but only what has been called 'genidentical' (see Lewin 1922: 7–20; 1923: 64; cf. Carnap 1928: §§ 128, 159).

[54] Note that this is the reason why we have to speak, somewhat clumsily, of 'an object a and an object b' instead of simply speaking of 'two objects'.

[55] See Hoche 1990: 120.

[56] I have to thank Dr. Øystein Linnebo, University of Bristol, an exchange of E-mails with whom prompted me to partly rewrite the concluding sub-sections 9.5 and 9.6. Nonetheless, he must not, of course, be held responsible for their present form, which in my eyes is still far from being optimal.

IV
CONSCIOUSNESS

Summary

The state of the discussion (1.1). – The aims of this essay (1.2.)

The term 'consciousness': A preliminary remark (2.1). – What we lose and regain by losing and regaining consciousness (2.2). – Comments on the consciousness-candidates just listed (2.3). – Intentionality and the status of bodily sensations (2.3.1). – The speech-act theoretical concept of human action. Why actions should be counted to be conscious experiences (2.3.2). – Why wanting and other propositional attitudes, though being 'intentional' in the technical sense of sect. 2.3.1, should *not* be counted to be conscious experiences (2.3.3). – Linguistic evidence for distinguishing between, e.g., fear as a propositional attitude and fear as a conscious experience, and for an epistemological asymmetry between one's own conscious experiences and those of others (2.3.4). – Dreaming and imagination. Bodily sensations as first-person ways of sensing one's own body. A third possibility besides numerical identity and numerical difference (2.3.5).

Seeing as an exemplary case of consciousness (3.1). – Seeing something, and seeing that something is the case (3.2). – Why we may concentrate on simple cases of seeing something (3.3). – Whenever I can truthfully assert that I (now) see, say, a dog, I can also specify the dog's way of now subjectively appearing to me (3.4). – Unity and multiplicity in what I can see (3.4.1). – Starting from an analogy: Linguistic types and linguistic tokens (3.4.2). – Visual objects and visual appearances (3.4.3). – The object-appearance distinction may be compared to the type-token distinction: Just as linguistic types are grasped through mediating tokens, which themselves as a rule go unheeded, visual objects are perceived through mediating appearances, which, too, use to go unnoticed. Neither types nor appearances can be counted parts of the material world (3.4.4). – Starting from appearances via material objects up to linguistic types and other universals, there is a gradation from concreteness to (relative) abstractness. Whereas the material objects make up *reality*, universals and appearances may be characterised as being *trans-real* and *cis-real*, respectively (3.4.5). – The gradation from the cis-real via the real to the trans-real is paralleled by a gradation from *subjectivity* to different *degrees of objectivity* (3.4.6). – Visual appearances, though usually going unheeded, can be noticed by a shift of attention (3.5). – The (naturalistic) painter's shift of attention (3.5.1). – The (non-naturalistic) consciousness theorist's shift of attention (3.5.2). – The – one and only possible – sense in which the manner of an object's being seen can be compared interpersonally (3.6). – In such a comparison, a distinction between qualitative and numerical identity need not be made (3.6.1). – In such a comparison, we can abstract from the onlooker's personal identity, from the time of his seeing, and also (if an exact double is provided for) from the object seen (3.6.2). – So the manner of an object's being seen is an abstraction, from which it follows that this manner of being seen is something different from the object's visual appearance (3.6.3). – A preliminary clarification of this difference (3.6.4). – The visual object in its *manner* of being seen (or 'the M-object') and the visual object in its *capacity* of [*as*; *qua*] now being seen by me (or 'the C-object') (3.6.5). – In contradistinction to the M-object, the C-object is not indifferent to being visually perceived, or else visually remembered, or else visually imagined (3.6.6). – In contradistinction to the M-object, as a rule the C-object is endowed, not only with theoretical, but also with emotional and in certain cases also with practical ('gerundive') features (3.6.7). – Just as we have, of course, to distinguish between the object (which is) now seen by me (or: by somebody else) and my (or: somebody else's) now seeing the object, we must also distinguish between the object in its *manner* of now being seen by me (or somebody else) and my (or the other person's) now seeing the object. However, so far we cannot make out any good reason for also distinguishing between the object in its *capacity* of now being seen by me in such-and-such a way and my now seeing the object (3.7). – Insisting on such a distinction would amount to making a distinction without a difference. My now seeing the dog may be taken to *be* nothing but the dog in its capacity of now being seen by me in such-and-such a way. There are several reasons for this identification (3.8). – This identification is much more natural than the merely hypothetical identifications of psychophysical reductionisms (3.8.1). – The mere fact that I cannot make out a temporal difference between my now seeing the dog and the dog in its capacity of now being seen by me in such-and-such a way is a sufficient reason for applying to them 'Ockham's Razor' (3.8.2). – It would be of no use to counter this argument by appealing to 'Leibniz's Law' (3.8.3). – A Peircean 'abduction' in favour of the identification in question (3.8.4). – In the spirit of verificationism and similar positions, the question 'What is my now seeing the dog?' may, and should, be given the more precise form: 'What is it that I must be given in order to be justified in asserting that I now see the dog?'. The answer to the second, and hence to the first, question has to run as follows: 'The dog *as*, *qua*, or *in its capacity of*, now being seen by me in such-and-such a way.' (3.8.5). – An extension and methodological interpretation of the analysis (3.9). – Visual and other kinds of remembrance and imagination. Non-theoretical conscious experiences such as emotions and actions as seen from my own, or first-person, point of view. The scope of pragmatico-semantic combination tests (3.9.1). – The position defended in this paper may be interpreted as a 'disappearing form' of a non-naturalistic 'identity-theory' (3.9.2). – The interpretation in question amounts to Husserl's 'noematic' conception of consciousness. Why this conception should be substituted for the traditional 'noetic' one (3.10). – In everyday life, we do, and must, abstract from the multiplicities of concrete noematic phenomena which ought to be the objects of a non-naturalistic research into consciousness. So, whereas such a research should be based on a systematic suspension of an abstraction which has become our second nature, the objects of everyday life and of science are but products of this abstraction. As we cannot at the same time *suspend* and *perform* this abstraction, noematic consciousness and the objects of nature are correlates of attitudes which are incompatible with each other. So noematic consciousness cannot be part of what we call nature (3.11). – The strict, reality-implying uses of verbs of perception, such as 'to see', prevail over their wider, sensation-centered uses (3.12). – On the other hand, the sensation-centered uses of verbs of pain seem to prevail over their reality-implying, or etiological, uses. This difference can easily be explained. Not only perceptions and pains but also most other kinds of conscious experience are characterised by the duality of a subjective and an objective aspect, or a first-person and a third-person authority (3.13). – Exceptions seem to be cases of imagining and dreaming; but all conscious experiences having to do with objective reality, including human actions, are neither purely private, or first-person, nor purely public, or third-person, affairs (3.14). – Two sacred cows slaughtered: For myself, my own consciousness is a multitude of noematic phenomena and thus no part of nature (cf. 3.11), and the consciousness of my fellow-men nothing but situated behaviour (3.15). – Some reasons for this 'semi-behaviouristic nothing-buttery' (3.15.1). – Rejection of a first standard objection: For myself, even the important distinction between somebody else's headache and his mere (and possibly fake) headache-behaviour has to be based on his perceived behaviour (3.15.2). – The 'neurobiological' versus the 'semi-behaviouristic' position (3.15.3). – Dudda's attempt to reduce 'semi-behaviourism' to absurdity, and to defend the view that conscious experiences of others are 'theoretical constructs' (3.15.4). – Rejection of a second standard objection: There is, indeed, more to your conscious experience besides mere behaviour – but only for *you*, not for *me*. For me, your conscious experiences *qua correlates of your first-person perspective* simply do not exist (3.15.5). – What we *speak* about, and hence intend to convey, is always something we can in principle *know* about. Linguistic evidence for this position (3.15.6). – That my and your detailed accounts of *my*, and my and your detailed accounts of *your*, conscious experience are not only disjunct but strictly incompatible with each other is, however, camouflaged by the use of the 'psychological verbs', which appears to be the same in the three grammatical persons as long as characteristic differences in depth-grammar are left out of consideration (3.15.7). – The standard objection that these differences are solely of 'epistemological' import and must not be given an 'ontological dignity' points to the fact that the concept of identification proper is missed (3.16). – A conscious experience and the correspondent behaviour differ from each other 'categorially' in that, for lack of a common 'counting-concept' under which both of them fall, it makes no genuine sense to say that they are either identical or numerically different (3.17). – A simpler argument against identifying conscious experiences with stretches of situated behaviour (or else central nervous occurrences, formal patterns of information processing, etc.): Reliable identity-criteria applicable to subjectively experienced conscious events as well as to objectively observable natural occurrences have so far neither naturally evolved nor been artificially elaborated (3.18). – At first sight, the upshot of all this seems to require us to deny human beings the status of a homogeneous natural kind. However, the 'sceptical problem' of solipsism admits of a 'sceptical solution', allowing us to say that my fellow-men, too, have their own subjective points of view. So the species of *Homo sapiens sapiens* is, after all, homogeneous, though not in the simpler way other species are. This is solely due to the fact that the species in question is precisely the one to which you and I belong (3.19).

1. Introduction

1.1. A note on the state of the pertinent discussion

Since the middle of the 20th century, the problem of consciousness has been mostly discussed in a naturalistic or physicalistic key; and more often than not, the results have been far from satisfying. To my mind, even the publication of Thomas Nagel's 'What is it like to be a bat?' (1974) and the revival of the 'qualia' discussion during the eighties did not change things considerably. In the last decade of the century, the novel approach of the London psychologist Max Velmans (esp. 1990; 1991; 1996a; 2000) seemed to raise new hope. For, rightly at first sight, he proposes to identify, say, 'one's percept of the cat' with 'the cat as-perceived', thus making a case for including 'physical objects as-perceived' (or the 'physical world as-perceived') within the 'contents of consciousness';[1] and, on this basis, at first sight he may appear to support a really promising – namely, a 'complementaristic' – solution to the mind-body problem.[2] However, on closer inspection it turns out that his conception of a 'physical object as-perceived' is insufficient, and that his 'complementarity' theory is nothing but a new variant of the time-honoured but unsatisfying 'dual-aspect theory (in the tradition of Spinoza)'.[3]

1.2. What the reader may expect of this essay

1.2.   In what follows, I am not going to criticise Velmans' conception of an object (or the world) 'as-perceived', or his conception of 'complementarity', in a straightforward and detailed manner. I have done so at some length in my paper ' "Reflexive Monism" versus "Complementarism". An Analysis and Criticism of the Conceptual Groundwork of Max Velmans's "Reflexive Model" of Consciousness' (Hoche 2007), and even more circumstantially in the following Essay V. Rather, in the present essay I shall try and develop the concept of consciousness in an independent way which, I do hope, is not only as simple as possible but also apt to avoid the grossest naturalistic prejudices regularly haunting the discussion of consciousness during the last fifty or sixty years. In so doing, I hope to be able to give cogent reasons in support of positions which seem, at first sight though *only* at first sight, to be the same as the ones advocated by Velmans: namely, that my perception of a physical thing is nothing but this thing 'as [*qua*] now being perceived by me (in such-and-such a way)', and that, as a consequence, the mind-

---

[1] Velmans 1990: 82f., 92–94; cf. 2000: 109–111, 125f., 134, 138 n. 25, 139f., 154, 165f., 169, 228, 262 n. 24.

[2] Velmans 1991: 667, sect. 9.3; cf. 1996a: 540 f.

[3] Velmans 1991: 717, sect. R 9.3; cf. 1996a: 541; 2000: 249–251, 254, 277, 281 n.5.

body (or mind-brain) problem calls for a solution which is 'complementaristic' in very much the sense of Niels Bohr's but not at all a dual-aspect theory.

2. The concept of consciousness

2.1. The term 'consciousness': A preliminary remark

The concept of consciousness is not only highly controversial but also surprisingly unclear in many respects. It is not even clear how philosophers use, or ought to use, the very term 'consciousness'. I think it best to tackle this question by first asking how this technical term is rooted in ordinary language. To be sure, this expression is rarely met with in everyday conversation, except for such well-known phrases as 'to lose [recover; regain] consciousness'. However, it is exactly these phrases that may give us our cue; for it seems to me that philosophers would be well advised if they made their concept of consciousness, or conscious experience, tally as much as possible with the totality of what we are debarred from when we have lost consciousness by fainting, falling asleep, or being anaesthetised.[4]

2.2. What we lose and regain by losing and regaining consciousness

So let us ask what I am prevented from enjoying and doing when I am in a state of unconsciousness, and what I regain when I become conscious, or come to myself, again. In this case, I am also said to come to my senses again; and in fact it is sense experience, or perception, which I am most obviously lacking while being asleep or otherwise unconscious. In cases like these, I cannot see, hear, etc., what is going on around me. However, in such cases I lack many other things as well: I do not, and cannot, feel anger, joy, grief, sorrow, remorse, shame, fear, and other emotions; I do not feel, or have, pain and all the rest of similar and dissimilar bodily sensations (although there are exceptions in highly extreme situations); I am unable to 'think' in the various meanings of this many-faceted word: I am deprived of the faculties of judging, inferring, reasoning and planning as well as of the faculties of remembering, imagining, and conceiving in other ways; and, last not least, I am unable to act by doing, or refraining from doing, or failing to do something. To this list of what I take to be consciousness-candidates, I shall propose to add dreaming, though this seems to occur precisely during sleep.[5]

---

[4] In what follows, I am not going to be concerned with the psychological (and, according to Chalmers 1996, relatively 'simple') problem of what, since Block 1995, has been called 'access consciousness' (see, e.g., Windmann & Durstewitz 2000: pp. 76f.). Rather, I shall confine myself to discussing the 'difficult problem' of 'phenomenal consciousness' or 'phenomenal experience' (see ibid.).

[5] See sect. 2.3.5, below.

Maybe other items ought to be added as well; but as I do not, in this essay, intend to devise a taxonomy of the multifarious sorts of conscious experience, we need not bother about that here.

2.3. Comments on the list of consciousness-candidates given in section 2.2

However, my list of consciousness-candidates is in need of a number of comments; for some of them may seem doubtful, whereas, on the other hand, some important possible candidates may seem to have been missed out.

2.3.1. A conscious experience is often said to be directed to, or aiming at, a thing or person, and this thing or person has been called (first by Franz Brentano, Edmund Husserl, and subsequent phenomenologists, and later on also by G. E. M. Anscombe and other linguistic philosophers) its 'intentional object'. The medieval, modern, and recent history of this technical term is rather complicated but of no relevance in the present context. However, it may be helpful to remember that the Latin phrase 'arcum intendere in [...]' was used in the sense of the archer's stretching his bow towards whatever he wanted his arrow to hit. Just as the archer is having in view, and taking aim at, a person, an animal, or an inanimate target, he who sees a neighbour coming, or hears a nightingale singing, or is afraid of a dog making up for him, or remembers a past event, etc., may be said to be aiming at, or intending (in the sense of having in view, or in mind), a certain 'object'. This 'intended', or 'intentional', 'object' may be taken to be a thing (such as an artefact, a living organism, or a human person), which then is denoted by a noun-phrase, or it may be taken to be a state of affairs, which then is denoted by a 'that'-clause. When I see somebody coming, I at the same time see that somebody is coming; when I hear a nightingale singing, I likewise hear that a nightingale is singing; when I am afraid of a dog, more specifically I may be afraid that the dog might bite me; and instead of saying that I remember a certain traffic accident, I may also say that I remember that, and even: how, (say) a big truck was crashing into a wall.

Now pains and other bodily sensations might perhaps be taken to lack such an intentional object; and this seems to be confirmed by the linguistic fact that, in speaking about such sensations, there is no room for any grammatical object – direct, indirect, or prepositional. So it may seem preferable to exclude all sorts of bodily sensations from our list of consciousness-candidates. Nonetheless I prefer not to do so; for perhaps it may turn out, on closer inspection, that bodily sensations, being not 'exteroceptive' but 'interoceptive' or 'proprioceptive', may be characterised as being 'intentional *sui generis*' – and if not, we are still free to distinguish between intentional and non-intentional conscious experiences. Moreover, pains have been a favourite topic of Wittgensteinian and post-Wittgensteinian research into the concept of consciousness.

2.3.2.   Similarly, one may object against my proposal to regard human actions as cases of conscious experience. As a matter of fact, it is still common philosophical usage to say that at least one component of human action is a bodily movement. For instance, according to Searle 'the whole action is an intention in action plus a bodily movement which is caused by the intention in action'.[6] Here, the term 'intention' is used in the stricter and more usual sense of intending to *do* something, and the bodily movement which is alleged to be caused by this intention is doubtless something quite different from what we are prepared to call a conscious experience. However, such component-theories of human action do not convince me for at least the following two reasons.

First, in ethics, the philosophy of law, and jurisprudence, an action may be an omission or a refraining from doing as well as a down-to-earth doing, and I think the philosopher of mind and action should not, without really excellent reasons, dispose of this important insight. Hence, as our refraining from doing something, and likewise our failing to do something, does not normally require any bodily movements, the latter ought not to be used in defining the concept of a human action. Instead, it seems to me preferable to define this concept in quite a different and more general way. In so doing, I think we can, and should, take advantage of the fact that a great many speech acts stand in a special relation to what we would not hesitate to recognise as human actions.[7] Strictly speaking, what I can promise is nothing but a *future*, and what I can apologise for is nothing but a *past, action* – doing, refraining from doing, or omission – of *my own*; and speech acts of asking, commanding, giving advice, etc., refer to *future*, and speech acts of thanking, praising, blaming, etc., refer to *past*, actions of *somebody else* (usually, though not always, the immediate hearer or addressee). So it stands to reason that we are well advised if we define a human action to be whatever one can promise or apologise for, or request, command, or forbid, or thank for, condemn, etc.[8]

Second, bodily movements are involved, not only in the bulk of our actions, but also in such uncontroversial conscious experiences as perceiving a thing or a state of affairs. To be sure, in, e. g., seeing or hearing something or someone, I do not normally pay attention to the movements of my eyes, my head, and so on; but nor do I normally pay attention to the movements of my hands, my arms, and my feet when I am driving a car, or playing the piano, or bowling, or writing a letter, or walking down the street. However, if somebody else is doing one or other of these things, I can know about this only by perceiving his or her situated bodily movements, or behaviour, linguistic as well as non-linguistic; but this is true not only of the actions but also of the perceptions, emotions, bodily sensations, reasonings, etc. of my fellow-men. As we rarely attend to this *similarity between*

---

[6] Searle 1983: ch. 3, esp. p. 106.

[7] Cf. Searle 1969: sect. 3.4, pp. 66f.

[8] Hoche 1973a: pp. 112–114; cf. Searle 1983: p. 81.

actions and perceptions, etc., and likewise to this *dissimilarity between my own case and that of others*, I think we may say that in point of fact we tend to model the concept of action after our fellow-men's case, and to model the concept of the rest of conscious experiences after respectively my own case, without being justified in so doing.[9] To this important point I shall return in due course. For the time being, let me confine myself to stating that I cannot conceive of a truly cogent reason for excluding human actions from the domain of consciousness.

2.3.3.   Now one may be tempted to say that, whether or not we are right in thinking actions to belong to conscious experience, in any case I ought to have listed, among the items of section 2.2, what is often taken to precede, and even to cause, human actions, namely, acts of deciding, wanting, wishing, intending, and the like. It is not easy to counter this objection without going into details. But let me state in few words what I think is wrong with it. First, most human actions cannot in fact be shown to be preceded, or otherwise accompanied, by such 'volitions', or 'acts of willing'. Second, as we ought to recognise since Ryle (1949) has devised his ingenious substitution tests,[10] it is indeed offensive to speak of 'acts' of willing. For the pertinent verbs seem to be used, never as 'occurrence words', which include action words, but only as either 'success words' ('to decide', 'to resolve', etc.) or 'disposition words' ('to want', 'to intend', etc.).[11] Third, as a rule, and for important linguistic reasons, we use post-success and other disposition words in such a way as to say even of them who are fast asleep or otherwise unconscious that they wish, want, or intend (somebody) to do something, or that they believe, know, hope, or are afraid, etc., that something is, or will or may become, the case. So whatever such disposition words stand for should not be counted a conscious experience – irrespective of the fact that mental dispositions of the kind in question, namely, the so-called 'propositional attitudes', may be said to be directed towards an 'intentional object'.[12] From this it follows that not everything 'intentional' in this technical sense of the term is a conscious experience; and as we had to leave open the possibility that some cases of consciousness, namely, bodily sensations, may be non-intentional, we have more than one reason to admit that the field of intentionality and the field of consciousness overlap to a high degree but do not coincide.[13]

---

[9] However, there seems to me to be a psychological explanation for this tendency. A great many actions are intended to *change* the objective world, but all the rest of our conscious experiences is characterised by *leaving* the objective world *as it is*. Changing objectivity, however, seems to be connected with physical movements in the most straightforward way.

[10] For a survey, see Hoche & Strube 1985: A.V.1.

[11] Disposition words include what I dubbed 'post-success' words, a prominent example being 'to understand'; cf. Hoche 1973a: §§ 36–37; Hoche & Strube 1985: pp. 159–163.

[12] See sect. 2.3.1, above.

[13] See ibid. – Velmans 2000: esp. 99 n. 20, 99f. n. 23, 244, 258, and ch. 7, insists that being 'representational' or 'intentional' is a *necessary*, though *not a sufficient*, condition for being a conscious

2.3.4.   I just claimed that even somebody fast asleep or otherwise unconscious may be said, according to the logical behaviour or 'depth grammar' of our disposition words, to be afraid of something. On the other side, I also claimed that somebody fast asleep or otherwise unconscious is unable to feel fear of something.[14] This may seem to be a square contradiction. However, I rather think that this points to an important ambiguity of some mental disposition terms. For instance, I may suffer from arachnophobia, i.e., be habitually afraid of spiders, without, at the moment, being scared by a particular spider. This is the way we are used to speak; and speaking differently would reduce the linguistic institution of disposition words to absurdity. For in the latter case we would have to say that arachnophobia obtains in precisely those moments in which I am actually feeling fear in the face of a spider – or, for that matter, that diamonds are hard when and only when someone is actually trying to scratch them.[15]

This difference between fear as a mental disposition and fear as an actual conscious experience is confirmed by subtle linguistic distinctions. Suppose I am showing fear of a spider approaching me. Then another person may interpret, and comment upon, my behaviour in at least two ways. He or she may say, either that I am feeling fear of this – small and harmless – spider, or that I am afraid of spiders, i.e., suffer from arachnophobia. To both statements (or reproaches, as the case may be) I can subscribe by simply saying 'Yes.'; but only in the latter case I can do so by saying 'Yes, *I know*.'. This linguistic fact tallies well with another one. Just as I can learn, discover, or find out that somebody else suffers from arachnophobia, I can learn, discover, or find out that I myself do; but whereas I may well be said to learn, discover, or find out that somebody else is feeling fear of a particular spider on a particular occasion, I cannot be said to learn, discover, or find out that I myself am. Both linguistic facts are closely related to each other. For, as Ryle aptly stated: 'To know something is to have discovered or learned something and not to have forgotten it.'.[16]

These two linguistic facts point to a difference which is of the utmost importance for understanding the concept of consciousness. Mental dispositions of my own as well as of others belong to the type of things I can learn, discover, or find out, and hence can know about; and so do actual conscious experiences of others; but my own actual conscious experiences do *not*. To this epistemological or cognitive 'asymmetry' between myself and others, and to the question of whether this is of any ontological import, I shall soon have to return.

---

experience. The first part of this claim has to do, of course, with the fact that he, unlike many others, takes even pains and similar bodily feelings to be *intentional* conscious experiences (ibid.: 98 n. 16; 2002: 12 fn. 9).

[14] See sect. 2.2, above.

[15] Cf. Hoche 1973a: § 30.

[16] Ryle 1962: p. 195; cf. 1949: sect. VII.4, passim.

2.3.5. But before so doing, I should like to briefly explain why I think we are justified in taking also dreaming to be a sort of conscious experience. At first sight, this may seem a matter of course indeed. For conscious experience is usually considered to be no different from subjective experience, and many people (and peoples) tend to find few subjective experiences more intimate and impressive than dreams. On second thoughts, however, we may feel tempted to argue that dreams, though being subjective, fail to belong to consciousness because they – allegedly – occur while the dreamer is asleep, i.e., in a state usually thought of as unconscious. But, as Norman Malcolm has shown ingeniously,[17] this line of argument is unsound in that it applies, not to the primary (familiar, or first-person), but to a secondary (third-person, or physiological) concept, say, the REM-concept, of dreaming. For if we adhere to the primary concept, 'the notions of the location and duration of a dream in physical time [...] have no clear sense'.[18]

Yet another way of arguing against dreaming as belonging to consciousness may be thought to remain. For apparently we cannot deny that the intentional objects of dreams differ considerably from those of the rest of conscious experiences. What conscious experiences of the perception, emotion, thinking, intending, and action types are 'intentionally' directed to, or aim at, might without exception be thought to hang together in the way of making up the real world and a number of ideal (logical, mathematical) and 'possible' (counterfactual) worlds all of which, in multifarious ways, refer back to the real (external, material) world. Even the intentional objects of pains and the other bodily sensations (if we are justified at all in ranking them as intentional, instead of non-intentional, conscious experiences)[19] may be regarded as belonging to the real world; for such sensations can be suitably understood as the first-person or 'inward' – 'interoceptive' and 'proprioceptive' – ways of sensing one's own body, which is part of the world.[20] Only dreaming, we might be inclined to say, is an exception. For dreams frequently do not refer at all to particular (individual) inhabitants of the real world, and when they do, they do so in a highly unstable manner, changing or confusing identities. But this line of reasoning, too, seems to me to be not convincing. For there is a major class of indisputable conscious experiences, falling under the rubric of 'thinking', which do not refer to the real world either. Acts of imagination or fiction – if we take these words in their purest and philosophically most important

---

[17] Malcolm 1959: esp. chs. 12–13.

[18] Ibid.: p. 70; cf. pp. 43, 76f., 79.

[19] See sect. 2.3.1 and sect. 2.3.3 with fn. 13, above.

[20] At present I shall content myself with this rough and ready remark. If we want to be more precise, however, we have, I think, to do justice to the fact that my body as 'sensed' from within is neither numerically identical with, nor numerically different from, my body as 'perceived' from without. I shall soon return to this point.

senses – do not 'intentionally aim' at individual objects residing in the real world (or any of its counterfactual variants). Rather, we ought to say, following Husserl, that they have to do with, or are directed to, mere 'quasi-individuals', of which it would be strictly nonsensical to say, either that they are numerically identical with, or that they are numerically different from, any real objects or any of their counterfactual variants.[21]

This is a first example of the general insight that sometimes there is a third way besides numerical identity and numerical diversity – an insight that will prove highly consequential for properly understanding the relation between consciousness, behaviour, and the brain processes.[22] At present, however, let me confine myself to stressing two more limited and less controversial points. First, there are, in addition to the real world, not only ideal worlds and 'possible worlds' in the sense of counterfactual variants of the real world, but also 'possible worlds' in the sense of fictional ('quasi'-)worlds.[23] And second, imagining and dreaming have at least so much in common that there is no convincing reason to count the former but not the latter among conscious experience.

3. The nature of consciousness

3.1. Seeing as an exemplary case of consciousness

Having outlined the *concept* of consciousness, i.e., clarified in a preliminary way how to use the technical term 'consciousness' in a suitable manner, now we have to consider the *nature* of consciousness, namely, the epistemological and ontological status of what we have decided the term 'consciousness' to stand for. Now, as we have seen, the domain of what we mean to call 'consciousness' is rather heterogeneous and of an intricate structure. So we shall have to proceed in an exemplary way and to shun premature generalisations; for, as Ryle once succinctly put it: 'In philosophy, generalisations are unclarifications.'.[24] Let us concentrate upon visual perception, i.e., seeing something or somebody. For seeing is, I take it, the most important and reliable form of human sense-perception, and sense-perception somehow or other seems to be at the root of most other forms of conscious experience. Once the case of seeing, in the most familiar and basic sense of perceiving by means of, or 'through', the eyes, will have been clarified, the rest may turn out to be rather plain sailing.

---

[21] Cf. Hoche 1990: sect. 9.6.

[22] See sect. 3.17, below, and Essays III and V of the present collection.

[23] For details, see Hoche 1990: ch. 9.

[24] Ryle 1951: p. 255.

3.2. Seeing something, and seeing that something is the case

So what we are after is the nature or, more precisely speaking, the epistemological and ontological status of seeing; and seeing is always somebody's seeing something or someone. For reasons which will become obvious in due course, let us first concentrate on enquiring, not into somebody else's, but into respectively my own seeing something or someone – or something being the case; for, in fact, whenever I can be said to see a thing (a body, animated or not), I can be said to see that something is the case, and vice versa.[25] Take, for instance, my present visual perception of a dog approaching me. This conscious experience of mine I may refer to by saying 'I see a dog approaching me.'. But this is ambiguous and can be interpreted, alternatively, as my seeing an animal or my seeing that something is the case: either as 'I see a dog which is approaching me.', or else as 'I see that a dog is approaching me.' ('I see a dog approach me.'). It is true that these two versions are by no means always interchangeable in conversation.[26] Nonetheless, whenever one of these statements is true, the other one is also true.[27] Even in the elementary case in which the words 'I see' are followed by a simple noun (instead of a composite noun-phrase), we can replace this noun with a 'that'-clause, proceeding, e.g., from 'I see a dog.' to 'I see that there is a dog around [near by; in front of me; in the vicinity; in the offing; in front of the church; etc.].'; and in the opposite direction, substitution is, of course, still easier.

---

[25] For the time being, we may disregard such untypical cases as looking at a conjurer's trick, or having illusions, or being the victim of a hallucination. In cases like these, one may be said to see (or to 'see') not a thing or material object, but a mere phantom, and to be confronted, not with a fact, but with a state of affairs merely mistakenly believed to really exist. For details, see sect. 3.12, below.

[26] See sect. 3.3, below.

[27] Whoever feels tempted to doubt this 'semantic equivalence', or mutual 'semantic implication', ought to make use of a method which I propose to call 'pragmatico-semantical combination tests' (see Essays I and II of the present collection and, for a number of methodologically relevant details, provisos, and caveats, Hoche 1981; 1990: sects. 8.2–8.5; 1992: sects. 1.5–1.12; Hoche & Strube 1985: A.IV.4; Dudda 1999: sect. 2.3). This method is a methodologically motivated refinement of a procedure frequently used by British philosophers since at least Moore 1903, and especially of the assenting tests inaugurated by Hare 1952. In the present case, we can convince ourselves that the modalized combination 'It is [counterfactually] possible that I [now] see a dog which is approaching me but that I do not [now] see that a dog is approaching me.' – taken to mean as much as 'I can conceive of a contrary-to-fact variant of the real world in which I [now] see a dog that is approaching me but in which I do not [now] see that a dog is approaching me.' – is false; and that the same holds true for the modalized combination with the relevant clauses interchanged (see the circumstantial definition of 'semantic implication' as a quite specific relation between completely interpreted ordinary-language sentences in Essay II: sect.2 of the present collection).

3.3. Why we may concentrate on simple cases of seeing something

Doubtless grammarians have researched into the speech-act theoretical differences between the alternative constructions just mentioned in section 3.2; but I do not think that details are of great import to our present purpose. According to my personal linguistic competence (which, in the more precise form of respectively my own combined imaginative and idiolectal competence, I take to be one of the philosopher's most effective tools),[28] one of the major differences, and the only one that need concern us here, mirrors a difference of *interest* and (hence) *attention*. When I say 'I see a dog which is approaching me.', I am primarily interested in, and attentive to, the dog itself and its appearances; but when I say 'I see that a dog is approaching me.', or 'I see a dog approach me.', I am focusing my interest and attention rather on what the dog is doing, and going to do, and perhaps also why it is behaving like this, and how I ought to react, etc. By the way, there is still a third grammatical variant, scil., 'I see how a dog is approaching me.', and in this case I seem to be interested rather in the manner it moves, how its movements depend on what is going on in its surroundings, etc. Very roughly speaking, we may say, perhaps, that the noun-phrase variant is at bottom 'aesthetic', the 'that'-clause variant at bottom 'practical' (or 'pragmatic'), and the 'how'-clause variant at bottom 'theoretical'. However, I think that in everyday conversation these distinctions tend to be frequently blurred. If this view of the matter may be accepted, the 'aesthetic' noun-phrase constructions seem to be basic in a way. So in the following enquiries I shall concentrate only on them, and even on their simplest (i.e., simple noun) variants.

3.4. Whenever I can truthfully assert that I (now) see, say, a dog, I can also specify the dog's way of now subjectively appearing to me

What makes these simple noun variants, i.e., statements such as 'I see a dog.', philosophically interesting is the fact that they can always[29] be expanded, not only into 'that'- and 'how'-constructions of the sorts just mentioned, but also into statements which will turn out to be of the utmost relevance to a non-naturalistic

---

[28] See esp. Hoche 1990: sect. 8.1.

[29] Instead of 'always', we could as well say 'necessarily': Whenever I see, say, a dog, I *necessarily* see this dog at a certain distance from me, from a certain point of view, under certain lighting conditions, etc., which together determine the shape and the colours in which the dog is being given, or subjectively appearing, to me at the moment in question. By saying that this is *necessarily* the case, I simply mean to say that I cannot even *conceive* of, or *imagine*, a situation in which I see an object, as it were, 'naked' or 'simpliciter', to wit, deprived of any specific mode of being visually given to me. (For important details concerning the questions of how to find out the boundaries between *conceivability* and *inconceivability* in the relevant senses, and of how *inconceivability* and *necessity* are related to each other, see Hoche 1990: chs. 9–10.)

theory of consciousness, to wit, into statements like 'I now see a dog (or whatever visual object) at such-and-such a distance, in such-and-such a perspective (or: from such-and-such a point of view; under such-and-such an angle), in such-and-such a degree of clarity and distinctness, in such-and-such a lighting condition, and in such-and-such colours.'. Let me explain this by means of the following considerations.

3.4.1.   Suppose you are looking at a certain building, say, a cathedral, from different points of view; and suppose, furthermore, that you are looking at it from one and the same angle, but first at noon and again at night. Then you may ask yourself whether what you see on these various occasions is always one and the same thing or rather something different in each case. I think it goes without saying that both answers can be admitted equally. Obviously, what you see on all these occasions may be said to be one and the same cathedral; but it is no less obvious that what you see may also be said to be something different in each case: first, the cathedral from (say) the north-east; second, the cathedral from (say) the west; third, the cathedral in broad daylight and (possibly) bright colours; and fourth, the cathedral – from exactly the same point of view – by night, flood-lighted or in gloomy hues, moonlit or darkened by clouds. In the first two of these four cases it is doubtless possible to say that you see one and the same church but different parts, sides, facets, façades, or surfaces of its. But in the last two cases this explanation does not work; for what you are now confronted with is not only one and the same church but also, according to our assumption, one and the same side or surface of the church. What then are the different things you see in the last two cases, and which, of course, you may alternatively be said to see in the first two cases, too?

3.4.2.   Before enquiring into this matter, let me call your attention to a formally analogous case which has become well-known in logic and the philosophy of language. Suppose somebody has written down the following words:

I HAVE TOOTHACHE.
I HAVE TOOTHACHE.

Then one may ask oneself whether what has been written down are three words or rather six words, or one sentence or rather two sentences, or whether what is in the second line is identical with, or rather different from, what is in the first one. All of these questions may be correctly answered in both ways, the preferable answer depending in each case on whether what we are thinking of is a so-called (word- or sentence-)'type' or rather a so-called 'token'.

That it is imperative to make such a distinction between a linguistic 'token' and a linguistic 'type' may be seen most easily from the fact that what we can meaningfully predicate of the one need not be meaningfully predicable of the other. When I say that the sentence 'I HAVE TOOTHACHE.' was a favourite example of Wittgenstein's in his Cambridge lectures during the early thirties, it is obvious that I am speaking, not of the sentence-token I have just been putting down (or you have been reading few seconds ago), but of the sentence-type. However, when, on a certain occasion, I say that the sentence 'I HAVE TOOTHACHE.' is hardly legible, or looks rather crawly, it is obvious that I am speaking of the sentence-token at hand rather than of the sentence-type. Or, to return to our initial questions: When I say that the second line, as compared with the first one, contains just the *same thing* once again, I am obviously speaking of the sentence-type; whereas, when in this case I say that someone has written down *six* words, or *two* sentences, I am obviously speaking of the linguistic tokens.

Once we have recognised, by means of clear-cut examples such as the ones just considered, that at least for theoretical purposes it is necessary to make this type-token distinction, we may, of course, regiment our way of speaking about linguistic objects in order to handle borderline-cases as well. When I say, for instance, that I have been writing down the words 'I HAVE TOOTHACHE.' on February 18, 1999, or in ink on hand-made paper, what I have in mind may be either the sentence-type or the sentence-token. To disambiguate such cases, we may – provided we think it useful for whatever purposes to do so – replace such ordinary-language expressions as 'to write [or: put] down', 'to utter', etc. with technical terms, saying, for instance, that in writing, or orally, we 'bring about' (or: 'produce') linguistic *tokens* but 'realise' (or: 'reproduce') linguistic *types*.

By such a terminological distinction, and especially by using the verb 'to realise' in the way just indicated, we make it very clear, furthermore, that linguistic types are no inhabitants of the real, material, three- or four-dimensional world; for doubtless they lack a temporal as well as a spatial location. In other words: They are not concrete but abstract objects;[30] or they belong, not in Popper's 'world 1' ('the physical world') nor in his 'world 2' ('the world of our conscious experiences'), but in his 'world 3' ('the world of the logical *contents* of books, libraries, computer memories, and suchlike'),[31] or in what Frege, more than half a century earlier and thus still in advance of the first beginnings of National Socialism in Germany, had in all innocence called 'a third Reich [realm]' ('ein drittes Reich').[32]

3.4.3.   Returning to our question at the end of section 3.4.1, above, let us first provisionally introduce a convenient term for the different things we see when we are looking, on different occasions and from different points of view or even

---

[30] For a penetrating discussion of 'criteria of abstractness', see Künne 1983: ch. 2.

[31] Popper 1972: 2.20; cf. ibid.: 3.1, where he also says: 'My third world resembles most closely the universe of Frege's objective contents of thought.'.

[32] Frege 1918: 69.

from one and the same point of view, at one and the same object, say, a cathedral. For my preliminary purposes, I propose to call these things 'views' or '(visual) appearances' but not to burden the latter term, which I think is not at all unusual in ordinary language, with terminological connotations taken from this or that part of the history of philosophy.[33]

That for certain purposes we have to distinguish between a (real, material) object and any of its visual appearances (or whatever else we prefer to call them) may best be seen, just as in the purely formal parallel considered in the preceding section 3.4.2, from the fact that it does not always make sense to predicate of the one what can be meaningfully predicated of the other. Take again the example of a building, say, Westminster Abbey. Of this church, but not of any of its visual appearances, we can meaningfully (and correctly) assert that it is chiefly made of stone; that it is more than 700 years old;[34] that most of its parts have been erected in early Gothic style; and that at least two famous queens have been buried within its walls. On the other hand, we can meaningfully (and correctly) assert of any of its visual appearances, but not of Westminster Abbey itself, that it continuously shades into others of that ilk; that it is respectively mine; that it disappears whenever I shut my eyes; and so on.

Again, once we have convinced ourselves by means of clear-cut examples like the ones just considered that at least for certain philosophical purposes we have to insist on distinguishing between a (real, material) object and its visual appearances, we may be well advised if we regiment our way of speaking about the one and the others. For it may seem inappropriate to use one and the same verb 'to see' in connection with things as dissimilar as material objects and their visual appearances – just as we possibly could have thought it inappropriate to state of linguistic types as well as of linguistic tokens that we 'utter' them, or 'write them down'. So our former distinction between 'bringing about' a linguistic token and 'realising' a linguistic type may be suitably paralleled by the proposal to reserve the everyday expression 'to see' for what we have to do with in everyday life, to wit, material objects (or to introduce instead the technical term 'to visually perceive'), and to

---

[33] From sect. 3.6.5 on, I shall be more specific and preferably speak, instead of an object's 'view' or 'visual appearance', of an object *as, qua, or in its capacity of* now being seen by myself, or, for short, a 'C-object'.

[34] Of course, I could have distinguished, moreover, between the Collegiate Church of St. Peter in Westminster as an ecclesiastical institution, dating back to the 8th century, and the extant building as we know and can see it now. This possibility has parallels in the linguistic case used, in sect. 3.4.2, as a formal analogue. Think, e.g., of the temporal difference between the typing and the printing of a computer-written sentence-token, or of the difference between, say, Shakespeare's *Hamlet*, a certain staging of its, and the performance of last Sunday. These differences are doubtless interesting and important in other connections; but at present I am only intent on clarifying the concept of an '(object-)appearance', which I should like to do in the simplest possible way.

stipulate terminologically that I do not *'see'* (or even 'visually perceive') a view or visual appearance but that I simply *'have'* it, or that I *'am given'* it.[35]

3.4.4. This terminological distinction is of much greater import than at first sight one might be inclined to think. For we can easily convince ourselves that a material object is always seen, or visually perceived, by means of, or mediated by ('through'), a more or less extended continuum of visual apperances, whereas our having, or being given, the latter is not at all mediated in any such way. In other words, our cognitive access to objects belonging to the material world differs from that to visual (or, for that matter, tactual, auditory, and other sensory) appearances, and so much so that we may take this divergence to be a second good reason for saying that appearances, whatever they may be, at any rate must *not* be classified as parts of the real (material) world.[36]

So here again we have a parallel with the linguistic case discussed in section 3.4.2, above. Neither linguistic types nor visual (and other sensory) appearances are material objects. By this I do not mean to say, of course, that appearances and types are kindred entities, which in fact they are not at all.[37] All they have in common is the negative property that they must not be counted to be *material* objects, and the positive property that they are none the less *objects*, if only in the purely formal sense of being something we can make true or false statements about.[38] As for the rest of their properties, I think it is even more illuminating to parallel types to real objects rather than to appearances, and to parallel appearances to tokens rather than to types – notwithstanding the fact that of course it is tokens but not types which belong to the real world. In particular, the main points of comparing the object-appearance distinction not, as it were, to a 'token-type' distinction but rather to a 'type-token' distinction seem to me to be the following ones.

---

[35] Many philosophers have insisted on making similar distinctions. But remember that I am intent on developing my distinctions as simply as possible, especially without appealing to more or less well-known – and for precisely this reason frequently misinterpreted – positions in the history of philosophy.

[36] For our first reason, see near the end of sect. 3.4.1, above: My visual appearances cannot even be identified with the *surfaces* of the material things I see. (Some philosophers have sometimes doubted, moreover, if *surfaces* of material things should be taken to be *parts* of these things. For this question, and other questions just touched upon, see Moore 1913–1914; 1918; 1953: ch. II.) This can be seen once more, and perhaps more simply, from a different type of example. If we have a uniformly coloured ball, all parts of its surface have, by definition, the same colour. In contradistinction to this, it practically never visually appears to me in a uniform way; unless we take great pains to avoid this, there are always various shades, reflexes, and the like.

[37] To believe otherwise would amount to missing the point of comparison, or the 'tertium comparationis'.

[38] Cf. Husserl 1913 [tr. 1931]: § 3, p. 15 [49], and § 22, p. 48 [80]; Carnap 1928: §§ 1, 18.

First, just as we see, i.e., visually perceive, real objects through the mediation of (continua of) visual appearances, in a way we mentally grasp linguistic types through the mediation of linguistic tokens. Suppose you are coming across (say, in a consciousness theoretical text written in English by a German philosopher) a linguistic construction that strikes you as unidiomatic or downright ungrammatical. Then as a rule you are not at all paying attention to the particular word- and sentence-tokens you have just been reading. Rather, as it were, you are 'looking through' these tokens, or 'penetrating' them, as if they were transparent, fixing your interest exclusively on the linguistic type of the unusual wording. Or, more precisely speaking: in this case you are automatically abstracting from the accidental occasion of your coming across the strange passage as well as from the accidental typographical shape which the written or printed words happen to have. In still other words: you concern yourself with the linguistically striking passage in a way which is invariant in respect to the particular tokens it happens to just have been realised by.[39] So these tokens are interchangeable and arbitrary; nothing depends on their individuality. In fact, their individuality becomes important only when we are interested in the tokens themselves, notably in cases in which we are unable to decipher them, or insist on having an autograph, and the like. – In basically the same way we can describe the visual perception of a material object. If we are interested in the latter, as in everyday life it is nearly always the case, we do not pay attention to the (continua of) visual appearances through which we see them, and again we 'look through', or 'penetrate', them as if they were transparent – for the simple reason that what concerns us is nothing but the real objects themselves. This is the reason why the visual (or, for that matter, the rest of the sensory) appearances here discussed may seem unfamiliar to many a reader. But in seeing material objects we can dispense with them as little as we can dispense with linguistic tokens when grasping linguistic types or such non-linguistic entities as (Fregean) thoughts, i.e., statements or propositions.[40]

Second, let me indicate a minor point parasitic upon the one just considered. Because as a rule we have little or no reason at all to concern ourselves with visual appearances or linguistic tokens, in the rare cases in which we nonetheless *do* we find it rather difficult to identify particular specimens of them by means of definite descriptions (not to mention proper names). Here we must resort to such clumsy descriptions as 'the last but one occurrence of the word "to" ', 'the second occurrence of the letter "c" in the last token of the word "occurrence" ', etc. on the

---

[39] In reading a text attracting our attention, we may be interested in the thoughts expressed in a way which is invariant in regard to the types as well as to the tokens; little then depends on the exact wording or, if we are bilinguals, even on the language used. Of course, by this remark I am alluding to what has been called (first by Peano) a 'definition by abstraction', particularly to such a definition of the concept of a (Fregean) thought.

[40] See the preceding fn. 39, above.

one hand, and 'the view I just have of Westminster Abbey', 'Westminster Abbey as [*qua*] now being seen by me', 'the dog in its capacity of visually appearing to me at the present moment in such-and-such a mode of being given', etc. on the other.[41]

3.4.5. The upshot of all this seems to me to be that we have to acknowledge a gradation from abstractness to concreteness of which only the following steps need concern us here. Just as we mentally grasp linguistic types and similar higher-order objects ('universals')[42] by way of abstracting from the particular tokens (specimens, exemplars) through the mediation of which we happen to have access to them, so we normally perceive a visible real object by way of abstracting from the particular visual appearances (views; sights; modes of givenness) through the mediation of which we happen to see it. And just as, in relation to the abstract type (or species of a different sort), the visible (or audible, etc.) real object deserves to be regarded as concrete, so in relation to the latter, which then in a way assumes a certain abstractness, the visual (or acoustic, etc.) appearance way well be taken to be 'even more concrete'.

That this view tends to run counter to our intuitions is easily to be explained. Because, as I repeatedly stated, in everyday life we have practically no motive whatsoever to concern ourselves with the appearances through which we perceive the material objects so important for us, we are very much inclined to think little, or even to deny the existence, of such appearances, and so *a fortiori* we are loath to grant them what we take to be the honorary title of concreteness. But once we have learned to see, in the way just outlined, that the philosophical term 'concrete' receives its meaning solely from the part a given thing plays in the process of abstraction, we ought to give up this irrational scruple.

So whereas types and other species are justly taken to be *more abstract* than ordinary things, to wit, real (material, physical) objects, sensory appearances should be considered to be *more concrete* than the latter. But what, in spite of this contrast, types and appearances have in common is that they are *not* ordinary

---

[41] Let me note in passing that we have a similar problem also in other cases in which little or nothing depends on the individuality of the object we are confronted with, especially if most objects of that sort look so much alike ('as like as two peas') that we can hardly know them apart. Think, e.g., of the robins and titmice in the park or your garden, which for exactly this reason we tend to treat as lowest ('infimae') species ('types') rather than as individuals ('tokens'). Only recently ethologists and producers of animal films have developed techniques which make it meaningful to bestow proper names upon individual wildlife animals.

[42] I take a linguistic type to be the lowest ('infima') species of its tokens, and this idea may be expanded in several directions. First, there are not only linguistic but also artistic (e.g., literary, musical, or sculptural) types and types of other kinds of artefacts (e.g., of motor-cars), which we may consider to be the lowest species of their exemplars. Second, frequently there are intermediate steps (cf. fn. 34, above). Third, there are higher species (say, 'letter' in relation to 'letter "n"', or 'motor-car' in relation to 'Austin Seven'), which I think are grasped in basically the same way.

things, or do *not* belong to 'reality', scil., the universe of real, or material, or physical objects. As it were, types and their like may be said to reside *beyond* reality (or to be 'trans-real'), appearances, however, to reside on *this* side of it (or to be 'cis-real').

3.4.6.   This gradation from the 'trans-real' via the 'real' to the 'cis-real' is paralleled by a gradation of being objective (in the sense of being intersubjective, interpersonal, transpersonal, or public). The 'real', no doubt, is objective. In principle, any material object accessible to me is also accessible to any other member of the real, factual, or historical community of communication I live in. Each of us can identify this very object individually (i.e., distinguish it from others of the same species), and in the process of this identification always a deictic or demonstrative element (at bottom, an act of pointing) is involved. The 'trans-real', however, is objective to still a higher degree. By a conceptual definition, which differs from an individual identification in that it does not depend on any deictic element, in principle we can make known a 'universal' to any member, not only of our real 'community of individual identification', but also of the ideal 'community of conceptual definition'. By the latter, I understand the all-embracing community of communication of all rational human beings and possibly of all rational beings at large, including even intelligent inhabitants of galaxies so distant from ours that we cannot come into contact with them materially, which, I think, is a precondition of pointing and hence of identifying individually.[43] On the other hand, the 'cis-real', i.e., the totality of the sensory appearances I can have, is completely deprived of being objective. As we had occasion to learn from Frege, Waismann, and Wittgenstein, I cannot compare any of the sensory appearances I am given with those of others,[44] for (crudely speaking) I have access only to my own appearances, which is to say in more precise terms: I cannot even *conceive* of, or *imagine*,[45] what it would be like to have access to anybody else's sensory appearances, and so *for me – for respectively myself* – such appearances do not even exist, since believing otherwise would remain without any sound sense.[46] In other words: The 'cis-real', i.e., the realm of the views and other sensory appearances I can have, is not objective, interpersonal, or public, but subjective, intrapersonal, or private.[47]

---

[43] Cf. Hoche 1975, tr. 1983: sect. III.

[44] See, e.g., Frege 1884, tr. 1950: §26, p. 36^e: 'We cannot know [our subjective sensation] to agree with anyone else's.' For a circumstantial discussion, see Hoche & Strube 1985: A. III.3.

[45] Cf. fn. 29, above.

[46] See esp. sect. 3.15, below.

[47] Not only *naturalistic* philosophers of mind may find this result repugnant. Even such influential exponents of *linguistic* philosophy as Wittgenstein and Ryle are often interpreted as having downright denied the existence of any subjective or private entities. However, I have tried and taken pains to show the latter interpretation to be untenable: see Hoche & Strube 1985: esp. A. III.2, A.V.2.a, A.VI.2.a–b.

3.5. Visual appearances, though usually going unheeded, can be noticed
      by a shift of attention

As I said already in section 3.4.4, above, in everyday life, which is normally
governed by practical interests, the respective mode of the visual object's appearing
or being given to me is not normally paid much attention to, and so much so
that it turns out to be extremely difficult to describe it in words and thus to fill in
a sentence-frame such as 'I see Westminster Abbey at *such-and-such* a distance,
in *such-and-such* a perspective, in *such-and-such* a lighting condition, and in *such-
and-such* colours.'. However, the mode or manner of an object's being visually
given to me at a certain moment of time can be easily noticed by means of a simple
shift of heed.

3.5.1.   *One* specific switch of attention, or change of attitude towards what I see, is
fundamental to the (naturalistic or realistic) painter's business, in contradistinction
to a child's, or an artistically ungifted adult's, obstinate habit of painting the trunk
of a tree uniformly bright brown, its leaves uniformly bright green, and the sky
uniformly bright blue. *Inter alia*, this well-known habit points – and is due –
to the fact that in everyday life we tend to be interested solely in the objective
colour (and the other objective properties) of a thing and to completely disregard
its varying subjective hues and appearances at large. Of course we do so for
perfectly good reasons. For in order to orientate ourselves in the world, we have
to lean on objective dispositional *properties*, which are more or less constant,
whereas objective dispositional *states*, that is, the states which an object, due to
its dispositional *properties*, takes in covariance with the (say, lighting) conditions
it is in, frequently change – not to speak of its subjective *appearances* which,
in correspondence with the slightest alterations of my point of view, are in a
continuous flux so that it is, as a rule, not even possible to give them distinctive
names (which is another reason why they are of no use in ordinary life).[48]

3.5.2.   It is precisely such subjective appearances, however, which we have to do
with when enquiring into the nature of seeing, or perceiving in general. Whereas
in everyday life we *do*, and *must*, abstract from these subjective modes of a thing's
being given to me at any single moment in time, in the theory of consciousness
it is imperative for us to suspend that abstraction, or, in other words, to take
what I see or otherwise perceive in its full concreteness, i. e., in the plenitude of all
the particulars in which it is subjectively appearing to me. So, in the special case
of seeing, on which I propose to concentrate for the time being, the basis of a
non-naturalistic (or at least unbiassed, non-reductive) research into consciousness
may at first sight seem to be exactly the same as the basis of *naturalistic* (or at least
realistic, non-abstract, representational) painting. However, there is a fundamental

---

[48] Cf. sect. 3.4.4, above.

though recondite difference the neglect of which suffices all by itself to frustrate
the attempt to supply consciousness research with a solid and sound foundation
(see the whole of the following section 3.6). Of course, there is also a much
more obvious difference in the way in which consciousness theorists and realistic
painters *deal* with their similar bases. Whereas the latter aim at picturing, or taking
a likeness of, what they see in the richness of all its visible details, the former
(provided they share my basic methodological tenets) are intent on clarifying and
analysing the concept of what it is that is being given to them, i. e., the concept of
an object *qua* now visually appearing to them in its respective mode of being seen
at the given moment in time.

3.6. The sense in which the manner of an object's being seen can be compared
      interpersonally. The object in its *manner* of being seen *versus* the object in
      its *capacity* of being seen

The fundamental but recondite difference I just referred to requires our going into
some more details. – Although we ought to have learned from Frege, Waismann,
and Wittgenstein that it would be unwarranted, nay, strictly nonsensical to claim
that what visually appears to me is either similar to, or else dissimilar from,
what visually appears to you or anyone else,[49] there is a well-established and
legitimate way of saying that the mode or manner in which a certain visual
object is subjectively appearing to me right now may be identical with its mode
of appearing, at some other moment of time, to somebody else with whom I
have changed position. The seeming contradiction between these two statements
can be easily dissipated. For in asserting that, e. g., the manner of Westminster
Abbey's being visually given to me at time t_1 is the same as the manner of its
being visually given to you at time t_2, we do not nonsensically imply that we have
been comparing your and my subjective visual impressions and found out that
they happen to completely coincide with each other (in the sense of being exactly
similar, or even in the sense of being the selfsame entity, i. e., numerically identical).
Rather, what we claim in this case is simply some such thing as the following. You
have painted the building, or taken a photo of it, or described it verbally at some
length, and I have done the same, and then we have assured each other, first, that
our respective pictures or verbal reports, to the best of our knowledge, fully meet
what we respectively saw, and second, that your representation of the building
fully tallies with mine. So here we are concerned, not with an alleged similarity
of two subjective impressions, one of which is mine and one of which is yours
(to assume which would be nonsensical in the strictest sense of the word), but
with the similarity of relevant stretches of your and of my objectively observable

---

[49] See sect. 3.4.6 with fn. 44, above.

behaviour and the similarity of their publicly accessible products, namely, the pictures or verbal reports. In this sense, and *only* in *this* sense, the manner in which a certain object is now being seen by me can be the same as the manner in which this object has been seen, or will be seen, by you at some other moment in time.

3.6.1.   This statement invites at least three comments. – First, in this special case the phrase 'the same as' can be replaced with either 'exactly similar to' or 'strictly (numerically) identical to'. For this is one of the cases in which it would be futile and even preposterous to insist on making this well-known distinction, which is important only as long as we have to do with material objects. As Wittgenstein and his followers rightly emphasised, in the cases of non-material objects such as colours, heights, gaits, etc. as a rule there is no difference between qualitative identity (exact similarity) and numerical identity (strict self-sameness).[50] For what on earth could it mean to say, e.g., that your height, or the colour of your hair, is exactly similar to mine but not strictly identical with it? Or, in other words, what could give us the right to speak of two exactly similar heights, or colours, instead of speaking of exactly one and the same height, or colour, and vice versa? Even if we do not want to exclude once for all the theoretical possibility that there might arise certain situations in which the need will make itself felt to *introduce* some such distinction for a specific purpose, at least we have to admit that so far such a distinction does not *obtain* in ordinary language. Obviously, the same is true of the manner in which a certain visual object is seen by you and by me. It makes no sense at all to say, e.g., that the manner in which Westminster Abbey is now being seen by you is *exactly similar*, though not *strictly identical*, to the manner in which Westminster Abbey was being seen by me a few seconds earlier. Such a conceptual differentiation has not yet been defined, and, if we recall what I just said in the opening paragraph of section 3.6, there seems to be not much reason to believe that the need of some such differential definition is ever to be expected.

3.6.2.   Second, in this connection it is by no means necessary that the object I see at t_1 is (numerically) identical with the one you see at t_2. For it seems to me to be obvious that doubles, replicas, 'Potëmkin' objects, identical (i.e., monozygotic) twins, clones, etc. would do as well in such cases. So the manner in which a certain object is being seen by a certain person at a certain time (if we stick to the sense of these words just indicated) is independent, not only of the person seeing, but also of the object seen, provided only that, in case two or more objects are involved, these objects look entirely alike. Furthermore, the manner in question is also independent of, or indifferent with respect to, the time of seeing, or being seen. For of course the manner in which, say, a dog is being seen by me at t_1 can

---

[50] For details and relevant sources, see Hoche & Strube 1985: A. III.3.

be exactly similar (or, what comes to the same, strictly identical), not only to the manner of the dog's (or its identical twin's) being seen by *you* at t_2, but also, if not *a fortiori*, with the manner of the dog's (or its twin's) being seen by *myself* at t_3. – Instead of saying that the manner in which an object is being seen by somebody at some time is *independent of*, or *indifferent with respect to*, the object seen, the person seeing, and the time of seeing, we can likewise say that, in describing the manner of an object's being seen, we may *abstract from* the object itself (as long as an exact double is provided for), from the onlooker's personal identity, and from the given moment in time.

3.6.3.   Hence, third, if being timeless in the sense of having neither a temporal position nor a temporal extension may be taken to be a sufficient condition for being an abstract object,[51] it follows that the manner of a visual object's being seen is certainly an *abstraction*. However, it seems to be, very roughly speaking, something like the 'negative abstraction' as compared with the everyday material object, which, in section 3.4, I took pains to characterise as being an abstraction as well. For whereas in conceiving a *material object* we use to abstract from the manner in which it just happens to be perceived by us, in conceiving the *manner in which a visual material object is being seen by us* we abstract from the selfsameness of the object seen, from the personal identity of the subject seeing, and from the moment in time at which it is being seen. At any rate this manner of being seen must be acknowledged to be an *abstract object*, and hence it must be something quite different from the *concrete object par excellence* I endeavoured to work out in section 3.4, above.

3.6.4.   It is not at all easy to know these two objects apart, i.e., the *concrete object* which I said is basic for a non-naturalistic theory of consciousness, and the *abstract object* which may be said to be basic for naturalistic painting. Obviously, both of them fail to be spatially localised in an objective way; but, in contradistinction to the latter, the former owns a definite temporal position. As it lacks an objective spatial localisation, this temporal position cannot be a position in space-time, i.e., an objective temporal position in the real world. Rather, it is a subjective temporal position within the field of my own conscious experiences. If we may compare the abstract object in question – i.e., the manner in which an object can be seen by myself or somebody else – to a normal photograph, which anybody may have taken at any time of a given object or any double, clone, or identical twin of its, the concrete object we are now turning to must correspondingly be compared to a photograph on which not only the precise time of its having been taken but also, as it were, the 'PIN' (the 'personal identification number') of the camera through which it was taken has been automatically printed. In other words: The manner in

---

[51] Cf. Künne 1983: sect. 2.1, p. 56f.

which an object is being seen by somebody at some time, which plays so decisive a role in the representational arts and may perhaps even be equated to what has been called the artist's 'subject' ('sujet'), may be considered to be an impoverished secondary product derived from a similar but richer object by abstraction, scil., by abstracting from – or leaving aside, or neglecting – the particular person or subject seeing as well as the subjective temporal position within this person's mental life, both of which we have to recognise as individuating characteristics of the primary (richer and, in fact, concrete) object. Besides, this primary object is also characterised by its reference to a particular, individually determined object seen, to the exclusion of the latter one's 'identical twins'. For in face of a particular person seeing, at a particular moment in time, the object which is being seen cannot be replaced with a double or 'clone' any more than, in the parallel we have just drawn, a double (or what not) could be substituted, at the very moment of the picture's being taken, for the object or person being photographed by means of a particular camera at a particular instant.

3.6.5.   Before going on to describe further important differences between the two objects in question – the primary, richer, and concrete one and the secondary, poorer, and abstract one –, we should perhaps try and give them distinctive and more suggestive names. To the latter (the representational artist's 'subject') I have already been referring as 'the manner in which an object is being seen by somebody at some time', or as 'a visual object's mode of subjectively appearing to somebody at some time', or, more specifically, as, e. g., 'the manner in which Westminster Abbey is now being seen by me'. Instead of using the last, specific description, we may, I take it, also speak of 'Westminster Abbey in the manner in which it is now being seen by me', or, replacing the phrase 'in the manner in which' with the simple particle 'as', of 'Westminster Abbey as it is now being seen by me'. However – at least according to the limited linguistic competence I have as a non-native speaker of English –, as soon as in the last wording we omit the two words 'it is', the meaning changes much more than just in a trifling way. I think we can say that, under certain circumstances, Westminster Abbey *as it is* now being seen by me may be the same as Westminster Abbey *as it is* being seen by me or somebody else at another moment in time; and we can say so on the basis of identity-criteria of the sort already outlined in the opening paragraph of section 3.6, above. But I don't think we would ever say that Westminster Abbey *as* now being seen by me is identical with Westminster Abbey *as* being seen by me or somebody else at some other time. The phrase (1a) 'Westminster Abbey *as* now being seen by me' seems to me to mean the same as the more circumstantial but also more precise phrase (1b) 'Westminster Abbey *in its capacity of* now being seen by me', whereas the phrase (2a) 'Westminster Abbey *as it is* now being seen by me' seems to me to be interchangeable with the phrase (2b) 'Westminster Abbey *in the manner in which it is* now being seen by me'. The mutual relation between the phrases (1b) and (2b), and so between (1a) and (2a), may perhaps be compared to the relation between the relevant phrases in such sentences as 'He spoke to me *in his capacity of* a friend.' and 'He spoke to me *in the manner of* a friend.', both of which, if we don't mind ambiguity, may simply be rendered as 'He spoke to me *as* a friend.'. In the latter example, the difference (or the ambiguity, as the case may be) is of considerable import even in everyday life; for everybody knows that the *manner* of a friend, in contradistinction to the *capacity* of a friend, can be easily feigned or pretended. In the former example, however, the difference is much less easily to be seen; for in everyday life few people are interested in artistic 'subjects', and practically no one is inclined to occupy himself with, or to admit the significance of speaking about, those primary and concrete entities of which the artistic 'subjects' are but secondary and abstract derivatives. In fact, these primary entities are of no interest whatsoever outside the field of research into consciousness, and even within this field most contemporary theorists are averse to taking them seriously. In other words, the semantic difference which in my view should be recognised as obtaining between the phrases (1a) and (2a) as well as between the phrases (1b) and (2b) is of little or no relevance at all to everyday life, and for this reason it seems to me to be well possible that even the idiolects of English native speakers do not entirely agree with each other in this respect. If so, the reader is certainly well advised if he takes recourse, not to demoscopic enquiries, but to his personal imaginative and idiolectal competence,[52] which, moreover, is always open to being adjusted to new conceptual challenges. What is important in the case at hand is solely that we realise the difference between what I called the 'primary' and the 'secondary' object in question, and that we make this difference verbally tractable by finding a suitable name for either one – in the last resort by inventing new technical terms. So it is but a suggestion of mine to refer to the 'primary' object as 'a visual object *as* [*qua*], i.e., *in its capacity of*, being seen by some person at some time', or rather – because here, as a rule, we ought to confine ourselves to the first-person case and the present tense – as 'a visual object *as* [*qua*], i.e., *in the capacity of*, now being seen by me' (or, as we may say for short, '*my C-object*').[53] In contradistinction, I shall speak of the 'secondary' object as 'a visual object *as it*

---

[52] See sect. 3.3 with fn. 28, above.

[53] With the abbreviation 'C', which I just introduced as standing for '(in its) *capacity* (of now being seen by me)', in what follows we may aptly associate the term '*consciousness*' as well; for, as we saw, the C-object ought to be basic in a non-naturalistic theory of (respectively) my own consciousness. – As the abbreviation 'my C-object' would badly need getting used to indeed, it seems to me preferable to speak explicitly of 'the visual object *as* [*qua*], i.e., *in its capacity of*, now being seen by me'. However, as the reader is likely to feel bothered by this somewhat lengthy and overburdened technical term, in most cases I will simply speak of either 'the object *in its capacity of* being seen by me' or 'the object *as* [or: *qua*] being seen by me'. But let me entreat the reader to keep in mind that in the latter case, too, what I will be speaking of is nothing but the object *in its capacity of* being seen by me right now and not, for instance, what *Max Velmans* means by the terms 'object as seen' or 'object-as-seen' (see

is, i.e., *in its manner of*, being seen by some person at some time' (or, for short, '*the M-object*').

3.6.6. Let me try and make clear in passing that the object in its *capacity* of now being seen by me (or, fort short, 'my C-object') differs from the object in its *manner* of now being seen by me (or, for short, 'the M-object') not only by involving, as individuating characteristics, (1) a particular, or individually determinate, subject seeing, scil., respectively myself, (2) a determinate instant of my seeing the object, and (3) a determinate object seen, which may not be replaced with a double.[54] Rather, my C-object is characterised by still more individuating traits which the M-object lacks. Take, e.g., its property of now being *seen* by me in the strictest sense of the word, scil., in the sense of now being visually *perceived*, as opposed to being visually *remembered* (called back to the mind) or visually *imagined* (conceived of, or formed in the mind). As a rule, at least, when I am paying attention to a visual object I am perfectly aware of whether I do so by way of perceiving it (either immediately, or mediated by, say, a live telecast), or of remembering it, or of only conceiving of it (my imagination being either in agreement with the facts I know, or else contrary to the facts, or else without any arbitrary restrictions).[55] So being visually given to me in either this or that one of these different ways is an inherent property of any object in its *capacity* of now being visually given to me. However, in derivating from the latter the corresponding object in its *manner* of being visually given, i.e., the artistic 'subject',[56] we abstract, among other things, also from this distinguishing feature of being either perceived or remembered or imagined – which perhaps may be best seen from the fact that, if I successfully try and truly paint what I 'see', the resulting picture may be exactly the same in any one of the different cases of visually perceiving, or remembering, or conceiving.[57]

3.6.7. Besides, more often than not an object in its *capacity* of now being visually given to me is imbued with multifarious emotional qualities such as attractive or repulsive 'forces' or positive or negative 'values'; and in case the object in question is given to me in the distinguished and primary form of being visually *perceived*, i.e., of being seen in the original and fundamental sense of the word, very often my C-object is additionally endowed with downright 'practical', 'imperative', or

---

sect. 3.8.5, fn. 90, below, and also Introduction: sect. 4, and Essay V: esp. sect. 1.3.3, of the present volume).

[54] See sect. 3.6.4, above.

[55] For these widely differing kinds of imagination, see Hoche 1990: ch. 9.

[56] See sect. 3.6.4, above.

[57] Certainly a fourth variant of 'seeing' is visually dreaming; however, because of the multifarious problems this mental phenomenon carries with it, in the present context I prefer to leave it out of consideration.

'gerundive' features.[58] For instance, a C-dog of mine may be subjectively given to me, not only as visually perceived from a certain distance in a certain perspective and under a certain lighting condition, but also as ugly, as dangerous, and possibly even as one which makes me run away or climb a tree in order to protect myself against it (as one 'to be fled by me' – or in the Latin gerundive: 'canis fugitandus'). All these emotional and practical features which my C-dog presents to me are strictly subjective, as is testified, first, by my fellow-men's possibly widely different behaviour towards the real dog, i. e., the animal in the world, and, second, by the fact that my C-dog's emotional and practical features cannot be incorporated into the corresponding M-dog, or artistic dog-'subject', any more than its feature of being visually perceived instead of being remembered or imagined (or dreamed of), or its feature of being seen in its own 'person' (and not through a double) by myself (and not by somebody else) right now (and not at some other moment in time).

3.7. There is no reason for distinguishing the object in its capacity of now being seen by me from my now seeing the object

Having introduced, elaborated, and discussed, in sections 3.4 through 3.6, the concept of 'my C-object', i. e., the concept of an object *'qua'* (*as*, or in its *capacity* of) now being seen by me, I now want to go on by attacking a time-honoured philosophical dogma concerning this basic concept of a non-naturalistic theory of consciousness. What I have in mind is the well-known and apparently well-entrenched conviction that an object 'qua' now being seen by me must needs be correlated to an act or process of my now seeing that object. It is true that this conviction at first sight seems perfectly natural, if not inescapable. For of course we have to make a difference between, say, the dog (which is) now being seen by me and my now seeing it. According to our well-established criteria of identity and non-identity, the dog now being seen by me (i. e., the dog which I now [can] see) is something quite different from my now seeing the dog. For the former is a dog, hence, an animal and as such a material spatio-temporal object out in the world, whereas the latter is a visual subjective experience of mine (whatever that means in detail; in what follows I will tackle this question in detail). While the dog is still there, sitting in front of me, I can at will interrupt the subjective experience just mentioned by simply closing and reopening my eyes; so the spaces of time in which my seeing the dog takes place are by no means congruent with the space of time in which the dog exists. Furthermore, my seeing the dog can vary (e. g., when I am walking around it) while the dog does not even change its position, and *vice versa*: while I am invariantly looking at, and see, the outwardly motionless dog,

---

[58] See Hoche 1973a: part II, *passim*; 1994: esp. sect. VIII; and the last paragraph of subsection 3.9.1, below. Cf. Aristotle, *De motu animalium*: 701a20, and Sartre 1936–1937: pp. 94, 97 f.

the latter as a rule is undergoing a multitude of physiological changes not to be seen from without. (This is even more obvious in the case of an inanimate thing, whose front side which I can see may remain unchanged while its interior or its back side, and so the thing itself, is wildly changing and perhaps disintegrating.) So, if an object A and an object B are not identical if they occupy (or exist during) distinct spaces of time and/or can undergo changes independently of each other, the dog I now (can) see and my now seeing the dog are not one and the same thing.

Similarly, although for a different reason, we must distinguish between the dog (which is) now seen by *you* and *your* now seeing the dog. The reason is in this case that, *for me*, your now seeing the dog may be taken to be nothing but that stretch of linguistic as well as non-linguistic behaviour of yours the perception of which gives me the ultimate right to believe or assert that you now see the dog;[59] and this behaviour of yours, though being situated in relevant surroundings, consists in movements of parts of your body, which of course do not occupy the same place as the dog. So, if an object A and an object B are not identical, either, if they occupy different places at the same time, the dog now seen by you and your now seeing the dog are not one and the same thing.

Furthermore, we also have to admit a distinction between my seeing the dog at a given time and the dog *as it is*, or in its *manner* of, being seen by me at this time. For, if we did not, by parity of reasoning we should also have to deny a distinction between your seeing the dog at a given time and the dog *as it is* being seen by you at this time – from which it would follow that, because the dog as it is being seen by me at a given time (say, my artistic dog-'subject') can possibly be identical with the dog as it is being seen by you at some other time (or your artistic dog-'subject'),[60] my seeing the dog at a given moment in time could possibly be identical with your seeing the dog at some other moment in time, which, of course, runs counter to our most ingrained intuitions concerning our pre-analytic concept of the subjective experience of seeing.

So at first sight it may seem most natural to take it for granted that we have to make a distinction, too, between my now seeing the dog and the dog in its *capacity* of now being seen by me. But so far, this is nothing but a prejudice; for do we really have any good reason for believing in such a difference? I think not. Furthermore, nearly all we know about this unfamiliar object, in contradistinction to the much more familiar dog *as it is*, or in its *manner* of, now being seen by me, is that it is a *concrete* object endowed with a *temporal position* which, however, is certainly *not a position in space-time* and so may best be thought to be a position within the field of my subjective conscious experience.[61]

---

[59] For a discussion, see sect. 3.15, below; cf. also sect. 2.3.2, above.

[60] See sect. 3.5–3.6, above.

[61] See sect. 3.6.4, above.

3.8. My now seeing the dog may be taken to be nothing but the dog in its capacity of now being seen by me

As a matter of fact, in what follows I shall make a case for saying that to distinguish between my now seeing the dog and the dog in its *capacity* of now being seen by me would amount to making a distinction without a difference. Inverting an ironical saying of Frege's,[62] we may say that in this case we would be following 'the principle of distinguishing what is not different'; and in fact it was Frege who stressed not only the importance of distinguishing what is different[63] but also the importance of *not* distinguishing what is *not* different.[64] Of course this amounts to emphasising a well-known principle of parsimony, to wit, *Ockham's Razor*; and what I now want to cut off, and dispose of, is the alleged act or process of my now seeing (say) a dog in such-and-such a mode of appearance as distinguished from, opposed to, and strictly correlated with, the dog *in its capacity of* now being seen by me in such-and-such a mode of appearance. As ought to be clear by now, I do not at all mean to propose by this that we should do away with the concept of my seeing something in a specific manner of appearing, or being given, to me. On the contrary, this concept is at the root of understanding conscious experience, and it is precisely for this reason that we must see to it that it be *properly analysed*.[65] To be quite explicit: I propose to say that my now seeing a dog in such-and-such a manner of appearing is neither a mysterious act being performed on an equally mysterious inner stage,[66] nor nothing at all, nor to be identified with specific goings-on in my central nervous system,[67] but that it is to be identified with the dog *in its capacity of* now visually appearing to me in such-and-such a way, i.e., with the dog *in its capacity of* now being seen by me in such-and-such a way of being subjectively given to me. – For this proposed identification I ought to offer very good reasons, indeed; and I hope the reader will find at least *some* of the following reasons sufficiently convincing.

3.8.1. A rather weak reason, but nonetheless a reason we should not pass over silently, seems to me to be suggested by the following rhetoric questions. If my now seeing something, which is perhaps the most familiar kind of a conscious

---

[62] Frege 1899: pp. VI, 17.

[63] Ibid., for instance.

[64] Frege 1897: p. 154.

[65] Think of a famous parallel case. It would be quite erroneous to see, in Hume's well-known considerations about causation, a *denial* rather than a *conceptual analysis* of this basic relation in the field of natural events.

[66] Cf. Ryle 1949: passim.

[67] For such an identification, in our preceding considerations we did not find even the slightest hint or evidence; and, furthermore, in what follows it will turn out that it would be not only unjustified but even illogical (see esp. sects. 3.11, 3.17, 3.18, below).

experience, has been made, by the combined efforts of recent 'neuro-philosophers' and cognitive scientists, downright unintelligible, but is nonetheless so basic and intimate a phenomenon that most of us are decidedly disinclined to simply deny its existence, then why should it be identified with some sort or other of a physical process, and not rather with the visual object *in its capacity of* now being given to me in its particular mode of appearance? For wouldn't it be by far more natural to identify a phenomenon which is given to me in my 'first-person perspective' with a phenomenon which is likewise given to me in my 'first-person perspective', instead of claiming – if only by way of an alleged 'empirical hypothesis', of which, by the way, it is completely unclear how it could ever be confirmed or disconfirmed – that it is identical to some physical process, our knowledge of which is obtained in the 'third-person perspective' of objective science?

3.8.2.   A much stronger reason seems to me to be that, say, my seeing a dog and the dog *in its capacity of* being seen by me occupy exactly the same stretches of time. This temporal congruence is testified by the fact that, whenever I close my eyes, 'both' entities (if they are really two) disappear, and whenever I reopen them – provided the dog is still there and has not moved in the meantime, and my eyes are converging towards it –, 'both' of them reappear. – It is true that we may be tempted to suppose that this congruence of their periods of existence, even if indubitable, is not a sufficient reason for asserting that they are one and the same thing. For – so the objection may be made more explicit – even if an object A and an object B exist in precisely the same span of time, they may do so in different places and hence, according to one of our most basic criteria of numerical identity and numerical difference, be two different objects which only happen to share their 'life-times'. In other words – so the objection may go on –, in order to show that my now seeing the dog and the dog *as* or *qua* now being seen by me are one and the same object, I have to show, not merely that they exist at precisely the same time, but rather that they exist at precisely the same time in precisely the same place. And – the objector might be tempted to conclude his argument – this cannot possibly be done; for my now seeing the dog is somehow going on within myself, whereas the dog *in its capacity of* now being seen by me is out in the world. – Here, however, gross prejudices are strikingly coming up to the surface. First, though the dog, as an animal and, hence, a material object, certainly is an inhabitant of the external world, there is no reason other than unwarranted habit and lack of conceptual precision for simply asserting the same of the dog *in its capacity of* now being seen by me. As a matter of fact, in section 3.6.4, above, I tried and made clear that the latter has no position in space-time and so is not situated in the external world. But we must also reject the claim that my now seeing the dog resides, in one way or another, within myself. For claiming this would either amount to simply reviving the 'internal world' or 'inner stage' fortunately disposed of by Ryle (1949), or else presuppose the identification of my seeing the dog with some processes in my central nervous system, which, as I just indicated, is not only unjustified but logically untenable.[68] So, instead of carelessly placing the dog *in its capacity of* now being seen by me in the external world, and my now seeing the dog either in some mysterious internal world or else in my central nervous system, we ought to realise that neither one can be meaningfully said to have an objective spatial localisation.[69] Because of this impossibility of attributing to either of them a spatio-temporal localisation in the objective world, the mere fact that I cannot make out a temporal difference between my seeing the dog and the dog *in its capacity of* being seen by me seems to me to be a sufficient reason for applying to them Ockham's Razor, i.e., for regarding and treating them as one and the same thing. This may be made even more perspicuous in the following way. Of my now seeing the dog, and of the dog *as* or *qua* now being seen by me, I would not only say that they *exist* in the same span of time, but also that I am *aware* of them strictly synchronously; for it would be utterly pointless to speak of their existence ('esse') over and above their being 'perceived' ('percipi') by me.[70] This coincidence of 'esse' and 'percipi' marks a striking difference between phenomena of this kind and material objects localised in objective space-time; and this difference suffices to make sure that the criteria of identity conventionally applied to the latter cannot simply be carried over to the former. In fact, there are no established criteria at all on the basis of which to decide whether my now seeing the dog and the dog *as*, or *qua*, now being seen by me ought to be considered one and the same phenomenon or two related phenomena taking place at the same time. At this point, I think, Ockham's Razor has to come into play. As long as we have no cogent reason for treating a phenomenon A and a phenomenon B as two distinct phenomena, for the sake of conceptual simplicity we should treat them as one and the same phenomenon; and, to repeat, I think this is the case with my now seeing the dog and the dog *in its capacity of* now being seen by me.

3.8.3.   But, it might possibly be objected, we *do* have a cogent reason for treating my now seeing the dog as something different from the dog *as*, or *qua*, now being seen by me; for I can significantly and truthfully say many things about the latter which I would hardly say about the former, e.g., that it is spatially extended, partly yellowish-white and partly dark brown, or looks dangerous, or

---

[68] See fn. 67, above, and sects. 3.11, 3.17, 3.18, below.

[69] See sect. 3.6.4, above. It should be noted, however, that the dog *as*, *qua*, or *in its capacity of*, now being, seen by me is spatially localised, and hence also spatially extended (cf. sect. 3.8.3, below), within the totality of my present views (visual appearances), which are subjective; for of course the dog is never seen alone, without some surroundings and some background.

[70] Moore 1913–1914: pp. 180–184 seems to call this in question; but in contradistinction to me, he takes it for granted that 'the entity which *is* experienced must in all cases be distinguished from the fact or event which consists in its being experienced; since by saying that it is experienced we mean that it has a relation of a certain kind to something else': ibid.: p. 169.

is constantly increasing (as the dog is approaching me). Obviously, the objector takes this argument to be an application of what logicians use to call 'Leibniz's law', according to which an object A and an object B are not identical unless anything that is true of the one must also be true of the other.[71]

However, it should be noted, first, that an object's having a certain property is not always the same as the possibility of ascribing to it this property on plausible grounds. If, for instance, a monstrous criminal pretends to be a nice young man, or even happens to have rescued a child from drowning, or if Dr Jekyll and Mr Hyde change back and forth between each other, or if one and the same planet poses as the morning-star at dawn and as the evening-star at dusk, then we are likely to say quite different things about them – as long as we have not learned to identify them with one another.[72] So the mere fact that we would not say of my now seeing the dog that it is partly yellowish-white and partly dark brown, etc., is not a decisive argument against its being the same thing as the dog *in its capacity of* now being seen by me. It is true that the latter phenomena – my seeing a thing and the thing *as* seen by me – always present themselves contemporaneously, whereas the cases of comparison just adduced present themselves strictly by turns. However, I think that this fact, far from impairing my point of comparison (or 'tertium comparationis'), is well suited to supply us with a further argument in favour of identifying the visual phenomena in question. For if we plead for identifying an object A and an object B which are strictly given by turns, the burden of proof is certainly on ourselves; but if we plead for identifying a phenomenon called A and a phenomenon called B which appear to us simultaneously without being spatially localised, the burden of proof seems to me to rest on the opponent's shoulders – and the more so if we are able to show up seeming psychological motives for believing that A and B are, or rather 'must be', two distinct phenomena and hence necessarily require two different names. Now I think that the present case is a clear-cut example of such a situation. For in matters of mind and action we tend to overlook important epistemological differences between respectively my own case and the case of my fellow-men, and to model the former case on the latter, or vice versa, which amounts to blending and so confusing the cases.[73] I think we may see that this tendency is at work also here. Take, for instance, *your* now seeing the dog. From *my* point of view, this may be rightly taken to be nothing but your relevant situated behaviour, linguistic as well as non-linguistic; for it is

---

[71] See, e.g., Flew 1979, p. 187. Historically, this seems not to be quite accurate (cf. Kretzmann 1967, p. 382). Furthermore, we ought to be alive to the fact that what is called 'Leibniz's law' is the *converse* of Leibniz's famous, though highly controversial, 'principle of the identity of indiscernibles'. But as I tried to make clear in Essay III: sect. 7 of the present collection, neither the former nor the latter, nor a sensible combination of them, can serve us as a universal *criterion* for (non-)identity.

[72] See again Flew 1979, p. 187.

[73] See sect. 2.3.2, above, and sect. 3.15, below.

this behaviour of yours, and nothing else, the perception of which gives me the right to speak of your now seeing the dog. Now taking your case as a model, I am prepared to consider *seeing* as something which is going on in an organism, namely, a set of bodily movements initiated by nervous processes starting from the retinas of the eyes. So of course I am strongly disinclined to say of my, as well as of your, now seeing the dog that it is partly yellowish-white and partly brown, or looks dangerous, or is constantly increasing, etc. On the other hand, we are subject to the reverse tendency to model the case of *what is seen* by somebody else on the case of what is seen by myself; for I have no immediate access to what you see: I can perceive your *seeing* the dog, scil., your appropriate behaviour, but not *what you see*, scil., the dog *in its capacity of* being seen by you (unless, of course, I mistake it for the dog *in its manner of* being seen by you, namely, your artistic dog-'subject', or even for the dog itself, namely, the animal in the world). So I might be ready to admit, for instance, that the dog *in its capacity of* now being seen by you is partly yellowish-white and partly dark brown, or constantly increasing as the dog is approaching you – although I think that this, strictly speaking, makes no genuine sense. So our tendency to model, in the field of perceiving and what is perceived, partly my case on yours and partly your case on mine – in other words: our tendency to blend and confuse these two cases, which epistemologically and, I take it, also ontologically[74] have to be strictly kept apart – may, I think, be made responsible for ingrained linguistic habits which are unwarranted and hence of no use in linguistic analysis.[75]

3.8.4.   To the preceding arguments in favour of my identifying my now seeing the dog with the dog *in its capacity of* now being seen by me, I am going to add two more reasonings, which, though considerably differing from each other in point of cogency, make use of more or less the same elements.

The first one I shall present in the form of a Peircean 'abduction', which in general may be given the following argumentative structure: 'The surprising fact, C, is observed; But if A were true, C would be a matter of course; Hence, there is reason to suspect that A is true.'[76] From this it is obvious that abductive reasoning is but a method of finding a promising explanatory hypothesis, which is still in need of an independent justification. Nonetheless abduction is a useful method in many areas, as is testified, for instance, by the successful manner of problem solving practised in countless cases by Sherlock Holmes, whom Arthur

---

[74] See sect. 3.16, below.

[75] In case the reader should be suspicious of my leaning on the two opposite tendencies just mentioned, he ought to remember the mind-body problem in its most spectacular but downright intractable variant, which arises, as Sartre (1943: pp. 365, 367) aptly put it, from our trying to join *my own* conscious experience to *another* person's material body.

[76] Peirce 1931–1935: 5.189.

Conan Doyle devised as a master abductionist par excellence.[77] However, what Peirce calls 'the surprising fact, C' need not always be as extraordinary as the traits, often unheard-of, in Holmes's mystery cases. In this respect, the famous detective's cases significantly contrast with the consciousness-theoretical case at hand, in which 'C' seems to be a 'surprising fact' only in the light of a stubborn philosophical prejudice. In virtue of this prejudice, many philosophers seem to consider surprising what, in the light of common sense, is a familiar fact of everyday life, namely, the well-known special status of my own perceiving in particular, and conscious experience in general, as compared, not only with my fellow-men's conscious experience in so far as it is accessible to myself, but also to anything else in the world.

This special status, as at least most non-philosophers easily recognise as soon as they pay attention to the issue at all, may be characterised as follows. The mere fact that there is, say, a dog in the garden does not at all suffice to justify my asserting that there is a dog in the garden; rather, I must also *see* (or perceive in some other way) that there is a dog in the garden. Similarly, the mere fact that you see that there is a dog in the garden does not at all suffice to justify my asserting that you see that there is a dog in the garden; rather, I must also *see* (or perceive in some other way) that you see that there is a dog in the garden. In contradistinction to this, however, the mere fact that *I* see that there is a dog in the garden *does* all by itself suffice to justify my asserting, not only that *there is* a dog in the garden, but also that *I see that there is* a dog in the garden. In other words: it would be preposterous to postulate that, in addition to my seeing that there is a dog in the garden, I must also *see* (or perceive in some other way) that I see that there is a dog in the garden.

In spite of this, many philosophers are so firmly in the grip of the prejudice that my own perceiving has, or rather 'must have', basically the same ontological properties as somebody else's perceiving and all other occurrences in the world, that they take it for granted that I cannot be aware of my perceiving something unless this alleged 'process' of perceiving is made itself the object of a further perception – an 'inner', 'introspective', or 'reflective' perception, as they are fond of calling it. Against the foil of this time-honoured philosophical prejudice, intellectuals of the last mid-century felt it to be a very release that Sartre, adopting some hints from Husserl's, restored the natural conception of a 'prereflective cogito' to its legitimate and innate position.[78] Seeing, and perception in general, and conscious experience at large, may be compared to a visible object that itself emits light and hence can be seen without being illuminated from without. But whereas nobody would be tempted to say that, for instance, a flame cannot be seen unless

---

[77] Cf. Sebeok/Umiker-Sebeok 1980.

[78] Sartre 1943: Introduction, sect. III; Husserl, esp. 1913, tr. 1931: sect. 45.

it is exposed to an outward source of light, many philosophers – being under the overwhelming and rarely questioned impression that my own consciousness, if it exists at all, 'must be' a part of nature and for this reason share, with the rest of her, at least the basic epistemological and ontological properties – take it simply for granted that I have no right to assert anything substantial about my own perceiving unless I make it the object of a special, higher-order perception. And on finding out that there is, indeed, not the slightest evidence for the existence of such a higher-order, or 'inner', or 'introspective' perception, they are ready to deny the very existence, too, of what was alleged to be given by means of the alleged introspection, rather than to call into question their 'unity of science' ideology and to revise their notion of subjective experiences. In a way, this, too, is a sort of abductive reasoning. Expecting from the very outset that I cannot possibly have any access to my conscious experiences, nor to anything else in the world, unless I make it the object of a suitable perception, they regard it as a surprising fact that, on closer inspection, nothing at all speaks in favour of a perception directed to one's own conscious experiences. Having recognised this fact, they tend to say to themselves: 'Indeed, if there really didn't exist such a thing as my subjectively experienced consciousness, then it would be a matter of course that we cannot find the slightest traces of a perception of such a spurious entity; hence, it seems to be a reasonable hypothesis that the supposed conscious experience does not exist at all, and that what traditional philosophers until now have always mistaken for it is in fact something quite different, as, for instance, a certain electro-chemical state of the central nervous system.'

As a less unpleasant alternative to such an application of abduction – which tries to make us believe that the first-person perspective, for many of us the most immediate, intimate, and sometimes overwhelming reality, is but a fake – I should like to suggest the following line of abductive reasoning, confining myself again to the special case of seeing something: 'If my now seeing, for instance, a dog were not some interior process, not something going on in an alleged 'inner world' of mine, but simply the dog *qua* now being visually given to me with such-and-such subjective traits, then it would be a matter of course that I cannot find a higher-order, or inner, or introspective, or reflective perception of my now seeing the dog, and that my now simply seeing the *dog* suffices all by itself to give me the right to assert, not only that *there is* a dog, but also that I now *see* (or see that there is) a dog; hence, it seems reasonable to suppose that my now seeing the dog is just the dog *in its capacity of* now being visually given to me.' Here, the first-person perspective has not been given up in favour of the third-person perspective, nor even called into question; but it has been cast into a different, more elaborate shape which seems to me to be truer to the phenomena really experienced. Nonetheless, our reasoning, being still abductive in Peirce's sense, belongs in the 'context of discovery' rather than in the 'context of justification', and thus is only of a limited cognitive value. I am confident, though, that its basic elements can be given quite a different and much more compelling argumentative form. I shall try to do so in the following sub-section.

3.8.5. What we are after in the present chapter is the *nature* of consciousness, and more specifically the nature of seeing, and still more specifically the nature of my now seeing something, say, a dog. In other words, what we want to answer are the questions 'What is consciousness?' (though not, of course, in the sense with which we occupied ourselves in the second chapter, scil., 'What is the *concept* of consciousness?', or: 'What phenomena do we count to be examples of consciousness?'), 'What is seeing?', and 'What is my seeing a dog?'. It seems to me to have been one of the major achievements of 20th century philosophy to replace such 'what is'-questions with questions of the form 'How, or under what conditions, do we (in fact) use the expression so-and-so?', and to replace at the same time nominal and nominalised verbal forms as radically as possible with finite verbal forms.[79] So the question 'What is my seeing a dog?' may, and should, be reworded as follows: 'Under what conditions are we, the native speakers of my mother tongue – or am I myself within the framework of my own idiolect – in fact prepared to say that I see a dog?'. As linguistic facts, at least in most respects, certainly adopt a 'normative force', I think we may as well substitute, for the aforementioned purely 'descriptive' wording, a 'normative' wording such as the following: 'Under what conditions am I entitled to assert that I see a dog?', or more precisely: 'What is it that, in respect of truth (though not necessarily in respect of speech-act theoretical suitability), gives me the ultimate right to assert that I see a dog?'.[80]

These questions may, of course, remind us of the 'verificationist' problems as they have been discussed since the prime of linguistic (or analytic) philosophy in the second quarter of the 20th century. However, the assertion in question, namely, 'I see a dog.', may in a way be thought to be of precisely that type in relation to which, according to a deep and highly important insight of Wittgenstein's, 'the question "How is that verified?" makes no sense'.[81] We encounter a similar problem if we think of Husserl's related but less restricted admonition that the philosopher should always try to go back to the 'things themselves' by making use of the relevant sort of 'originarily giving consciousness' (or 'primordinal dator consciousness'; in German: 'originär gebendes Bewusstsein'), which is the 'ultimate source of legitimacy of all rational assertions'.[82] For in using, as a generic

---

[79] See, e.g., Austin 1950: sects. 1–2.

[80] Cf. Landscheid 1997: esp. 18–22, and 2000: esp. 162–174, who stresses the difference between what he calls 'descriptive' and 'normative explanations' in a still stronger way.

[81] Moore 1954–1955: p. 266. – I shall discuss this topic at some length in sects. 3.12–3.14, below.

[82] Husserl 1913, tr. 1931: sect. 19. – In rendering Husserl's technical terms, in cases of doubt I shall follow Cairns 1973 rather than W. R. Boyce Gibson, who translated Husserl 1913, tr. 1931 into English.

term to be applied to 'originarily giving consciousness of any kind whatsoever', the expression 'immediate "seeing"' ('das unmittelbare "Sehen" [νοεῖν]'),[83] Husserl chooses an expression which, in connection with statements of the type 'I see a dog.', is as much out of place as the word 'verification'. If it is true[84] that I cannot 'verify' that I see a dog because my seeing a dog is given to me in too immediate a manner for admitting of a – mediated – procedure of verification, I cannot 'see' – or νοεῖν, i.e., perceive, learn, find out, and the like – that I see a dog, either. For as a rule we use the latter terms only in those cases in which my *immediately perceiving something* presupposes my *being immediately given something else* – irrespective of how philosophers prefer to call, or rather to interpret, this 'something else': as a 'phenomenon' in the (not 'transcendental' but 'empirical') sense of Kant's ambiguous term 'Erscheinung',[85] or as a 'phenomenon' in the sense of Husserl's term 'Noema',[86] or as a 'sense datum' or 'sensible' in anyone of the various meanings of these words,[87] or what not. So in the present case we ought to speak, not of 'verification', 'perceiving', and 'seeing', but of 'being given' or 'being confronted with', and to transform our leading question – 'What is my seeing a dog?' – into something like the following question: 'What must be given to me, or what is it that I must be confronted with, in order for me to be entitled to assert that I see a dog?'.

Thus posing our question in terms of being given instead of seeing, or perceiving in general, we achieve quite a number of positive results. Leaving aside the historical gain of bringing about full harmony with Kant's basic but frequently overlooked distinction between an object's being given and its being perceived,[88] from a systematic point of view we thus gain at least two assets, the first of which will become clear in the remainder of the present section, whereas the second one will be made use of in extending the analysis to other kinds of conscious experiences besides seeing, and perceiving in general (see section 3.9, below). For suppose the wording of our question were, not: 'What is it that I must *be given* in order to be entitled to assert that I see a dog?', but: 'What is it that I must *see*, or otherwise *perceive*, in order to be entitled to assert that I see a dog?'. In this case, we couldn't help replying: 'A dog.', i.e., 'What I must *see*, in order to be entitled to assert that I see a dog, is a dog.'. To be sure, this answer is doubtless correct; for as we found out in section 3.8.4, the purely schematic alternative to this answer, scil., that I have to see, or otherwise perceive, that *I see* a dog, would be neither warranted nor acceptable. Nonetheless, that correct answer would be of no help

---

[83] Ibid.

[84] Cf., however, sects. 3.12–3.14, below.

[85] As opposed to Kant's term 'Phänomen'; for the important difference, see esp. Prauss 1971: § 1 (and *passim*); Hoche 2007: sect. 7.2 with fn. 20; Essay V: 1.8.2 with fn. 35, below.

[86] See sects. 3.10–3.11, below.

[87] See, e.g., Moore 1913–1914, 1918, 1953: ch. II.

[88] See esp. Prauss 1971: § 2.

whatsoever in our present enterprise, namely, in searching for an answer to the question 'What is my seeing a dog?'. For if we were inconsiderate enough to try to do justice to verificationism, or to Husserl's watchword of going back to the 'things themselves' with the help of the relevant sort of 'seeing', by stipulating that my seeing a dog is precisely that which I have to *see*, or otherwise *perceive*, in order to have a sufficient reason for asserting that I see a dog, then we would be left with identifying my seeing a dog with a dog, to wit, with the dog I see. This, however, would be unacceptable for at least two obvious reasons. First, we are doubtless unwilling to identify my seeing a dog with a dog, i.e., with an animal out in the real world; and second, whereas the dog I see right now and the dog I saw a moment ago can and must, under appropriate circumstances, be taken to be one and the same thing (animal, or physical object), we are certainly not prepared to consider my seeing a dog at the present moment and my seeing a dog – either a different or the selfsame one – a moment ago to be identical.

For all that, however, we need not, and should not, unconditionally give up the attempt to answer our leading question – 'What is my seeing a dog?' – in terms of the empiricists' notion of 'verification' or of Husserl's generalised concept of 'seeing'. Rather, what we ought to do is to suitably adapt, or to adjust, the remarkable philosophical potential of these ideas to the case of my own conscious experience, which does not admit of criteria of verification, nor of being perceived in the usual sense of the word (which we would be well advised not to blur). I am speaking, of course, of the substitution just mentioned, scil., of substituting, for the terms 'seeing' or 'perceiving', the term 'being given'. If we carry out this substitution, our leading question turns into the question: 'What is it that I must *be given* in order to be entitled to assert that I see a dog?'. To *this* question, however, we have to give some such answer as this: 'A dog *in its capacity of* being seen by me at the moment.', or, *in precisely this sense*, 'A dog in its specific way of being visually given to me right now.', or: 'A dog in, or with, its specific subjective mode of now visually appearing to me.'.

Nobody, I take it, will be seriously tempted to identify a dog in, or with, its momentary mode of subjectively appearing to me, or a subjectively appearing dog *as such*, i.e., *as subjectively appearing to me right now in such-and-such a way*, with a real dog, which is an inhabitant of the physical world. Again, although under appropriate circumstances we can and must say that a dog I see at time t_1 is identical with a dog I see at time t_2, nobody, I take it, is inclined to say that a dog *qua* being seen by me at t_1 may be identical with a dog *qua* being seen by me at t_2. For if we remember that we are wont to identify a physical object A with a physical object B if and only if the continua of their modes of being given meet specific conditions all of us are intimately acquainted with from our earliest childhood,[89]

---

[89] For some details, see the following Essay V: 2.2.3, of the present collection.

then we cannot but recognise that the possibility of identifying a physical object (say, a dog) A with a physical object B is an immediate consequence of, and thus dependent on, the fact that A and B are given to me in more or less changing modes of subjective appearance. But a physical object in, or with, its transient mode of subjectively appearing to me (say, a dog *as*, or *qua*, now being seen by me in such-and-such a way) is never given to me in higher-order modes of appearance, and so there is simply no legitimate basis for identifying, say, a dog *qua* being seen by me at t_1 with a dog *qua* being seen by me at t_2.

Remembering now what we observed above, namely, that also my seeing a dog at t_1 is never considered to be identical with my seeing a dog at t_2, we can easily realise that also the second, and chief, obstacle which prevented us from identifying my now seeing a dog with the dog (which is) now being seen by me is not in the way to identifying the former with the dog *qua* now being seen by me, or the dog in its subjective mode of visually appearing to me right now. By making this latter identification, we stick to the basic and sound idea of verificationism, and also to the basic and sound idea of Husserl's admonition to go back to the 'things themselves' by means of the relevant sorts of 'originarily giving consciousness', without being involved in absurdities. If, in the spirit of doing philosophy in a well-founded way, we replace our leading question, scil., 'What is my seeing a dog?', with the question: 'What is it that I must be given in order to be entitled to assert that I see a dog?', and if to the latter question we have to reply: 'A dog *in its capacity of* (now) being seen by me.', or: 'A dog in, or with, its specific subjective mode of visually appearing to me at the given moment.', then these answers are also appropriate to the former question. So a cogent reason for identifying my (now) seeing a dog with the dog *qua* (now) being seen by me – or the dog in is mode of (now) visually appearing to me – seems to me to have been established in a consistent as well as convincing manner.[90]

3.9. An extension and methodological interpretation of the analysis

The fecundity of our having replaced, in section 3.8.5, the squarely verificationist question 'What exactly is it that I must *see*, or otherwise *perceive*, in order to be justified in asserting that I now see a dog?' by the more appropriate question 'What exactly is it that I must *be given* in order to be justified in asserting that I now see a dog?' may be appreciated once more when we now try and extend our

---

[90] This identification of my (visually) perceiving an object with the object as (*qua*) being (visually) perceived by me cannot but remind the informed reader of Max Velmans's identifying our perceiving an object, or the 'percept of an object', with what he calls the 'object perceived' ('object as perceived', 'object-as-perceived'). However, I have taken pains to show that what Velmans has in mind is something quite different from what I just tried to work out in sections 3.7–3.8: see sects. 1.1–1.2, above, Essay V of the present collection, and Hoche 2007: esp. sects. 2, 6–8.

analysis to sorts of my own conscious experience other than seeing, or perceiving in general.

3.9.1.   Take, for instance, my now – visually – *remembering*, or calling back to my mind, something that happened some time ago. Obviously it would be quite futile to ask: 'What exactly is it that I must *perceive* in order to be justified in asserting that I am just calling back to my mind what happened on this or that occasion?'. For my present remembrance does not in the least require my presently perceiving anything.[91] But now let us again replace the squarely verificationist question with the improved version: 'What exactly is it that I must *be given* in order to be justified in asserting that I now (visually) remember, say, the squirrel that plundered the hazel this morning?'. To this question – and hence to the question: 'What is my now (visually) remembering the squirrel that plundered the hazel this morning?' – we have to reply: 'The squirrel *in its capacity of having been seen by me* when it plundered the hazel this morning'.

Let me add incidentally that this agrees well with the linguistic fact that we would hardly speak of *remembering* an animal or a human being that we believe to be still alive – *unless*, and this *proviso* is of the utmost importance to the issue at hand, what we have in mind is the animal or the human being *in its [her; his] capacity of having been perceived by me on a certain occasion*. The same holds true, of course, of any material object whatsoever. If I say, for instance, that I can remember the house in which I spent my early childhood, either what I have in mind – i.e., what I say I am able to call back to my mind – is that house *as it used to appear to me at that time*, or else I take it for granted that the house in question does not exist any longer. For if I believe that it still exists, I would either say that I can *remember* (call back to my mind) that house – in which case I am thinking of *the house in the particular way it once, or usually, looked to me in my childhood* – or else that I can *conceive*, or *imagine* (form in my mind) that house – and then I am thinking of that house in an unspecified way, i.e., without relating it to any particular time and perspective of appearance, or of that house as it may look from any arbitrary point of view and at any arbitrary moment in time, say, right now.

If this is true, then remembering a material object always amounts to remembering *that object in its capacity of having been perceived by me on a particular occasion*, or, as we would not hesitate to say instead, to remembering *my having perceived that object on a particular occasion*. In order to convince ourselves of the legitimacy of this interchange, we ought to make use of the method of 'pragmatico-semantical combination tests' (or 'assenting tests') in general and of the

---

[91] Of course, in a great many cases – although certainly not in every case – it requires my *having* seen, or heard, etc., something *in the past*; but this is of no relevance to our present issue.

definition of 'semantic implication' in particular.[92] According to the testimony of my personal imaginative and idiolectal competence, to which the reader may or may not subscribe,[93] the modalized combination 'It is (counterfactually) possible that I remember the squirrel *qua* having been seen by me this morning but that I don't remember my having seen the squirrel this morning.' is certainly false, and so is the statement with the relevant clauses interchanged. From this we have to conclude that the two clauses 'I remember the squirrel *qua* having been seen by me this morning.' and 'I remember my having seen the squirrel this morning.' semantically imply each other, and thus are semantically equivalent. But note that from this it does *not yet* follow that the two phrases 'the squirrel *qua* having been seen by me this morning' and 'my having seen the squirrel this morning' are semantically equivalent, *too*. For the method of pragmatico-semantical combination tests does not suffice by itself to enable us to define a relation of semantic equivalence that may be also applied to phrases below the level of whole propositions (in the sense of completely interpreted sentences of ordinary language). So we cannot take advantage of that method for producing an *additional* argument in favour of my suggestion to interpret, for instance, my now seeing the dog as being nothing but the dog *in its capacity of* now being seen by me, or my now – visually – remembering the squirrel that plundered the hazel in the morning as being nothing but the squirrel *in its capacity of* having been seen by me when it plundered the hazel in the morning, or my now – visually – imagining (or visualising) a unicorn as being nothing but a unicorn *in its capacity of* being possibly seen by me or, to be more precise, being seen by me within the framework of a fictional (quasi-)world.[94]

To the latter three examples we may add, of course, the interpretation of (say) my *acoustically* perceiving (remembering; imagining) something as being nothing but the given object or quasi-object *in its capacity of* being *heard* (having been *heard*, being possibly *heard*) by myself. Furthermore, in view of what I outlined in section 3.6.7, above, we may, I take it, go as far as interpreting my now being afraid of the dog which is approaching me as being nothing but the dog *qua presenting to myself, inter alia, the emotional feature of being dangerous*, and even my running away from it as being nothing but the dog *qua presenting to myself, inter alia, the practical, 'imperative', or 'gerundive' feature of being something to be fled*.

3.9.2.   In order to call a spade a spade, let me add that any such *interpretation* of items of my own consciousness (including my own actions) – in so far as they are accessible from my own first-person perspective – *as being nothing but*

---

[92] See fn. 27, above, and Essays I and II of the present collection.

[93] See fn. 28, above.

[94] By a fictional world I suggest to understand a *fictionally*, as opposed to a *counterfactually*, possible world. For details, see Hoche 1990: ch. 9, and sect. 2.3.5, above.

(quasi-)objects *in their capacity of* presenting themselves to me in specific ways may be regarded as sort of *identification* of the former with the latter. However, in thus advocating some form of an 'identity theory' – though clearly not a 'mind-brain identity theory' but rather what, in default of a better term, might be called a 'noesis-noema identity theory'[95] – I do not mean to say that here, just as in other, more familiar cases of identifying something with something or someone with someone, we have an object *a* which is given to us in *one* mode and an object *b* which is given to us in *another* mode such that, on the strength of a well-entrenched criterion of identity,[96] we nonetheless can (and must) identify *a* to *b*, and *vice versa*. Rather, the noesis-noema identity theory I wish to defend may be compared to what Rorty called the '*disappearance* form' of the mind-brain identity theory.[97] 'It would seem that the verb in such statements as "Zeus's thunderbolts are discharges of static electricity" and "Demonical possession is a form of hallucinatory psychosis" is the "is" of identity, yet it can hardly express *strict* identity. The disappearance form of the Identity Theory suggests that we view such statements as elliptical for e.g. "What people used to call 'demonical possession' is a form of hallucinatory psychosis", where the relation in question *is* strict identity.'[98] Similarly, according to Rorty's suggestion we are supposed to analyse such identity-theoretical propositions as 'Sensations are identical with certain brain processes.' as 'What people now call "sensations" are identical with certain brain processes.'.[99] Analogously, I should like to suggest that, say, 'My now seeing the dog is nothing but the dog *in its capacity of* now being seen by me.' should be paraphrased or restated[100] as 'What philosophers and psychologists use to call (the 'noetic' act of) my now seeing the dog is (identical with; nothing but) the dog *in its capacity of* now being seen by me.'. Let me finally add that strict identity-statements of this kind can be considered to be explications (i.e., explicative definitions) of the multifarious specific segments of my own conscious life insofar as it is being experienced by myself, or accessible from my own first-person perspective.

---

[95] See sect. 3.8.1, above, and sects. 3.10–3.11, below.

[96] In my view, such a criterion can never be of a universal validity; rather, it is always valid for all and only the objects of a specific 'category'; see the preceding Essay III: esp. sects. 6–7.

[97] Rorty 1965: esp. sect. II. This 'disappearance form' has been argued for by, e.g., Paul Feyerabend, Wilfrid Sellars, and Richard Rorty himself (cf. ibid.: 189, fn. 5).

[98] Ibid.: 190; Rorty's italics.

[99] Ibid. – By suggesting this analysis, Rorty aims at 'avoiding the charge of "category-mistake"', which can be directed against all 'cross-category' identifications, without being entangled in the notorious problems of what has been called 'topic-neutrality': ibid. This motivation is, I take it, not relevant to my adopting Rorty's strategy.

[100] Note, however, that 'no philosophical argument can lead to the conclusion that an expression must be banished from the language': Passmore 1961: 192 (cf. 190–192).

3.10. Why Husserl's 'noematic' conception of consciousness should be substituted for the traditional 'noetic' interpretation

Following Husserl (1913, and subsequent writings), henceforth I shall refer to this kind of interpretation as the *'noematic'* conception of consciousness.[101] It is true that Husserl himself (from 1907 on, and at least prior to 1934–1937) advocated a dual-aspect conception of conscious experience, allowing of a 'noetic' aspect alongside the 'noematic' one. As we could see in sects. 3.2 and 3.4, above, this may seem obvious enough. Whenever, in virtue of a visual perception, I can truthfully say that *there is a dog* in my neighbourhood, I can truthfully say two more things: first, that *I see a dog*, and second, that *I see a dog in, or with, its particular mode of appearing or being visually given to me right now*. So whenever I see a dog it seems only too natural to say that I am aware of the dog, aware of my seeing the dog, and aware of the dog's particular way of appearing or being given to me (i. e., the dog *qua* being seen by me at the very moment). Hence it is not surprising that Husserl for a very long time took it for granted that I could be interested in three different things: either in the dog itself, or else in my now seeing the dog, or else in the dog *qua* now being seen by me in such-and-such a way; and that, accordingly, in Husserl's opinion there were three different attitudes I have to adopt in turn if I intend to do justice to, or satisfy, each of these interests: first, the 'straightforward attitude' of everyday life, in which I am immediately absorbed in, or smitten with, the dog itself; second, the 'noetic reflection' in the sense of that deflection from the straightforward attitude in which I focus on what Husserl called a 'noesis'[102] such as my now seeing the dog; and, third, the 'noematic reflection' as a second kind of deflection from the straightforward attitude, namely, that one in which I attend to what Husserl called a 'noema', or 'noematic phenomenon',[103] such as the dog *qua* now being seen by me in such-and-such a manner.

Now, as far as this terminology is concerned, Husserl's Greek-based 'noesis'/ 'noema' distinction is, I think, neither linguistically convincing nor suggestive. So for explanatory purposes it may be useful to remember an equivalent predecessor terminology dating back to Husserl 1907, scil., the Latin-based distinction between

---

[101] In view of Ryle 1932, 1949, and 1962, and of Wittgenstein's considerations concerning the problem of a private language (1953: esp. §§ 154, 202, 243, 246f., 253, 256, 258–261, 271f., 293, 304–308, 580, and passim; cf. Kripke 1982) some readers might wonder how we can speak about noematic phenomena in our common language. I discussed this question in Hoche 1979a, though in this paper (see esp. sects. 2.4–2.8) I still failed to pay attention to the difference between a C-object and an M-object. More felicitously, I think, I dealt with the problem in Hoche & Strube 1985: A.VI.2, the upshot being that, in the respects relevant to the present question, noematic phenomena do not differ from subjective experiences in the sense which even Wittgenstein and Ryle did not call into question (ibid.: p. 197).

[102] See, e.g., Husserl 1913, tr. 1931: sects. 87–96.

[103] Ibid.

'cogitatio' and 'cogitatum qua cogitatum', which may be suitably translated as 'conscious experience'[104] and 'what is consciously experienced *as such*, i.e., *as being consciously experienced* (by myself)'.

To the best of my knowledge, this 'cogitatum qua cogitatum', or 'noema', and the 'noematic reflection' as the appropriate manner of grasping it, had never been clearly noticed before; and I think it was an epoch-making idea of Husserl's to discern them from their 'noetic' counterparts. In fact, I think it is hardly an exaggeration to say that the significance of this distinction may be well compared to that of Kant's discerning between 'phenomena' ('Phänomene', or 'Erschein-ungen' in the 'transcendental' sense[105] of this ambiguous term) and 'things in themselves' ('Dinge an sich [selbst betrachtet]'). However, just as Kant did not succeed in completely getting rid of the latter, Husserl[106] did not realise that we are scarcely justified in clinging to noetic phenomena, and to noetic reflection, once noematic phenomena, and noematic reflection, have come into view. But let us note the following point of difference. We can easily see why it was an enormous philosophical progress to replace things as they might be (or might be viewed) 'in themselves', i.e., irrespective of our having cognitive access to them, with things considered as objects of human knowledge; for this amounts to doing philosophy, not any longer from an alleged, or hypothetical, divine point of view, but from the human point of view. But what on earth is the use of substituting the noematic view on consciousness for the noetic one? At first sight, the consequences seem indeed to be much less spectacular; but on closer inspection, things begin to look different.

For the notion of a noetic phenomenon, such as my now seeing the dog, is apt to arouse a picture which leads us astray,[107] namely, the picture of an inner world or stage,[108] and of enigmatic goings-on within myself to which I have access by means of an 'internal perception' such as 'introspection' or classical (i.e., noetic)

---

[104] Cf. Descartes 1641: sects. III.1, III.5. (Descartes' influence on Husserl may best be seen from Husserl 1929b.)

[105] Cf. sect. 3.8.5 with fn. 85, above.

[106] At least prior to 1934–1937; for a circumstantial discussion see Hoche 1973a: ch. I. – As this discussion of mine appears to have been widely neglected at least in Germany, it took me with some surprise to find, in Flew 1979: p. 146 (entry 'Husserl'), the statement that 'no distinction can be made between what is perceived and the perception of it'. If one takes this at face value, it seems to me to describe precisely the position of my '*purely noematic* phenomenology'; for in contradistinction to Velmans's use (see sects. 1.1–1.2 and fn. 90, above), in the statement quoted the words 'what is perceived' certainly cannot mean as much as 'the object (which is) perceived' but only something like 'the object *qua* being perceived (by myself at such-and-such a moment of time in such-and-such a way)'.

[107] Cf. Wittgenstein 1953: §§ 422–427.

[108] Cf. Ryle 1949: passim.

'reflection'. That this picture leads us wildly astray is testified, I think, by at least three conspicuous facts. First, this picture is likely to make us believe that an introspection, or a noetic reflection, being itself a noetic phenomenon, may again be subjected to introspection or noetic reflection; and in fact Husserl conceived of 'higher-order reflections'[109] (which, although they need not necessarily lead to a vicious regress, at any rate seem to me to lack any phenomenal evidence). Second, this picture arouses the tendency, betrayed by quite a number of recent philosophers, to doubt the very existence of subjectively experienced phenomena simply on the score of being unable to trace any such higher-order reflections.[110] And third, philosophers have frequently asked how an 'inner' phenomenon, such as my now seeing the dog, should ever be able to reach its intentional object 'outside', such as the animal in the external world. If, however, I conceive of my now seeing the dog as precisely the dog *qua* now being seen by me in such-and-such a way, I would, first, never feel invited to launch an iteration of the type 'the dog *qua* now being perceived by me *qua* now being perceived by me, etc. etc.'; nor would I, second, be taken aback by the fact that in being aware of the dog I am simultaneously, and without any introspective ado, aware that I see the dog; nor would I, third, find it difficult to understand the intimate relation between the dog *qua* now being seen by me and the dog itself. As for the first of these three cases, it would seem obvious that an object in, or with, its mode of subjective appearance cannot itself be given in this or that mode of subjective appearance, and that to expect an iteration of appearing would amount to committing a category-mistake in very much the Rylean sense. As for the second case, it would seem obvious that I am aware of the dog's being given to me in, or 'through', *some or other* mode of visual appearance, even if I do not heed the *particular* mode of appearing, and focus my interest on the dog itself. And as for the third case, it would seem obvious that the dog *qua* now being seen by me in a particular way is only one out of a strictly continuous multiplicity of possible modes of appearance in, or 'through', which the dog itself can be visually given to me.

3.11. For myself, my own – noematic – consciousness is *not* part of nature

So I propose to take Husserl's discovery of the noema seriously, but to go beyond him in treating what he called the *noesis* as kind of a Wittgensteinian 'ladder',[111] i.e., to throw it away after having used it for reaching the level of the *noema*. Consciousness then presents itself as *purely noematic*, and this in the following

---

[109] See, e.g., Husserl 1913, tr. 1931: sect. 77.

[110] Cf. the last but one paragraph of sect. 3.8.4, above.

[111] Cf. Wittgenstein 1922: 6.54.

way.[112] When I see a dog, the relevant conscious experience is to be regarded as the dog *in its capacity of* being seen by me at the given moment in the respective particular way, or, *in this very sense*, as the dog in, or with, its present mode of appearing, or being given, to me – or, generally speaking, as a *complete* noema, that is, as a noematic phenomenon *in its full concreteness*. This noematic phenomenon is but one out of a 'noematic multiplicity' or 'manifoldness',[113] i.e., out of a continuum of noematic phenomena which are related to each other in a specific way which allows me to interpret them as 'intentionally' referring to one and the same 'noematic unity', in this case the dog itself as the 'object pure and simple', which may be considered to be the ultimate noematic 'core' or 'nucleus'.[114] In the 'straightforward attitude' of everyday life, I am absorbed in, smitten with, or 'nuts about' (Husserl: 'verschossen in') the noematic object pure and simple (the noematic unity, core, or nucleus), to the total exclusion of attending to the continuous change of its transient modes of noematically appearing to me. So I think we may say that in this attitude we abstract from these modes, i.e., from the noematic multiplicity. Accordingly, I consider noematic reflection as a cancelling or suspension of this everyday abstraction, which has become our second nature, i.e., as an uphill attempt to take the noematic phenomenon in its full concreteness; and although such an attempt can certainly be made in different degrees of decidedness, it doubtless defies iteration. In principle – to wit, once I have acquired the necessary skill and practice – it is easy to switch to and fro between the straightforward attitude, centered on noematic unities, and the reflective attitude, attending to the noematic multiplicities. But it seems to me to be out of the question to *simultaneously* focus on a noematic unity and on a member of a noematic multiplicity, namely, a noematic phenomenon in its full concreteness. So I take it that the different fields of abstract noematic unities and of concrete noematic phenomena, excluding each other to the point of being well comparable to the 'incompatible observables' of quantum mechanics, define the concepts of objectivity[115] and subjectivity. From this it follows that I consider subjectivity in

---

[112] For further details, see Hoche 1973a: 'Einleitung' (pp. 15–38) and ch. II; 1982: sects. 2–2.3.3.2; 2007: *passim*; and the following Essay V: esp. sect. 1.7. – In translating Husserl's technical terms, again in most cases I shall follow Cairns 1973.

[113] See, esp., Husserl 1913, tr. 1931: §§ 88–91, 128–132.

[114] The just-mentioned modes of subjective appearance specifically relating to each other may be well compared to a bunch, or bundle, of rays or straight lines intersecting each other in one and the same point, which, for its part, would then correspond to the noematic core or nucleus, i.e., to the noematic unity or noematic object itself.

[115] It should be noted that my noematic unities or objects are *truly objective* or *intersubjective* entities. For in most cases I intentionally refer not to single noematic objects in separation from each other but to constellations of objects, or states of affairs. For instance, when I see a dog, more often than not I do not see the dog alone but, say, the dog barking at a cat which is afraid of it, or the dog playing with other dogs, or the dog being called back by its master, etc. Hence as a rule I interpret

the strictest sense of the word, i.e., my own conscious experience insofar as it is accessible to myself, to be different from all objects in the natural world to such a degree that we may downright call it 'the negative' of objective reality (see Hoche 1986). In this sense – which coincides with Husserl's to a certain extent but by no means completely – I cannot but *deny that consciousness is a part of nature*. In so saying I may seem, of course, to place myself in flagrant opposition to all serious contemporary philosophers, including even the most 'soft-line' exponents of non-reductive and non-physicalistic theories of consciousness.[116] But I trust that things will look much better as soon as I shall have laid hands on a second sacred cow of present-day philosophy.

3.12. The reality-implying uses of verbs of perception prevail over their
        sensation-centered uses

But before I will do so (in discussing, in section 3.15, below, the nature of *somebody else's* consciousness as seen from *my* point of view), let us round off what I have said so far about the nature of *my own* consciousness, and return to a topic which I touched upon without entering into details. In section 3.2, note 25, above, I mentioned some non-standard cases of 'seeing' something, such as having a hallucination, or having an illusion, or 'seeing' what a conjurer is only pretending to do, which attest to the fact that there are situations in which I am justified in saying that *I see* a dog without being justified in saying that *there is* a dog (in my visual field). The question is how to appropriately describe such well-known situations. For instance, if a conjurer succeeds in pretending that he is changing a rabbit into a dove, in all probability he does not literally make us *believe* that; but does he make us *see* it, or only *'see'* it? A moment ago, I decided in favour of the inverted commas version. But it should be noted that this version, say in the

---

a dog or any other noematic object of mine as being seen, heard, feared, acted upon, etc., not only by myself but by other human beings and animals as well.

[116] Velmans adduces a revealing reason why scientists researching into consciousness *empirically* are likely to find my denial that consciousness is a part of nature simply out of the question: 'Few contemporary students of consciousness would agree with [Hoche], as this would block its investigation by any natural means.' (Velmans 2007: 420). By the way, Velmans here seems to be playing on the ambiguity of the word 'natural', thus making my non-empirical ('noematic') method of researching into my own consciousness appear 'unnatural' also in the sense of being unsuitable for its purpose. No less revealing is the rationale Velmans ascribes to my position: 'Hoche's attempt to dismiss consciousness from nature based on a behaviourist understanding of other minds sounds very much like a lone voice from the past.' (ibid.: 421). Psychological behaviourism is in fact hopelessly obsolete; but my 'attempt to dismiss consciousness from nature' is, of course, *based on a noematic understanding of my own consciousness*. Nonetheless Velmans's mistake is illuminating; for ist shows once again that his – through and through non-behaviourist – position in psychology includes the view that, for myself, consciousness of my fellowmen is of essentially the same nature as my own consciousness.

sentence 'I "see" a dog.', is sometimes also used in the sense of 'I seem to see a dog.', which, for its part, may be taken to mean as much as 'I fancy I see a dog.', or 'I am visualising a dog.';[117] and obviously this use is not now intended. Rather, when I say that we do not *see*, but only *'see'*, the conjurer's 'transformation', I want to point to the linguistic fact that by and large we are wont to use phrases of the form 'to see an S' (i.e., 'to see something of sort S') only in situations in which there is an S – a real or genuine S – to be seen. If this were always true, however, the statement, say, 'I see a dog.' would entail the statement 'There is a dog (to be seen).', and this seems not to be the case. For as a rule I trust my eyes so firmly that I am prepared to say, e.g., that I can see the teacup on my desk without corroborating my present visual perception by means of succeeding visual perceptions, or tactile perceptions, or reported perceptions of other people present. However, in the few cases in which afterwards I find out that there really was no teacup to be seen on my desk (e.g., that I mistook something else for a teacup, or that I was deluded by a kind of 'Potëmkin' teacup, or by a mirror trick, etc.), I do not hesitate to admit that I did not really see a teacup but was only misled into thinking I saw one. So, although we spontaneously tend to say on the evidence of a single short glance that we see a certain thing, we are prepared to retract this statement as soon as, on the strength of richer or intersubjective evidence, we cannot but convince ourselves that we only erroneously believed that there was a thing of the appropriate sort in our visual field. Thus the reality-implying use of the verb 'to see' obviously prevails over its wider, sensation-centered (or inverted commas) use, and this agrees well with the fact that, from the standpoint of learning to master our common language, the former use is clearly the primary and the latter a derivative one. Before I have learned in what situations I am entitled to assert that somebody else *sees*, let us say, a (genuine) *dog*, I am not in a position to assert on solid grounds that somebody else only *'sees'* an (only seeming) *'dog'*. For asserting the latter, relatively complex, fact is plainly parasitic upon being able to make the former, relatively simple, statement. The same is true of my own 'seeing' a 'dog' in relation to my seeing a dog; but one minor difference should be noted. Whereas my assertion that somebody else only 'sees' a (seeming) 'dog' is logically and pragmatically compatible with the assertion that they – *mistakenly* – believe that there is a dog in their visual field, my (present tense) assertion that I myself only 'see' a (seeming) 'dog' pragmatically implies that I do not believe that there is a dog in my visual field.[118]

---

[117] Cf. Ryle 1949: sect. VIII.3.

[118] This pragmatic implication, which is a counterpart of 'Moore's paradox' and differs characteristically from semantic implication (entailment), may be shown in detail by applying pragmatico-semantical combination tests – or assenting tests – of the sort touched upon in fn. 27 and sect. 3.9.1, above, and elaborated in Essays I and II of the present collection.

3.13. The sensation-centered uses of verbs of pain prevail over their
       reality-implying, or etiological, uses

If it was correct to say, in the preceding section 3.12, that the reality-implying
use of the verb 'to see' prevails over its wider, sensation-centered (or inverted
commas) use, then by asserting, say, that I see a dog I usually make a statement,
not only about a conscious experience of mine, but at the same time about a piece
of objective reality. In this case, however, the statement 'I see a dog.' has a kind
of 'hypothetical' character in a sense used not only by Popper 1934 but also, in
the early thirties, by Wittgenstein.[119] If this is true, my seeing a dog admits of the
distinction between appearance and reality, and if so, I can meaningfully say that
I *seem* to see a dog in a sense which differs from the Rylean one just mentioned
in 3.12, scil., that it *seems* to me that I see a dog. Furthermore, in this case it
makes sense to talk of my *knowing that*, or *not knowing if*, I see a dog, and to
ask me *how I know* that I see a dog. Hence, if Wittgenstein was right to say, in the
early thirties, 'that "It seems to me that I have toothache" is nonsense', and 'that "I
don't know whether I have toothache" is always absurd or nonsense', and that 'the
question "How do you know that you have toothache?" is nonsensical',[120] then
an important correspondence between statements about my seeing something
and statements about my being in pain – a correspondence which may be taken
to point to the central feature of my own consciousness – seems to break down.

In fact, however, this supposed breakdown is only a seeming one. For there are
more parallels between seeing and being in pain than most philosophers hitherto
seem to have attended to. These parallels become obvious once we recognise
the ambiguity of such words as 'toothache', 'stomach-ache', or 'pain in my right
knee'. At least before naturalistic philosophers adopted the – by now outdated –
physiological theory of C-fibres firing, practically nobody doubted that he or she
alone was the only, or at least the final, authority on deciding whether or not he
or she had a pain, and a pain, ache, or twinge of the sort he or she felt. In fact,
it would be ridiculous to try and correct somebody else by saying 'You haven't
got a toothache; you are suffering from headaches.'. And yet it is obvious, though
frequently overlooked, that in an important way it is the medical expert who
often has the last word in these matters, namely, by finding out and instructing
her patient that he has not an aching stomach but, say, an aching pancreas or an
aching heart. So we have to distinguish between feeling a bodily pain and feeling
an aching, or hurting, organ; or between feeling a pain in a certain part of the body
and feeling a hurting organ in that part of the body. On the former, the painful
bodily sensation, the patient is the authority; but on the latter, the precise cause,
origin, and localisation of that painful sensation, certainly the medical expert is. In

---

[119] See Moore 1954–1955: esp. 261 f., 266.

[120] Ibid.: 307; cf. 261, 266.

other words, the problem of bodily pains has a sensational aspect, which requires a 'first-person' authority, and an etiological aspect, which requires a 'third-person' expert. Wittgenstein, in the passages quoted above, focussed exclusively on the sensational or first-person aspect, and this seems to me to be natural enough; for, as far as I can see, the sensational, or sensation-centered, use of the terms of pain prevails against their etiological, or reality-implying, use. As I tried to show in section 3.12, above, the reverse is true of the terms of seeing – and, we can safely add, of perceiving in general. This is a linguistic fact which, once it is stated, permits of a simple explanation. Expertness in judging whether an object supposedly perceived is a real or only a specious one is easier to obtain and at the same time more important for surviving, and hence arising in an earlier stage of biological and cultural development, than expertness in the aetiology of pains. So it is not surprising that, despite the indubitable first-person or subjective character of one's own perceiving, feeling a pain, and having any other kind of conscious experience, the additional third-person or objective aspect is far more conspicuous in the cases of one's own perception than in those of one's own bodily sensations. But this difference arises on the basis of fundamental parallels, to wit, the parallel between feeling *a pain* and seeing *something*, on the one side, and the parallel between feeling *a hurting organ* and perceiving *a real object*, on the other. Therefore, on the one hand one may feel inclined to talk about perceiving – say, seeing – in just the manner Wittgenstein talked about pains, namely, to assert that it is nonsense to say such things as 'It seems to me that I see a dog.', 'I know [= have learnt; have discovered; have found out; etc.] that I see a dog.', 'I don't know if I see a dog.', 'How do you know [= how did you find out, or discover, etc.] that you see a dog?' – although, near the beginning of the present section, we could convince ourselves that at least very often it makes a perfectly good sense to say so. On the other hand, by now we should also recognise that it may be perfectly meaningful (although, of course, not always perfectly tactful) to say about pains what Wittgenstein declared to be nonsensical, for instance, to ask somebody – say, the victim of a car-accident who has just regained consciousness after an amputation and is suffering from a phantom-pain – 'How do you know [or: are you really sure] that you have a pain in your knee?'. So in cases of feeling pains as well as in cases of seeing, or perceiving in general, it depends on the given point of view, which in spoken language is normally made clear by emphasis and intonation, whether or not we find a string of words nonsensical. Asking, for instance, 'How do you know that you see a *wolf*?', or 'How do you know that you have an ache in your *stomach*?' may be very often meaningful, whereas asking 'How do you know that you *see* a wolf?', or 'How do you know that you have an *ache* in your stomach?' as a rule seems to be nonsensical. (An exception present those few cases in which a purely terminological question is being discussed, say, the question of whether 'ache' or 'smart' is the more appropriate word in the case at hand.)

I think that these results may be carefully generalised. Prior to a piecemeal examination, we may certainly and safely suppose that all conscious experiences of mine which have to do with objective reality – in the more precise sense of 'intentionally aiming' at something which belongs to the real world[121] – show the dual-aspect character just indicated. They certainly have a subjective aspect, or can be seen in a subjective perspective, that is due to the given *kind* of conscious experience. But they also have an objective aspect, or can be seen in an objective perspective, that is due to the given *intentional object* in question.[122]

3.14. All conscious experiences having to do with objective reality are neither purely private, or first-person, nor purely public, or third-person, affairs

In a way, a certain duality between the intentional *kind* and the intentional *object* is to be found in *all* of my intentional conscious experiences, that is to say, even in those which are intentionally directed to something which is *not* part of the real world, say, in instances of imagining or conceiving in the pure and absolute sense which is relevant to philosophical and literary theories of fiction.[123] In these cases, however, the third-person expert is out of place, and saying such things as 'It seems to me that I am just imagining a pink elephant.' or 'How do you know that you are imagining, not a lilac mammoth, but a pink elephant?' seems to me to be always nonsensical, even if we should advocate the intricate position that members of natural kinds, taken *as such*, can never be made the object of a pure or absolute imagination.[124] Still more difficult are some problems connected with dreaming in the primary, strictly first-person, or 'non-REM' sense of the word.[125] At first sight it seems to be nonsense to say such things as 'It only seems [or: seemed?] to me that tonight I was dreaming of Morgan le Fay [or: of my mother; etc.].'. If we remember, though, the writings of Freud and others, our initial conviction that here there is no room for a third-person expert may very soon be shaken.

But leaving such questions aside, and returning to clear-cut cases of conscious experiences of mine in (or through) which I intentionally refer to, or 'aim' at,

---

[121] See sect 2.3.5, above.

[122] This duality has been worked out in detail by Husserl, who distinguished, within the complete or concrete 'noematic phenomenon', between the 'intentional quality' or 'positional characteristic', on the one side, and the 'objective' or 'noematic sense', on the other. For sources and details, see Hoche 1973a: § 2; 1982: sects. 2–2.3.3.2. The analogy between this consciousness theoretical distinction and the speech-act theoretical distinction between 'illocutionary force' and 'propositional content' may perhaps best be seen from Searle 1983.

[123] See sect 2.3.5, above.

[124] For related problems, see Hoche 1990: sect. 10.7. Cf. also Kripke 1972: 763–765, Addendum (a).

[125] See again sect 2.3.5, above.

objects in the real world out there, we can safely say that the duality between the first-person authority and the third-person authority is indubitable. Take, in addition to the cases of perceiving and feeling a bodily sensation, which we already discussed in detail, cases from the most conspicuous class of my own actions, namely, actions in (or through) which I intend to change something real. At first sight it may seem as if it makes no sense at all to speak of my being in doubt whether, or my finding out that, I am splitting logs, or drinking a cup of tea, or kissing my wife, or stealing a book from the library, etc. But if we remember that, according to Popper,[126] not only universal 'all'-statements but even such particular statements as 'Here is a glass of water.' defy strict verification; or that, as has been shown in science-fiction movies, it is logically possible (or, as I think is preferable to say: purely conceivable) that extraterrestrial aliens, unbeknownst to the respective husbands, have replaced wives with exactly similar and highly refined robots – then we cannot help seeing that, in principle, even in such everyday cases the first-person authority is not enough. However, in many, if not all, cases it is needed; that is, the third-person authority does not suffice, either. This is easily seen in such cases as stealing something. For an action does not count as stealing unless it is done from a certain motive, particularly with a certain intention, and the access to intentions and other motives is, at least *in practice*, mostly a matter of the first-person view. But the same seems to me to be true of all the other examples of action just mentioned. For the overt bodily movements of him who is splitting logs, or drinking a cup of tea, or kissing his wife, do not count as actions thus named, and not even as actions at all, if the person alleged to be acting is not fully aware of them (as may be the case in sleepwalking), and hence can be held responsible for them.[127] What I just said of 'bodily' actions holds true also with regard to 'linguistic' actions, that is, speech acts. Indeed it seems to be common knowledge among contemporary linguists, literary theorists, and philosophers of language that neither the speaker (or writer) alone nor the hearer (or reader) alone is in a position to finally settle all questions of the precise illocutionary force and the exact propositional meaning of a given speech act. Furthermore, at least in principle every human action whatsoever admits of some true description which cannot be known by the actor himself because it can be coined only in historical hindsight, famous examples being Petrarch's climbing Mont Ventoux on April 26, 1336 (or giving birth to Renaissance), and the Sarajewo assassination of the Austrian Archduke Francis Ferdinand (or 'triggering' World War I). So I think we may conclude with some confidence that all human actions and other instances of consciousness, provided that they intentionally 'aim' at some objective reality, are neither purely private, or first-person, nor purely public, or third-person, affairs,

---

[126] Cf. esp. Popper 1934, tr. 1959: sect. 25.

[127] Think of the speech-act criterion of human action suggested in sect. 2.3.2, above.

and that they have, though being a person's subjective experiences, to stand the test of intersubjectivity.

3.15. For myself, the consciousness of others *is* part of nature.
       'Semi-behaviourism'

Let me take up this cue and turn to the problems of *somebody else's* consciousness, the discussion of which I had postponed so far. By applying myself to this task, I return to the 'second sacred cow' alluded to at the end of section 3.11, above. What I am having in mind is the ingrained prejudice that, for myself as well as for anybody else, my own consciousness and the consciousness of others must needs be of essentially the same nature, and is, in this sense, something 'objective' and existing 'in itself'. In passing, I tried already to do away with this prejudice and to suggest that *my own conscious experiences* and the *conscious experiences of others* are not fish from the same kettle; for in a number of my preceding remarks (see sects. 2.3.2, 3.5, and 3.8.3, above) I advocated the position that, from *my* point of view, the conscious experiences of *others* do not admit of a noematic interpretation but rather should be considered to be nothing but stretches of relevant situated behaviour, linguistic as well as non-linguistic. For short, I will dub this position 'semi-behaviourism'. It should be noted, however, that by this terminological allusion to a well-known though by now doubtless obsolete psychological theory of the first half of the 20th century I do not in the least commit myself to any of the opinions advocated by J. B. Watson, B. F. Skinner, or their followers in both psychology and philosophy.[128]

---

[128] The importance of this proviso can be seen from the following objection raised by Velmans (2007: 421), which in the light of what I just said is irrelevant: 'Given behaviourism's traditional opposition to incorporating conscious phenomenology into psychological science, or even admitting to its existence, Hoche's transcendental phenomenology and his "semi-behaviourism" make strange bedfellows.'. I do appreciate the brilliance of these words, but I find them irrelevant in still another respect: Though my transcendental phenomenology and my "semi-behaviourism" may indeed be called 'bedfellows', *noematic consciousness* and *behaviour* certainly may *not*; for bedfellows are of necessity two (or possibly more) of them, whereas my own noematic consciousness as it is experienced by myself is not numerically different (nor, of course, numerically identical) to the behaviour of others I can perceive and observe. Rather, as will soon become clear in what follows, 'they' – here we almost inevitably fall victims to one of the proverbial 'pitfalls' of our ingrained linguistic habits – are what I call 'categorially different': see the preceding Essay III: sect. 9, and sect. 3.17, below. Understandably enough, this conception is not familiar to, and probably hard to be grasped by, a typical exponent of psychology, even a philosophically highly ambitious one. This is remarkably true of Velmans, who stubbornly adheres to 'things themselves' in the sense of 'a reality lying behind phenomenal appearances' (ibid.: 420) *without even the trace of an attempt to ontologically challenge this naïve concept* and hence expectedly cannot help missing the concept of complementarity proper, anthropological or otherwise.

3.15.1. The reasons why I think I ought to defend, if only in this strictly limited version, sort of a behaviourist 'nothing-buttery' are easily stated. First, nowadays very few people are prepared to admit that we have immediate access to another person's subjective conscious experiences (be it via 'introjection' or 'empathy', be it via Husserl's 'appresentation' or 'analogising apperception' – not to mention the obsolete 'argument from analogy').[129] Second, as we should have learned from Frege, Waismann, and Wittgenstein,[130] it does not even make sense to say that somebody else has, or *probably* has, or *possibly* has, or possibly has *not*, conscious experiences similar to my own, from which it follows that all traditional and modern 'inverted spectrum' speculations, and even recent reasoning about 'inverted', 'absent', 'fading', and 'dancing qualia',[131] lack a sound foundation.[132] Third, which is but a corollary, the attribution of consciousness, *in the sense of subjective experiences*, to other people and higher animals is neither verifiable nor falsifiable; hence it is not even open to purely empirical hypotheses and, thus, to an assessment of 'probability'. And fourth, as we speak about ourselves and our fellow-men in strictly the same interpersonal terminology of 'psychological' (or 'psychical') verbs and hence are definitely disinclined to flatly *deny* the existence of 'other minds', the best option which I think we have is identifying somebody else's perceiving, sensing, feeling, wanting, intending, acting, and the like, with precisely that stretches of their situated verbal or non-verbal behaviour on the strength of whose observation all of us are *in point of fact wont* to assert, and for this very reason have an *inalienable right* to assert,[133] that they are perceiving, sensing, feeling, wanting, or intending something, or acting in such-and-such a way, and so forth.

3.15.2. A first standard objection against this identification consists in pointing out that, whenever we say, for instance, that somebody else has a headache, feels glad about a gift, or intends to see a movie tonight, we certainly do not want to say that they display a headache behaviour, or behave like they feel (or even: as if they felt) glad about a gift, or show all outward signs of intending to see a movie tonight. This is all perfectly true, of course, and should go without saying. And it is even true that sometimes we are quite sure that somebody else is suffering from a headache while displaying not the slightest trace of a verbal or non-verbal headache behaviour, or, on the contrary, that somebody else only pretends to have a headache. But in such cases, too, we have nothing to rely upon except this person's non-verbal or verbal behaviour. So, whether we speak about someone else's having a headache, or feeling glad, and so on, or whether we speak about

---

[129] For trenchant criticisms, see esp. Carnap 1932–1933: sect. 4.B (pp. 118–120); Malcolm 1958.

[130] See sect. 3.4.6 with note 44, above.

[131] Cf. Chalmers 1996: ch. 7.

[132] See sect. 3.19 with note 160, below, and Hoche 1990: sects. 3.6, 7.2–7.3; cf. also sect. 3.15.5, below.

[133] Cf. sect. 3.8.5 with note 80, above.

this person's behaving *as if* he or she had a headache, or felt glad, and so on, what gives us the epistemological or rather the speech-act theoretical[134] right to make such an assertion is invariably the perception of this person's behaviour, the main differences consisting in a gradation of carefulness and expertness of observation and the taking into account of either shorter or longer stretches of behaviour, the latter of which in extreme cases may last throughout the person's life. In fact, sometimes we are definitely and forever unable to decide whether somebody else is behaving sincerely or only pretending. An excellent example of this can be found in Louis Buñuel's film *L'objet obscur du désir*, the protagonist of which has been brought to the verge of endlessly oscillating between believing and disbelieving in a young woman's love for him.

3.15.3.   Perhaps experiences like these lie at the root of our indubitable inclination to identify the conscious experiences of others, not with their outwardly perceivable behaviour ('macro-behaviour'), but with goings-on in their central nervous systems, which, at least in principle, can be observed by physiologists and other scientists ('micro-behaviour'). I do not want to find fault with this inclination, which conforms well with the spirit of present-day science and is apt to give rise to fertile research projects. Furthermore, whereas at present scientists still have to lean on rather gross brain imaging techniques such as positron emission tomography (PET) or magnetic resonance imaging (MRI), in the nearer or farther future it may be well possible to correlate stretches of 'macro-' and 'micro-behaviour' to each other with increasing precision, and perhaps so much so that stretches of outward behaviour scattered over a whole lifetime could be associated with brain processes taking place during a definite temporal span. Hence I think it possible that some fine day this 'neurobiological' position may successfully compete with my 'semi-behaviouristic' one, without, however, having to call into question what I consider my basic tenet, to wit, that there is an ontological difference between my own consciousness and that of others. But today it would be premature to adopt 'neurobiologism', i. e., to identify conscious experiences of one's fellow-men with observable occurrences in their central nervous systems. Not just *premature*, however, but principally *misguided* seems to me to be the widespread tendency, to be found on the part of those who simply refuse to see or to acknowledge the essential differences between my own conscious experiences and the conscious experiences of others, to extend such 'mind-brain identity theories' to one's own consciousness, too.

3.15.4.   Recently, Friedrich Dudda claimed that 'semi-behaviourism' of the type I am inclined to advocate can be reduced to absurdity, and therefore found it preferable to count statements about conscious experiences of others, not among

---

[134] Cf. Hoche 1990: sect. 7.4.

observation-statements, but among purely 'theoretical propositions' (2006: 5.2.1). However, I take it that his efforts to substantiate this claim suffer from making light of the important difference between shorter and longer stretches of actually perceived (or observed) overt behaviour which I mentioned in subsection 3.15.2, above. I think this is due to his silently presupposing that someone's propositions about *conscious experiences* of others and someone's related propositions about their relevant *behaviour* must needs refer to precisely the same spans of time. Now at first sight this presupposition looks plausible, indeed. Nonetheless, it seems to me to be far from being a matter of course. Suppose, for instance, that I think or say that someone has recognised me on a certain occasion without at that moment showing even the slightest trace of having done so. Then of course I think or say so solely on the ground of his subsequent behaviour towards myself or others with whom I communicate, and 'subsequent' here means as much as, say, 'after an arbitrary, shorter or longer, lapse of time'. From this we may infer that I take it for granted that the 'success' of someone else's having recognised me on a given occasion is followed by a lasting 'post-success' disposition to behave in certain ways dependent on certain situations.[135] Hence it seems to me to be questionable and highly difficult to decide whether, when I say, for instance, that Jones has recognised me last night, what I primarily have in mind is his 'success' at, say, 11:30:57 p.m. last night or rather his permanent 'post-success' disposition which had its origin at that moment in time.[136] I think what I just said can be cautiously generalised. Hence Dudda's attempt to reduce my 'semi-behaviourism' to absurdity must at any case be heavily refined, and I hope he will take first steps in this direction himself before publishing his book on 'The Language of Subjectivity'. So let me say that as yet at least he didn't succeed in showing my position to be untenable. Nevertheless his idea of considering conscious experiences of others to be but theoretical constructs might be interesting – provided he can bestow a truly satisfying sense upon the concept of assigning theoretical constructs of this sort a temporal position in objective space-time. Furthermore, Dudda (2006: 7.1.6) tried to show that his interpretation of conscious experiences of others as theoretical constructs prevails over my semi-behaviouristic position in point of *prognostic relevance* or *fecundity*. So far, I cannot find his arguments really convincing, either; but at least he must be credited with having raised this interesting methodological question. It ought to be noted, though, that even if it should turn out to be possible to substantiate Dudda's suggestions, this would be detrimental solely to my 'semi-behaviourism' (to which I don't cling), but not at all to my much more basic and

---

[135] The well-known concept of 'success verbs' dates back to Ryle 1949. For the much less well-known concept of 'post-success verbs', see Hoche 1973a: §§ 36–38, esp. pp. 315–319.

[136] Possibly, a first answer may in part depend on whether we say 'Jones *has* recognised me.' or simply 'Jones recognised me.'. But to confirm or reject this linguistic hypothesis I must leave, of course, to native speakers of current English.

consequential claim that *my own conscious experiences* and the *conscious experiences of others* are two very different kettles of fish, and that they have no relation to each other besides being 'categorially different', 'incompatible entities' (given Dudda's interpretation, the technical term 'incompatible *observables*' would, of course, be entirely out of place), and 'complementary' – to all of which Dudda seems to fully subscribe. But for the time being, let me stick to my 'semi-behaviouristic' position, for which I think I can adduce three more reasons which seem to me to have some weight. First, my option well accords with the parsimony principle of 'Ockham's Razor'. Second, identifying, from *my* point of view, the conscious experiences of *others* with their overt behaviour is another application of the methodological principle discussed and applied already in section 3.8.5, above, for instance, a replacement of the question 'What, as seen from *my* point of view, is *your* being scared by the dog approaching you?' with the question 'What is it that I must be confronted with (be given, experience, or perceive, as the case may be) in order for me to be justified in asserting that you are being scared by the dog approaching you?'. And third, whoever can make friends with my suggestion to count actions among conscious experiences instead of contrasting the two (see section 2.3.2, above) would surely find it strange to be expected to regard the actions of others as theoretical constructs rather than as empirical observables, to wit, perceivable behaviour in certain situational surroundings.

3.15.5.   For all that, it certainly remains a fact that we have a strong aversion to 'reducing' our fellow-men's conscious experience to their (overt or secret) behaviour; for, so the story goes, there is always more to it besides mere bodily movements. Now of course I do not hesitate to admit that *for you* there is more, and *enormously* more, to your conscious experience besides doing and saying a multitude of things. But I am equally prepared to deny that *for myself*, in my role as a casual onlooker and sometimes even as an attentive observer, there is really anything more to it. For whenever I try to describe, say, your seeing a dog approaching you, and your feeling frightened of it, my description can be made virtually complete without including the dog's being given to you in such-and-such transient modes of subjective appearance, visual as well as emotional and possibly 'gerundive'. What is more, I could not even *conceive* of 'enriching' my account of your seeing and being afraid of the dog by adding to this objective and 'semi-behaviourist' description any subjective features. For I have not the slightest idea of *where* on earth and *how* on earth – as it were, by means of what sort of 'adapter' – I could bring about such a connection between objective bodily movements and subjective conscious experiences.[137] Such things as your

---

[137] Of course, the same is true of my own case, although in the reverse sense. For in the subjective description of the dog's appearance in such-and-such modes of being visually and emotionally given to me, there is no conceivable room or 'enclave' whatsoever in which to accommodate some such

subjective conscious experiences *as such*, that is to say, as being something which resembles in nature my own experienced consciousness, simply *do not exist* in my world – not even as entities detained, if you will, in a camp surrounded with walls I am in principle unable to overcome. For within *my* world there is, as it were for 'topological' reasons, no thinkable 'enclave' whatsoever where to accommodate *your* subjective experiences as such. Hence subjective conscious experiences of yours *qua data of your first-person perspective* exist neither in the (objective) world which is the correlate of my third-person point of view nor, I take it, in the (noematic) world which is the correlate of my first-person point of view.

3.15.6.   Nonetheless it would never occur to me that you, our common fellow-men, and even higher animals might be automata lacking consciousness. On the contrary, in my opinion all of us speak about their own conscious experiences and the conscious events of others with precisely the same certainty. For unless 'the native hue' of language 'is sicklied o'er with the pale cast of thought' (*Hamlet*, III.1), what we *speak* about in the indicative or assertive mood seems to me to be restricted to what we can in principle *know* about (or, more generally speaking, what in principle we have a cognitive access to). Hence what, if we are using language in the ordinary way, we mean (to say), have in mind, or intend to convey is, I take it, always something we are either immediately aware of (to wit, our own present or recent consciousness) or something we can in principle find out and possibly verify (to wit, everything else). Only if our ordinary language use has been systematically misinterpreted by philosophical prejudices, we can be misled into believing that sometimes we want to speak about, and hence have in mind, what in principle we have no access to – such as Kant's ('transcendental') *'things in themselves'*, which by definition are objects considered as entirely independent of our coming to know them;[138] or *future events as such* (Aristotle's 'contingentia futura'), that is to say, events still to come as opposed to their present or past indicators (on which not only a trustworthy weather forecast but also the sound prediction of, say, a naval battle leans); or *conscious experiences of others* (or higher animals and even advanced robots) *qua correlates of somebody (or something) else's first-person perspective*.[139]

Arguably, we may find sort of an empirical confirmation for this philosophical position of mine in the linguistic fact that there are languages, for instance Tuyuca

---

ethological and physiological strangers as the movement of my eyes, my pausing and withdrawing, and what is going on in my nerves and my brain. So my and your detailed accounts of my, and my and your detailed accounts of your, conscious experiences are strictly disjunct, nay, incompatible. See Hoche 1987: esp. 4.6–4.9.

[138] See the following Essay V: subsects. 1.7.2 and 1.8.1–1.8.2, of the present collection.

[139] In such cases, too, we should remember what Hume (1739: 162) stated in the context of causation: "'tis more probable, that these expressions do here lose their true meaning by being *wrong apply'd*, than that they never have any meaning" (Hume's italics).

and Aymara in South America, in which a speaker has always to indicate by means of a suffix from which source he is drawing his assertion, for instance, whether he has seen himself, or has heard himself, or has logically derived himself, or knows only from hearsay what he is speaking about. In such a language it makes sense to metaphorically place the past, which is already known, in our visual field, that is, in front of us, and the unknown future behind us, as can be gathered from Aymara gestures.[140]

3.15.7.   However, the fact my and your detailed accounts of my, and my and your detailed accounts of your, conscious experiences are strictly disjunct and even incompatible is usually camouflaged by our being wont from infancy to employ, irrespective of the first, second, or third grammatical person, such uniform open sentences (or 'propositional functions') as '[…] see(s) a dog approaching […] and feel(s) scared by it'. To be sure, this way of speaking is unobjectionable and above doubt in everyday life. But in doing philosophy, it should not make us blind to the truth of what Wittgenstein emphasised in his Cambridge lectures in the early thirties, namely, that the epistemological and ensuing linguistic properties – the logical behaviour or depth grammar – of the statements 'I have toothache.' and 'He has toothache.' are so different that we had better say 'that they are not both values of a single propositional function "x has toothache"'.[141]

3.16. Why, a commonplace-argument notwithstanding, the generally accepted 'epistemological asymmetry' of psychological verbs ought to be given an 'ontological dignity'

However, there seem to be only few post-Wittgensteinian philosophers who are not convinced that this conclusion is a grossly unprofessional exaggeration. The great majority, although quite willing to admit, under the fashionable label of '*epistemological* asymmetry', the conspicuous epistemological differences between first-person and second- or third-person accounts of human consciousness, stead-fastly refuse to commit the alleged professional blunder of bestowing upon these differences the dignity of an '*ontological* asymmetry'. Rather, they are likely to assure us that conscious experience is but another example for the well-known fact that *one and the same object* can be accessible in *multifarious* ways. Now of course all of us know that we can reach the peak of a mountain via more than only one single route, or (what may seem to be even more to the point) that already in our early childhood we have learned how to identify something felt with something seen. But I think the decisive question is whether we have also

---

[140] See Núñez & Sweetser 2006.

[141] Moore 1954–1955: p. 307; for a discussion, see Hoche & Strube 1985: A.V.2 and A.VI.2. Some of the relevant depth-grammatical differences have also been indicated in sect. 3.13, above.

learned to identify, say, a subjectively experienced headache with an objectively perceived headache-behaviour. In a way, of course, we have; for irrespective of the first, second, or third grammatical person we use to speak of 'having a headache'. But this seems to me to be not a case of identification proper, and we are well advised if we pay attention to the grave difference between 'identifying' a headache and a headache-behaviour on the one hand, and identifying, say, my tea-cup seen with my tea-cup touched, or my alarm clock heard with my alarm clock seen (or touched), on the other. The latter I can achieve *all by myself*; for I can immediately perceive the thing seen as well as the thing felt, or heard, whereas the former requires the co-operation of *others*. As far as my own headache and headache-behaviour is concerned, I can focus on either this or that one but not on both together (which is even more conspicuous in such cases as my seeing, or being scared of, a car threatening to run into me, and my corresponding behaviour);[142] and in the case of somebody else, I have no access whatsoever to their subjectively experienced pain, visual perception, fear, and so on. So all I can do is associating my own subjective experience with the perceived behaviour of others, which can only be brought about by means of the medium of our common language. For this reason I tend to say that a subjective experience and the objective behaviour we have been trained from infancy to regard as its correlate can only be identified *inter*personally, or *inter*subjectively, which is to say that it cannot be identified at all in the primary, to wit, the strictly *intra*personal or *intra*subjective sense of the word.[143]

3.17. My own conscious experiences and the corresponding 'macro'- and 'micro'-behaviour differ from each other 'categorially'

Furthermore, as I tried to expound in the preceding Essay III of this collection, we have cogent reasons to state that a subjective conscious experience and the correspondent objective behaviour, for lack of an appropriate common concept under which both of them could be subsumed, are so fundamentally, or 'categorially',

---

[142] See Hoche 1973a: esp. pp. 179f., 236–238, 241f., and sect. 3.19, note 161, below.

[143] For details, see Hoche 1995a: esp. 5.3–5.5; 2007: pp. 406f.; and the subsequent Essay V: 2.7. – Note that my terminological distinction between an *intra*subjective and an *inter*subjective identification may be found misleading. For of course most of the identifications we perform are *inter*subjective identifications in that we take it for granted that, e.g., the cup or saucer I (can) see is identical, not only with the cup or saucer *I* (can) touch and use, but also with the cup or saucer which *you* and lots of *other people* (and even *cats* and *dogs*) can touch and use. But I think it goes without saying that identifications of this kind – which certainly are not foreign to higher animals, either – are not brought about by means of *that* specific form of intersubjective co-operation that depends on a use of *human language*, which *is* foreign even to higher animals. For recent researches seem to have shown that animal languages profoundly differ from ours, and so much so that the attributes 'human' and 'animal' *modify* or *qualify* rather than *determine* or *specify* the noun 'language'.

different from each other that, in virtue of the structure of the logical paraphrases of positive and negative identity-statements of ordinary language, it does not even make sense either to affirm or else to deny their numerical identity.[144] However, it is an intricate question precisely *what* conditions an 'appropriate' common concept has to fulfil in this case. It does certainly not suffice to demand the non-formal, or material, character of such a concept (so that we need not delve, in the present connection, into the problem of how to define the difference between formal and non-formal concepts). For a subjective conscious experience and a piece of objective behaviour share not only the concept or property of being 'something', or an 'entity', or an 'object', in the purely formal sense of being something we can make a true or false statement about,[145] but also the non-formal concept or property of being considered, and hence called, an item of 'human consciousness' or 'human action'. As I stressed time and again in this essay, my own seeing a dog, or being afraid of it, or running away from it, and so on, presents itself (to me) as a conscious experience given to me in the first-person perspective, whereas somebody else's seeing a dog, or being afraid of it, or running away from it, and so on, presents itself (to me) as a piece of situated behaviour. Hence such phrases as the ones just used – 'seeing a dog', 'being afraid of a dog', 'running away from a dog' –, and likewise the general terms 'human consciousness' and 'human action', must be regarded as names for concepts, and certainly non-formal ones, under which we are wont to subsume subjective experiences in our own cases and objective bodily movements in the cases of others. However, in speaking of an 'appropriate' common concept I was thinking of a concept, or property, or (in the extensional reading) of a kind, class, or set, the members of which have something more in common than a mere linguistic label which has been brought into use by the way we have learned how to apply so-called 'psychological' terms to ourselves and to others.[146] For a concept, property, or kind which can fulfil the function of a hidden (or overt) conceptual unity in a sound positive or negative identity-statement has to be a 'counting-concept', that is, a concept to which a finite natural number can be assigned.[147] This seems to me to be reasonable especially for the following reason. If we may say with Frege that 'affirmation of existence is in fact nothing but denial of the number nought',[148] we may certainly say with the same right that affirmation of numerical identity is nothing but denial of the number two (or, more precisely speaking, of any natural number greater than one), and that affirmation

---

[144] For a definition of the concept of 'categorial difference', see Hoche 1990: sect. 6.8, p. 120, and the preceding Essay III: sect. 9, of the present collection.

[145] See sect. 3.4.4 with fn. 38, above.

[146] See sect. 3.15.1, above.

[147] See Frege 1884, tr. 1950: esp. §54; Hoche 1975, tr. 1983; and Essay III: sects. 4–6, of the present collection.

[148] Frege 1884, tr. 1950: §53.

of numerical diversity, or difference, is nothing but denial of the number one (whereby in both cases the denial of the number nought is silently presupposed). As I took pains to show in section 4 of the preceding Essay III of the present collection, a 'counting-concept' must be a concept which is *both* 'sortal' *and* open to what I call an 'individual binding'. In the case at hand, it might be difficult to decide whether such specific concepts as 'seeing a dog' or 'running away from a dog', and such generic concepts as 'human consciousness' and 'human action', are strictly *sortal*. Fortunately, we need not bother to research this issue. For it seems to me to be clear that in any case they don't admit of an *individual binding*, and this for the following reason. In my own case, I have to do with *experienced consciousness*, in the case of others with *perceived (or observed) behaviour*, and I cannot conceive of any principle of individual binding which could be possibly applied to the *former* and to the *latter* alike. For a piece of *perceived behaviour* – be it linguistic or non-linguistic – is invariably the objective, bodily behaviour of a real person and thus takes place in the material, four-dimensional world. So it only allows of an individual binding with respect to a particular person inhabiting the physical world, and hence, basically, of an *inter*personal or *inter*subjective spatio-temporal binding. In contradistinction to this, a piece of *experienced consciousness* is always part of my subjective or 'noematic' world, which, in section 3.11, above, I have tried and shown to be utterly different from the objective or physical world. Hence the indubitable – though strictly *intra*personal or *intra*subjective – spatio-temporal structure of the former must by no means be mixed up with, or even downright mistaken for, the *inter*personal or *inter*subjective spatio-temporal structure, which is characteristic for the latter, and the latter alone.[149] So, to sum up, a subjective conscious experience and a corresponding piece of objective behaviour cannot be said to be *numerically* identical or else *numerically* different because they do not share any 'counting-concept' under which both of them fall alike.

3.18. A simpler argument against identifying my own conscious experiences with stretches of situated behaviour or neural occurrences

For all that, the whole issue might still be taken to lack final clarity. So let me briefly add another and perhaps more familiar argument against identifying conscious experiences and bodily movements (or stretches of situated behaviour). For different sorts of entities, say, material objects, physical events, moments in time, real numbers, and colours, we have to apply different criteria when we are to decide whether an entity A and an entity B are one and the same thing or two separate things; and the criterial differences are sometimes neither trifling nor easily recognised. The first of these two points may be illustrated by the fact that

---

[149] See also sect. 6.1, note 22, of the preceding Essay III.

in relation to some sorts of entities we can, and definitely should, discern between 'identical' in the sense of 'the very same', or 'the selfsame', and 'identical' in the sense of 'exactly similar', or 'exactly alike' (as in 'identical twins'), whereas in relation to other sorts of entities, say, colours, it would be vain, if not preposterous, to insist on making this distinction.[150] As to the second point, the precise meaning of such an everyday expression as 'simultaneous', or 'happening at the same time', had not been satisfactorily clarified before Einstein had devised his Special Theory of Relativity. So it should be obvious that all of our conventional criteria of numerical identity and numerical diversity have evolved (or, in few cases, have been invented) in strict relation to a given ontological domain, or sort or set of entities, and that none of these criteria are valid in a 'universal', 'absolute' or 'topic-neutral' way.[151] And most certainly no reliable identity-criteria have ever been worked out which might be indiscriminately applied to all members of an ontological domain which is supposed to include objectively perceived bodily movements, or pieces of situated behaviour, and subjectively experienced conscious events alike. For this reason, too, we ought to be suspicious of all attempts to simply proclaim either the identity with, or else the *numerical* difference from, any piece of subjective consciousness with any piece of objective behaviour, or with any neurological pattern of central nervous occurrences, or with any purely formal pattern of information processing, and the like;[152] and the more so as it seems to be reasonable to consider subjectively experienced consciousness – or, in other words: the field of my own noematic phenomena – to be the ontological 'negative' of all objective reality, and hence no part of nature.[153]

3.19.   A 'sceptical solution' to the 'sceptical problem' of solipsism.
Man as a natural kind *sui generis*

Now, if it can be accepted that all items of my subjective consciousness, in the sense of noematic phenomena such as the dog *qua* now appearing to me in a given way, are immediately experienced by me, whereas I come to know all items of objective reality, such as the dog itself, in a mediate way, namely, through the medium of multiplicities of noematic phenomena, and that therefore subjective consciousness may be regarded as the 'negative' of, or at the very least shares no common 'counting-concept' with, objective reality and hence cannot maintain any numerical identity or diversity relations to it – then it is no use insisting on

---

[150] See sect. 3.6.1, above.

[151] See sect. 7 of the preceding Essay III.

[152] Note that this is highly consequential, not only for all 'mind-brain identity theories', but also for the concept of an alleged 'psychophysical', or 'physiopsychical', causation; for cause and effect are normally taken to be numerically different events. See the following Essay V: sects. 2.3–2.5.

[153] See the end of sect. 3.11, above.

the purely epistemological character of these differences ('epistemological asymmetry') and refusing this asymmetry an 'ontological dignity'.[154] Hence I think
we have to face the awkward situation that *my own* ('subjective') 'consciousness',
or my noematic phenomena, and the ('objective') 'consciousness' of *others*, to
wit, their situated behaviour, belong to different ontological domains the disparity
of which can hardly be overestimated. But what makes this situation appear so
unpleasant if not flatly unbearable is a small carelessness of wording. For what
I had in mind when I was writing down the last sentence was, of course, my
'consciousness' as it presents itself to *myself*, and the 'consciousness' of others
again as it presents itself to *myself*.

Now it would be extremely unreasonable to defend the 'solipsistic' position
that other human beings (and some 'higher' non-human animals) are so gravely
different from myself as to fail to be themselves subjects endowed with a subjective
point of view from which *my* consciousness presents itself as situated behaviour
and *their own* consciousness presents itself as subjective experience, or multiplicities of concrete noematic phenomena.[155] Of course, it might appear that we
cannot consistently argue either for or against solipsism; for, as I indicated above,
it seems to make no sense to say that others may, or must, have conscious experiences 'similar' to, or 'dissimilar' from, my own, or conscious experiences at all,
or *no* conscious experiences at all.[156] However, this 'sceptical doubt' can be given
a 'sceptical solution' very much in the sense of Hume's solution to the sceptical
problem of causation, or of Wittgenstein's solution to the sceptical problem of
following a rule. According to Kripke's valuable interpretation, 'a *sceptical* solution of a sceptical philosophical problem', as opposed to a '*straight* solution' of it,
'begins […] by conceding that the sceptic's negative assertions are unanswerable.
Nevertheless our ordinary practice or belief is justified because – contrary appearances notwithstanding – it need not require the justification the sceptic has shown
to be untenable'.[157]

In the present case, what I ought to concede is that I have no access to the
subjective experiences of others, and what I ought to realise is that nonetheless
I have a right to credit my fellow-men with a subjective point of view, and with
subjective experiences in the sense of noematic multiplicities. This right, I think,
can be based upon facts such as these. Among (non-naturalistic) philosophers,
we can make ourselves sufficiently understood when discussing such topics as
the present one; among (naturalistic) painters, we can estimate the propriety of
perspective, drawing, and colouring; and in everyday life, we are used to saying
that somebody else can see something in exactly the way I do if they can describe

---

[154] See sect. 3.16, above.

[155] Let us forget for a moment that this is a rough and ready wording; I shall soon improve on it.

[156] See sect. 3.4.6 with note 44 and sect. 3.15.1 with note 130, above.

[157] Kripke 1982: p. 66.

it by the same words, or paint it with the same colours. In fact, the example of colour is perhaps best suited for illuminating the decisive core of the issue.[158] We are justified in saying that a visual object presents itself to me and to you in the same colours, not of course if my and your subjective colour impressions are completely, or at least nearly, alike (for there is no possibility at all to find this out, and hence no genuine sense in speaking thereof in the first place), but if we use, in describing it, the same colour words, or if we dip, in painting it, our brushes in the same colour-pots. In – at least – this sense we may say that 'an "inner process" stands in need of outward criteria';[159] and hence it makes no sense to admit, if only in the sense of a 'logical' possibility, that somebody else, as compared with myself, could have an 'inverted spectrum', or 'inverted qualia', while the outward criteria are exactly the same.[160] Nevertheless, it would be unreasonable to maintain the sceptic position that solipsism can be neither proved nor disproved; for demanding a disproof over and above the one indicated would reveal, I think, a fundamental misunderstanding of the problem. So we may say with confidence that respectively my fellow-men, too, have their own subjective points of view and that, what I can say on the strength of my conscious experience, they may have a right to say on the strength of perceiving my situated behaviour.

However, two provisos ought to be added. First, at least in the last sentences I deliberately avoided downright saying that my conscious experience presents itself to others in the shape of my situated behaviour; for, as I took pains to make plain in sections 3.16 through 3.18, above, we cannot simply identify pieces of subjective consciousness with pieces of objective behaviour. Second, so far my argument against solipsism works only for human beings but not for higher animals such as other primates, horses, or dogs. For most of the relevant 'outward criteria' I share only with my fellow-men; and particularly our communicating by means of speaking, drawing, or painting has not been significantly extended yet to non-human animals (nor to 'intelligent' machines, if there really are such things). But this does not in the least impair my present purpose, namely, an enquiry into the concept and the nature of *human* consciousness.

And as far as *this* is concerned, now it finally turns out that, a previous impression notwithstanding, human consciousness yet makes up a sort of natural kind. This, however, differs from other, garden-variety natural kinds in a fundamental respect. It is the only natural kind known to us the members of which admit of a dual epistemic or cognitive access, namely, from a subjective, *intra*personal,

---

[158] For bibliographical and substantial details, see Hoche 1990: 3.6, 4.2, 7.2–7.3; Hoche & Strube 1985: A. III.3.

[159] Wittgenstein 1953: § 580; cf. Kripke 1982: 14, 44, 98–102, 120 fn.; Hoche & Strube 1985: A.III.4.c.

[160] See Plato: *Theaitetos* 154a; Locke 1690: bk. II, ch. xxxii, sect. 15; Shoemaker 1982; Chalmers 1996: ch. 7.

or first-person perspective and from an objective, *inter*personal, or second- and third-person one. Now this exceptional position, or special status, ought not to surprise us. For what is in question is nothing less, and also nothing more, than our own nature. After all, from my own point of view – and if we disregard the well-known cases in which I look on (parts of) my body as if I were somebody else[161] – I *am* my subjectively experienced consciousness, and, again from my point of view, others *are* bodies which (or, rather, *who*) behave in specific ways depending on specific circumstances or situations. Nor should it be suspected that my insisting on that special status of human beings betrays a human 'speciesism'. For I think it is plausible to *feel*, though it might be strictly nonsensical to *claim*, that what I, being human, have said of *my* species, *homo sapiens sapiens*, could, other things being equal, also be said, of *their* species, by any member of any species endowed with the faculty of speech and knowledge.[162]

---

[161] I am thinking, first, of looking at myself, in real time, in a mirror or on a monitor. It must be noted, however, that by this means I can only see my bodily appearance, the appearance of my passive corporeal body, but not my actions, or myself acting in a given way, from outside, i.e., in a third-person perspective; for any action is gravely disturbed, distorted, and even nullified by my simultaneously trying to observe it. For details and examples, see Hoche 1973a: esp. pp. 179f., 236–238, 241f. Second, we have also to think of such cases as my seeing previously taken photos or motion pictures of mine, where I can see *past* actions, perceptions, and other conscious experiences of mine as if they were somebody else's. But these cases require a different interpretation. See Essay VI: sect. 4.1, fn. 39 of the present collection.

[162] See Hoche 1973a: p. 247f.

V

THE PURELY NOEMATIC APPROACH *VERSUS* MAX VELMANS'S 'REFLEXIVE MODEL' OF CONSCIOUSNESS

Summary

In the last decade of the 20th century, the London psychologist Max Velmans developed, in a number of books and papers, what at first sight may appear to be one of the philosophically and scientifically most promising contemporary attempts to understand consciousness. According to what he calls his 'reflexive model' of phenomenal consciousness, the subjective *experience of an object* is nothing but the *object (as) experienced*. As such, it is neither something going on 'in the mind', that is, on a Rylean 'inner stage', as the average 'dualist model' would have it, nor something neural going on in the central nervous system, as the average 'reductionist model' claims. Rather, it is, in the exemplary and fundamental case of an exteroception, something 'out in the world'. This view gives rise to intricate questions such as the relation between the 'object (as) experienced' and the 'object itself', the details of Velmans's 'reflexive monism', the precise character of the 'complementarity' of what is given in the first-person and in the third-person perspectives, and the puzzling issue of 'psychophysical causation'. The conceptual framework of this 'reflexive model' of consciousness needs to be carefully analysed. For only on the basis of such an *analysis and clarification* it is possible to subject Velmans's theory of consciousness to a *constructive criticism*. But I think it is worth while taking pains to try and do both, and it is my aim to make at least a beginning in the present essay. In what follows, I shall mainly concentrate upon Velmans's *Understanding Consciousness*, which appeared in the very last year of the 20th century. Unless stated otherwise, references will be made to this book (Velmans 2000).

1. The conceptual framework of Velmans's theory of consciousness

1.1. Velmans's 'reflexive model' of consciousness I

Max Velmans opposes his *'reflexive model* of perception' to the *'dualist model'* and the *'reductionist model'* (see 2000: Figures 6.1–6.3, pp. 106f., 110): Whereas the latter two locate the perception, or 'percept', of an object in the (non-physical) *mind* or the (physical) *brain* of the perceiving subject, respectively, the reflexive model locates it where the perceived object is supposed to be located, say, 'out in the world' or 'out in space' (pp. 109, 111, 133–135, 197, 230, 246). As Velmans doesn't seem to see any reason to call psychophysical causation into question (see esp. ch. 11, pp. 236, 248, but also, e.g., pp. 108f.), he does not hesitate to agree with the 'conventional assumption' (p. 166) of both dualists and reductionists that there is a 'causal sequence' initiated by 'some entity or event', say, light rays reflected by a cat sitting in front of a subject S, which innervate S's optic nerves, then leading, step by step, to 'neural representations' of the cat in S's brain, and finally producing S's 'visual experience' of the cat, i.e., S's seeing the cat. However, whereas dualists and reductionists believe that this visual experience of S takes place in her mind or her brain, respectively, Velmans claims that, 'while S is gazing at the cat, her only visual experience *of* the cat is *the cat she sees out in the world*. [...] That is, an entity in the world is reflexively *experienced* to be an entity in the world' (p. 109). Similarly, for instance, '[the] damage produced by a pin in the finger, once it is processed by the brain, winds up as a phenomenal pain in the finger, located more or less where the pin went in. That is why the entire process is called "reflexive" ' (ibid.). According to Velmans, in all such cases we *project*, as it were, our perception of an object or event onto the place where the relevant causal origin of this perception, to wit, the perceived object or event itself, is 'judged to be' (p. 118). He is convinced that the evidence for this psychological effect, which he terms 'perceptual projection', is abounding (pp. 115, 197, 230f.).

1.2. 'In terms of *phenomenology* there is no actual separation between the perceived body and experiences *of* the body'

From what I just quoted in section 1.1, we can already gather that, according to Velmans, a subject's 'visual experience *of* the cat' is no different from '*the cat she sees out in the world*' (p. 109). This important finding is confirmed by a large number of passages, some of which should be quoted here, too. Experiences are *not* 'quite different from the perceived body and the perceived external world' (pp. 110 f.); rather, 'in terms of *phenomenology* there is no actual separation between the perceived body and experiences *of* the body or between the perceived external world and experiences *of* that world' (p. 111).[1] Taken together, 'inner experiences ['such as verbal thoughts, images, feelings of knowing, experienced desires and so on'], bodily sensations [such as pains] and external experienced entities and events [such as cats] comprise the contents of our consciousness – which are none other than our everyday phenomenal world' (p. 111; cf. pp. 110, 225–229). Hence, 'what we normally think of as being the "physical world" is *part of* what we experience. It is not *apart from* it. And there is no mysterious, *additional*

---

[1] Cf. p. 174, explanation of Figure 8.2: '[I]n terms of their *phenomenology* there is no actual difference in the subjective vs. objective status of the light "experienced" by the subject and the light "observed" by the experimenter.' – '[I]n terms of *phenomenology* there is no difference between "observed phenomena" and "experiences" ': p. 175. – 'In terms of their *phenomenology* the perceived "physical world" and percepts *of* the physical world are one and the same': p. 154. – See also pp. 246, 254. – Unless stated otherwise, italics in quotations are adopted from Velmans (or whichever author cited).

experience *of* the world "in the mind or brain" ' (p. 139; cf. pp. 125f., 133–135, 189, 260 n. 9).

1.3. Velmans's use of the term 'phenomenology'

These quotations stand in need of being explained in more than one respect. First, in rejecting an actual separation between the perception of a body and the body perceived, what exactly does Velmans mean by the qualification 'in terms of *phenomenology*' (p. 111; cf. p. 125/6)? And second, in speaking of an 'actual separation' or an 'actual difference', what exactly does he mean by the qualification '*actual*' (pp. 111, 174)? Let us deal with the first question first.

1.3.1.   Velmans seems to give us a clue in speaking of 'an experience of pain (phenomenal pain)' and asserting, only two lines later, that '[in] terms of its phenomenology, the pain really is in the finger and *nowhere else*' (p. 109). In the very same context, when speaking of a subject's 'phenomenal cat', he adds the parenthesis '(her "cat experience")' (ibid.). So I take it that we may say that Velmans, by using such terms as 'phenomenal pain' or 'phenomenal cat', is trying to make it clear once again that he is referring, not to the (physical) pain 'itself' or the (physical) cat 'itself' (see sects. 1.7–1.8, below), but to the pain *felt* or the cat *seen* – or otherwise *perceived* – by a certain subject. Instead, I think, Velmans might as well have spoken of the *experienced* pain or the *experienced, or perceived*, cat.[2]

1.3.2.   As for the term 'phenomenology', Velmans seems to use it as sort of a technical term but nonetheless in a rather loose way. In some cases, by the expressions 'phenomenology' and 'this rich phenomenology' he seems to refer to a subject's 'inner conscious life',[3] i. e., to the totality of the subject's 'phenomenal experiences', 'conscious experiences', 'conscious appearances', or 'phenomenal consciousness', given to her in her first-person perspective.[4] In other cases, by the term 'phenomenology' at first sight he seems to understand the *way* phenomenal consciousness is given, or appears, to the subject in her first-person perspective.[5]

---

[2] In fact, at least once he seems to me to be doing so in stating that the '*perceived* lightning is a phenomenal representation of L (*phenomenal* L) produced by the visual system', where 'event L' is an 'event out in the world': p. 45, n. 14 (my italics).

[3] Ibid: p. 130; cf. p. 46 n. 14.

[4] Ibid.: pp. 66, 133, 135, 137 n. 21.

[5] That the 'definitions of consciousness' offered by traditional consciousness theorists 'start more from some *theory* about its nature than from the *phenomenology of consciousness itself*' amounts to putting 'the cart before the horse': p. 6. – 'Once a given reference for the term "consciousness" is fixed in its *phenomenology*, the investigation of its nature can begin, and this may in time transmute the meaning (or sense) of the term': p. 7. – Importing '*nonconscious* information processing operations into the ordinary meaning of "consciousness" [makes] it more difficult to be clear about how the

In still other cases, it seems rather difficult to decide which of these two interpretations is to be preferred.[6] In point of fact, however, this apparent classification cannot be maintained for the following reason: In the case of a subject's conscious experiences, there is no point in making a distinction between their reality, existence, or being ('esse'), on the one hand, and their appearing or being given *to*, or their being 'perceived' ('percipi') *by*, the subject in question, on the other.[7] Hence, as a term used by Velmans, *'phenomenology'* perhaps may simply be taken as standing for the totality of a subject's conscious experiences as they are appearing, or given, to her in her first-person perspective, or simply (what amounts to the very same thing) for *the totality of a subject's conscious experiences*. However, from my above quotations it seems to be also clear that Velmans sometimes is prone to give way to certain connotations of the word which do not do justice to his better insight. Alternatively, perhaps, we may take him to let the word 'phenomenology' oscillate between standing for a subject's *'inner conscious life'* given to her in her first-person perspective, on the one hand, and for her *systematic scrutiny and/or description of this life*, on the other. Possibly, quite a number of the passages I have quoted in the foot-notes of the present section can also be seen in the light of this interpretation.

1.3.3.   Anyway, I think, we are on the safe side if we return to what I said at the end of subsection 1.3.1, above, and refine it a bit. By claiming that, 'in terms of [its] phenomenology', there is no actual separation between the object which a given subject is experiencing and her experience of this object, Velmans subscribes to the view that *the object as being experienced by the subject cannot be actually separated from her experience of this object*. In fact, there are a number of passages that clearly

---

phenomenology of consciousness *relates* to such nonconscious information processing': p. 8 n. 2. – An '*experienced lightning* – in the form of a perceived flash of light in a phenomenal world' – may be said 'to *represent* the same event in the world that physics describes as a motion of electrical charges. But the *phenomenology of the experience itself* cannot be said to be nothing more than the motion of electrical charges': p. 38. – 'It is reasonable to suppose that the phenomenology of perceived lightning also has *neural correlates* in the visual system': p. 46 n. 14. – '[B]oth dualist and reductionist accounts misdescribe the phenomenology of most ordinary experiences': p. 108. – 'In short, under normal conditions first-person consciousness is just *phenomenal consciousness* and its phenomenology reveals no added "consciousness as a vehicle"': p. 133.

[6] 'Some reductionist philosophers claim that psychologists are not interested in phenomenology. [...] [However,] some psychologists *are* interested in consciousness. [...] [I]n some areas of psychology, conscious phenomenology *is* an investigable issue and always has been': p. 45 n. 13. – 'In sum, eliminative and reductive versions of computational functionalism [...] largely dismiss the phenomenology of the phenomenon (conscious experience) that they seek to explain': p. 87.

[7] See the preceding Essay IV: sect. 3.8.2 with fn. 70, of the present collection. – Velmans subscribes to this view; for on p. 131, he quotes from Searle 1992: p. 122 (sic!), that 'consciousness consists in the appearances themselves. *Where appearance is concerned we cannot make the appearance-reality distinction because the appearance is the reality*', and then adds in a footnote (p. 137 n. 21): 'In this quotation Searle neatly summarises the underlying thrust of the argument I develop above.'

bear witness to this: 'an object as experienced' is 'one and the same as an experience *of* an object' (p. 134); 'physical objects as perceived are *not* quite distinct from our percepts *of* those objects' (p. 139); 'experiences *of* objects and objects *as perceived* are phenomenologically identical' (p. 140, and likewise pp. 165/6). All in all, I take it that for Velmans there are two *basic* forms for expressing *one and the same* important insight: (1) *Phenomenologically*, or *in terms of phenomenology*, there is no actual difference between a subject's *percept (experience) of an object* and the *object (which is) perceived (experienced)* by that subject; (2) there is no actual difference between a subject's *percept (experience) of an object* and the *object as perceived, or experienced*, by that subject. Additionally, once in a while Velmans uses two more forms for expressing the same thing, the first of which seems to me to be redundant, if not tautological (3), whereas the other one (4) leaves out an important aspect and hence may be easily found misleading: (3) 'experiences *of* objects and objects *as perceived* are phenomenologically identical' (pp. 140, 165/6; cf. pp. 169, 125/6, and 262 n.24); (4) a subject's 'only visual experience *of* the cat is the *cat she sees out in the world*' (p. 109); here, however, Velmans immediately continues by adding: 'If she is asked to point to this phenomenal cat (her "cat experience") [!], she should point not to her brain but to the cat as [!] perceived, out in space, beyond the body surface.', and so a possible misunderstanding is blocked at the very beginning.[8]

1.3.4.   In sum, the important insight we have Velmans to credit with may perhaps best be summarised in the following way (for the sake of simplicity, I confine myself to cases of exteroception [see p. 134], and for the sake of clearness, I am going to speak in first-person terms, i.e., in terms of my own first-person perspective): For myself, *my percept of a physical object is nothing but the physical object as being perceived by me*. In section 1.7.4, below, I will be going to suggest that the latter should more precisely be taken to be *the (physical) object qua, or in its capacity of, being perceived by me*, or, in still other words, *the (physical) object in so far as I perceive it*.

1.4. 'Actual' versus 'conceptual' differences

Before turning to the question of what exactly it is to which Velmans opposes the physical object thus qualified, i.e., the object '*as* perceived', we still have to deal with another qualification already mentioned (see sect. 1.3, above): What exactly is the kind of separation or difference to which Velmans opposes an 'actual' separation or difference (pp. 111, 174)?

---

[8] See also p. 111, where the claim that 'there isn't a phenomenal cat "in the mind" *in addition* to the cat one sees out in the world' is embedded in a context which is clearly seen to be formulated 'in terms of *phenomenology*'.

1.4.1.   By explicitly stating that there is no *'actual'* separation or difference between my percept, or experience, *of* an object and the object *as* perceived, or experienced, Velmans obviously hints at the fact that in *some other way* my percept of, say, a cat and the cat as perceived by myself can, and should, well be distinguished. Let me first quote a note of his which makes what he seems to have in mind very clear: 'Of course, the phrase "an object as experienced" does not have quite the same *meaning* as the phrase "an experience of an object", for the reason that these phrases focus our attention in different ways. The first phrase places the *observed* in the foreground, which, in the reflexive model, is the initiating stimulus. If we are interested primarily in what is going on in the world, this is appropriate. The second phrase draws our attention to the results of perceptual processing – that is, to the resulting experience. If we are interested primarily in what is going on in the subject, this is appropriate. But this does not alter the fact that when we look at an object in the world, we experience only an object in the world, whichever way that experience is conceived' (p. 138, n. 25).

1.4.2.   From the last sentence of this quotation, we may gather that Velmans is aiming at the notion of a *'conceptual* difference', which, in fact, in traditional philosophy is the standard opposite to the notion of an *'actual* difference'. Although there is no *actual* difference between, say, a given subject S's *seeing the cat* and the *cat as (being) seen* by S, in the sense that both of them must needs exist at the same time and at the same place, we can *think, conceive,* and hence, *speak* of them *differently,* which is testified by the fact that as a rule we are inclined to call the first of these entities the 'event' or 'process' of S's seeing an object and the other one the 'object' (as) seen by S.

1.4.3.   Furthermore, from the quotation in subsection 1.4.1 it becomes plain that Velmans stresses the conceptual distinction between the 'initiating stimulus' and the 'resulting experience'. For an external observer, say experimenter, E, the 'initiating stimulus' is 'the observed', say, the cat he can observe. Of course, besides the cat out in space, E can observe much more, namely, what is going on in the body (especially in the retinae, the afferent nerves, and the cortex) of the observed subject, S. However, the external observer E cannot possibly observe the 'resulting experience', that is, S's *conscious experience* of *perceiving* the cat; he 'can only *infer* the existence of the experiences themselves' (p. 186; cf. p. 187).

1.4.4.   But of course *'the roles of S and E are interchangeable'* (p. 175). So far, the cat or, for that matter, the light[9] was taken to be observed by E and experienced, or perceived, by S. But once S becomes interested in E's seeing the cat or light, the cat

---

[9] I take it that Figure 8.2 (p. 174), in which an *electric-light bulb* is taking the role of the object, is virtually the same as Figure 6.3 (p. 110), where a *cat* is featuring as the object. The only difference worth noting seems to me to be the hyphenated form 'as-perceived' (and possibly the use of capital

or light is taken to be observed by S and experienced, or perceived, by E. Similarly, '[o]nce E reflects on his own experience, he adopts the role of the "subject"', and then 'the light that E can see is the experienced *effect* of [his] own perceptual processing. Once he sees it, the processes that enable him to see it have already operated. If he switches back to being an external observer, he quite rightly *regards* the light as the cause of what S experiences (it is, after all, his own perceptual representation of the stimulus that causes S's perceptual processing). However, whether he *thinks* of the light as the "perceptual effect" (of his own processing) or the "cause" (of S's processing), its *phenomenology* remains the same' (p. 188). 'In short, whether we *regard* a phenomenal light in the world as an "experience" or a "physical cause" of an experience depends entirely on whether we adopt the role of the subject or that of the external observer [...]. If we take the role of the subject, the light we can see out in the world is a "perceptual effect" of our current perceptual processing. If we adopt the role of an external observer, we regard the same light we can see as the initiating cause of perceptual processing in someone else' (p. 187).

1.4.5.   In other words, 'there can be no actual difference in the subjective versus objective status of the light *phenomenology* "experienced" by S and "observed" by E' (p. 175; cf. p. 174, explanation of Figure 8.2); or, more generally speaking: 'in terms of *phenomenology* there is no difference between "observed phenomena" and "experiences"' (p. 175).[10] Hence, 'there is no actual conscious content–physical phenomena separation. For everyday purposes it is useful to think of the phenomena we observe as the "physical causes" of what other people experience. However, once we have observed such physical phenomena, they are *already* aspects of what we ourselves experience. That is, physical phenomena are *part of* what we experience rather than *apart from* it' (p. 189).[11]

---

letters in the word 'CAT') in the latter. I shall briefly return to this subtlety in section 1.5.2, fn. 14, below.

[10] Cf. p. 254: '[I]n terms of *phenomenology* there is no difference between a given individual's "observations" and "experiences"; p. 246: 'In terms of their *phenomenology*, my observations of your brain states are just my visual experiences of your brain states'; p. 192: 'In terms of *phenomenology*, the light E observes and the light E experiences are one and the same [...]; I [...] claim experiences of the light as such to be phenomenologically indistinguishable from the observed light out in the world'; p. 190: '[T]he *whole* of science may be thought of as an attempt to make sense of the phenomena we observe or experience'.

[11] 'To avoid ambiguity, I reserve the term "a physical phenomenon" for physical events *as experienced* (or physical events *as observed*), and use the term "events as described by physics" (or other sciences) to refer to the more abstract representations of the same events given within physics (or other sciences)': p. 136, n. 17.

1.5. Velmans's 'reflexive model' of consciousness II

From some of the passages just looked at, particularly that of p. 188 quoted in subsection 1.4.4, at first sight we may feel tempted to gather that it is one and the same entity, say, the light I see out in the world, that I am at liberty to regard as *my own experience* of the light or else as the *initiating cause of somebody else's experience* of the light.

1.5.1.   However, we should take a closer look at the *parenthesis* inserted in the quotation from p. 188: The light that the external observer, E, can see 'is, after all, his own perceptual representation of the stimulus that causes S's perceptual processing'. But in point of fact, what 'he [E] quite rightly regards [...] as the cause of what S experiences' is certainly 'the stimulus that causes S's perceptual processing' and not 'his own [scil., E's] perceptual representation of the stimulus'.

1.5.2.   In this respect, not only in the citation in question Velmans sometimes seems to me to speak somewhat loosely. In raising this piece of criticism, I am not so much thinking of his interchangeable use of expressions of the type 'the perceived object' (i.e., 'the object perceived'), 'the object as perceived' and 'the object as-perceived'.[12] Rather, I am thinking of his terminological use of the expression '*reflexive*' in his basic labels 'reflexive model of consciousness' and 'reflexive monism' (esp., pp. 223, 233). I suppose that Velmans's use of the term 'reflexive' is not entirely independent of the use it has long since been given in the logic of relations: 'A relation R is *reflexive* if "aRa" holds for all a that are members of the field of R.'[13] For if we look at the illustrations of his 'reflexive model of perception' which he offers on pages 110 (Figure 6.3) and 174 (Figure 8.2), we can easily convince ourselves that, in each of these drawings, the object 'as perceived [or: as-perceived] by S' and the object 'as perceived by an external observer [(E)]' is represented by one and the same picture (of a cat and a light or electrical bulb, respectively). Figures 6.3 and 8.2 are doubtless suited to make us believe that, according to Velmans's reflexive model of perception, it is one and the same object that (a) is emitting light rays towards the eyes of subject S and (b) is being perceived by S. Moreover, Velmans explicitly says so:[14] 'The cat as perceived by

---

[12]   See sect. 1.3.1 with fn. 2 and sect. 1.4.4, fn. 9. – A particularly clear-cut case of this interchangeable use is to be found on p. 159, where, under the heading: 'Question 3: What does *the world as experienced* represent?', Velmans says 'it seems reasonable to assume that *the experienced world* produced by perceptual processing is a partial, approximate but nonetheless useful representation of what is "really there"' (my italics).

[13]   Edwards 1967: Vol. 5, p. 74, entry 'relation'.

[14]   For clearly seeing my point, the reader should bear in mind that in Figure 6.3, p. 110, the (drawing of the) cat is characterised twice over as being 'a CAT as-perceived by S' (*above* the cat-picture) and 'a CAT as perceived by an external observer' (*beneath* it). Similarly, in Figure 8.2, p. 174, the (drawing of the) electric-light bulb is characterised twice over as being 'A light as perceived by S' (*above* the

S is the same cat as perceived by E (albeit viewed from S's perspective rather than from E's perspective)' (p. 109). If we let the letter 'o' stand for 'the object (as) perceived (by S and/or E)' and the letter 'C' for 'the subject S's cognitive-processing device' (or, in short, her body and brain), then Velmans's 'reflexive model of perception' (or of 'consciousness' at large), which is the central part of what he calls his 'reflexive monism', may perhaps aptly be symbolised by the formula 'oCo', which, at least typographically, closely resembles the formula 'aRa' frequently used in defining the 'reflexivity' of a logical relation.

1.6. Velmans on 'representations', 'intentionality', and '(phenomenal) consciousness'

Nonetheless, what I said in subsection 1.5.1, above, should be taken seriously. If we are *at all* justified in speaking in terms of a psychophysical (or rather physiopsychical) *causation*, which in Velmans's opinion we clearly are,[15] then it is obvious that 'the stimulus that causes S's perceptual processing' is not an external observer E's 'perceptual representation' *of* some entity but *the entity itself of which it is a representation.*

1.6.1. To be sure, Velmans is perfectly alive to this. The 'distinction between the *phenomena* perceived by any given observer and the stimulus entity or event *itself*' is important. Perceived phenomena *represent* things-themselves, but are not identical to them' (p. 176); 'the experienced world is not the world *in itself* – and [in playing billiards] it is not our experience *of* the balls that governs the movements of the balls themselves. Balls as experienced and their perceived interactions are *representations* of autonomously existing entities and their interactions, and conscious representations (of what is happening) can only be formed *after* the occurrence of the events they represent' (p. 256; cf. p. 258). But Velmans does not scruple to say that although conscious experiences 'are only *representations* of events and their causal interactions, for everyday purposes we can take them to *be* those events and their causal interactions' (p. 257). 'In everyday life we [...] behave as "naïve realists". That is, we take the events we experience to *be* the events that are actually taking place [...]. For everyday purposes the assumption that the world just *is* as we experience it to be serves us well' (p. 256). We shall have to return to this point in due course.[16]

---

bulb-picture) and 'A light as perceived by an external observer (E)' (*beneath* it). – I take it that the typographical differences – two capitalisations and (only) *one* hyphenation in Figure 6.3 – may be neglected; at least, Velmans gives us no hint at a possible import. Most probably, the capitalised 'CAT' as well as the hyphenated 'as-perceived' are but relics of the readings he preferred in his first pertinent publication; see Velmans 1990: esp. pp. 82f., 92–94, and Figures 2–4.

[15] See sect. 1.1, above.

[16] See, for instance, fn. 19, below.

1.6.2.   Before so doing, we should take a closer look at Velmans's concept of 'representation', which is pivotal to his theory of consciousness. For according to this theory, 'consciousness is intimately bound up with representation. Phenomenal consciousness is always *of* something' (p. 258; cf. p. 244). Nonetheless, 'consciousness in humans is not *co-extensive* with [...] representation [...]. There are many forms of representation in the brain that are preconscious or unconscious' (p. 258.). Nor is human consciousness co-extensive with *intentionality*. Opposing Searle (1990), Velmans *denies* 'that only conscious states are truly intentional (truly about something)', and expressly speaks of a 'dissociation between intentionality and phenomenal consciousness' (p. 99f., n. 23). '[I]ntentionality (in the sense of being about something) has to be teased away from "consciousness"'; for although 'consciousness is always consciousness of something [...], it also appears to be true that unconscious states – for example, in human memory – are genuinely about something to the person who has them' (p. 99 n. 20). However, for Velmans the properties of being *representational* and of being *intentional* seem to be mutually co-extensive in that both properties alike coincide with the property, as it were, of '*about-ness*' or '*of-ness*'. 'Normal human conscious experiences are representational (phenomenal consciousness is always *of* something)' (p. 244). '*[A]ll* conscious states are "about something" for the reason that they are fundamentally *representational* in nature', and this is even true of pains and similar bodily feelings which Searle and many others take to be *non-intentional* conscious experiences (p. 98 n. 16).[17] And still more conspicuously, Velmans reminds us of the fact that in 1990 he coined the term 'general representationalism' for 'the view that *all* experiences are intentional. That is, inner experiences, bodily experiences and experienced external phenomena represent entities or events (from a first-person perspective) which can, in principle, be given alternative (scientific) representations, viewed from a third person perspective' (p. 136 n. 15). In sum: For Velmans, being *representational* or, what amounts to the very same thing, *intentional* is a *necessary*, though not a sufficient, *condition for being a conscious experience*.

1.6.3.   What then, if not being representational or intentional, is, in Velmans's theory, the *defining* property of conscious experience? It is '*phenomenal content*'. Velmans takes it that, according to 'everyday understanding [...], [a] person, or other entity, is conscious if they experience *something*; conversely, if a person or entity experiences nothing, they are not conscious. Elaborating slightly, we can say that when consciousness is present, phenomenal content is present.

---

[17] Cf. Velmans 2002: fn. 9 on p. 12: 'A feeling of pain [...] represents (in one's first-person experience) actual or potential damage to the body, and it is usually quite accurate in that it is normally subjectively located at or near the site of body damage. A feeling of anxiety is a first-person representation of a state of one's own body and brain that signals actual or potential danger, and so on. Viewed this way, *all* conscious states are about something.'

Conversely, when *phenomenal content* is absent, consciousness is absent' (p. 6). Hence, this particularly important concept of consciousness can aptly be characterised as '*phenomenal consciousness*', and can thus be terminologically contrasted with other uses of the term 'consciousness' to be found in psychology (p. 8 n. 2). As 'there is nothing to prevent organised discussion of a *specific* usage of "consciousness" […], [one may] restrict the term "consciousness" to situations where phenomenal content is present (where one is conscious *of* something […]) (p. 33). In this sense, 'consciousness can partly be defined in terms of the presence or absence of phenomenal content' (p. 16). So, 'the presence (or absence) of subjective phenomenal contents becomes the *only* difference between conscious and unconscious representational states' (p. 100, n. 23).[18]

1.6.4.   Let me add that, for Velmans, *phenomenal consciousness* is intimately connected with the individual '*first-person perspective*' of the subject in question. '[C]onsciousness is in essence a first-person phenomenon. Only I have direct access to what my own conscious states are like and only you have access to yours. How close can I get to your conscious states by observing your brain? No closer than their neural correlates!' (p. 243). 'I know something about your mental states that you do not know (their physical embodiment). But you know something about them that I do not know (their manifestation in experience). Such first- and third-person information is *complementary*. […] I have access to the neural correlates of what you experience, and you have access to what it is like to have that experience' (p. 247). 'Does the absence of a third-person function for consciousness raise doubts about its existence, evolution or importance? No. […] Given its first-person nature, it is appropriate to assess its importance to life and survival *from the perspective of the beings that have it*' (p. 278). At least as far as the *kernel* of this view is concerned, I fully subscribe to it. However, I have to take exception to the following wording that Velmans gives to it: 'The external observer can *observe* the causes of a subject's experiences but can only *infer* the existence of the experiences themselves' (p. 186). Convincing though this doubtless appears at first sight, speaking of the *observable causes* of a subject's experiences seems to me to be highly dubious, and so does taking it for granted that one can '*infer*' the existence of conscious experiences of others, especially if that is to say that, given certain conditions, one can *infer* that somebody else has experiences similar to one's own (cf. pp. 176f., 184f., 194, 254, 266). I will return to these issues in due course (see sections 2.2.5–2.2.9, below).

---

[18] ' "Intentionality" ', Velmans adds in the following sentence, 'may then be thought of as a functional property to do with "symbol grounding" ' (ibid.), that is, with 'linking the symbols to real events in the world, via internal iconic representations of sensory input', which is not *based* on consciousness but on the contrary *productive* of it in that it finally *leads* to 'meaning', 'understanding [a language]', and 'trad[ing] in ideas' (and 'not just in words'): pp. 89f. (and p. 78); cf. p. 91.

1.7.   Velmans's distinction between 'phenomenal things' and 'things themselves' compared to Kant's distinction between 'phenomena' and 'things-in-themselves' and to the noematic distinction between 'phenomena' and 'things themselves'

Let us now focus our interest on the important result, obtained in subsection 1.6.2, above, that, for Velmans, all conscious experiences are intentional, that is, representational. Of course, 'this does not make sense unless there is something there to represent. Unless representations are *of* something, they are not representations. But *what* are they representations of?'.

1.7.1.   Velmans's answer is that 'they represent (in our experience) what the world itself "is like". [...] This implies that there is a "reality" which is like something. I use the term "thing itself" to refer to this implicit reality' (p. 163, cf. p. 162) – to 'the "real" nature of the world' (p. 166). 'Like all forms of representation, experienced phenomena can misrepresent actual states of affairs (for example, in illusions and hallucinations). However, in general, what we experience corresponds in some useful way to what is "actually there". [...] Observed phenomena are partial, approximate, species-specific but useful representations of the "thing itself" ' (p. 162, cf. pp. 159, 166).[19] In Velmans's view, this 'ultimate reality' (p. 165) is not only *represented by* our conscious experiences. In cooperation with our perceptual processing device, it is also *productive of* them. 'Observed phenomena [...] result from an interaction of an observer with an observed (a thing itself)' (p. 162; see also p. 166); 'the experienced world' is 'produced by perceptual processing' (p. 159).[20]

---

[19]   A handful of Velmans's formulations may be apt to lure the reader into thinking that, for Velmans, this 'thing itself' is identical to 'the world described by modern physics (the world of quantum mechanics, relativity theory, grand unified theory, and so on)' (p. 139). What I have in mind are statements such as these: 'the world described by physics is translated, by our biology, into a world as experienced' (p. 141); 'altered mappings of events as described by physics into events as perceived have met with varying degrees of success in the rehabilitation of the blind and the deaf [...]. The possibility of translating physical energies into non-normal phenomenal worlds is within current technological means' (p. 148); *'what we take to be "normal perceived reality" has more to do with what enables successful interaction with the world than with any immutable, one-to-one mapping of the events described by physics into events as perceived'* (p. 149). Taken as a whole, however, what Velmans says in Chapter 7 makes it plain that, in his eyes, the world described by physics is but another, more thorough and systematic, representation of the underlying 'thing itself' – a representation systematically aiming at overcoming the 'species-specific' constraints of the world as represented by us humans in everyday life. Velmans 2004 expressly confirms this latter interpretation, adding that 'the world described by current physics is just another representation [of the thing or world itself] that is likely to be superseded by some future physics'.

[20]   Cf. p. 134: Velmans's 'reflexive model accepts that, for many explanatory purposes, it is useful to distinguish the *observer* and the *observation* from the *observed object itself*. For example, in cases of exteroception of the kind shown in Figure 6.3 [p. 110], the *object itself* is the source of the stimuli

1.7.2.   In speaking of 'the', or 'a',[21] 'thing itself', Velmans admits that he has 'bor-rowed Immanuel Kant's term, the "thing itself" ' (p. 138, n. 26), that is, Kant's Ger-man term 'Ding an sich selbst (betrachtet)', which, by English-speaking philoso-phers, is also often translated by 'thing-in-itself'. However, he is eager to add that he, 'unlike Kant', regards 'the thing itself [as] knowable'; 'in fact, it is the only thing we *can* know' (ibid.). 'In the reflexive model, things themselves are the true objects of knowledge. [...] [T]he thing itself *is all there is to know*' (p. 166). So it may seem doubtful whether Velmans was well advised in referring to Kant *at all*, which, in fact, he does not only terminologically but also in respect of the very core of his theory. More than once, he unmistakably implies that the rela-tion he sees between *things themselves* and *things (as) perceived*, or '*phenomenal*' things, closely resembles the relation between Kantian '*things-in-themselves*' and Kantian '*phenomena*'.[22] In at least two respects Velmans is right. First, Kant too, though certainly being quite inconsistent in doing so,[23] assumes – and in a way *has* to assume for his critique of pure theoretical reason to run smooth – that the things-in-themselves causally contribute to the production of the phenomena, that is, the phenomenal world, in that they are the material sources of our 'sensa-

---

that initiate visual processing. These stimuli interact with the perceptual and cognitive systems of the observer to produce the observation, an object *as seen*. Barring hallucinations, this perceived object (a phenomenal cat in 3-D space) *represents* something that actually exists beyond the body surface. But it does not represent it fully, as it is *in itself*'. I must confess that I have a problem with this passage. In the first sentence, or so it seems to me, Velmans is (partly) speaking of the (not *actual*, but) *conceptual* difference between (an observational form of) *perception* and the *object (as) perceived* (see the whole of sect. 1.4, above); but then he switches to the '*object itself*' which is emitting stimuli that interact with a given subject's perceptual and cognitive device, thus producing an 'object *as seen*', that is, an observation. The joint which makes this inadvertent switching possible is, of course, the mixed up wording '*observed object itself*'. For its part, this way of speaking seems to me to be supported by a loose, 'naïve realistic' way of expressing oneself which, in everyday life, Velmans is prepared to tolerate: see sect. 1.6.1, above.

[21] When speaking of the Kantian 'things-in-themselves' (or 'noumena'), one is always at a loss for using the plural or rather the singular form. For the Kantian 'categories', among them the categories of 'quantity', are as little applicable to things-in-themselves, or the thing-in-itself, as are the 'forms' of sensory experience, space and time. In Velmans's theory, there is no problem with this. When he is characterising what he calls his 'reflexive monism' by claiming that 'there is *one* universe (the *thing itself*) with relatively differentiated parts in the form of conscious beings like ourselves' (p. 233; cf. p. 229), then he is doubtless using the term interchangeably with the terms 'the world itself' and 'implicit reality', which admit of no plural forms (p. 162f. – see sect. 1.7.1, above). On the other hand, when stating that observed phenomena 'result from an interaction of an observer with an observed (a thing itself)' (p. 162 – see again sect. 1.7.1, above), then he is plainly using the term as standing for something properly countable.

[22] See, for instance, pp. 111, 133, 164; 1990: p. 83.

[23] The categories of *cause and effect* are as little applicable to things-in-themselves as are the categories of *quantity* and the rest of the Kantian categories; see fn. 21, above.

tions'. And second, Kant too regards the phenomena as 'species-specific'[24] rather than subject-specific (or, more precisely speaking, subjectively *particularised*), i.e., individualised by reference to any given single subject at any given moment in time.

1.7.3.   It seems to me, however, that Velmans, at least in *Understanding Consciousness* (2000), *at the same time* advocates a view which *can*, and possibly *must*, be taken to be rather *different* from the one just described. Immediately after having told us that he 'use[s] the term "thing itself" to refer to [the – I take it, *one* and *single*] implicit reality' mentioned in section 1.7.1, above, he goes on as follows. 'The thing itself may also [!] be thought of as a "reference fixer" required to make sense of the fact that we can have multiple experiences, concepts or theories of the *same thing*. How this page looks, for example, depends on whether one views it in darkness or light, with unaided vision, a microscope or an electron microscope. One can think about it as ink on paper, as English text, a treatise on the "thing itself", etc. Which is it 'really'? *It* is as much one thing as it is the other. [...] The critical realism I adopt assumes [...] that there really is something there *to experience or to think about*, whether we perceive it, have thoughts about it, or not. [...]. [T]here has to be some *thing* which underlies the various views, concepts or theories we have about it' (p. 163f.). In fact it seems to be reasonable enough to say that any given subject can at any given moment in time be representing, or 'intentionally referring' to, one and the same given object, that is, perceiving it (e.g., by way of seeing, hearing or feeling it), adopting emotional attitudes towards it (e.g., by way of loving it, despising it or being scared of it), dealing with it (e.g., by way of fighting, shunning or painting it), theorising about it, etc.[25] If, for the sake of simplicity, we confine ourselves to the case of my own seeing an object out in the world, say, a cat, we need to distinguish the cat itself from the countless different percepts I can get of it from different perspectives and under different lighting conditions at different moments in time.

1.7.4.   Now the relation that obtains between those *multifarious experiences* and the *one and same object* of which they are experiences could also, and more suitably, be described in terms of 'transcendental phenomenology', especially in the 'purely noematic' version of it which I pleaded elsewhere.[26] On the face of

---

[24] See sect. 1.7.1, above.

[25] For the sake of simplicity, here I am neglecting some subtleties I will discuss in detail in sect. 2.2, below.

[26] See Hoche 1973a and the preceding Essay IV: esp. 3.6.5–3.6.7, 3.10–3.11, of the present collection. – This variant of Edmund Husserl's transcendental phenomenology is 'purely noematic' in that it gives up the seemingly natural idea of a thoroughgoing 'parallelism' between 'noetic phenomena' (or 'noetic multiplicities') and 'noematic phenomena' (or 'noematic multiplicities') in favour of the latter. Such a parallelism between a stream of 'noetic' *experiences* (or '*cogitationes*') taken to be going on 'in the mind', that is, on a kind of Rylean 'inner stage', and 'noematic' *objects as experienced*

it, the defining characteristic of such a 'purely noematic phenomenology' (or 'pure noematics') is the very point Velmans tries and drives home, namely, the assumption that, contrary to first appearances and ingrained prejudices, we are not genuinely justified in making a distinction between a given subject's *conscious experience of an object* at a certain moment of time and this *object as experienced* by that subject at that moment. Unlike Velmans,[27] however, the advocate of such a purely noematic view of consciousness takes the terminological distinction between 'the object (experienced)' and 'the object *as* experienced' to be highly significant. A simple case in point is again Velmans's example of my own seeing a cat. When I see a cat, the relevant conscious experience, to wit, my visual perception of it – or, speaking more down to earth: my seeing it – should again be considered to be the cat *as* seen, but unlike Velmans by these words I suggest one ought to understand, not simply the cat (which is) seen, that is, the cat as a *Kantian* 'phenomenon', but the cat *as, qua,* or *in its capacity of* being seen by me at the given moment in the given particular way, that is, as a '(noematic) phenomenon' in the *Husserlian* sense. Instead of speaking of the cat *as, qua,* or *in its capacity of* now being seen by me in such and such a way, we could likewise speak of the cat *in,* or *with,* its present *mode of appearing,* or being given, to me. From a purely noematic point of view, this cat *as* (or *qua*) now being seen by me is an example of a *complete* noema, or of a noematic phenomenon *in its full concreteness.* As such, it is but *one* out of an exuberant 'noematic multiplicity' or 'manifoldness',[28] to wit, out of a continuum of complete noematic phenomena of mine which are related to each other in a specific way[29] which makes me interpret them as 'intentionally' referring to one and the same 'noematic unity', in this case to the cat itself as the 'object pure and simple', which may be considered to be the ultimate noematic 'core' or 'nucleus'.[30]

(or '*cogitata qua cogitata*') has been supported by Husserl at least between 1907 and 1929. Only in his very last work, the *Krisis* (1934–1937), I am not able to spot any longer a vestige of his former 'noetic-noematic parallelism'. As far as I can see, it is true that Husserl nowhere expressly retracts this 'parallelism'; but nonetheless I have come by the strong impression that in his *Krisis* he takes *all multiplicities* of conscious experiences to be as much of a *noematic* character as the corresponding *unities*; see Hoche 1973a: pp. 27 f. and §§ 8–9.

[27] See esp. sect. 1.5.2 with fn. 12, above, and sect. 1.7.5 with fn. 31, below.

[28] See, esp., Husserl 1913, tr. 1931: §§ 88–91, 128–132; 1920: sects. 18–19.

[29] To all of us, this 'specific way' is familiar from infancy, and for exactly this reason its precise description is as difficult as it is, at least in the present context, unnecessary. See, however, sect. 2.2.3, below.

[30] The just-mentioned noematic objects in or with their modes of subjective appearance specifically relating to each other may be well compared to a bunch, or bundle, of rays or straight lines intersecting each other in one and the same point, which, for its part, would then correspond to the noematic core or nucleus, that is, to the noematic unity or noematic object itself.

1.7.5.   So it seems to me that Velmans, without being truly alive to it, uses his terminological distinction between the 'thing (as) perceived' (or 'phenomenal thing') and the 'thing itself' in two quite different ways, namely, first, for something at least *roughly* resembling the *Kantian* dichotomy of 'phenomenon' and 'thing-in-itself' (or 'noumenon'), and, second, for something which *rather closely* resembles the *phenomenological* dichotomy of '(concrete or complete noematic) phenomenon' and '(noematic) thing itself'. His *original* distinction seems to me to have been aiming at the *Kantian* distinction. It is true that his early, hyphenated spelling 'objects [events; the world] as-perceived' in his paper 'Consciousness, brain and the physical world' (1990: esp. pp. 82, 92–94) at first blush appears to point in the opposite direction. But as soon as we compare with each other two nearly parallel statements to be found in this paper – 'percepts *of* objects and objects as-perceived are one and the same' (1990: p. 94), and: 'our percepts *of* physical objects, and the physical objects we perceive around us are one and the same' (1990: p. 82) – it becomes quite obvious that Velmans, at least in that early paper, makes no conceptual difference at all between 'objects as-perceived' and 'objects we perceive'. Moreover, in this paper we cannot find any other hint at something like a quasi-noematic reading of the terminological distinction in question.[31]

1.8.   Why Velmans's *quasi-noematic* reading of the dichotomy of 'phenomenal things' and 'things themselves' should be preferred to his *quasi-Kantian* one

None the less, as I tried to show in section 1.7.3, above, there *is* sufficient evidence that, later on at least, something like a noematic interpretation of his terminological distinction between the 'thing (as) perceived' and the corresponding 'thing itself' must have occurred to Velmans. If so, the question should be asked how these different interpretations could be harmonised with each other as neatly as possible.

1.8.1.   Comparing the *Kantian* distinction between a 'phenomenon' and the corresponding[32] 'thing-in-itself' with the *phenomenological* distinction between a '(complete noematic) phenomenon' and the corresponding '(noematic) thing itself', we may be tempted to think that *each* of these dichotomies leaves out something important. In the *former*, we might miss the conceptual distinction between a 'species-specific' phenomenon, that is, an object as it is apt to appear to any arbitrary member of the human species in more or less the same way,

---

[31] Velmans 2004 explicitly agrees to this.

[32] Possibly, it is not quite correct to speak, in this case, too, of 'correspondence'. This has to do, of course, with the problem of whether Kantians should speak of *a* thing-in-itself or rather of *the* thing-in-itself; see sect. 1.7.2 with fn. 21, above.

on the one hand, and an object as it is (being) perceived by a particular human subject in a particular manner at a particular moment of time, that is, a percept *of* the object, on the other. In the *latter*, however, we might miss the conceptual distinction between a noematic thing itself as the core, or unity, of a certain set of my actual and potential noematic phenomena, on the one hand, and something corresponding to Kant's thing-in-itself, that is, an object as it exists irrespective of being perceived by myself, by other humans, and by any other intelligent beings, on the other.

1.8.2.   As for the distinction that *Kant* apparently failed to make, I take it that it is simply not true that he should have neglected to distinguish between the 'object of experience', that is, the 'phenomenon' out in space, and 'experience' itself. To be sure, sometimes it may *seem* as if he tends to identify the one to the other.[33] In point of fact, however, he *does* distinguish between the two, and contrary appearances arise from the fact that Kant, unlike Descartes, Hume, and others, is convinced of the predominance of the 'external sense' as against the 'internal sense', that is, that the 'affection' of the former is a prerequisite for the 'affection' of the latter.[34] So I take it that in Kant the dichotomy of 'phenomena' and 'things-in-themselves' is imbedded in a trichotomy of 'perceptions', 'phenomena', and 'things-in-themselves', and hence, that Velmans is mistaken if he thinks that Kant identified 'perceptions' to 'phenomena' in the prevailing terminological use this expression has acquired in transcendental philosophy done in a Kantian key.[35]

1.8.3.   As for the distinction that *transcendental phenomenology*, including its *purely noematic* variant, in point of fact refrains from making – namely, the distinction between 'phenomena' and 'things-in-themselves' in the (not *empirical* but) *transcendental* sense which these terms have acquired in the philosophy of

---

[33] See, for instance, Paton 1936: Vol. I, p. 283 fn. 5 and p. 285.

[34] See, for instance, Hoche 1964: pp. 66–69, 72; Prauss 1971: esp. pp. 147–151, 257f., 285–301. The best-known *locus classicus* is Kant's famous 'refutation of (psychological or material) idealism' in his 'Preface' to the 2nd edition of his *Critique of Pure Reason*.

[35] It is, of course, plausible to believe that this mistake is strongly supported by the fact that Kant uses the German term 'Erscheinungen' in two quite different ways (an *empirical* and a *transcendental* one): first, for the various modes in which one and the same empirical object can be given to me, that is, for '*perceptions*' ('Wahrnehmungen') or 'appearances' ('Apparenzen') in the specific sense of subjective or private 'sensations' ('Empfindungen') insofar as they have been already unified by means of the categories of quantity and quality; and, second, for the intersubjective or objective '*phenomena*' ('Phänomene') brought about by an application to those 'perceptions' of the categories of relation. Whereas Kant's '*phenomena*' are opposed by him to 'things-in-themselves' in the *transcendental* sense, that is, to 'noumena', Kant's subjective or private '*perceptions*' are opposed by him to 'things-in-themselves' in the *empirical* sense, that is, to the intersubjective objects all of us have in common, which are nothing but the 'phenomena' just mentioned before. This interpretation has been convincingly pleaded in detail by Prauss 1971: esp. § 1 ('Erscheinung und Phänomen'); cf. my Summary in Hoche 1973b: pp. 96f.

Kant[36] –, there are good reasons indeed to dispose of it. For Husserl rightly suggests that an ontology which is justified in claiming not to content itself with mere abstractions – in other words, a 'fully concrete ontology' – has to take into account each and every feature that is essential to objects we can speak about; and certainly an essential and basic feature of objects which we have a genuine right to *speak* about is that we are able to *know* about them, or that they are epistemologically accessible to us. Hence it would be a contradiction in terms to speak of objects as they are, or might be, 'in themselves', that is, irrespective of our possibly having any knowledge of them.[37] Hence for phenomenologists of a Husserlian provenance there is an unexceptional and thoroughgoing correlation between basic types of *objects* and basic types of *gaining knowledge of objects*, or between *ontological* and *epistemological* categories (in a non-Kantian sense which we need not dwell upon in the present context).[38]

1.8.4. Taking together the results of sections 1.8.2 and 1.8.3, above, we may say that Velmans's quasi-noematic interpretation of his terminological distinction between the 'thing (as) perceived' and the corresponding 'thing itself' is certainly an improvement on his original quasi-Kantian interpretation. For as compared to the genuine Kantian *trichotomy* of 'perceptions', 'phenomena', and 'things-in-themselves' I spoke about in section 1.8.2, Velmans's quasi-Kantian *dichotomy* of 'phenomena' and 'things (-in-) themselves' leaves something out, as it were, on its 'left edge'; and in the light of the unexceptional phenomenological correspondence between *objects* and our *gaining knowledge of objects*, on the 'right edge' of Velmans's dichotomy there is something '*de trop*', something superfluous and to be disposed of, provided Velmans uses the term 'thing itself' in the sense of Kant's *transcendental* use of the term 'thing-in-itself'.[39] So I think that Velmans

---

[36] See sect. 1.8.2 with fn. 35, above.

[37] See also Frege 1884, tr. 1950: § 26 (at the very end): '[W]hat are things independent of the reason [Vernunft]? To answer that would be as much as to judge without judging, or to wash the fur without wetting it.'

[38] See, for instance, Husserl 1913, tr. 1931: § 138: '*To every region and category* of would-be objects corresponds phenomenologically [...] a *basic kind of primordial dator-consciousness*'; § 142: '*To every object "that truly is"* there intrinsically corresponds [...] the *idea of a possible consciousness* in which the object itself can be grasped in a *primordial* and also *perfectly adequate* way. Conversely, when this possibility is guaranteed, the object is *eo ipso* "that which truly is".' (Boyce Gibson's 1931 translation of Husserl's *Ideas* does not at all conform yet to the standards set later on in Cairns's *Guide for Translating Husserl* [1973]; but for our present purposes I think we need not bother to improve on it.)

[39] To be sure, Velmans is well aware of differing from Kant in a fundamental respect; for he repeatedly says that for him, the 'thing itself' is not unknowable but, on the contrary, the *true* and *only* object of knowledge (see sect. 1.7.2, above). Nonetheless it can hardly be doubted that what Velmans has in mind is the *transcendental* rather than the *empirical* use of the Kantian term 'thing-in-itself' (see sect. 1.8.2 with fn. 35, above).

would be well advised if he 'shifted' his dichotomy towards the left side of the Kantian trichotomy, that is, to the distinction between (Kantian) 'perceptions' ('appearances') and 'phenomena' or, for that matter, between (noematic) 'things *as (qua)* perceived' and 'things themselves'. This would perfectly square with what Velmans says about his 'things themselves': They are the true and sole objects of knowledge – not only of human knowledge of the everyday brand, but also of the perceptual knowledge that, for instance, the blind or deaf can acquire, and of knowledge as it is striven for in modern natural science, and even of non-human knowledge researched into by animal psychology, ethology, and so on.[40] More or less the same can be said about the noematic 'things themselves',[41] and also about Kant's 'phenomena' in the *transcendental* sense of the word, that is, his 'things-in-themselves' in the *empirical* sense, which must be taken to be the *inter-subjectively knowable* objects *all of us have in common*.[42] By the way, this alone suffices to show that Kant's (transcendental) 'phenomena', being *intersubjective*, can hardly be compared to Velmans's phenomenal consciousness, which is only accessible from the *first-person* point of view, and hence is definitely taken to be *subjective*.

1.8.5.   Let me try and arrange the items just discussed in section 1.8.4 in the following table, which ought to make it quite plain how much Velmans would gain by the above-mentioned 'shift towards the left':

KANT	PERCEPTION (subjectively experienceable)	PHENOMENON (intersubjectively knowable)	THING-IN-ITSELF (unknowable)
NOEMATICS	THING *as* PERCEIVED (subjectively experienceable)	THING ITSELF (intersubjectively knowable)	
VELMANS		THING (AS) PERCEIVED (subjectively experienceable)	THING ITSELF (intersubjectively knowable)

---

[40] See Velmans 2000: ch. 7.

[41] See sect. 2.2, below.

[42] See sect. 1.8.2, fn. 35, above.

2. Some second thoughts about Velmans and pure noematics

2.1. The relation between the 'world itself' and the 'thing itself' as a 'reference fixer'

In section 1.7.3, above, we saw that Velmans regards the 'thing itself' not only as 'the "real" nature of the world' (Velmans 2000: p. 166), or the 'world itself', but also 'as a "reference fixer" required to make sense of the fact that we can have multiple experiences, concepts or theories of the *same thing*. [...] The critical realism I adopt assumes [...] that there really is something there *to experience or to think about*, whether we perceive it, have thoughts about it, or not. [...]. [T]here has to be some *thing* which underlies the various views, concepts or theories we have about it' (p. 163f.). As I already stated,[43] on the face of it there is no problem with using the expression 'thing itself' partly as standing for something *uncountable*, to wit, *the world itself*, and partly for something *countable*, to wit, each and every intersubjectively knowable *thing, object, or entity itself* which, in any one given case, we are 'intentionally' referring to. There may, however, arise a problem as soon as we take interest in the *relation* between *a* given thing itself and *the* thing itself. Are the separate *things, or objects, themselves* simply divided parts of the whole of *the thing, or world, itself*? Remember that such a simple part-whole relation has been called into question by many philosophers, for instance by Ludwig Wittgenstein, who, at the very beginning of his *Tractatus*, insisted that 'the world is the totality of the facts, not of the objects', or by Edmund Husserl, who regards the world not as the *totality* of objects but as the unlimited '*horizon*' inevitably surrounding any single object we intentionally refer to (that is, have in mind or have to do with).[44] Remember, furthermore, that many philosophers and linguists use to hint at the fact that it is some *interest* – and possibly more often than not a *practical* one – we take in certain parts of the world which is at the root of forming the *sortal concepts* we need not only for *counting* but also for simply *identifying* individual things.[45] I do not intend to dwell upon this issue; but let me say at least this much. As we are rarely interested in the totality of the world *as such*, it seems plausible to regard a given single object of interest as the *primary* thing itself we have to do with. In what follows, I will therefore make a terminological distinction between the 'world itself' and a 'thing itself', by which henceforth I will always understand an individual 'reference fixer'. Such an object, however – at least

---

[43] See sect. 1.7.2, fn. 21, above.

[44] Wittgenstein 1922: 1.1; Husserl, esp. 1913, tr. 1931: §§ 27–28.

[45] See Essay III: sect. 4 of the present collection. – The role of sortal concepts in *counting* things has first been stressed by Frege 1884, tr. 1950: esp. §§ 46–54, 68. The role of such concepts even in simply *identifying* individual objects I tried to work out in detail in my paper 1975, tr. 1983.

as far as a *material* or *concrete* object 'out in the world' is concerned[46] –, cannot even be *imagined* without a surrounding, or external (outside),[47] '*horizon*' which can be seen to be essentially unlimited. Hence, the individual outside horizons of each and every concrete object merge into one comprehensive horizon, common to all material objects, which should be taken to be *the* thing or world itself. The greater part of this world-horizon is certainly undetermined; but in principle it can be researched into successively and thus increasingly determined, and this may be taken to be the global task of natural science.

2.2. The thing itself, experiences of my own, and 'experiences' of others

2.2.1.   If we now focus our interest on a given thing itself out in the world, say, the cat which I see sitting in front of me, there is little doubt that we are very much inclined to regard this cat itself as the underlying unity, not only of *my own* varying visual percepts, or views, but also of the (real or potential) views of *others*.[48] Again, at first sight it seems natural enough to go on and regard it, moreover, as the unifying core of multiplicities of real or potential visual *and/or* non-visual (say, acoustic, haptic, or olfactory) percepts and also of multifarious emotions, evaluations, and actions of *others* as well as of *myself*. For it is indeed part of the very essence of the things we encounter out in the world that they can be perceived, sensed, estimated, and acted upon *intersubjectively*, and it is certainly tempting to believe that this essential insight could be likewise stated by saying that these things themselves (in Velmans's and the noematic sense of the word) may be taken to be *intersubjective unities* of varieties of real or potential multiplicities of conscious experiences of different human beings and even certain non-human animals. Nonetheless I think we should hesitate to simply speak, in all these cases alike, of '*intersubjective unities*'. For if we want to avoid Husserl's highly problematic conception of a 'transcendental intersubjectivity', we should pay due attention to the fact that we can neither *experience* or *observe* nor, strictly speaking, even *infer* the conscious experiences of others.[49] Hence we should scrutinise the precise situational circumstances which make us say, in any one case in point, that it is 'one and the same' object that I and others (including possibly certain animals) intentionally refer to.

---

[46] At least *some* of the so-called abstract objects, for instance *numbers* of various mathematical kinds, are likewise embedded in comprehensive horizons, say, the 'world' of natural numbers. But within our present considerations we need, and should, not bother about this problem.

[47] Husserl justly distinguished between the *external* (outside) and the *internal* (inside) horizon of a material object; but this, too, is not now any concern of ours.

[48] 'The same entity (now thought of as a differentiated or countable part of the thing-itself) can be viewed in different ways by different people *or* in different ways by the same person – and still remain the same thing-itself': Velmans 2004.

[49] See sect. 1.6.4, above.

2.2.2.   In such a scrutiny, we should preferably use the methods of what John L. Austin once suggested to call 'linguistic phenomenology' – rather than simply ' "linguistic" or "analytic" philosophy or "the analysis of language" ' – in order to make it quite plain that '[w]hen we examine what we should say when, what words we should use in what situations, we are looking […] not *merely* at words (or "meanings", whatever they may be) but also at the realities we use the words to talk about'.[50] This method of systematically varying selected imaginary situations and asking ourselves in each case what we should – or rather: would[51] – say with respect to the given imagined variant has also been frequently used by Ludwig Wittgenstein, Gilbert Ryle, Richard M. Hare, and other 'ordinary language philosophers'. It also bears very close similarities to the phenomenological method of an unconstrained variation in pure or 'eidetic' imagination ('unbeschränkte Phantasievariation') often discussed and applied by Edmund Husserl.[52] What the linguistico-phenomenological and the Husserlian (or 'transcendentally phenomenological') variation in pure imagination have in common is, inter alia, that they can be aptly characterised as methods of systematically probing the *limits* of what can be imagined and is in this sense possible,[53] and consequently that they have to do, neither simply with what is *possible* nor simply with what is *real*, but in the first place with what is *impossible* and, correspondingly, with what is *necessary*, from which it follows that they are *non-empirical* methods of investigation.[54]

2.2.3.   Turning now to the problems touched upon in section 2.2.1, above, let us first ask about the relation that obtains between a given thing *as* (*qua*; *in its capacity of*) now being seen by myself (that is, a given visual phenomenon or percept of mine) and the thing itself I regard as its noematic core.[55] We are no sooner asking this question than we realise that it would be much more natural to ask about the mutual relation which obtains between any two visual phenomena or percepts of mine which I take to be related to, or intentionally referring to, one and the same

---

[50]   Austin 1956: 130.

[51]   It should be noted that in such cases we are engaged, not in *normative*, but in *empirical* (or rather *quasi-empirical*) studies of what *I myself*, in the *personal idiolect* I have acquired since my early childhood, am *wont* and hence *inclined* to say in the presence of what type of situation (cf. the preceding Essay IV: 3.8.5 with fn. 80, of the present collection). I take such studies to be applications of what I call my personal combined 'imaginative and linguistic [or, more precisely speaking: idiolectal] competence' ('Phantasie- und Sprachkompetenz'); see, for instance, Hoche 1990: pp. 141, 146, 148.

[52]   See Introduction: sect. 11 of the present collection of essays, and Hoche 1983; 1990: ch. 10.

[53]   See Hoche 1990: ch. 9 ('Möglichkeit und Vorstellbarkeit' ['Possibility and imaginability']).

[54]   It should go without saying that what is *necessary* – what cannot even be 'imagined away' – also strongly bears on what is *real*, and hence that non-empirical investigations do not rival, or 'compete' with, empirical research but rather found, complement, or 'complete' it.

[55]   See sect. 1.7.4 with fn. 30, above.

thing itself, say, the cat just sitting in front of me.[56] For what we take to be the unifying core of different visual percepts (or 'views'), that is, 'the one and same thing itself' of which they are views, is but an *abstraction*. The *concrete* data given to me are nothing else but objects *as* – or *qua*, or *in their capacity of* – being seen (or otherwise perceived) by me at a certain moment and in a certain way, or, as we may likewise say, objects endowed with their respective modes of visually (or in whatever way) appearing or being given to me. Now if any two such concrete visual data (or views) of mine – which cannot but being given to me at different moments in time – are to qualify as visual percepts of *one and the same* thing itself, they need to be *elements* ('slices') of a temporal *continuum* of views successively emanating from each other; or, in other words, each view is to proceed from a former one by a *continuous* change, that is, a change which admits of no *leaps*, *breaks*, or *ruptures*. Note that it would be no use asking for a *proof* of this; we are concerned, not with *proving that* in certain cases we refer to one and the same thing, but with *trying to understand*, by way of using our personal 'imaginative and idiolectal competence',[57] *how* we use language, to wit, *in what cases* we are *wont to say* that we refer to 'one and the same' thing.

2.2.4.   Suppose now that we *interrupt* such a continuous change of views, for instance by taking a nap or simply shutting our eyes. In such a case, we are no longer in a position to decide whether what we see now – say, the cat sitting in front of us – is the same object that we saw before; for we have forfeited the possibility to apply the only *genuine* linguistico-phenomenological identity-criterion applicable to material objects we possess. To be sure, it would be ridiculous to presume that my copy of Velmans's *Understanding Consciousness*, which I left on my desk over night, might in the meantime have been replaced with a different copy of that work, especially if, to the best of my remembrance, all my notes, commentaries, and all the other countless vestiges of having been intensely used are still in place. But none the less it is not downright impossible, though highly improbable, that somebody felt like playing a trick on me. So, strictly speaking, the *only* identity-criterion for material objects that we can *actually* apply without any temporal restrictions – to wit, a combination of suitable circumstances and 'exact similarity' – lacks the degree of reliability that can be ascribed to the *genuine* identity-criterion mentioned before, that is, to the criterion of visual continuity.

---

[56] It would indeed sound a bit strange if we used the plural form 'different *things* as seen by me' – say, 'different *cats* as seen by me' – when we take it for granted that what we have to do with are *different* *percepts* of *one and the same* object (cat). However, I take it that, in point of fact, that way of speaking would be no stranger than calling the percept of a thing 'the thing as perceived', as both Velmans and a purely noematic phenomenology would have it.

[57] See sect. 2.2.2 with fn. 51, above.

2.2.5.   This criterion of a continuous shading of my visual percepts or views into each other is even less applicable if we extend our considerations so as to include also the 'views' of *others*. Strictly speaking, in this case we are not justified in using the same word any longer, and hence I just put it in inverted commas. For as I already indicated at the end of section 1.6.4, above, I very much feel like *objecting* to the idea that I can possibly '*infer*' the existence of somebody else's conscious experiences – especially if that is to say that I can 'infer' that somebody else has experiences 'similar' to my own. Velmans takes a different view. 'As [an external observer or experimenter] E does not have direct access to [another subject] S's experience […] and vice versa, there is no way for E and S to be *certain* that they have a similar experience, whatever they might claim. E might nevertheless *infer* that S's experience is similar to his own on the assumption that S has similar perceptual apparatus, operating under similar observation arrangements, and on the basis of S's similar observation reports. […] It is important to note that this has not impeded the development of physics and other natural sciences, which simply ignore the problem of "other minds" (uncertainty about what other observers actually experience). They just take it for granted that if *observation reports* are the same, then the corresponding *observations* are the same. The success of natural science testifies to the pragmatic value of this approach' (Velmans 2000: p. 184; cf. pp. 176f., 184f., 194, 266). Now what guarantees the success of *natural science* need not necessarily guarantee the success of *philosophy*, part of which is 'philosophical anthropology' or the ontology of human beings. On the contrary, philosophy – if it is done in the spirit of a 'linguistic phenomenology', which essentially proceeds in a non-empirical way[58] – often has to take into account certain subtleties dealing with which would only complicate, if not obstruct, empirical scientific research.[59]

2.2.6.   Leaving generalities aside and turning to the particular case in question, in the first place I should like to state that, for principal reasons, I have no access to somebody else's *subjective or conscious experiences as such*. Up to this point, Velmans and I *basically* agree. Humans, says Velmans, 'can only access the experiences of others indirectly via their verbal descriptions or nonverbal behaviour' (p. 184).

---

[58] See sect. 2.2.2 with fn. 54, above.

[59] A case in point has been mentioned in sect. 1.8.3, above. Ontology, as a part of philosophy, cannot abstract from the fact that it is part and parcel of the very essence of material objects we can meaningfully speak about that they are *cognitively accessible* to us. Physicists, however, need, and possibly should, not be alive to this feature in each and every theory and experiment they are engaged in, and maybe classical and contemporary physics mainly differ from each other in that the latter – think of relativity theory and quantum mechanics – have been successful by paying attention to the problems of *cognitive access*, too. Similarly, the facts that inorganic matter can develop into *living matter*, and that highly organised parts of the latter can somehow 'correlate' with *subjective consciousness*, possibly need and should not be taken into account in (basic parts of) physics and chemistry.

But I have to explain my qualification, *'basically'*. I rather demur at speaking of an 'indirect' access; for by using this expression one is likely to be understood to imply that in principle it is *meaningful* to think also of a 'direct' access to the experiences of others, which, however, *happens* to be *permanently blocked* – as if somebody else's experiences are housed in sort of an 'enclave' which, though being part of my own 'topology', that is to say, having common boundaries with my 'ontological territory', nonetheless is off limits to me. This picture, however, is misleading in that my 'topology', my 'ontological territory', leaves no room, no 'topological niche', where to lodge the subjective experiences of others: there is simply no space left for such an 'enclave'. For my description of, say, somebody else seeing a cat is *complete* without taking resort to any such things as 'visual percepts',[60] of which I know only from my own case or, to speak more properly, of which *it makes sense to speak* only in my own case. There is nowhere any sort of *'adapter'* to be seen by means of which to connect my description of someone else's verbal and nonverbal behaviour to a description of their alleged 'visual percepts'.[61]

2.2.7.   It is important to note that, in section 2.2.6, above, I did not mean to *deny* the existence of conscious experiences of others – as if it were *false* to assume that others have suchlike, too. Rather, I wanted to insist that it is *meaningless* to make such an assumption, or that *it makes no sense* to ascribe to *others* conscious experiences *as such*. If this can be accepted, of course it doesn't make sense, either, to believe that on certain conditions I can 'infer' that others have experiences more or less 'similar' to the ones I have myself. But even if what I said in section 2.2.6 appears to be dubious, one can take exception to such an 'inference' on indepen-

---

[60] To *this*, as should be expected, Velmans fully subscribes. 'Viewed from my perspective, an account of your brain states seems to be a *complete* account of what is going on, and the neural correlates of your experiences fill any gaps that your experiences might fill' (Velmans 2000: p. 254; *my* italics). I think this view of 'completeness' should be preferred to the one advocated in Velmans 1991: p. 667: 'Information processing models and other third-person perspective models are incomplete in so far as they do not encompass the subject's first-person perspective. Conversely, a subject's first-person account of his actions (based on what he experiences) is incomplete in so far as is does not encompass information available to an external observer.'

[61] Conversely, I take it that my – phenomenological – description of *my own* seeing a cat is *complete* without taking resort to my 'verbal descriptions', if there are any, to my 'nonverbal behaviour', or to the neural activities going on in my body, and that here, too, there is no sort of 'adapter' by means of which to integrate a description of the latter into the description of my visual percepts (I tried to work this out in detail in Hoche 1986: 3.4–3.5; 1987: 4.7–4.8; see also the preceding Essay IV: 3.15.5, of the present collection). To *this*, too, Velmans subscribes. '[T]he phenomenology of a 'wish' includes no details of where our motor neurons are located, let alone how to activate them' (Velmans 2000: p. 19); 'Viewed from your perspective, an account of what is going on in terms of what you experience seems to be *all* that you need to explain what is going on "in your mind" ' (p. 254; *my* italics).

dent grounds. Frege repeatedly did so: '[…] if we blur the boundary between the subjective and the objective, […] also what is subjective takes on the appearance of being objective. For instance, one speaks of this or that representation [German: Vorstellung], as if it could be seen in public, severed from the representing subject. And yet nobody has somebody else's representation, but only his own, and nobody even knows to what extent his representation – for instance, his representation of something red – agrees with the one of somebody else; for what is peculiar to the representation which I connect with the word "red" I cannot make known. In order to be in a position to compare the representations of one subject with the representations of another one, one would have to have unified them in the same consciousness, and one would have to be sure that they did not change in the process of being carried over' (translated from Frege 1894: p. 317). And even more distinctly: If a companion of mine suffers from red-green blindness, 'the colour impression he gets from the strawberry does not differ noticeably from the one he gets from the leaf. Now does my companion see the green leaf red, or does he see the red berry green? These are unanswerable or, more properly speaking, nonsensical questions. For the word "red", if it is not to indicate a property of things but to characterise sense impressions belonging to my consciousness, is only applicable in the sphere of my consciousness; for it is impossible to compare my sense impression with somebody else's. This could not be done unless a sense impression belonging to one consciousness and a sense impression belonging to another consciousness were unified in one consciousness. […] At any rate it is impossible for us human beings to compare representations of others with our own'.[62] Friedrich Waismann and Ludwig Wittgenstein elaborated these Fregean ideas,[63] the upshot of which it is, inter alia, that the alleged possibility of an 'inverted spectrum' or of 'inverted qualia', apparently still accepted even by some renowned contemporary consciousness theorists,[64] on closer inspection turns out to be rather an *impossibility*.[65]

---

[62] Translated from Frege 1918: p. 67; see also Frege 1884, tr. 1950: § 26, p. 36; Frege 1892a, tr. 1952: p. 29f.

[63] See my discussion in Hoche & Strube 1985: A.III.3, pp. 77–82 ('Können verschiedene Personen "die gleichen" Empfindungen haben?' ['Can different persons have "the same" sensations?']).

[64] See, for instance, Martine Nida-Rümelin (pp. 259–282, passim) and David J. Chalmers (pp. 368–370) in Metzinger (ed.) 1995, but also Velmans 2000: p. 85 with n. 11 on p. 98.

[65] See Hoche 1990: pp. 59–61, 126–131. – As Velmans's conception of 'inferring' the 'similarity' as well as the existence of conscious experiences of others certainly has to do with time-honoured ideas of 'analogy', let me add in passing that Carnap 1932–1933: pp. 118–120, and Ryle 1949: II.9, offered remarkable reasons why 'arguments from analogy', which in some connections are in fact unobjectionable and useful, must not, under penalty of incurring nonsense, be applied to the problem of 'other minds'. I take it that such considerations likewise speak against the conception of 'analogising *apperceptions*' – that is, analogising *interpretations* – which Husserl substituted for the older conception of 'analogising *inferences*'. However, here there is no room to discuss these

2.2.8.   If what I just said in sections 2.2.6 and/or 2.2.7 is acceptable, it is plain that we must not say that the 'cat itself' which I see is the common unifying core of my own cat-views *and of the cat-views of others as well*; for by so saying we would, as it were, cross 'the bounds of sense', or trespass upon the field of *'non-sense'*.[66] By stressing this point I do not intend, of course, to deny that the cat I see can be seen, touched, liked, or acted upon *intersubjectively*. Rather I take it that saying, for instance, that the cat I now see is at the same time, or at some other moment of time, being seen also by somebody else – or that it is being chased by myself and a dog alike – simply amounts to saying that I and some other human being or non-human animal nonverbally (and sometimes also verbally) *behave* in specific and highly familiar ways which can be described in objective terms, and which I think we need not dwell upon in the present context.

2.2.9.   *Mutatis mutandis*, the same can be said with respect to the intersubjective character of science, including the science of consciousness. Although empirical science cannot dispense with the subjective experiences of individual researchers,[67] it would never become *objective* science unless, for instance, the subjective experiences of meter reading were *intersubjectively* repeatable (reproducible) by different scientists as well as *intrasubjectively* repeatable (reproducible) by one and the same scientist at different moments in time. So far I agree with Velmans (and others, too, of course). Because of what I just said in sections 2.2.6 and 2.2.7, however, I cannot follow him in grounding this view on an alleged intersubjective 'similarity' of subjective experiences, as I take him to do, for instance, in the following four quotations. 'If the perceptual, cognitive and other observing apparatus of different observers is similar, we assume that their experiences (of a given stimulus) are similar. In this special sense, experienced phenomena may be *public* in so far as they are *similar or shared private experiences*' (Velmans 2000: p. 177; cf. p. 176 f.). '[I]t is important to note that different observers cannot have an *identical* experience. Even if they observe the same even[t] at the same location at the same time, they each have their own, unique experience. *Inter*subjective repeatability resembles *intra*subjective repeatability in that it merely requires observations to be sufficiently similar to be taken for "tokens" of the same "type" ' (p. 180). 'If, given a standard stimulus and standardised observation conditions, different subjects give similar reports of what they experience, then (barring any evidence to

---

questions at any more length.

[66] Cf. the quotations from Frege in sect. 2.2.7, above.

[67] Cf. Velmans 2000: p. 254: 'One cannot reduce first-person experiences to third-person observations for the simple reason that *without first-person experiences one cannot have third-person observations*! Empirical science *relies* on the "evidence of the senses". Eliminate experiences and you eliminate science.' This important insight is central in the philosophical doctoral dissertation of the natural scientist Heiner Schwenke (1992: esp. sects. 3–4) and has found a particularly convincing shape in Schwenke 2005.

the contrary) it is reasonable to assume that they have similar experiences [...]' (p. 185). 'If we access observed events in similar (symmetrical) ways, we are likely to experience/observe them in similar ways. Conversely, if we access given events in different (asymmetrical) ways, we are likely to observe/experience them in different ways. Asymmetries typically arise when observed events are within a given subject's body or mind/brain' (p. 254).[68] These statements doubtless deserve a much more circumstantial discussion than there is room for in this essay, but let me confine myself to saying that similar experience-reports on similar conditions certainly should be regarded as a *defining characteristic* of what we sometimes *feel like calling* an 'intersubjective similarity of subjective experiences', or as a means of *giving sense* to this otherwise senseless expression, rather than as a *base for* 'assumptions' or 'inferences' to this effect.

2.3. Consciousness and causation I

2.3.1.   That said, let me add that *of course* we are very much *inclined indeed* to follow Velmans in saying that sometimes, and on specific conditions, we can 'infer' the existence of certain conscious experiences of other humans and higher animals, and hence the existence of experiences more or less *similar* to our own (for at least *some* degree of alleged similarity seems to me to be a prerequisite for believing that we have to do with somebody else's 'subjective consciousness' in the first place). To say so need not be taken to contravene what I just said in section 2.2. For, adopting a terminological distinction once used by Kant in quite a different connection, we may properly say that objecting to arguments from analogy (or to analogising 'apperceptions') as part of a *'strict science'* of 'other minds' is not tantamount to denying intersubjective analogising as a *'natural tendency'*.[69] However, I think that giving in to this natural tendency might be compared to connecting an idle cog-wheel to the machinery of our theorising about 'other minds'. We pay a high price for it in that it is apt to impede a sober outlook on the problem of what consciousness of others should be taken to be *from my point of view*, i.e., as it presents itself, not to themselves, but to me; and yet nothing is gained by it. For instance, I cannot convince myself that such an analogising view of our fellow-men should be a prerequisite for treating them humanely, as some philosophers would make us believe. Nor can I find it necessary to postulate subjective experiences as causes or effects of overt behaviour or electrochemical goings-on in our central

---

[68] As I tried to indicate in sect. 2.2.7, above, the question of whether certain subjective experiences of *one* subject *resemble* certain subjective experience of *another* subject is *void of meaning* (provided we do not simply mean to ask whether both subjects behave similarly under similar objective conditions). *If so, it is not possible to meaningfully ask whether a potential answer to it is true, false, or possible ('likely')*; cf. Carnap 1932–1933: p. 121 f.

[69] See sect. 2.2.7 with fn. 65, above, and Hoche 1986: 3.3.

nervous systems. Rather, it seems to me that all of us are familiar, from our early childhood, with the *genuine* criteria for knowing conscious beings and 'their opposites' apart (however the latter should be precisely defined or delineated); and though, just *because* of this intimate familiarity, it is again[70] difficult to describe these criteria in detail, I, for one, do not doubt that something like an 'introjection' of subjective experiences into the bodies – or whatever 'non-bodily organs' – of my fellow-men does not play any part in the criteria in question.[71]

2.3.2.   My adopting a sceptical attitude towards mind-body as well as body-mind causation which I just mentioned in passing in subsection 2.3.1 is not only due to the fact that we have no genuine ('immediate') access to the experiences of others. For although we have such an access to our own experiences, and *in a way* also to our own overt behaviour, I am likewise reluctant to recognise a causal relation between *my* subjective experiences on the one hand and *my* 'macroscopic' (overt) behaviour, or the 'microscopic' neuro-chemical occurrences in *my* body, on the other. Now one may think that my sceptical attitude towards psychophysical causation might be based on an inadequate concept of causation, say, the idea that causation has essentially to do with a transfer or flux of energy; for in this case, the assumption of a psychophysical causation might well be incompatible with the assumption that the physical world is 'causally closed', which I share with Velmans[72] and the mainstreams of today's philosophy of mind as well as of empirical science. However, like Velmans I am inclined to think of a 'cause' in terms of 'necessary and sufficient conditions' for the 'effect' in question,[73] which, I take it, basically agrees with Hume's ingenious and well-known analysis of causation.[74] Why, then, do I so decidedly dislike the conception of a psychophysical causation, whereas Velmans, as I indicated in section 1.1, above, clearly does *not*? I think this difference may be explained by surmising that Velmans, though perfectly alive to the fact that here, as everywhere in the borderland of science and philosophy, 'we need to separate the empirical problems from the conceptual ones' (Velmans 2000:

---

[70] See sect. 1.7.4 with fn. 29 and sect. 2.2.3, above.

[71] Believers in ESP ('extra-sensory perception'), spiritualists, etc. will have to oppose to this. Personally, I find it difficult to take a rational stance towards them. I feel that I have no right at all to flatly deny that they are right; but ought I therefore to *take into account* their alleged findings, using them, for instance, as falsifying evidence against my philosophical conceptions? I started discussing this question in Hoche 1990: 2.7.

[72] Cf. Velmans 2000: pp. 17, 238, 252f., 258, 276; 2002: pp. 7, 10.

[73] See Velmans 2000: pp. 239, 243; cf. p. 25. – In adopting Velmans's wording, I do not intend of course to deny that a cause is usually taken to be what Mackie 1965 called an 'INUS condition', that is to say, 'an *insufficient* but *necessary* part of a condition which is itself *unnecessary* but *sufficient* for the result' (ibid.: p. 16; cf. Hoche 1990: 10.6).

[74] The importance of Hume's analysis of the concept of causation to understanding consciousness I tried to work out in detail in Hoche 1995a.

p. 241), and though squarely facing what he calls 'a familiar *conceptual* problem' of the relevant sort (p. 243), *does not go far enough* in the *conceptual analysis* that is needed – and which, in fact, is the business of philosophers rather than that of psychologists and other empirical scientists.

2.3.3.   Now the 'familiar *conceptual* problem' just mentioned consists in the fact that the brain, the rest of the body that can be researched into scientifically, the rest of the physical world, and, last not least, the overt bodily behaviour of humans and non-human animals can only be examined 'from an external third-person perspective' whereas 'consciousness is in essence a first-person phenomenon' (Velmans 2000: p. 243). 'Once we arrive at the end of a third-person physical or functional account of how a brain or other system works, we still need some credible way to cross the "explanatory gap" to conscious experience. Luckily, in the human case this is not really a *practical* problem, for the reason that we naturally have access to *what lies on both sides of the gap*. We can observe what is going on in the brains of others or in our own brain from an external third-person perspective (via exteroception, aided by a little physical equipment). And we naturally have first-person access to what it is like to have the experiences that accompany such observable brain activity. For many explanatory purposes we just need to switch from one perspective to the other at the appropriate place, and add the first-person to the third-person story in an appropriate way' (p. 245). And in a note he adds: 'Actually, we are so accustomed to this "perspectival switching" that we often do it without noticing that we are doing it. However, recognising when such switches occur is one important step in making sense of the causal stories that we tell about the interactions between consciousness and brain' (p. 260, n. 7). Another important step in making sense of psychophysical (and/or physiopsychical) causation – in Velmans's view, I take it, actually *the only* remaining step – is understanding what he calls the 'complementary' relation between our first-person and third-person findings: 'While *perspectival switching* from a third-person account of neural events to a first-person account of correlated experiences allows one to cross the "explanatory gap", we still need to understand how such accounts relate to each other' (p. 246). 'I know something about your mental states that you do not know (their physical embodiment). But you know something about them that I do not know (their manifestation in experience). Such first- and third-person information is *complementary*. We need your first-person story and my third-person story for a complete account of what is going on' (p. 247).

2.3.4.   In what follows, I will try and show that Velmans's conception of *per-spectival complementarity* is basically sound, whereas he makes too light of the problems connected with the conception of crossing what he calls the 'explanatory gap' between complementary first- and third-person data by means of *'perspectival switching'* and *'mixed-perspective'* explanations (Velmans 2000: pp. 248, 249, 251).

2.4. Psychophysical complementarity

2.4.1.   When calling first-person and third-person information 'complementary', in the first place Velmans means to say that what is seen from the first-person perspective and what is seen from the third-person perspective *complement*, or *complete*, each other in the sense that either perspective is required if we want 'to broaden our theories of mind' (2000: p. 278; cf. p. 135 n. 2) and to get a comprehensive view of it: '[T]he information available to [a subject] S *complements* the information available to [an external observer] E. To obtain a complete account of visual perception one needs to utilise *both* sources of information' (p. 185; cf. pp. 186, 189, 247–250, 277 f.). 'The clinician merely reports what he or she observes or infers about what is going on (using available means), and the patient does likewise. Such first- and third-person accounts of the subject's mental life or body states are complementary, and mutually irreducible. *Taken together*, they provide a global, psychophysical picture of the condition under scrutiny' (p. 248; cf. pp. 250, 278).

2.4.2.   For Velmans, the aim of obtaining such a global, complementary view is *to understand the nature* of the 'explanatory gap' mentioned in sections 2.3.3 and 2.3.4, above. 'We can cross the explanatory gap by switching between a subject's perspective and an external observer's perspective in an appropriate way, but this says little about the nature of the gap that we cross. [...] What dwells within the "explanatory gap"? Ontological monism combined with epistemological dualism assumes that there must be some thing, event or process that one can know in two complementary ways. There must be something that grounds and connects the two views we have of it. Let us call this the "nature of mind" ' (2000: p. 249). '[T]he nature of the mind is revealed as much by how it appears from one perspective as from the other. If so, the nature of mind is not *either* physical *or* conscious experience, it is at once physical *and* conscious experience. For lack of a better term we may describe this nature as *psychophysical*' (p. 250). 'If consciousness and its physical correlates are actually complementary aspects of a psychophysical mind, we can close the "explanatory gap" in a way that unifies consciousness and brain while preserving the ontological status of both. It also provides a simple way of making sense of all four forms of physical/mental causation. Operations of mind viewed from a purely external observer's perspective ($P \rightarrow P$), operations of mind viewed from a purely first-person perspective ($M \rightarrow M$), and mixed-perspective accounts involving perspectival switching ($P \rightarrow M$; $M \rightarrow P$) can be understood as different views (or a mix of views) of a single, psychophysical information process, developing over time. In providing a common psychophysical ground for brain and experience, such a process also provides the "missing link" required to explain psychosomatic effects' (p. 251; cf. pp. 236, 248–250).

2.4.3.   From the last quotation it becomes obvious that Velmans, 'naturalising' Spinoza, favours a '*dual-aspect theory*' of mind, taken to be 'a single, psychophysical information process' (see 2000: esp. pp. 23 f., 239, 249 f.). According to Velmans, there is a mental entity which is *unknowable* in so far as we cannot have *a single, unifying, integrated view* of it, and yet *knowable* in so far as we can access it from *two quite different perspectives* – the first- and the third-person perspective – which *complement* each other. Velmans points to remarkable parallels between his psychophysical dual-aspect theory and what he takes to be comparable theories in micro- as well as in macrophysics: Maxwell's theory of electromagnetism and Bohr's conception of 'complementarity' in quantum mechanics (p. 250). But he also stresses 'important differences between psychophysical complementarity and the wave-particle complementarity of quantum mechanics', for instance the fact that in physics the complementary data 'are both observable from a third-person perspective' (p. 261, n. 19; cf. Velmans 1991: p. 669, n. 18).

2.4.4.   There is one problem, however, which, I take it, he pays no attention to. He seems to take it for granted that complementary data in microphysics, such as a light-wave and 'the corresponding' photon, or an electron endowed with a precise location and 'the same' electron endowed with a precise momentum, should be regarded as different aspects of *one and the same* underlying entity (as our way of speaking in point of fact seems to require). Correspondingly, his ways of speaking about psychophysical complementarity make it quite plain that he thinks of *one and the same* psychophysical entity ('mind') that can be seen from *either* the first-person *or* the third-person perspective. 'For some purposes, third-person accounts are more useful, but for other purposes, first-person accounts may be more useful. And when these accounts are accurate and *of the same thing*, they need not conflict' (Velmans 2000: p. 277; my italics).[75] '[D]ual aspects have to be aspects *of* something. Consequently, my own analysis adopted a form of nonreductionist monism (ontological monism combined with epistemological dualism). That is, the one thing is the "nature of mind" – which can be known in complementary first- and third-person ways' (p. 281 n. 5; cf. pp. 249 f., 254). This position looks highly attractive in that it may be easily taken to help us understand alleged body-mind and mind-body causation[76] and, moreover, appears to be downright forced upon us by our ingrained ways of speaking. However, let me briefly mention some doubts concerning this intricate point. First, the argument from linguistic constraints on our thinking or forming concepts must not be overestimated; on the contrary, Frege, Wittgenstein, Austin, Hare, and other 'ordinary language philosophers' have often warned us of the 'pitfalls' of lan-

---

[75] See also 2000: pp. 67, 204, where Velmans quotes from George Miller.
[76] See sect. 2.5.3, below.

guage.[77] Second, though it is true that Niels Bohr himself at least once spoke in passing of 'complementary aspects of one and the same thing',[78] at least *some* of the contemporary interpreters of quantum mechanics seem to me to take it that speaking of 'one and the same' quantum-mechanical object 'in itself', that is, without any reference to the experimental arrangement in question, is void of meaning.[79] Third, let us remember that, according to Bohr, certain descriptions of quantum-mechanical phenomena are 'complementary, *but mutually exclusive*' (although 'not contradicting each other'),[80] and that what is given in views which are complementary in this strict sense are 'incompatible quantities'. If so, from a logical analysis of our ordinary-language identity-statements we can infer that such complementary data can be neither numerically identical nor numerically different to each other. Rather, they stand to each other in the unique relation of what I call a '*categorial difference*' – a difference which is peculiar to precisely such entities that cannot be subsumed under *a common sortal concept admitting of being individually bound, that is, a common concept that allows the counting of objects.*[81] For these reasons I decidedly doubt that we are truly justified in speaking of '*dual aspects*' as well as of '*one and the same thing*' of which they are aspects. All the same it remains true that it is not at all easy to replace this everyday way of expressing oneself with a more appropriate one.

2.4.5. My misgivings concerning the conception of *one and the same* psy-chophysical entity ('mind') different *aspects* of which may be seen either from a first-person or from a third-person perspective are confirmed by the mutually exclusive character of these perspectives, which I just mentioned in section 2.4.4. Velmans himself hints at this mutual exclusiveness. Having stated that 'psycholog-ical complementarity would seem to be nonexclusive – that is, [that] third-person observations of neural correlates by an external observer would not exclude simul-taneous first-person observations by a subject of correlated experiences', he rightly adds that 'self-observation (by a subject observing his or her own neural correlates via an autocerebroscope) might be governed by *exclusive complementarity*. That is, *it might be impossible simultaneously to observe the neural correlates of a given experience and to have that experience*' (2000: p. 261, n. 19; my italics). I believe that the import of this very last conjecture can hardly be overestimated. Unless I am very much mistaken, in fact there are only *few* conscious experiences the neural correlates of which I can *research into* while I am *having* or *undergoing* these expe-

---

[77] For a discussion, see Hoche & Strube 1985: A.II.1.b (pp. 46–48).

[78] Translated from Bohr 1933: p. 246; for a discussion of the pros and cons of 'dual-aspect' conceptions see Hoche 1990: 11.8

[79] See, e. g., Drieschner 1974: p. 117; 1981: pp. 109, 121, 131; 1984: pp. 58f.; Holton 1981: pp. 149f., 165.

[80] Translated from Bohr 1927: pp. 38f. For a discussion, see Hoche 1990: 11.7.

[81] See sect. 2.1, fn. 45, above; Essay III of the present collection; and Hoche 1990: p. 120.

riences – to wit, only non-visual (say, auditory, haptic, and olfactory) percepts. For by means of a simple thought-experiment I can easily convince myself that, as a rule at least, I cannot simultaneously *see* something happen out in the world and *scrutinise* the correlates of my visual percepts going on in my central nervous system. The same seems to me to be true if we think of non-perception experiences, say, emotions or actions. An emotion such as being afraid of a situation or being in love with someone can hardly go 'unscathed' if *at the same time* we try and make use of an autocerebroscope; and likewise an action such as writing a letter, playing the piano (even if it is done by heart), drinking a glass of water or simply walking up and down the garden-path is at least seriously impaired by our *simultaneously* trying to pay attention, with the help of whatever appropriate devices, to its neural correlates.[82] This situation strongly differs from the well-known cases in which we have access to a material object by means of two or more different senses, say, by simultaneously seeing, touching, hearing and smelling *one and the same* thing (as we would unhesitatingly say). If so, I find it hard to see how to bring about something like the 'unity' of *one and the same* 'psychophysical entity', or how to justify the view that complementary perspectives yield different 'aspects', 'faces', 'facets', or 'sides' of *one and the same* underlying reality.

2.5. Consciousness and causation II

2.5.1. To be more precise: If in the bulk of pertinent cases we cannot simultaneously *have* (*undergo*, or '*live*') a conscious experience and *perceive* (or, what is more, *observe* or even *scrutinise*) what we are used to regard as its neural correlate, then we cannot help admitting that the following is the case. *Either* it is simply not true that, in the majority of concrete situations which are to the point, we have access to *all* of the complementary data (that 'we […] have access to *what lies on both sides of the* [explanatory] *gap*', as Velmans puts it),[83] *or* the data given from *one* perspective *disappear*, or *cease to exist*, as soon as, by means of a 'perspectival switching', we manage to bring the data given from the *other* perspective *into view*. Or more simply: In the case of what we call '*other minds*' or take to be the 'conscious experiences' of our *fellow-men*, I have to content myself with the neural correlates of their 'experiences' as well as the observable, overt behaviour on the basis of which I ascribe to them these 'experiences'. And in *my own* case I have a first-person access to *all* of my conscious experiences (for if I had not, what is in question would be, not conscious experience, but something 'preconscious'

---

[82] Focussing on the corresponding *overt behaviour* instead of the corresponding *neural events*, I tried to point out such 'interferences' in Hoche 1973a: pp. 179–184; 1990: p. 213 fn. 560. But see also Velmans 2002: p. 13: 'While you maintain your focus on the imaged scene, you cannot observe its neural correlates in your own brain (you would need to use my equipment for that).'

[83] See the quotation from Velmans 2000: p. 245, in sect. 2.3.3, above.

or 'unconscious' or what not) and, presumably, a *simultaneous* third-person access to *only a handful* of their neural correlates as well as, possibly, a *retarded or delayed* access to the (records of the observations of the) neural correlates of the rest of my subjective experiences. In a word: Apart from a few exceptions,[84] in my own case I can access *either this* side of what Velmans calls the 'explanatory gap', *or else* what lies *beyond* it. But if what is given from the *one* perspective does not temporally *coincide* with, or *closely follow*, what is given from the *other*, then it seems to me to be doubtful whether we should speak or think of a 'causal' relation between the two sets of data. For temporal *coincidence* or *succession* is, I take it, at the very root of causation (though surely not *all* that is essential to it; see Hoche 1977).

2.5.2.   Furthermore, if we were really prepared to follow Velmans in regarding a conscious experience and what he takes to be its neural correlate as only *two* 'aspects' of *one and the same* 'psychophysical mind',[85] then I would find it rather strange that *one aspect* of *one and the same entity* should be the 'cause' (or the 'effect', as the case may be) of *another aspect* of it. However, this is a very intricate question of *linguistic analysis* which, I think, here we need not discuss.

2.5.3.   But of course Velmans thinks he has a very good reason for adopting his 'dual-aspect theory' of the human mind. To begin with, what definitely looks like body-mind and mind-body causation is not only a highly familiar everyday phenomenon. There is, furthermore, 'extensive experimental and clinical evidence that conscious experiences can affect brain/body processes'.[86] 'The most well accepted evidence for the effect of states of mind on medical outcome is undoubtedly the "placebo effect".'[87] But '[h]ow can one reconcile the evidence that conscious experiences are causally effective with the principle that the physical world is causally closed? One simple way is to accept that for each individual there is *one* "mental life" but *two* ways of knowing it: first-person knowledge and third-person knowledge'.[88] For instance, '[w]hen we image ourselves in green grass on a summer's day and feel relaxed we are usually right to assume that the

---

[84] I am speaking of the non-visual percepts mentioned in sect. 2.4.5, above. Even in these rare cases, however, the fact that I am in a position, say, to *see*, by means of an autocerebroscope, the neural correlates of what I *simultaneously hear, touch, smell*, or *taste*, is, I think, of no help whatsoever in understanding the nature of the relation between the experiences involved and their neural correlates.

[85] By the way, speaking of one and the same 'psychophysical mind' seems to me to be not much more informative than speaking point-blank of one and the same '*Je ne sais quoi*' or '*I dunno what*'. For if 'we know little about the physical nature of the neural correlates of conscious experiences' (Velmans 2002: p. 11), then we certainly know much less about the enigmatic whole allegedly consisting of conscious as well as neural constituent parts.

[86] Velmans 2002: p. 10.

[87] Ibid.: p. 5; for further examples, see pp. 4–7.

[88] Ibid.: pp. 10 f.; cf. sect. 2.3.2 with fn. 72, above.

mental state that is represented in our imagery has produced a real bodily effect. For everyday life, it doesn't matter that we don't understand how such imaged scenarios are constructed by preconscious mental processes'.[89] Provided that we are justified in saying that, 'from a third-person perspective', these 'preconscious mental processes' not only '*look like*' but in fact *are* 'neurochemical and associated physical activities in our brains'[90] – and I cannot see a point in insisting on a conceptual difference in this case –, and given that our conscious experiences are in fact, as Velmans repeatedly says,[91] '*constructed*' or '*generated*' by 'preconscious mental processes' and hence by 'neurochemical and associated physical activities in our brains', it now turns out that, for Velmans, in the last instance it must be the latter that are causally effective, and hence that the alleged *mind-body* causation should be frankly taken to be just a mediated variant of *body-body* causation. So Velmans's dual-aspect theory may at first sight appear to be extremely fertile indeed. But at least two things seem to me to speak against this view. First, a dual-aspect theory is untenable for the conceptual reasons I tried and outlined in subsections 2.4.4–2.4.5, above. And second, in assuming a '*construction*' or a '*generation*' of conscious experiences by neuronal events Velmans still relies on a genuine *body-mind* causation which, I take it, contravenes the principle of the causal closedness of the physical world as much as a genuine *mind-body* causation would do.

2.6. The methodological problem of correlating conscious experiences to neural events

2.6.1. By now, even a reader who is not very good at reading between the lines may have got the suspicion that I doubt, not only a *causal relation* between conscious experiences and what are commonly taken to be their neural correlates, but even the *propriety of speaking of neural 'correlates'*. To be quite frank, it never occurred to me that this way of speaking might be improper until I became acquainted with the recent neurobiological conception of 'distributive representation' in the human brain, which by the late eighties of the 20th century seems to have superseded the older model of 'gnostic neurons' (jokingly also called

---

[89] Ibid.: p. 19.

[90] Cf. ibid.: p. 20: 'We habitually think of ourselves as being our *conscious selves*. But it should be clear [...] that the different facets of our experienced, conscious selves are generated by and represent aspects of our own preconscious minds. That is, we are *both* the preconscious generating processes *and* the conscious results. Viewed from a third-person perspective our own preconscious mental processes look like neurochemical and associated physical activities in our brains. Viewed introspectively, from a first-person perspective, our preconscious mind seems like a personal, but "empty space" from which thoughts, images, and feelings spontaneously arise. *We* are as much one thing as the other [...].'

[91] Ibid.: p. 20, passim.

'granny neurons') dating back to the well-known researches of D. H. Hubel and T. N. Wiesel.[92] According to the conception of a '*distributive* representation' (or a '*distributive* processing' of stimuli), 'neither a *single* neuron nor a *local* neuronal network is able to represent a complex perceptual content in all its aspects'; rather, the neuronal 'activity pattern' – revealed by means of novel brain imaging techniques such as positron emission tomography (PET) or magnetic resonance imaging (MRI) – with which we can correlate a more or less complex cognitive process 'is traversing, in a selective way, the *whole* brain'.[93]

2.6.2.   If we have to take this seriously, which I think we certainly do, there seems to me to come up a grave methodological problem, the problem, to wit, of how to exactly correlate neural events to conscious experiences, or the observation of neuronal activity patterns to 'introspection'. Let me say in advance, first, that in my opinion we would not be truly justified in assuming that such a correlation *exists* (or *is likely to exist*, or *should be postulated to exist*) if there were no actual or potential *workable methods* of *coming to know* such a correlation,[94] and, second, that such methods certainly cannot be speculative but have to be *empirical* and, more specifically, *experimental*. Nonetheless I think that there are a number of *conceptual problems* concerning such *experimental methods*, and that a philosopher, even if not conversant with the details of psychological and psychophysical experiments *really carried out*, yet in his capacity of being conversant with *conceptual analyses* ought to be allowed to try and devise some *thought-experiments* concerning those *real experiments*.[95] – The latter can in principle be carried out by either an *external* experimenter or the subject to be examined *herself*.

2.6.3.   Let us begin with the latter sort of experiments, that is, with psychophysical *self-experiments*, and suppose that in such a *self-experiment* I am up to correlating, say, my visual imagining[96] my favourite granny's face – which certainly

---

[92] See, for instance, Roth 1992: esp. pp. 301f., 306f., 308f., 312f., 314f., 317–319.

[93] Translated from Roth & Schwegler 1995: §§((8)), ((9)), and ((27)) (my italics); cf. Roth 1992: pp. 312f.: '[P]robably, the unity of perception can only be constituted by a heterarchical connection of all [cortical and subcortical] areas taking part in the actual processing of the stimuli' (my translation); p. 318: 'The complete perception at a given moment in time is represented in the simultaneous activity of the centres which, in different ways, take part in the bringing forth of information' (my translation).

[94] See sect. 1.8.3 and also sect. 2.2.9 with fn. 68, above.

[95] I think that a considerable part of doing conceptual analysis may be subsumed under the title of a 'thought-experiment', which, however, as Tobias Knobloch recently brought to my attention, is not as it were 'protected by law'. – Undoubtedly, my following considerations can only be a modest beginning which should be propped up and further developed by the constructive criticisms of psychological practitioners.

[96] I am intentionally choosing an example of *imagining* instead of visually *perceiving*, or *recognising*, a certain person's face; for otherwise the argument I am about to develop could be cut short by

does not exemplify an altogether trivial case of a conscious experience – with the concomitant neuronal activity pattern.

2.6.3.1. To achieve this, I have to concentrate upon the imagined face and, more or less simultaneously, upon the corresponding image on the monitor. In this case, what I can see on the monitor is an image, not just of the neuronal activity pattern corresponding to my focussing on my granny's face, but of the 'sum' of this pattern *plus* the pattern corresponding to my focussing on the result of the imaging procedure.[97] To avoid this undesirable *interference*, one might think of making use of the small temporal span which is taken to extend between the taking place of the conscious experience and the appearance of the finished image on the monitor.[98] But suppose that I am trying to concentrate, *first* upon my granny's imagined face, and *afterwards – to wit, a couple of seconds later –* on the PET- or MRI-image. Certainly I cannot leave this switching of attention to chance. That is, while I am occupied with my first task, namely, with concentrating on the imagined face, I must (a) be prepared to turn, after a couple of seconds, to my second task, namely, to scrutinising the image on the monitor, and (b) try as I can not to think of my second task – but here, (b) would obviously *contradict* not only (a) but already itself.

2.6.3.2.   Now one might think of having recourse to 'the "subtraction method" commonly used today in order to be able to distinguish specific from unspecific raisings of metabolism due to a raised brain activity (Posner, 1993). For instance, in the first phase of an experiment a test person is asked to read certain words *purely mechanically*, but in the second phase she is supposed to read them *and at the same time think about their meaning*. By subtracting the spatial activity patterns and their intensities from each other [sic], one gets a "pure" representation of the neuronal processes which are the basis of grasping the meaning of the words.'[99] But I cannot see that resorting to the 'subtraction method' would be of much help to our present problem. For if I intend to apply this method in order to make seen the 'pure' neuronal representation of my imagining my granny's face, I have to

---

pointing to the fact that I cannot (visually) *perceive*, that is, *see* a face and at the same time (visually) take notice of a PET- or MRI-image on a monitor (cf. sects. 2.4.5 and 2.5.1, above).

[97] This 'undesirable disturbance' may perhaps be compared to the older (by now, I take it, partly out-dated) quantum-mechanical conception that the *act of measuring* the location of a sub-atomic particle inevitably disturbs or prevents *measuring* 'the same' particle's momentum (cf. sect. 2.4.4, above).

[98] Experts say that it takes around 30 seconds to bring about a PET-image, and in the case of MRI-images there are comparable temporal spans: cf. Roth & Schwegler 1995: §((9)). As Dr. Jane F. Utting was kind enough to point out to me, it should be emphasised that alone the time between the electrical response of a neuron and the blood flow response – the last of which is what in MRI and many PET imaging experiments is being measured – varies from one to about three or four seconds.

[99] Translated from Roth & Schwegler 1995: §((9)). I changed 'Posner, 1994' into 'Posner, 1993'.

try, either at the same time or at a later time, to 'subtract' the spatial distribution and intensity of the activity pattern that corresponds to my observing the PET- or MRI-image on the monitor from the spatial distribution and intensity of the activity pattern corresponding to the *interference* mentioned before. However, a *simultaneous* 'subtraction' is impossible because the attempt to achieve one would obviously result in an additional interference and hence in iterating the problem.

2.6.3.3.   The alternative would be a *subsequent* 'subtraction'; but such a procedure seems to me to be impossible for the following reason. Isolating the activity pattern that corresponds to *my attempt to grasp the activity pattern corresponding to my imagining my granny's face* surely is as little possible as isolating the activity pattern that corresponds *to my imagining my granny's face*, and on the same grounds. To be sure, it might well be possible that, in a neurobiological self-experiment in which I apply an imaging procedure to myself, I exclusively pay attention to the question of what activity pattern is going to emerge in the next moment. However, the activity pattern thus emerging would be the pattern corresponding to my attentively expecting *any* activity pattern *whatsoever* and not the pattern corresponding to my attentively expecting the activity pattern *corresponding to my imagining my granny's face*. And as yet I cannot see any old way how to decide whether or not these two patterns coincide; as far as I can see, neither a *self*-experiment nor testing *somebody else* would do. – Finally, one might think of taking recourse to the possibility of subsequently comparing a *recorded* PET- or MRI-image of a cognitive process of one's own with the *recorded* '*introspection-report*' about this very cognitive process. But then one would have, not simply to *perform* this cognitive process in the first place, but to *perform and at the same verbalise* it; and this certainly would be a more complex cognitive achievement, to which therefore a different PET- or MRI-image would be likely to belong.[100]

2.6.4.   Turning now to psychophysical experiments conducted by an *external* experimenter, we have first to face the fact that the latter has *no first-person access* to the conscious experiences of his test person, or that he is barred from 'introspecting' them.[101] As a substitute, we may first think of the 'introspection'-*reports* delivered by the subject to be tested. But the problem connected with the use of such reports in *self*-experiments which I just outlined at the end of section 2.6.3.3 obviously adheres to psychophysical experiments *as such*. To be sure, one may think of delivering the report, not *simultaneously* with having the conscious experience in question, but a short time *later*, that is, from *memory*. But then novel

---

[100] The methodological problems just considered in subsections 2.6.3.1–2.6.3.3 have already been sketched in Hoche 1995b: §§ ((8))–((10)).

[101] I prefer to put the terms 'to introspect' and 'introspection' in inverted commas as they seem to me to be dictated by the erroneous view that conscious experiences are 'in the mind', which Velmans rightly rejects (see esp. sect. 1.2, above).

problems are likely to arise, among them the problem of the exact dating of the experience and the uncertainties and inaccuracies of memory. But surely the external experimenter can do *without* 'introspection'-reports. For instance, he may ask the test person to think about, remember, imagine, or look at certain objects, or to seek for as much gains as possible in a certain game of hazard, or he may simply offer to her selected pieces of sensory input – say, well-defined optic or auditory stimuli. But in such cases I think it will be difficult, if not impossible, for him to assess the efficacy of hosts of possible collateral experiences such as expectations, distractions, excitement and similar emotions, forcible attempts at isolating, or focussing attention to, single experiences,[102] etc., the neuronal activity patterns corresponding to which will be 'interfering' with those belonging to the subjective experiences provoked by, or however else associated with, the attempt to fulfil the task proper – although, perhaps, comparing with each other the results of tests with different persons may lead to statistically significant similarities (see Posner 1993: p. 673).

2.7. The correlation between conscious experiences, neural events, and overt behaviour

2.7.1.   Calling into question the very concept of a strict correlation between given conscious experiences and given neural events can hardly be the last word; but how to continue the story? To begin with: Why do we tend to take it for granted in the first place that such a correlation exists, nay, '*must* exist'? For this firm belief of ours, the following two reasons may be prominently responsible. First, some rather close correlation exists between certain *conscious experiences I undergo* and certain pieces of *my overt behaviour which others can observe*, and in fact some such correlation *must* exist in order to account for the indubitable fact that we can, and nearly always do, communicate with each other about our mutual thoughts, emotions, pains, intentions, actions, etc. Second, the triumphs of the exact natural sciences promoted the – certainly warranted – conviction that the basic and decisive processes of life take place on the molecular level (which, for its part, depends on occurrences in the atomic and subatomic levels), and that therefore the behaviour of humans and other animals that we can immediately observe ought to be causally explained by, and hence in the first place correlated to, simultaneous or nearly simultaneous events that can be researched into by the neural sciences.

---

[102] It should be noted that as a rule we undergo a vast *multitude* of conscious experiences at the same time.

2.7.2. Now a correlation of the *latter* sort, that is, a correlation of *overt behaviour* with *neural goings-on*, is, I take it, no *crucial* problem in that, in principle, it can be brought about in one and the same fundamental attitude, namely, from a purely third-person perspective. What we are supposed to correlate in *this* case is, as it were, some 'ethologically' observable stretch of 'macro-behaviour' on the one hand and a stretch of 'micro-behaviour' that is open to electrochemical, biochemical, and physiological research on the other.

2.7.3. So the crucial problem seems to me to reside in the question of how to correlate certain *conscious experiences I am having* with certain pieces of *my overt behaviour which others can observe and on the strength of which they are in a position to find out that I am having those experiences*. At first sight, here all the difficulties appear to be bound to recur which I discussed in section 2.6, above; for *others* can *only* observe my overt behaviour, and *I* cannot observe my overt behaviour as though it were somebody else's (say, by means of a looking glass or a monitor) *while I am having or carrying out* 'corresponding' conscious experiences – such as cognitions, emotions, intentions, or actions – without severely distorting and damaging the latter.[103] But as I tried to make plain elsewhere,[104] these difficulties can be overcome if we try to solve them in a way analogous to Hume's attempt to justify the concept of causation, that is, on the formal model of what Hume called his 'Sceptical Solution' of the 'Sceptical Doubts Concerning the Operations of the Understanding'.[105]

2.7.4. Saul A. Kripke aptly characterises such a method as follows. 'A *sceptical* solution of a sceptical philosophical problem begins [...] by conceding that the sceptic's negative assertions are unanswerable. Nevertheless our ordinary practice or belief is justified because – contrary appearances notwithstanding – it need not require the justification the sceptic has shown to be untenable.'[106] Along these lines, Kripke exposes an analogy between 'Wittgenstein's argument against *private* language' and 'Hume's argument against *private* causation'.[107] Likewise, a structural similarity between the latter and a possible 'argument against the *private* correlating of subjective consciousness and objective behaviour' may be sketched, in its barest outlines, in the following way.[108] In a first step we have to concede that the sceptic is right when he asserts that neither *a subject S* nor *an external observer E* is in a position to simultaneously have S's subjective experiences and observe S's

---

[103] See sect. 2.4.5 with fn. 82, above.

[104] See Hoche 1995a.

[105] Hume 1748: headings of sects. IV and V; but note that his 'Sceptical Solution' does not reach its summit before sect. VII, part 2.

[106] Kripke 1982: p. 66.

[107] Ibid.: p. 68 (my italics).

[108] I have tried to develop this sketch at considerable more length in Hoche 1995a.

objective behaviour and thus to correlate them to each other. But in a second step we have to realise that such a *'private correlating'* by either S or E *alone* is not at all required. Rather, the correlating *must*, and also *can*, be done *intersubjectively*: Since my earliest years, I have learnt how my elders speak in the same terms about *their, my, and somebody else's* perceptions, emotions, intentions, actions, etc., and thus by the mediation of our common language there is brought about a 'customary connexion'[109] between a number of subjective data I can obtain from my first-person (or 'internal') perspective and a number of objective data I can obtain, *in a non-interfering way*, from my third-person (or 'external') perspective.

2.7.5.   Such intersubjectively achieved correlations, sufficient though they certainly are for most or all of our everyday purposes, possibly may be not fine-grained enough to be of much help for reaching the ambitious aims of contemporary neuroscience. Nonetheless at least a gross correlating of conscious experiences, overt behaviour, and neural goings-on seems to be possible in the way just indicated.

2.8.   The relation between *things as experienced* and *things themselves*

2.8.1.   If we now turn to the question of how conscious experiences, that is, *things as experienced* (or, in the phenomenological jargon: fully concrete *'noematic phenomena'*) are related to *things themselves* (or to noematic *'objects pure and simple'*, that is, abstract noematic 'cores', or 'nuclei'),[110] then it should be plain that this *relation* is *not a correlation* in that what we are seeking for is not a one-one correspondence but a relation between 'bald' *unities* and 'exuberant' *multiplicities* intentionally referring to them.[111] For instance, we have various percepts of one and the same cat (various 'cats *as* perceived')[112] and the cat itself of which they are percepts, or to which they intentionally refer (at which they 'mentally aim'). The cat itself, the animal out in the world, I can see from my third-person (or 'external') perspective, whereas the various cat-percepts are given to me from

---

[109] Cf. Hume 1748: p. 78: 'customary connexion in the thought or imagination'; p. 78, note: 'customary connexion between the ideas'. It is important to see that Hume is here rightly speaking of a 'connexion' and not a mere 'conjunction'.

[110] See sect. 1.7.4 with fn. 30, above.

[111] See ibid. – It should by now be plain that 'intentionally' referring to something has nothing to do with acting 'wilfully' or 'on purpose'. Rather, the medieval technical term 'intentio', which was revived by the 19th century Austrian psychologist and philosopher Franz Brentano and then adopted from the latter by phenomenologists, ordinary language philosophers, and psychologists, seems to derive from the Latin expression for an archer's taking aim at something, namely, 'intendere arcum in aliquid'. In fact, the term 'intentionally referring to' could be explained as meaning some such thing as 'mentally aiming at'.

[112] Cf. sect. 2.2.3, fn. 56, above.

my first-person (or 'internal') perspective. For this reason the cat itself and the cat-percepts are *complementary* data and, therefore, *neither numerically identical* with *nor numerically different* from each other. All I can meaningfully say about their relation is that they are *different qua being given from mutually exclusive perspectives*, hence *incompatible with each other*, hence unable to be subsumed under *a common sortal concept* – that is, *a common concept that allows the counting of objects* –, and in this sense '*categorially different*'.[113] As I tried to make plain in the present paper, the same relation holds between my percepts of the cat on the one hand and their behavioural and neural correlates in my body on the other. But this ought not to be found surprising. For the cat I see, the neural correlates of my seeing it, and my overt behaviour on the strength of which others can say that I see it are all of them third-perspective data, and at least in principle an external observer can ascertain in exactly what way they causally relate to each other.

2.8.2.   So I think we have 'objectivity' or 'nature', comprising material objects out in the physical world including animate bodies with their neural goings-on and their overt behaviour, on the one side of what Velmans calls the 'explanatory gap',[114] and 'subjectivity' or 'conscious experience' on the other. As both sides are only accessible from complementary perspectives, the 'explanatory gap' cannot be satisfyingly bridged over by 'perspectival switching'[115] and causation; for what the former brings into view are 'incompatible entities', which are '*categorially different*' from each other, whereas the latter requires a *numerical* relation of either difference or identity between cause and effect.

2.8.3.   For the same reason I think we ought to conclude that Velmans's conception of 'reflexive monism'[116] cannot be maintained. In subsection 1.5.2, above, I tried to illustrate this conception of his by means of the schema 'oCo', where 'C' is to stand for a subject's cognitive-processing device (her body and brain); but what should be to the left and to the right of 'C' is not one and the same object 'o' twice over but the *object itself* on the one side and the *object as experienced* on the other, which, as I just stated in subsection 2.8.1, are not numerically identical with each other but *neither numerically identical nor numerically different*. Nor do I find it helpful to suggest that 'there is *one* universe (the *thing itself*) with relatively differentiated parts in the form of conscious beings like ourselves, each with a unique, conscious view of the larger universe of which it is a part. In so far as we are parts of the universe that, in turn, experience the larger universe, we participate in a reflexive process whereby the universe experiences itself.'[117]

---

[113] See sect. 2.4.4, above.

[114] See sects. 2.3.3–2.3.4 and 2.4.2, above.

[115] See ibid.

[116] See sects. 1.5.2, 1.7.2 fn. 21, 2.4.2 and 2.4.4, above.

[117] Velmans 2000: p. 233; cf. p. 229.

This old and in a way undoubtedly attractive conception of a universe 'in itself' which in the course of its evolution becomes increasingly aware of itself, and thus a 'Being for itself' in much the Hegelian sense of the term, is bound to draw upon the conviction that it is meaningful to speak of 'things in themselves' in the *transcendental* Kantian sense,[118] that is, in the sense of being quite independent of someone's having access to them. This conviction, however, has been seriously called into question not only by transcendental phenomenologists but also by contemporary interpreters of quantum mechanics.[119] So we should rather follow the clues of our better insight and acknowledge that it makes no sense to speak of a universe which is *not* potentially knowable or, as it were, connected to a potentially perceiving subject by sort of a transcendental 'umbilical cord',[120] and hence that there are as many 'universes' as there are conscious beings.

2.8.4.   I am well aware that this view at first sight must seem revolting to a natural scientist. But the 'universes' I was just speaking of are, of course, the surrounding 'life-worlds' we have to do with in everyday life and of which each of us is, as it were, the 'centre', whereas natural science is interested in the 'uncentred' universe abstracted from our individual, 'centred' life-worlds. Furthermore, philosophy as well as empirical science should see to it that they can perform their different tasks each in an optimal way, and this includes a *basically abstractive attitude in science* and an *entirely non-abstractive (concrete) attitude in philosophy*.[121] And as I already let myself lure away into the field of speculation, I should like to finish this essay with a highly speculative consideration which nonetheless is likely to be of personal interest to each of us. None of us knows what dying looks like from their first-person perspective; but let me guess that it *would* be a complete loss of the experienced world if only this loss were not *so* complete as to include the loss of the experiencer himself, which means to say that after all it is not a loss at all, which always requires a 'loser'. I do not intend to go any deeper into this case of a 'coincidence of the opposites', but one thing at least ought to be clear. The universe which may be expected to cease to exist the moment I die is 'only' my concrete, individual life-world of which I am the centre, but not the abstract, centre-less universe which is the global object of science; and *in this sense* it is certainly true that the earth will go on revolving around the sun when I will be dead.[122]

---

[118] See sect. 1.8.2 with fn. 35, above.

[119] See sects. 1.8.3 and 2.4.4 with fn. 79, above.

[120] See. sect. 1.8.3, above.

[121] See sects. 1.8.3 and 2.2.5 with fn. 59, above. – For three further fundamental differences between the attitudes of the empirical sciences and non-empirical philosophy, see Hoche 2002.

[122] For some related questions concerning sense, nonsense, and contradiction in terms, see Hoche 1990: 8.1, esp. the exemplary sentence (37).

VI

A BRIEF OUTLOOK: THE TWO
COMPLEMENTARY PERSPECTIVES ON
THE BODY-MIND-WORLD PROBLEM
AND ON HUMAN ACTION

Summary

As for the body-mind-world relation, two pseudo-problems tend to impose them-selves upon us (1). – The time-honoured mind-body pseudo-problem (1.1). – The mind-world pseudo-problem (1.2). – The body-consciousness-world problem as seen from the third- and the first-person perspectives (2). – The scientific body-consciousness-world problem (2.1). – The phenomenological body-consciousness-world problem. Changing philosophical amazement into insight (2.2). – Human action in the third- and the first-person perspectives (3). – The actions of others as seen from my point of view. Overt behaviour (3.1). – My own actions as seen from my point of view. Gerundive features of my noematic phenomena (3.2). – Actions and intentions in action (3.3). – The complementarity of freedom and determinism in human action (3.4). – A plea for the coexistence of the two complementary perspectives (4). – Why the third-person perspective seems to be 'the scientifically correct' one (4.1). – However, the first- and the third-person perspectives do not contradict each other; so there is no question of a primacy among them (4.2). – We are in need of a novel conceptualisation of the phenomena of so-called 'psy-chophysical interaction' (5). – Perceiving and acting are no proper examples for an alleged psychophysical interaction (5.1). – The placebo effect. Views of some medical experts (5.2). – *Subjective* effects of placebo treatments (5.3). – *Objective* effects of placebo treatments (5.4) – Causation as a flux of energy *versus* Humean causation (5.5). – 'Moore's see-saw'. 'The work of analysis and distinction is often very difficult' (5.6). – The human and the divine points of view (6). – The origin of the world as seen from the human and the divine angles (6.1). – The world of science and our personal life-worlds (6.2).

1. Pseudo-problems concerning the relations between body, consciousness, and the world

Strictly speaking, the headline of this concluding essay is incorrect; for there is not 'the' – that is to say: not just *one* – body-mind-world problem. Rather, it is a consequence of the considerations of the preceding chapter that there are *two* genuine problems besides the much more familiar pseudo-problem concerning the relations between body, consciousness, and the world. Furthermore, in all three cases the relation between body and consciousness and the relation between consciousness and the world as a rule are discussed separately, whereas the relation between body and world is mostly taken for granted and therefore neglected.

Ironically, though on plausible psychological grounds, it has regularly been the pseudo-problem most of us automatically think of whenever the terms 'body-mind-world problem' or, in the usual narrowing down, 'mind-body problem' is being thrown into philosophical and scientific debates.

1.1.   This can be seen already in the following passage from Saint Augustine, which has proved to be enormous influential up to now: 'Modus quo corporibus adhaerent spiritus [...] omnino mirus est nec comprehendi ab homine potest – et hoc ipse homo est': 'The manner in which minds adhere to bodies is altogether enigmatic and cannot be comprehended by man – and this is man himself' (*De civitate Dei*: XXI, 10). Similarly, and expressly referring to Augustine, Blaise Pascal stated in his *Pensées*: 'What makes our inability to apprehend things complete is that they are simple in themselves and that we are composed of two opposite and essentially diverse natures, soul and body [...], spirit and matter [...]. This mixture [ce mélange-là] [...] is [...] what we understand less than anything else. Man is to himself the most amazing object of nature; for he cannot conceive what the body is, and still less what the spirit is, and least of all how a body can be united with a spirit. This is the summit of his difficulties, and yet this is his own being'.[1] In our time, Josef Seifert, following Bonaventura and John Henry Cardinal Newman,[2] goes as far as to consider this seemingly impossible fact a manifestation of divine omnipotence. '[T]he fact of the "transition", the "connection" between the nervous system and the soul, is incomprehensible and a thoroughly *inexplicable* natural "miracle" [...]. Certainly it is already surprising that physiological occurrences in the body can have "psychic effects". But that purely causal occurrences in the body can enter into relations with the fundamentally different, sense-imbued reality of the perception of the external world – that is, taken all by itself, an argument for the existence of God.'[3]

Having in view what I tried to make clear in the preceding chapters, we should find it easy to spot the origin of such considerations. It is a confounding of two complementary perspectives incompatible with each other, to wit, the first-person and the third-person perspectives – a confounding which, after all, might seem to be justified on the ground that, contrary impressions notwithstanding, human beings – even though in a unique way – make up a natural kind.[4] Or, as Sartre concisely put it: The insurmountable difficulties in question result from the attempt

---

[1] Translated from Pascal 1669: II, No. 72, pp. 92f.

[2] Seifert 1973: pp. 201–208.

[3] Ibid.: p. 203 and p. 238, respectively.

[4] See Essay IV: sect. 3.19 of the present collection.

to unite my consciousness not with *my* body (as I experience it myself) but with the body *of others* (as I can perceive it).[5]

1.2.   Similarly, the relation between consciousness and the world (or rather the objects singled or, as it were, crystallised out from it) more often than not has been discussed in the form of what I take to be a mere pseudo-problem. What I have in mind is the frequently posed question of how consciousness, being something 'internal', is in a position to 'transcend itself' and get hold on the essentially different and 'consciousness-independent'[6] material objects of the 'external' world. What is presupposed in this time-honoured style of dealing with the 'transcendence of consciousness' has still been shared even by Sartre, who, notably in his notorious 'ontological proof' ('preuve ontologique'),[7] fundamentally distances himself from Husserl, whose intentionality, in his opinion, is but the 'caricature' of the true transcendence looked for.[8]

2. Two genuine body-consciousness-world problems

Much less spectacular than the two pseudo-problems just outlined are a number of genuine and respectable problems which likewise concern the relations between body, consciousness, and the world. The reader may already gather that what I have in mind is the widely ramified complex of body-consciousness-world problems as conceived solely from the *third-person perspective* on the one hand and the similarly ramified complex of body-consciousness-world problems as conceived solely from the *first-person perspective* on the other. The former is the domain of psychologists, physiologists, and a number of other scientists, on

---

[5] '[…] d'insurmontables difficultés […] proviennent de ce que je tente d'unir ma conscience non à *mon* corps mais au corps *des autres*. En effet, le corps dont je viens d'esquisser la description n'est pas *mon* corps tel qu'il est *pour moi*. Je n'ai jamais vu ni ne verrai mon cerveau, ni mes glandes endocrines' ['Insurmountable difficulties arise from fact that I try to unite my consciousness not with my body but with the body of others. In effect, the body the description of which I just sketched is not *my* body such as it is *for myself*. I have never seen, and I will never see, my brain or my endocrine glands']: Sartre 1943: p. 365; cf. 367: '[…] l'origine de ce faux problème: c'est que l'on a voulu lier *ma* conscience des objets au corps de *l'autre*' ['this spurious problem originates from trying to join *my* consciousness of objects to *another person's* body']. (Sartre's italics.)

[6] It should be noted that the 'independence of consciousness' rightly ascribed to material things in the world is a highly ambiguous matter. Up to now, this ambiguity tends to be neglected; see Hoche & Strube 1985: pp. 27f.

[7] Sartre 1943: pp. 27–29.

[8] Ibid.: pp. 145, 152f. – Opposing this verdict, I do think that Husserl lucidly pleaded for something which might perhaps called a 'transcendence within the immanence'; in an especially succinct and felicitous way he did so in Husserl 1907: esp. Lectures II and III. (The *term* occurs in Husserl 1913, tr. 1931: § 57, where it has a different meaning, though.)

which, however, the 'neurophilosophers' of our days use to poach, too.[9] The latter is one of the three natural domains of philosophy[10] and has mostly been dealt with by phenomenologists, especially in the fields of transcendental phenomenology and existential ontology.

2.1.   As *perceived* from the *third-person* perspective, the relations obtaining between body, consciousness, and the world need not be attended too much by the *philosopher at work*, that is to say, by the philosopher during his 'office-hours' – or so I, for one, believe. Intricate and time-consuming though the empirical inquiries into the manifold facets of these relations doubtless are – I am sure there will remain, and still newly arise, a lot of fascinating research-projects for many centuries to come –, their most basic features can, I think, be quite simply sketched. There is a human subject amidst the material world, of which he, being (from the third-person point of view) himself a material object among others, is part, and other material objects exert multifarious causal influences on his body. For instance, light rays of different wave-lengths, reflected in this or that way by visible things, stimulate his retinae; the resulting electrochemical impulses are conveyed, by afferent neurons, toward his central nervous system; in his brain, countless interactions with contributions (say, 'engrams') of other parts of his nervous system (and his biological body at large) take place; and the resulting nervous impulses are conveyed, by efferent neurons, to effectors such as muscles which become active and produce, say, speech, gestures, or bodily movements which exert immediate causal influences on material objects (including other human beings) in the world surrounding him.

2.2.   As *experienced* from the *first-person* perspective, however, the relations between *my* body, *my* consciousness, and *my* world define a field of philosophical – not only, but for the most part: phenomenological – research which certainly is no less complicated than the scientific field of research just outlined. From the very beginnings of phenomenology in Husserl and, arguably, Brentano, the relation of consciousness to the objects we encounter in the world has been a central topic. In modern psychology and philosophy, Franz Brentano was the first to revive the medieval technical term 'intentio' and to speak of an 'intentional object', and Husserl is certainly the one who did most to clarify this tricky and controversial concept.[11] From the point of view of a pure noematics, the question

---

[9]   It remains to be seen how the contributions of the latter, as opposed to the contributions of scientists proper, will eventually be judged by the scientific community.

[10]   See Introduction: sect. 10, of the present collection of essays.

[11]   Later on, this concept has been adopted by G. E. M. Anscombe and other linguistic philosophers; see Essay IV: 2.3.1, of the present book. Arguably in a closely related sense Max Weber 1913: sect. III, p. 439, introduced the concept of a 'subjective referent' ['subjektiver Bezogenheitsgegenstand'] into his 'Verstehende Soziologie'; cf. ibid.: pp. 427–440 and Weber 1921: pp. 541–570.

of how consciousness can intelligibly 'reach' its intentional objects has been dealt with in section 3.11 of Essay IV of the present collection.

What is perhaps less well-known in the circles of more analytically or scientifically minded consciousness theorists is the fact that the relation between my consciousness and my body *as I myself am aware of them* has likewise been made the topic of extended phenomenological research. This has notably been the case in French phenomenology, which, however, seems to me to have left the sober Husserlian spirit far behind, and with the recent developments of which I am not conversant; but this can also be illuminatingly done within the framework of a pure noematics.

For it can be shown in detail that even in my completely unrestricted imagination I cannot possibly conceive of my subjective conscious experiences in separation from my experienced or 'functioning' body, that is, my body as it is accessed by myself, or from my first-person standpoint. By appropriately applying the method of free phenomenological variation,[12] we can convince ourselves that, if only we consistently stick to the first-person point of view, the close connection or unity of consciousness and body – far from being an *impossibility* (and yet a fact, which hence seems to be only explainable by recourse to God's omnipotence)[13] –, on the contrary is a *necessity* in that its negation or contradictory, the mutual separation of consciousness and body, is strictly inconceivable and in this sense impossible.[14] So here we have, I think, an important 'paradigm-case' confirming Aristotle's conviction, illustrated by means of examples mostly taken from mathematics and physics, that philosophy and science begin with our being amazed that things are as in fact they are and that, if we finally succeed in coping with the issue at hand, this amazement gives way to our seeing that, on the contrary ('enantíon'), things cannot be otherwise – in short: that our *amazement about a fact seemingly impossible* can be transformed into the *insight into a necessity*.[15]

That my consciousness is permeated with bodily (corporeal, somatic) features may be most easily seen from the fact that I cannot possibly perceive, or even conceive of, a material object which does not appear to me in a certain direction, distance, and perspective, so that we may say that my body is present in each and every sensual perception in the function of being the centre or zero point of my

---

[12] See Introduction: sect. 11, of the present collection of essays.

[13] See sect. 1.1, above.

[14] In Hoche 1990: ch. 9 ('Möglichkeit und Vorstellbarkeit [Possibility and conceivability]') and ch. 10 ('Vorstellbarkeit und Unvorstellbarkeit [Conceivability and inconceivability]'), *inter alia* I tried to deal with familiar qualms concerning the relation between (in)conceivability and (im)possibility, which I think are based on insufficient distinctions. (As Moore 1903: p. VII, concisely put it: 'the work of analysis and distinction is often very difficult'. In Hoche & Strube 1985: A.I, I dedicated a whole chapter to appreciating the great importance of this statement.)

[15] Aristotle: *Metaphysics*, Book I, 982b11–983a21; cf. Hoche 1983.

noematic world perspectively arranged around myself – as my 'geometrical eye', as Wittgenstein once or twice illuminatingly put it. Furthermore, an object perceived or imagined by me is always perceived or imagined in a given sensory quality, to wit, as being seen and/or heard and the like, and by changing my position, looking in a different direction, closing my eyes, stopping my ears, etc., I can easily modify the details and even the sensory quality of what I am perceiving. As far as the voluntary actions (or, frequently, reflex actions) just mentioned are concerned, although they often go unnoticed, I can in principle become aware of them through my kinaesthetic or motion sense.[16]

Let me add, however, that the role of kinaesthesia in the awareness of my own actions has, I think, often been overestimated; what in my view is much more relevant are the 'gerundive' traits the objects of my personal noematic world present to me.[17] Not surprisingly, these practical features, too, reveal the bodily structure of my consciousness; for whenever a noematic object of mine appears – and appeals – to me as being, say, an apple *to be plucked by myself right now*, this gerundive feature refers to my arms and hands presently being able to reach and grasp it, or my hands and legs enabling me to climb the tree or fetch a ladder, etc. But let me deepen the issue of human action as being an important form of consciousness in the following section.

3. Human action in the third- and the first-person perspectives

I think we may safely say that to our *fellow-men* we ascribe a certain action – as well as a certain perception, emotion, body feeling, etc. – on the basis of our seeing, hearing, or otherwise perceiving how they nonverbally and/or verbally behave ('act' and 'react') in a given situation. This may seem to be simple and uncontroversial indeed. But the difficulties begin as soon as we take a closer look and try to work out a detailed description of what precisely we are doing in such a case; and the difficulties become even greater once we pose the '*what is*'-question, namely: 'What is (are), from my point of view, somebody else's action(s)?'. Again, as always in philosophy, we must proceed exemplarily and piecemeal; for I think that Ryle's dictum 'In philosophy, generalizations are unclarifications.'[18] can hardly be taken seriously enough.

---

[16] That we are aware, not only of objects out in the world, but also of our own body (physical sensations, pains, sexual desire, and so on) is important but a different story which, I think, does not immediately contribute to the 'bodily structure' of many of my conscious experiences.

[17] See Essay IV: sects. 3.6.7, 3.9.1, and 3.15.5 of the present collection, and sections 3.2–3.3, below.

[18] Ryle 1951: 255.

3.1.   Therefore let us first ask how to describe what precisely we are doing when we say in a given speech-act situation that someone else (say, Jane) is making a coat. Normally in this case we are performing an illocutionary act of assertion, which is governed by rules of which only what Searle called the 'preparatory rule' seems to me to be of interest in the present context. According to Searle's suggestion, which I will adopt for the purpose at hand, the preparatory rule for speech acts of asserting is this: '[The speaker] S has evidence (reasons, etc.) for the truth of [the asserted proposition] p.' What exactly is my evidence for the truth of the proposition 'Jane is making a coat.'? It is my perception of Jane's relevant behaviour or, what in my eyes amounts to the same thing, Jane's relevant behaviour *as*, *qua*, or *in its capacity of* being perceived by myself.[19]

But what pieces or stretches of Jane's behaviour are *relevant* in this case? I think we may reply: All and only those stretches of her verbal and/or nonverbal behaviour I have learned, from infancy, to connect with what all or most of us use to call the making of a coat. It would be extremely difficult to describe such pieces of behaviour without using the verbal phrase 'to make a coat', and certainly this is not the place to try to go into further details. Therefore I suggest to speak in this case simply of a 'coat-making behaviour' – just as in the great majority of other such cases we could only speak, say, of a 'reading-a-book behaviour', a 'stealing-a-book-from-the-library behaviour', a 'writing-a-letter-to-Jane behaviour', a 'being-pleased-by-the-flattery behaviour', a 'having-fallen-in-love behaviour', a 'having-headache behaviour', and so forth. All these types of behaviour can adopt a legion of divergent features which I think it is virtually impossible to specify.

What is important, however, is the *consistency* of the relevant behaviour. For we would be at a loss if, say, stretches of someone else's 'reading behaviour' would alternate with stretches of 'not-reading behaviour' or 'only-pretending-to-read behaviour'. In some such cases we would downright say that our fellow-man is just pretending to read, in some others that he only seems to be reading, and in still others we would be unable to say what precisely he might possibly be doing in the presence of the opened book before his eyes. To have a short term for what I have in mind, and what the reader should not find difficult to understand at least in principle, I should like to speak of a *consistent* behaviour of the sort in question, or of a *consistent relevant behaviour*.

On this basis I think we may say that my *criterion* for asserting that Jane is making a coat is my perceiving a behaviour of Jane's which I judge to be a consistent coat making behaviour. More generally speaking: The *criterion* on the basis of which I ascribe to somebody else an action of type *a* is my percep-

---

[19] See Essay IV: sect. 3.6.5 of the present collection.

tion of a consistent relevant behaviour, that is, of a consistent *a*-behaviour of theirs.[20]

Let us now try to answer the tricky question, posed at the beginning of the present section 3: 'What is (are), from my point of view, somebody else's action(s)?' I touched already on the problem of how to properly understand and deal with 'what is'-questions in general.[21] In particular I discussed the question of whether or not to consider conscious events of my fellow-men – and possibly also of higher non-human animals – to be nothing but their relevant perceivable (observable) behaviour, nonverbal and/or verbal, in specified situations. Though I warned against making light of Dudda's suggestion to treat conscious events of others as mere theoretical constructs, I decided, if subject to further research, in favour of a 'semi-behaviouristic nothing-buttery'.[22] This decision of mine can only gain in plausibility if we think of *actions*, which I suggested not to contrast with but to count among conscious experiences.[23]

For it would be strange indeed to regard the actions of others not as empirical observables but as theoretical constructs. Furthermore, my suggestion to *definitionally identify* the actions of others with certain stretches of their overt behaviour in a way accords with, or at least seems to come rather close to, the position of some renowned contemporary philosophers for whom a human action, irrespective of whether it is accessed from the third-person or the first-person perspective, is a composite entity consisting of 'an intention in action plus a bodily movement [...]'.[24] I would definitely prefer, of course, to say instead that a human action (performed at time *t*) *as seen from the point of view of somebody else* is a bodily movement *which either takes place or fails to take place (at time t)* – for an overt behaviour need not be a *movement*, or a *set of movements* – plus an intention in action. And I would add that an intention in action, *as seen from the point of view of somebody else*, is nothing but the totality of the agent's relevant observable behaviour *before*, *during*, and *after* his carrying out, or failing to carry out, the movement at time *t*. For *with what intention* somebody else is doing whatever he is doing at time *t* I can only gather from what he has said and done *before t*, is saying and doing *at t*, and will say and do *after t* – provided, of course, that his sayings and doings are relevant to the action in question. In short: For myself, the action of somebody else – just as any other piece of consciousness of others

---

[20] This seems to me to be in accordance with the normal use of the term 'criterion'; see, for instance, Malcolm 1959: pp. 24, 44, 56, 60; Birnbacher 1974: esp. sect. 3.3.3; Hoche & Strube 1985: pp. 193 f.; and sect. 3.2 with fn. 26, below.

[21] Esp. in Essay IV: sect. 3.8.5 of the present collection.

[22] See Essay IV: sect. 3.15, esp. subsect. 3.15.4, of the present collection.

[23] See Essay IV: sect. 2.3.2 of the present collection.

[24] Searle 1983: p. 106; cf. esp. pp. 101, 107 f., 125.

– is nothing but their relevant overt behaviour in a given situational environment ('behaviour-in-situation').[25]

3.2.   The criterion on the basis of which I ascribe to *somebody else* an action of type *a* is, to repeat, my perception of a consistent relevant behaviour, that is, of a consistent *a*-behaviour, of his or hers. It seems to me to be obvious, however, that to *myself* I ascribe a certain action not on the basis of such a behavioural criterion, and in fact not on some criterial basis in the first place. For a *criterion* is usually considered to be an *evidentiary* or *verificational criterion*,[26] and in the case of my own actions I can speak neither of *evidence* nor of *verification* (as long as we abide by the normal juridical, scientific, and philosophical uses of these technical terms).[27] So each of us should seriously doubt whether he is well advised if he considers his own actions, insofar as they are accessed from his own first-person point of view, to be something like his relevant overt behaviour in a given situation, or some form of behaviour at all.

If so, how else should we characterise our own actions as accessed from the first-person point of view of each of us? In Essay IV of the present collection, I suggested to consider a given conscious experience (say, an action) of mine, insofar as it is accessible from my own first-person perspective, to be *nothing but* one of my personal – simple or complex – objects of reference ('intentional objects') *as*, *qua*, or *in its capacity of*, being given to me in one of its constantly varying subjective modes of appearance, that is, as a 'noematic phenomenon' in very much the Husserlian sense.[28] By any such noematic phenomenon I am confronted with a vast array of subjective features, and according to the given type of conscious experience these features may be only *theoretical* ('indicative') ones, or *theoretical* as well as *emotional* ones, or, in the case of actions, *theoretical* and *emotional* and also *practical* ('imperative' or 'gerundive') ones.

According to this *purely noematic conception of consciousness*, from my own point of view my own action of, say, catching the tram should be taken to be nothing but *the tram to be caught by me*,[29] and similarly my action of making a

---

[25] It might be suspected that this definition is circular in that the term 'relevant' which it contains would have to be spelled out as 'relevant to the (type of) action, or whatever conscious event, in question'. This is not correct, however; for in the second paragraph of the present subsection 3.1, I introduced the expression 'relevant behaviour' as an abbreviation for 'behaviour I have learned, from infancy, to connect with what all or most of us use to *call* an action, or whatever conscious event, of the type in question' – for instance, 'making a coat', 'reading a book', or 'having headache'.

[26] Cf. sect. 3.1 with fn. 20, above.

[27] Cf. Moore 1954–1955: p. 266; Strawson 1959: pp. 99–112 (esp. 108), 134; Austin 1962b: pp. 115–117, 140–142.

[28] See esp. Essay IV: sects. 3.5–3.10 of the present collection. For the special case of actions, see ibid.: sects. 3.6.7 and 3.9.1, and the much more detailed considerations in Hoche 1973a: part II, *passim*.

[29] Cf. Sartre 1936–1937: p. 94; cf. pp. 97 f. For a discussion, see Hoche 1973a: § 16.

coat would be nothing but *a coat to be made by me*. I have borrowed the latter example from Aristotle, who may perhaps be taken to have been the first to envisage a gerundive and for that matter sort of a noematic conception of action. For Aristotle, the conclusion ('tò sympérasma') of a practical syllogism is an action ('prâxis'), and such an action he once characterises as being, say, the coat to be made or produced ('tò himátion poietéon'): 'kaì tò sympérasma, tò himátion poietéon, prâxís estin'[30] – 'the conclusion, the coat to be made, is an action'.

3.3.   So, whereas I take a *fellow man's* action to be a nonverbal and/or verbal 'behaviour-in-situation' of his or hers and hence a specific event in nature, I take an action of *mine* to be essentially a system of gerundive characters of my subjective noematic phenomena; and I took pains to show that such phenomena are *not* part of nature.[31] So, as in the case of conscious experiences other than actions, on pain of utter confusion we must carefully see to it that we do not mix up, or blend into each other, these two complementary perspectives on human action. I think this is already done if we say, using Searle's words, that a human action is a 'composite entity' which consists of 'an intention in action plus a bodily movement [...]'.[32] I have no objections indeed against saying that in human actions – actions of others as well as actions of my own – it may be highly useful to distinguish between the action proper and the intention with which it is being carried out; but in both perspectives action proper and intention in action belong to the field of *one and the same* perspective, as can be outlined in the following way.

An action of mine, insofar as I have access to it from my own first-person perspective, is a system of gerundive features of my noematic phenomena. Normally, such features appeal to me only in the light of my beliefs as well as my personal motives, notably my intentions or 'forward-looking motives'.[33] Only on

---

[30] *De motu animalium* 701a20. Cf. Hoche 1973a: p. 172 with fn. 165. It should be noted that, for my noematic interpretation of my own actions, nothing depends on whether or nor I properly interpret Aristotle's doctrine of the practical syllogism, which since many centuries and up to our time has been discussed highly controversially.

[31] See Essay IV: sect. 3.11 of the present collection.

[32] See sect. 3.1 with fn. 24, above, where I tried to disentangle the confusion likely to arise from Searle's lapidary statement. – The revealing term 'composite entity' is being used in Searle 1983: Subject Index, entry 'action'. Similarly, Searle (ibid.: p. 101) speaks of 'the complex event which constitutes the action'. See also ibid.: p. 106, where he says that 'the whole action is an intention in action plus a bodily movement which is *caused* by the intention in action' (my italics). Under both perspectives on action, speaking of *causation* seems to me to be at best misleading.

[33] See Anscombe 1957: §§ 12–14. I take it that, from my own point of view, these motives of mine can and should *themselves* be interpreted as being higher-order gerundive features of my noematic phenomena (or smaller or greater sets of them). This issue certainly has to do with the traditional distinctions between what I intend to do for the sake of some other purpose and what I intend to do for its own sake ('entelécheia'), and between what is good in respect to some other good and good in itself. But this is not the place for a discussion of these problems. – The co-operation of

condition I intend to do something specific (say, to make a coat), certain objects in my surroundings (say, a piece of woollen cloth, a pair of scissors, or a sewing-machine) adopt specific gerundive features (say, the features of being something *to be purchased by me, to be looked for by me,* or *to be handled by me*) – provided, of course, I believe these objects to be suitable for the purpose at hand. Or, to take some other examples: Unless I were hungry or planned to provide for the next winter by making jelly, etc., and unless I took them to be edible, my property, etc., the apples on the tree wouldn't take on the gerundive character of being fruit *to be plucked by me*; only if I am going to take the bus, this vehicle assumes the gerundive trait of being a means of transportation *to be reached by me in time* (provided I believe it is the right line); and only in the light of my proposing to call somebody up on the spot (and my belief that the person in question lives in my town), the local telephone directory can present to me the gerundive feature of being a book *to be paged through by me right away.*[34] Certainly it would be an untenable prejudice to believe that the intentions of mine need to precede my actions in time.[35] But they are at work from the very beginning, and I cannot even start performing a determinate action unless I am aware of my intention. – In the case of actions of others, however, I can gather the intention with which they are being done only from the overt behaviour before, during, and after the action in question; and again, I think, there is reason to definitionally identify their intentions with their relevant behaviour-in-situation.[36]

3.4.   Let me add in passing that, once we take the separation and incompatibility of the two complementary perspectives seriously, there is no reasonable justification whatsoever for transferring to my own actions, as I have access to them myself, the determinism to which, again from my point of view, the actions of others, just as the rest of at least the macrophysical and 'mesophysical' occurrences in the physical world, may be rightly taken to be subjected. So I think we

---

intentions and *beliefs* in the practice of acting is not a central topic in Anscombe's booklet; but it has often been noticed by others, e. g., MacIntyre 1969: pp. 50–52; Stegmüller 1969: pp. 404, 409f. Even *theoretically* intention and belief cannot be treated in separation from each other; see Hoche 2004.

[34] In the last example, I deliberately added the words 'on the spot' and 'right away'. For although in the case of my present actions an addition of this kind is always to be silently understood, there are also certain action-related noematic features which should be distinguished from gerundive features proper and which therefore I suggest to identify, not with my actual actions as experienced by myself, but, for instance, with so far only potential actions which appeal to me in varying degrees so that I more or less seriously consider them for realisation in the nearer or farther future. These are fine-grained distinctions which, furthermore, are rendered still more difficult to survey by the tricky problem of how to distinguish between several phases of an action and how to determine the boundaries of what may be called my 'present' action. All of these questions I have circumstantially dealt with in Hoche 1973a: esp. §§ 32 and 35.

[35] See ibid.: §§ 29–31.

[36] See sect. 3.1 (last paragraph), above.

have to conclude that my own actions for myself, in contradistinction to actions of others for myself and arguably to my actions for others, are not subjected to natural causation. So my own actions as accessed from my own first-person perspective seem to me to be distinguished by precisely that 'independence of empirical conditions' which, according to Kant's *Critique of Pure Reason* (A 553), is nothing but 'freedom' in a 'negative' sense. In this sense we may also speak of a complementarity of freedom and necessity, or determinism, in human action.[37]

4. A plea for the coexistence of the two complementary perspectives

Throughout the essays IV, V, and VI of the present collection, I have been trying to disclose the fundamental difference between the first- and the third-person perspectives, and to defend the view that an entity given in the one of them can be neither identical with nor numerically different from an entity given in the other. Rather, they stand to each other in the relation of what I call a 'categorial' difference. Hence we cannot properly say that 'the *two* entities' are categorially different from each other; and, strictly speaking, even referring to an entity given in the one perspective and an entity given in the other perspective by means of the plural form 'they' – as I inadvertently though, I hope, pardonably just did (and which, without breakneck verbal acrobatics, we can in fact hardly avoid) – ought to give us linguistic qualms. So it is not surprising that this important kind of difference, which, I think, has to be accepted alongside the familiar relation of numerical difference, has been notoriously neglected in philosophy and science. And yet in this case – as in a lot of others which notably Frege and Wittgenstein called our attention to – we cannot avoid struggling with the pitfalls and snares of language if we want to escape confusion and reach philosophically satisfying results.

4.1.   Suppose we shun this struggle against ingrained linguistic habits (the 'engrams' of our ordinary language use since early childhood, as it were) and regard the distinction between numerical identity and numerical diversity as an exhausting dichotomy, and suppose, furthermore, that we take it for granted that human conscious experiences – say, the perception of an approaching car and the ensuing action of jumping out of its way – are sort of 'things in themselves' which exist

---

[37] See Hoche 1994. – It should be noted that freedom in this 'negative' sense is not the kind of freedom, however it is to be defined in detail, that is of interest in everyday life, especially to lawyers, judges, jurors, educators, and so on. The latter concept of freedom is applicable not just to my own actions as I experience them from my first-person perspective but likewise to the actions of others as I come to know them in my third-person perspective. Therefore, this is not the place to discuss it.

autonomously, that is to say, which 'are there' independently of someone having cognitive access to them.[38] In this case, I think, we are inevitably misled into believing that the first- and the third-person perspectives must needs contradict each other, and that one of them is specious and has to give way to the other. Most of the many present-day believers in such a contradiction share with each other the conviction that the third-person approach to human consciousness – that is, the approach to the consciousness of others or to one's own consciousness as if it were the consciousness of somebody else[39] – is the 'scientifically correct' one. As far as I can see, an explicit reasoning to this effect can be rarely (if ever) found; but it seems to me that this conviction is silently based on some such considerations as the following one. My own consciousness is, at it were, outnumbered by the innumerable 'consciousnesses' of my fellow-men and many higher non-human animals, and it is not at all problematic to communicate with others about the sensations, perceptions, convictions, emotions, intentions, actions, etc., of arbitrarily many third persons – whereas I am principally unable to share with anybody else my own cognitive approach to my own sensations, perceptions, convictions, intentions, and actions, and could not even speak about them in a public language (which is the only language we have) unless I had access to the consciousness of others, too. So the primacy of the third-person view on consciousness seems to be secured.

4.2.   But let me call your attention to the following two facts. First, our most familiar everyday-life experience as well as an abundant literature in philosophical, psychological, and other fields of knowledge has taught us that I can likewise

---

[38] Cf. Introduction: sect. 7, of the present collection of essays.

[39] I cannot *see* my presently seeing something, say, a tree. To start with, I cannot see my eyes converging toward the tree I see. Even a mirror or monitor cunningly installed in the tree would be of no help; for what I would see in such cases would be my eyes converging, not toward the tree, but toward an image of themselves. (What I can see, with or without the help of looking glasses and so on, is, of course, my passive corporeal body, or part of it. But this is a different story; for here we are concerned with my perceptions, actions, and other conscious experiences of my own.) However, I am *immediately and unquestionably aware* of my presently seeing the tree, and so much so that it would be pointless to say that I *seem* to see, or that I *know* that I now see, the tree. Similarly, I cannot doubt, cannot meaningfully say that I 'know', need not 'find out', etc., that I saw the tree *a more or less short time ago*. (For a necessary case distinction and a more thoroughgoing discussion, see Essay IV: sects. 3.12–3.13 of the present collection.) But suppose we are looking at photographs or motion pictures taken *a long time ago*. Then it is quite common indeed to say such things as 'I seem to see the girl looking out that window [to wit, then and there].', or 'It seems that I am making a coat [to wit, then and there].' And in such a situation I might quite naturally also be asked: 'How do you know that you are seeing the girl looking out that window [to wit, then and there]?' or 'How do you know that you are making a coat [to wit, then and there]?'. This phenomenon makes it plain that in such cases I take a third-person view on my own (past) perceptions, actions, etc., as if they were the perceptions, actions, etc., of somebody else; cf. Essay IV: sect. 3.19 with fn. 161 of the present collection.

communicate with a fellow-man about *his* and *my own* conscious experiences and their phenomenal properties in a way that enables us to perfectly rationally assent to, doubt, or contradict our mutual statements or considerations. (At least I do hope that the reader will find what I said so far either contravening his or her own experience or, preferably, at least basically acceptable and worth further consideration, but not literally nonsensical, that is, void of intelligible meaning!) Second, the very basis for raising the question of primacy in the first place is unsound. For the only collision which at first sight might perhaps seem possible could occur between *my* experiencing *my* perceptions, emotions, intentions, actions, and so on, and *somebody else's* perceiving *my* perceptions, emotions, intentions, actions, and so on – but as I am not, and cannot possibly be, somebody else as well as myself, this supposed 'collision' does in fact, and of necessity, not occur. So there is no collision and hence no contradiction between what is viewed from the first- and from the third-person perspectives. In other words: The first-person and the third-person approaches to a 'target consciousness' are not open to one and the same person (or 'source consciousness'). I can (and must) choose the first-person attitude with respect to myself and to nothing else, and I can choose the third-person attitude only with respect to anything else, that is, to the objective world including my fellow-men, higher animals, and their conscious experiences; and it seems reasonable to generalise and say[40] that anyone else can take the first-person view only on himself and the third-person view only on me and the rest of the world. From this it follows that to each of us his or her own subjective and yet bodily structured[41] consciousness is accessible in *one* specific way and the objective world, including the 'objectified' consciousness we ascribe to others, in *quite another* specific way. Neither one's own consciousness nor someone else's consciousness can be given to anyone of us in *either this or that* way to be freely chosen, and so a conflict cannot come up. For any two persons P_1 and P_2 it holds true that P_1's view on P_1's consciousness or on P_2's consciousness cannot be combined with P_2's view on P_2's consciousness or on P_1's consciousness so as to yield a common, unified, or integrated view, and hence there exists no way in which P_1's consciousness or P_2's consciousness can be accessible to P_1 and P_2 alike. For this reason, the correlates of the two views on human consciousness can never coexist,[42] or exist side by side, as being two numerically different ones; for as soon as we catch sight of the *one* of them we lose sight of the *other* – and, to repeat, I take it that they do not exist autonomously as sort of Kantian 'things-in-themselves'. Rather, a correlate of the first-person view and a correlate

---

[40] See Essay IV: sect. 3.19 of the present collection.

[41] See sect. 2.2, above.

[42] It should be noted that what in a way coexists, or should coexist, are the two – *numerically* different – approaches to, or perspectives on, consciousness, but not the – *categorially* different – correlates of each of these views.

of the third-person view are[43] *categorially* different from each other and in this sense '*complementary*' data, which, being unable to be either one and the same or two different entities, cannot causally interact, either.

5. Phenomena of alleged psychophysical interaction

The last remark cannot fail to provoke the question of how to deal with the plethora of everyday as well as medical, for instance, psychosomatic phenomena apparently exemplifying psychophysical and physiopsychical causation. It would be preposterous, of course, to try to explain these phenomena away. But I think it would be no less preposterous to offhand regard them as our principal witnesses against the conception of psychophysical complementarity in particular and anthropological complementarity at large. Instead of rashly throwing in the towel, we should rather regard this tricky problem as a challenge to try and launch a novel conceptual analysis of what seems to be psychophysical 'interaction'. As I tried to make plain, there are two complementary and incompatible body-con-sciousness-world complexes;[44] and in the preceding essay I went into a couple of pertinent details at some more length.[45] So I am confident that a solution to this purely conceptual (and hence non-empirical) problem which will turn out to be more satisfying than the traditional and time-honoured ones may be found in the long run – not, I daresay, in the near future, and certainly not in the rest of the present essay. I even think it possible that, in this case, too – as in the closely related case of a 'connection' or 'unity' of consciousness and body –, some day we will find ourselves in a position to transform *amazement about a fact seemingly impossible* into an *insight into a necessity*.[46] But this is a dream of the future, and at present I cannot do more than roughly sketch a few thoughts I take to be helpful.

5.1.   If we say, as in fact we often do, that perceiving a dog consists in the effect of physical stimuli on our nervous system which, 'somewhere in the brain' and in a way 'we do not yet understand', are 'processed' or changed into psychical events, then we seem to have adduced one of the most common examples for a *physiopsychical* causation. And if we say, for instance, that my seeing the dog, my feeling scared by it, and my trying to evade it make me act (to wit, overtly behave) in such-and-such a way, say, run away or climb a tree, then we seem to have given one of the most common examples for a *psychophysical* causation. But if we remember what I have said so far, then we cannot fail to see that describing

---

[43] Cf. the linguistic remarks in the first paragraph of the present section 4.

[44] See sect. 2, above.

[45] Essay V: sects. 2.3–2.7 of the present collection.

[46] See sect. 2.2 with fn. 15, above.

perceptions and actions *like this* is nothing but the result of illegitimately blending the first- and the third-person perspectives. As I tried to make plain above,[47] the descriptions given in each of these perspectives are self-contained in that they offer neither 'enclaves' to accommodate first-person data in a third-person view, or vice versa, nor 'adapters' for bringing the two views together. In the case of actions, moreover, I suggested to say that, from *my* point of view, intentions and other motives of *others* are but stretches of their overt behaviour, and that, again from my own point of view, what 'causes' my own acting are not events and other objects *themselves* but events and other objects *qua being subjectively given to me in a certain way* (noematic phenomena).[48] For instance, I am trying to evade the dog, not because it *is* on the verge of attacking me, but because *I believe (rightly or not), or have the impression,* that it is so; and this 'motivational causation' must be carefully distinguished from 'natural (or physical) causation'.

5.2.   Now one might try to interpret other cases of alleged 'psychophysical interaction' on precisely this model. 'The most well accepted evidence for the effect of states of mind on medical outcome is undoubtedly the "placebo effect".', says Velmans.[49] On the basis of his 'dual-aspect' theory, he has, of course, no serious problems to find a plausible explanation for this effect. But as I endeavour to avoid this low-price competitor of what I take to be complementarity properly understood, I have to search for another solution.

However, let us first have a brief look at what medical scientists have to say about the placebo effect. The London physiologist Patrick D. Wall emphasises the fact that in the case of 'jaw tightness (trismus) and swelling after the extraction of wisdom teeth […] the placebo therapy not only reduced the pain report [sic!] but also improved the ability to open the mouth and reduced the swelling'[50] and concludes that the placebo effect 'is evidently a common and powerful phenomenon which needs explanation'.[51] However, in a more recent meta-analysis the authors of the study come to a quite different conclusion.[52] As I had no opportunity yet to read this paper myself, I have to rely on the summary given in *Wikipedia*:[53] '[…] there was no significant placebo effect in studies in which objective outcomes (such as blood pressure) were measured by an independent observer. The placebo

---

[47] See Essay IV: sect. 3.15.5, and Essay V: sect. 2.2.6 of the present collection.

[48] See Essay IV: sects. 3.9.1, 3.10–3.11, 3.14–3.15 of the present collection, and sects. 3.2–3.3, above.

[49] Velmans 2002: p. 5; for further examples, see pp. 4–7. See Essay V: sect. 2.5.3 of the present collection

[50] Wall 1996: p. 164; his source is Hashish, Finman, & Harvey 1988.

[51] Wall 1996: p. 171.

[52] Hróbjartsson & Gøzsche 2001.

[53] *Wikipedia*, entry 'placebo' (November 29, 2007); the italics are partly mine. – I am well aware of the fact that *Wikipedia* is often taken to be unciteable in scientific and philosophical contexts; but I also remember having come across a comparative study which considerably relativises this prejudice, even in comparison with the renowned *Encyclopedia Britannica*.

effect could only be documented in studies in which the outcomes (improvement or failure to improve) were reported by the subjects themselves. The authors concluded that the placebo effect does not have "powerful clinical effects" (*objective* effects) and that patient-reported improvements (*subjective* effects) in pain were small and could not be clearly distinguished from bias. *These results suggest that the placebo effect is largely subjective.* This would help explain why the placebo effect is easiest to demonstrate in conditions where subjective factors are very prominent or significant parts of the problem. Some of these conditions are headache, stomachache, asthma, allergy, tension, and the experience of pain [...].'

5.3.   I take it that '*subjective* effects' of a placebo treatment, if there should be any clear-cut cases of them (see section 5.2, above), could be easily shown to be compatible with my strictly complementaristic position. If I have swallowed a pill I erroneously believe to be a pharmacologically effective remedy against headaches, and if a little bit later my headache is in fact mitigated or disappears, then I can describe the process, thanks to the subjective access I have to my own conscious experiences, as an out-and-out first-person-perspective affair: My *(subjectively) believing or expecting* something is followed by my *(subjectively) sensing* a decrease of pain. But the process can also be described as an out-and-out third-person-perspective affair: I credibly report to an investigator that I took a certain pill (of which he knows that it is pharmacologically inert), that I believed it to be an effective remedy, and that my (feeling a) headache has in fact diminished or disappeared; and the investigator comes to know about all this on the basis of what he hears (and possibly sees), that is, on the basis of his intersubjectively reproducible perceptions and observations.[54]

5.4.   So what deserves a deeper discussion are only '*objective* effects' of a placebo treatment. Let us suppose, for the sake of argument, that there are any such effects (see again section 5.2, above), that is to say, cases in which my believing in the efficacy of some medication or other sort of treatment, say, an ultrasound therapy,[55] has an influence, not only on my subjective feeling, but on the objectively observable state of my physical body. In the third-person view, a case in question may, I think, be described as follows. A subject has been treated, under clinical or laboratory conditions, in a certain way known to specialists to be objectively ineffective, but the patient has been told by the investigator that this way of dealing with his disorders is effective, and the investigator can convince himself that the subject believes it; and after some time, a positive change of his bodily (physiological and possibly also anatomical) condition can in fact be observed. Again a research report can be based on intersubjectively reproducible perceptions and observations alone – just as it ought to be.

---

[54] This kind of a third-person report is what is normally found in medical journals.
[55] See Wall 1996: p. 164.

It is true that a purely first-person description is not possible in this case; for even if I have the opportunity to observe with my own eyes which changes have, or have not, taken place in my physical body, these observations are throughout third-person-perspective observations:[56] I am looking at my own body as if it were somebody else's. But what about a mixed first-and-third-person description in such a case? According to what I have claimed so far, such a blending of descriptions which are partly based on a first-person and partly on a third-person view should inevitably lead to utter confusion and hence are inadmissible. And yet here there appears to be, at least at first sight, no way of avoiding such a supposedly impossible description; for certainly it appears that (or: as if) the following facts obtain(ed): First, I have an immediate first-person experience of what I did and what I believe (in this respect I neither need nor can rely on my perceiving what others tell me); second, at the same time I have a sensorium-mediated third-person perception of what has happened to my physical body; and third, I cannot help stating a coincidence or 'conjunction' of the two disparate cognitions which in favourable cases – and these alone would justify our speaking of a full-blown placebo effect – is sufficiently 'regular' for producing a case of Humean causation.

5.5.   In the preceding essay, I took sides with precisely this interpretation of causation.[57] However, as can be seen from their *practice*, the majority of present day scientists appear to be not satisfied with this, as it were, minimal form of causation. Rather, they seem to regard natural or physical causation, not only as a Humean regular conjunction or coincidence, which certainly is a necessary ingredient of this relation, but additionally as sort of an energetic flux, which, of course, must be taken to be restricted by the laws of conservation of energy and matter.[58] It is true that Hume rightly stressed that we never see a 'power or force' or an 'efficacy or energy' operating in objects in general and in the clearance between cause and effect in particular.[59] But I think it is equally true that scientists, in their search for causal relations, rarely if ever content themselves with a mere regular coincidence of events which diverge from each other to such a degree that a reasonably 'intelligible connection' between them is nowhere to be seen. Rather, whenever they are confronted with a pair of strikingly disparate events which nonetheless seem to stand to each other in a Humean relation of cause and effect, they are intent on filling in the gap between them with as many intermediate steps as possible; and this is doubtless one of the most effective stimulants for engaging

---

[56] In fact, I take it that speaking of a first-person-perspective *observation* would be a contradiction in terms.

[57] Essay V: sect. 2.3.2 of the present collection.

[58] If we adopt this view, the following apologetic considerations can be dispensed with.

[59] '[…] in all these expressions, *so apply'd*, we have really no distinct meaning, and make use only of common words, without any clear and determinate ideas': Hume 1739: p. 162; cf. 1748: p. 74.

in further research. But such intermediate steps (or 'missing links', as it were) can be hardly found in the case of a subjective belief of mine on the one hand and a physiological and/or anatomical change of my biological body on the other.[60]

If we are determined to abide by a flawless Humean view on causation, *this* way out is, of course, blocked. Nonetheless, *another one* remains wide open even under these aggravated conditions. For Hume doubtless thought of *two* – that is, two *numerically different* – events that stand to each other in the relation of cause and effect; and although beliefs and other 'propositional attitudes' are not conscious experiences in the strict sense,[61] my belief in the efficacy of a placebo on the one hand and physiological or even anatomical changes occurring within my biological body on the other are surely *categorially different* in that they lack a common sortal genus. So, after all, they can play the role of cause and effect not even under the auspices of an orthodox and devout Humean point of view.

5.6.   Having reached this point, however, we ought to be alive to the fact that a stout defender of mental causation would be strongly inclined to react by thinking: 'So much the worse for the conception of a categorial difference between physical and mental events!'. In other words: We have reached a situation of the type which has sometimes been called 'Moore's see-saw'. For Moore was notoriously indecisive ('see-saw') as to which of two possible conclusions to draw in a given case; therefore, he repeatedly stressed[62] that if 'p' and 'q' are likewise appealing though mutually incompatible propositions, so that we have '$\neg(p \,\&\, q)$', which is logically equivalent to both '$p \rightarrow \neg q$' and '$q \rightarrow \neg p$', then we have to decide whether to conclude that '$\neg q$' (since we take 'p' to be 'more certain') or rather to conclude that '$\neg p$' (since we take 'q' to be 'more certain'). Obviously, our present case is a striking example. Let 'p' be the proposition 'First- and third-person data stand to "each other"[63] in the relation of a categorial difference.', and let 'q' be

---

[60] The momentousness of (the search for) intermediate steps seems to me to be likewise presupposed by many philosophers of science. For I think this idea is the basic rationale behind the frequently stressed conviction that the physical world is 'causally closed' (see, for instance, the preceding Essay V: sect. 2.3.2 with fn. 72 and sect. 2.5.3 with fn. 88), which for its part is a crucial constituent of many contemporary mainstream discussions of the mind-body problem (see, for instance, Bieri 1981: pp. 5, 9).

[61] See Essay IV: sect. 2.3.3 of the present collection.

[62] See, for instance, Moore 1925: p. 40.

[63] Our language is imbued with 'numerical' traits. One of them is the linguistic fact that we have no alternative besides choosing between the grammatical 'numbers' *singular* and *plural*. For historical as well as for conceptual reasons, even having at our disposal the ancient (or partly obsolete, partly obsolescent) '*dual* number' would be of no help whatsoever. Another one is the fact that we cannot possibly avoid saying that an entity '*a*' and an entity '*b*' which differ categorially stand to 'each other' in this unique relation, or that the categorial difference obtains 'between' the 'one' and the 'other'. These facts certainly help explain why it is so difficult to mentally get hold of the unique relation of a *categorial*, i.e., *non-numerical* difference. But we should not allow language to take us hostage.

the proposition 'First- and third-person data can stand to each other in a causal relation.'. Then whoever takes the possibility of psychophysical interaction ('q') to be 'more certain' than the categorial character of the difference 'be-tween' first- and third-person data ('p') cannot help denying the latter, that is, concluding that '¬p'; but whoever finds my arguments in favour of a categorial difference 'be-tween' first-person and third-person data 'more certain' ('p') cannot help concluding that '¬q', and consequently has to look for a novel conceptual interpretation of the indubitable empirical phenomena of what at first sight seems to be 'psychophysical interaction'.

At present, I am neither willing nor in a position to go into any more details. Suffice it to say that certainly a lot of analytical work has still to be done in this field, and that a lot of conceptual distinctions are still waiting for being made.[64] What, more than hundred years ago, Moore has said in view of ethics is still worth heeding, and especially so with regard to our present problem:

> [T]he work of analysis and distinction is often very difficult: we may often fail to make the necessary discovery, even though we make a definite attempt to do so. But I am inclined to think that in many cases a resolute attempt would be sufficient to ensure success; so that, if only this attempt were made, many of the most glaring difficulties and disagreements in philosophy would disappear. At all events, philosophers seem, in general, not to make the attempt; and, whether in consequence of this omission or not, they are constantly endeavouring to prove that 'Yes' or 'No' will answer questions, to which *neither* answer is correct, owing to the fact that what they have before their minds is not one question, but several, to some of which the true answer is 'No', to others 'Yes'.[65]

Thinking about the implications of these words should also prevent us from rashly discarding the research project of anthropological complementarism proper.

6. The human and the divine points of view

6.1.   Let me conclude this essay with calling your attention to still another intriguing case of transforming amazement into insight. One of Aristotle's own examples of philosophical amazement is the problem of the origin of the universe ('génesis toû pantós': *Metaphysics*, 982^b17). In broadly this sense, Leibniz posed the famous

---

[64] One of these distinctions certainly has to be made between the supposed interaction between conscious experiences (such as perceiving) and their alleged neural correlates on the one hand and the supposed interaction between mental dispositions (such as expecting relief) and occurrences taking place in the biological body (such as the reduction of swelling) on the other; see sect. 5.2 with fn. 50, above.

[65] Moore 1903: p. vii (Moore's italics).

question: 'Why is there something rather than nothing?', which Heidegger later on declared to be the basic question of metaphysics.[66] However, the justification for asking this question which Leibniz immediately added – 'Car le rien est plus simple et plus facile que quelque chose.' ('For the Nothing is simpler and more facile than something.') – seems to me to break down in view of the fact that we can show, by means of the method of free phenomenological variation,[67] that even in our fully unrestricted imagination we do not succeed in conceiving of something like 'the Nothing' ('le rien') as the mere negative of the being of the world. That nonetheless one is frequently tempted to believe that it is easier to conceive the existence of nothing than the existence of something, and that Leibniz thought he could base a cosmological argument for the existence of God ('argumentum a contingentia mundi') on this alleged fact, now seems to be amazing to *me*; but again I think we can change this amazement into an insight into a necessity of sorts – if only the insight into a psychological or anthropological compulsion we cannot easily get rid of. What I have in mind is our deeply ingrained addiction, resulting perhaps from false modesty which, in philosophising, is a bad adviser, to view ourselves and the world not from our native and natural human standpoint – to wit, as being the correlate of each one's own noematic, 'transcendentally constituting' consciousness – but to adopt instead, as it were, an extramundane 'view from nowhere', or from 'God's eye's' position.[68] By thus changing, more or less unwittingly, our points of view, we make ourselves believe, for instance, that the earth (not to speak of ourselves) is but a dust particle in the universe, or that our own personal problems are so insignificant as to be negligible – or, to return to the case under consideration, that it must be an enormous and virtually infeasible task to create the world from nothing ('ex nihilo').[69]

6.2. It should be added, however, that 'the view from nowhere'[70] is certainly the natural perspective to be taken by the 'positive' sciences, which, in contradistinction to philosophy, need and should (under pain of becoming intractable) not

---

[66] Leibniz 1714: p. 602, § 7: 'Pourquoi il y a plutôt quelque chose que rien?'; Heidegger 1929: pp. 20f., 38.

[67] See sect. 2.2 with fn. 12, above, and the Introduction: sect. 11, to the present collection of essays.

[68] I think we may reasonably say that this is precisely the view which Husserl wanted to overcome by applying the method of what he called 'transcendental' or 'phenomenological reduction'. After Kant's conception of 'phenomena' as opposed to 'things-in-themselves' (see the preceding Essay V: sects. 1.7.2 and 1.8.1–1.8.2 of the present collection), this method of Husserl's seems to me to be the second epoch-making attempt to replace philosophising from a divine point of view with philosophising from a human – and, in the end, from each one's own – point of view, which is, I take it, the only one we can reliably adopt in doing philosophy.

[69] I elaborated on this question in Hoche 1983: sect. VIII.

[70] This is, of course, an allusion to Nagel 1986.

take into account the, as it were, transcendental 'umbilical cord' of the physical world. From this purely scientific point of view – which, by the way, should not be mixed up with what I called the 'third-person perspective' –, it is certainly quite appropriate to think that the world takes priority over consciousness of non-human and human animals and that the latter (just as organic life) gradually 'emerges' from (inorganic) matter in the course of evolution. As viewed from this angle, the whole well-known story about the evolution of the universe, of life, and of the species should, I think, be accepted without ifs and buts – pending, of course, further scientific progress and corrections necessitated by it. But we have to tell quite a different story once we adopt the philosophical point of view. For if we do so (or, to use the more appropriate singular form: if *I*, for one, do so), I cannot even *imagine* the material world in separation from my noematic and bodily structured[71] consciousness – just as little as I can imagine, say, a perception of mine in separation from a material object and the material world,[72] of which I am the centre or zero point.[73] If we adopt, however, the purely scientific point of view, then we have to do with an abstract, theoretically constructed, centre-less universe which is neither *my* nor *your* personal world;[74] and this universe of science may well be taken to have existed before I was born and to persist after my death.[75] From this point of view, which is rightly adopted by scientists but wrongly usurped by 'neurophilosophers', human and animal consciousness depends on the world. From a non-abstract ontological point of view, however, which endeavours to do justice to the full wealth of the concrete phenomena (or, in this sense, 'to save the phenomena'), each one's noematic world in a way depends on his or her 'transcendentally constituting' consciousness. On the whole, both perspectives,

---

[71] See sect. 2.2, above.

[72] The latter we may, I think, aptly define as being the all-embracing and in principle unbounded 'outside horizon' ('Aussenhorizont') of any arbitrarily chosen material object. This conception, and also the technical term, go back to Husserl; see, e.g., Husserl 1913, tr. 1931: §§ 27, 47; 1923–1924: pp. 145–152; 1929b: § 19; 1934–1937: pp. 160–162, 165; 1948: §§ 8, 33. Defining the world this way seems to me to be at least as fertile as defining it as the totality of the facts or existing states of affairs (Wittgenstein 1922: 1.1, 1.2, 2.04) – not to speak of the totality of objects. For instance, I think that the 'horizontal structure' of perception and imagination can be made use of in a promising way if we want to deal with the sophisticated traditional problems of substance and causation; see Hoche 1964: §§ 28–29; 1983: sects. VII–VIII; 1990: sects. 10.5–10.6. But note that Wittgenstein's conception of the world is fruitful, too. For instance, in Essay IV: sect. 3.11, fn. 115, of the present collection I made use of the fact that normally we intentionally refer, not to single objects, but to constellations of objects, or states of affairs. See also ibid.: sect. 3.2, where I stated that whenever I can be said to see a thing (a body, animated or not), I can be said to see that something is the case, and vice versa.

[73] See sect. 2.2, above; Hoche 1973a: pp. 33f., 226–228, 328f.

[74] In somewhat this sense, Husserl and others have distinguished between the 'world of science' and our 'life-world(s)'.

[75] Cf. the preceding Essay V: sect. 2.8 of the present collection.

the philosophical and the scientific ones, should be taken to have equal rights, if each in its proper field – just as the first- and the third-person perspectives (which, as we cannot stress frequently enough, must not be mixed up with the other pair of perspectives) do not contradict but fruitfully complement each other and hence deserve to be equally respected.

THREE AFTERTHOUGHTS

1. In the foregoing essays, I took pains to show that a precise logical analysis of our basic ways of speaking – which, on penalty of making a conceptual mess, not even the highly specialised philosopher is allowed to tamper with – requires us to accept and defend the following positions. First, any entity accessible from the third-person perspective and any entity accessible from the first-person perspective belong to those entities which differ from 'each other' not numerically but in a way I suggest to call 'categorial'. From this it follows, second, that any objectively observable bodily occurrence and any part of my subjectively experienced consciousness cannot be considered either one and the same entity or else two different entities. Therefore, third, a bodily occurrence and a conscious experience of mine can neither be substantially 'united' ('connected') nor stand in a causal relation of 'psychophysical interaction'. This, however, may seem to be squarely belied by such well-known phenomena as psychosomatic diseases, placebo effects, and, above all, our everyday experiences with taking drugs, alcoholic drinks, and even any drinking and eating of the garden variety. Hence my claims may seem counterintuitive to such a degree that some of my readers might feel like reminding me of Hamlet's words

    > There are more things in heaven and earth, Horatio,
    > Than are dreamt of in your philosophy.[1]

    I must admit that, in the course of devising the foregoing essays, I more than once quoted these famous words to *myself*.

2. It should be noted, however, that trying to make a *self*-critical use of Hamlet's statement would amount to no less than falling back into bad philosophical habits. What I am having in mind is the following backslide. If the words cited are to be strong enough to carry the weight of an effective *self*-criticism of the sort just mentioned in my first afterthought, they cannot but make up what I called a '*pragmatic*' contradiction. For saying to *myself* what Hamlet said to Horatio would *semantically* imply that there is at least one thing in heaven or earth that is not (even) dreamt of in my (own) philosophy. If so, however, I am implying – pragmatically, and likewise in the everyday sense of the word 'imply' – that I am deprived of the speech-act theoretical *right* to assert (or, if you will, of a 'legal ground' or 'verifying evidence' for asserting) what in fact I *am* asserting.[2]

---

[1] Shakespeare, *Hamlet*, I.5.

[2] See, e.g., Essay II of the present collection. – From this it follows that Horatio, or whoever is the addressee of Hamlet's words, can never assent to them without entangling himself in a pragmatic contradiction, or uttering a fine specimen of 'Moore's paradox'. There are kindred examples, such

3. But it might appear as if the modified version could be transformed into a sound statement by simply subjecting it to a 'possibilisation', yielding, say,

> There may be more things in heaven and earth
> than are dreamt of in my philosophy.

Now to a certain extent this is true, and a truism at that. For although the words 'There may be things of the existence of which nobody *can have* the least idea.' – sometimes uttered as an alleged demonstration of one's scientific and philosophical modesty – seem to me to be again pragmatically (or, arguably, even semantically) self-contradictory,[3] their variant 'There may be things of the existence of which nobody *has* (in fact) the least idea.' is a perfectly consistent and true statement. Nonetheless, this certainly does not hold of entities – or, more precisely speaking: of alleged entities – which I cannot conceive of even in pure (eidetic) imagination. Especially, this is true of such pseudo-entities the very concept of which is inconsistent, for instance, of the professed 'things in themselves' in Kant's 'transcendental' sense. Speaking of a 'body-mind *unity*' or a 'psychophysical interaction', however, seems to me to amount to abstracting from the point(s) of view from which we could possibly come to know about them and their constituents, and hence to treating them as 'things in themselves'.

---

as all statements of the form 'You erroneously believe that *p*.'. Though this may well be true, the addressee cannot consistently assent to it by saying, e.g., 'You are quite right; on second thoughts I must in fact concede that I erroneously believe that *p*.'.

[3] See Hoche 1990: 8.1, esp. the discussion of the exemplary sentence (36).

BIBLIOGRAPHICAL REFERENCES

ANSCOMBE, G. E. M. 1957: *Intention*. Oxford: Blackwell.

AUSTIN, John Langshaw 1950: Truth. Reprinted in: Pitcher 1964, pp. 18–31.

- 1956: A Plea for Excuses. Reprinted in: J. L. Austin, *Philosophical Papers*, ed. by J. O. Urmson & G. J. Warnock, Oxford: University Press, 1961, pp. 123–152.

- 1962a: *How to do things with Words. The William James Lectures delivered at Harvard University in 1955*. Ed. by J. O. Urmson. Oxford: Clarendon 1962.

- 1962b: *Sense and Sensibilia*. Reconstructed from the manuscript notes by G. J. Warnock. Oxford University Press paperback, 1964.

BIERI, Peter (ed.) 1981: *Analytische Philosophie des Geistes* [Analytic philosophy of mind]. Königstein (Taunus): Hain.

- 2007: Was bleibt von der analytischen Philosophie? [What remains of analytic philosophy?] In: *Deutsche Zeitschrift für Philosophie* 55 (2007) 333–344.

BIRNBACHER, Dieter 1974: *Die Logik der Kriterien. Analysen zur Spätphilosophie Wittgensteins* [The logic of criteria. Analyses concerning Wittgenstein's later philosophy]. Hamburg: Felix Meiner.

BLAU, Ulrich 1978: *Die dreiwertige Logik der Sprache. Ihre Syntax, Semantik und Anwendung in der Sprachanalyse* [The trivalent logic of language. Its syntax, semantics, and application in linguistic analysis]. Berlin & New York: de Gruyter.

BLOCK, N. 1995: On a confusion about a function of consciousness. In: *Behavioral and brain sciences* 18 (1995) 227–287.

BOHR, Niels 1927: Das Quantenpostulat und die neuere Entwicklung der Atomistik [The quantum postulate and the recent development of atomism; Bohr's lecture delivered at the Como congress on September 16, 1927]. Reprinted in: Werner Heisenberg & Niels Bohr, *Die Kopenhagener Deutung der Quantentheorie*, Stuttgart: Battenberg, 1963, pp. 36–61.

- 1933: Licht und Leben [Light and life; German translation of Bohr's lecture delivered at the Copenhagen congress on August 15, 1932]. In: *Die Naturwissenschaften* 21, No. 13 (March 31, 1933) 245–250.

- 1958: Quantum Physics and Philosophy. Causality and Complementarity. In: R. Klibansky, ed., *Philosophy in the Mid-Century, I: Logic and Philosophy of Science*, Florence, 1958, 3rd ed. 1967, pp. 308–314.

BORST, C. V. (ed.) 1970: *The Mind-Brain Identity Theory*. London & New York: Macmillan & St. Martin's Press.

CAIRNS, Dorion 1973: *Guide for Translating Husserl*. The Hague: Nijhoff.

CANTOR, Georg 1885: Review of Gottlob Frege, Die Grundlagen der Arithmetik [i. e., Frege 1884, tr. 1950]. Reprinted in: G. Cantor, *Gesammelte Abhandlungen mathematischen und philosophischen Inhalts*, ed. by E. Zermelo and A. Fraenkel. Berlin, 1932; reprint edition: Hildesheim, 1962, pp. 440–442.

CARNAP, Rudolf 1928: *Der logische Aufbau der Welt*. 3rd ed., Hamburg: Felix Meiner, 1966.

- 1931, tr. 1959: The Elimination of Metaphysics Through Logical Analysis of Language, tr. by Arthur Pap, in: A. J. Ayer, ed., *Logical Positivism*, Glencoe, Ill., 1959, pp. 60–81. –

German original: Überwindung der Metaphysik durch logische Analyse der Sprache, in: *Erkenntnis* 2 (1931) 219–241.

- 1932–1933: Psychologie in physikalischer Sprache. In: *Erkenntnis* 3 (1932/33) 107–142. (English translation: Psychology in Physical Language, tr. by George [i.e., Frederick] Schick, in: A. J. Ayer, ed., *Logical Positivism*, Glencoe, Ill., 1959, pp. 165–198.)

- 1934, tr. 1937: *Logical Syntax of Language*, tr. by Amethe Smeaton, London 1937. – German original: *Logische Syntax der Sprache*. Wien: Julius Springer, 1934.

- 1947: On the Application of Inductive Logic. In: *Philosophy and Phenomenological Research* 8 (1947) 133–147.

CASTAÑEDA, Hector-Neri 1975: Identity and Sameness. In: *Philosophy* 5 (1975) 121–150.

CHALMERS, David J. 1996: *The Conscious Mind. In Search of a Fundamental Theory.* Oxford & New York.

CORNMAN, James 1962: The identity of mind and body. Reprinted in: C. V. Borst 1970, pp. 123–129.

DESCARTES, René (1641): *Meditationes de prima philosophia.* Paris, reprinted in: *Œuvres de Descartes*, ed. by Charles Adam & Paul Tannery, Paris 1897–1910, Vol. 7.

DIOGENES LAERTIUS: *Lives of Eminent Philosophers*, 2 vols. With a Translation by R. D. Hicks. London & New York: Loeb Classical Library, 1925.

DRIESCHNER, Michael 1974: Objekte der Naturwissenschaft [Objects of natural science]. In: *Tendenzen der Wissenschaftstheorie* (Neue Hefte für Philosophie, No. 6/7), Göttingen: Vandenhoeck & Ruprecht, 1974, pp. 104–128.

- 1981: *Einführung in die Naturphilosophie* [Introduction to the philosophy of nature]. Darmstadt: Wissenschaftliche Buchgesellschaft.

- 1984: Physik a priori? [Physics (as a science) a priori?]. In: Bernulf Kanitscheider (ed.), *Moderne Naturphilosophie*, Würzburg: Königshausen & Neumann, 1984, pp. 41–61.

DUDDA, Friedrich 1999: *Die Logik der Sprache der Moral* [The logic of the language of morals]. Paderborn: mentis.

- 2006: *Die Sprache der Subjektivität* [The language of subjectivity]. (Professorial dissertation, submitted to the Fakultät für Philosophie, Pädagogik und Publizistik [Department of philosophy, education, and journalism] of the Ruhr-Universität Bochum, 2006). Berlin: Logos (forthcoming).

- 2007: Gettier-Beispiele und eine Gebrauchsdefinition des Begriffs des propositionalen Wissens [Gettier examples and a usage-oriented definition of the concept of propositional knowledge]. Lecture, delivered at the Institute of Philosophy, Ruhr-Universität Bochum, Germany, on June 6, 2007. In: Facta Philosophica 9 (2008); forthcoming.

DUMMETT, Michael 1963: Realism. Reprinted in: Dummett 1978, pp. 145–165.

- 1969: The Reality of the Past. Reprinted in: Dummett 1978, pp. 358–374.

- 1978: *Truth and Other Enigmas.* London: Duckworth.

EDWARDS, Paul (ed.) 1967: *The Encyclopedia of Philosophy*, Vol. 1–8. New York and London: Macmillan. Reprint edition 1972.

FAHRENBERG, Jochen 1979: Das Komplementaritätsprinzip in der psychophysiologischen Forschung und psychosomatischen Medizin [The principle of complementarity in psychophysiological research and psychosomatic medicine]. In: *Zeitschrift für Klinische Psychologie und Psychotherapie* 27 (1979) 151–167.

– 1981: Zum Verständnis des Komplementaritätsprinzips [On understanding the complementarity principle]. In: *Zeitschrift für Klinische Psychologie und Psychotherapie* 29 (1981) 205–208.

– 1989: Einige Thesen zum psychophysischen Problem aus der Sicht der psychophysiologischen Forschung [Some theses concerning the psychophysical problem from the point of view of psychophysiological research]. In: W. Marx, ed., *Philosophie und Psychologie: Leib und Seele – Determination und Vorhersage*, Frankfurt, 1989, pp. 9–35.

FLEW, Antony (ed.) 1979: *A Dictionary of Philosophy*. New York: St. Martin's Press.

FORSTER, T. E. 1992: *Set Theory with a Universal Set. Exploring an Untyped Universe*. Oxford.

FREGE, Gottlob 1879, tr. 1952: Begriffsschrift, tr. by Peter Geach. In: Frege 1952. – German original: *Begriffsschrift, eine der arithmetischen nachgebildete Formelsprache des reinen Denkens*. Halle (Saale), Nebert 1879.

– 1884, tr. 1950: *Die Grundlagen der Arithmetik. Eine logisch-mathematische Untersuchung über den Begriff der Zahl / The Foundations of Arithmetic. A logico-mathematical enquiry into the concept of number*, ed. and tr. by J. L. Austin. Oxford: Basil Blackwell, 1950, 2nd revised ed. 1953. – German original: Breslau, Koebner 1884; German reprint: Darmstadt, Wissenschaftliche Buchgesellschaft, 1961.

– 1891, tr. 1952: Function and Concept, tr. by Peter Geach. In: Frege 1952. – Pagination according to the German original: *Funktion und Begriff*. Jena, 1891.

– 1892a, tr. 1952: On Sense and Reference, tr. by Max Black. In: Frege 1952. – Pagination according to the German original: Über Sinn und Bedeutung, in: *Zeitschrift für Philosophie und philosophische Kritik* 100 (1892) 25–50.

– 1892b, tr. 1952: On Concept and Object, tr. by Peter Geach. In: Frege 1952. – Pagination according to the German original: Über Begriff und Gegenstand, in: *Vierteljahrsschrift für wissenschaftliche Philosophie* 16 (1892) 192–205.

– 1893: *Grundgesetze der Arithmetik, begriffsschriftlich abgeleitet* [The basic laws of arithmetic]. Vol. 1, Jena 1893. Reprint edition: Darmstadt, Wissenschaftliche Buchgesellschaft, 1962.

– 1894: Rezension von: E. G. Husserl, Philosophie der Arithmetik. I [Review of: E. G. Husserl, Philosophy of Arithmetic. I]. Reprinted in: Frege 1967 (references follow the original pagination).

– 1897: Logik [Logic]. In: Frege 1969, pp. 137–163.

– 1899: Über die Zahlen des Herrn H. Schubert [On the numbers of Mr. H. Schubert]. Reprinted in: Frege 1967 (references follow the original pagination).

– 1918: Logische Untersuchungen, Erster Teil: Der Gedanke [Logical investigations, Part I: The thought]. Reprinted in: Frege 1967 (references follow the original pagination).

– 1952: *Translations From the Philosophical Writings of Gottlob Frege*, ed. by Peter Geach and Max Black. Oxford.

– 1967: *Kleine Schriften* [Minor works]. Ed. by Ignacio Angelelli. Darmstadt: Wissenschaftliche Buchgesellschaft.

– 1969: *Nachgelassene Schriften* [Posthumous papers]. Ed. by H. Hermes, F. Kambartel, E. Kaulbach. Hamburg: Felix Meiner.

GOODMAN, Nelson 1954: *Fact, Fiction, and Forecast*. London. 3rd ed. 1973.

GRICE, H. P. 1961: The Causal Theory of Perception. Reprinted in: G. J. Warnock (ed.), *The Philosophy of Perception*, Oxford University Press, 1967 (Oxford Readings in Philosophy), pp. 85–112.

–   1975: Logic and Conversation. In: P. Cole & J. L. Morgan (eds.), *Syntax and Semantics*, Vol. 3, New York: Academic Press, 1975, pp. 41–58.

HARE, Richard M. 1952: *The Language of Morals*. Oxford: Clarendon.

–   1959: A School for Philosophers. Reprinted in: Hare, *Essays on Philosophical Method*, London & Basingstoke: Macmillan, 1971, pp. 38–53.

–   1960: Philosophical Discoveries. Reprinted in: Hare, *Essays on Philosophical Method*, London & Basingstoke: Macmillan, 1971, pp. 19–37.

–   1963: *Freedom and Reason*. Oxford University Press.

–   1966: Some Sub-Atomic Particles of Logic. (Circulated manuscript; lecture given at the University of Canberra, 1966.)

–   1971: Some Sub-Atomic Particles of Logic. (Lecture, delivered at the University of Leeds, 1971; unpublished notes.)

–   1981: *Moral Thinking. Its Levels, Method, and Point*. Oxford: Clarendon.

–   1989: Some Sub-Atomic Particles of Logic. In: *Mind* 98 (1989) 23–37.

HASHISH, I., FINMAN, C., & HARVEY, W. 1988: Reduction of postoperative pain and swelling by ultrasound: a placebo effect. In: *Pain* 83 (1988) 303–311.

HEIDEGGER, Martin 1929: *Was ist Metaphysik?* [What is metaphysics?]. Sixth edition, Frankfurt: Klostermann, 1951.

HEISENBERG, Werner 1964: Erinnerungen an Niels Bohr aus den Jahren 1922–1927 [Reminiscences of Niels Bohr from the years 1922–1927]. In: W. Heisenberg, *Schritte über Grenzen. Gesammelte Reden und Aufsätze*, Munich: Piper, [3]1976, S. 52–70.

HICK, John 1960: Theology and Verification. Reprinted in: B. Mitchell (ed.), *The Philosophy of Religion*, Oxford 1971 (Oxford Readings in Philosophy), pp. 53–71.

HOCHE, Hans-Ulrich 1964: *Nichtempirische Erkenntnis. Analytische und synthetische Urteile a priori bei Kant und bei Husserl* [Non-empirical knowledge. Kant and Husserl on analytical and synthetic judgements a priori]. Meisenheim am Glan: Hain.

–   1973a: *Handlung, Bewusstsein und Leib. Vorstudien zu einer rein noematischen Phänomenologie* [Action, consciousness, and (the functioning) body. Preliminary studies concerning a purely noematic phenomenology]. Freiburg & Munich: Karl Alber.

–   1973b: Review of Prauss 1971, in: *Archiv für Geschichte der Philosophie* 55 (1973) 96–100.

–   1975, tr. 1983: How Substance-concepts function in Indicating and Counting Objects, tr. by Gerhard Heyer. In: D. E. Christensen et al., eds., *Contemporary German Philosophy*, Vol. 2, University Park and London, 1983, pp. 200–211. – German original: Über die Rolle von Substanzbegriffen beim Zeigen und Zählen von Gegenständen, in: *Zeitschrift für allgemeine Wissenschaftstheorie / Journal for General Philosophy of Science* 29 (1975) 337–348.

–   1976: Vom "Inhaltsstrich" zum "Waagerechten". Ein Beitrag zur Entwicklung der Fregeschen Urteilslehre [From the 'content-stroke' to the 'horizontal (one)'. A contribution concerning the development of Frege's theory of judgement], in: Matthias Schirn (ed.), *Studien zu Frege II: Logik und Sprachphilosophie / Studies on Frege II: Logic and Philosophy of Language*, Stuttgart: frommann-holzboog, 1976, pp. 87–102.

- 1977: Kausalgefüge, irreale Bedingungssätze und das Problem der Definierbarkeit von Dispositionsprädikaten [Causal sentences, counterfactual conditionals, and the problem of how to define disposition predicates]. In: *Zeitschrift für allgemeine Wissenschaftstheorie / Journal for General Philosophy of Science* 8 (1977) 257–291.

- 1979a: Husserls Phänomenbegriff im Lichte sprachanalytischen Philosophierens [Husserl's concept of a phenomenon in the light of philosophising in a linguistic key]. In: *Phänomenologische Forschungen / Phenomenological Studies / Recherches Phénoménologiques*, ed. by Ernst Wolfgang Orth, Vol. 8 (Studien zur Sprachphänomenologie), Freiburg & Munich: Alber, 1979, pp. 65–90.

- 1979b: Does Goodman's 'grue' Serve Its Purpose?, tr. by Gisela Shaw. In: *Ratio* 21 (1979) 162–173.

- 1981: Zur Methodologie von Kombinationstests in der analytischen Philosophie [On the methodology of combination tests in linguistic philosophy]. In: *Zeitschrift für allgemeine Wissenschaftstheorie / Journal for General Philosophy of Science* 12 (1981) 28–54.

- 1982: Beziehungen zwischen der Semantik Freges und der Noematik Husserls [Relations between Frege's semantics and Husserl's noematics]. In: *Archiv für Geschichte der Philosophie* 64 (1982) 166–197.

- 1983: Philosophisches Staunen und phänomenologische Variation [Philosophical amazement and phenomenological variation]. In: *Archiv für Geschichte der Philosophie* 65 (1983) 283–305.

- 1985: Sein und Heissen. Modalprobleme der Identität [Being, and being called. Modal problems of identity]. In: *Zeitschrift für allgemeine Wissenschaftstheorie / Journal for General Philosophy of Science* 16 (1985) 287–303.

- 1986: Subjektivität [Subjectivity]. In: Julie Kirchberg & Johannes Müther, eds., *Philosophisch-Theologische Grenzfragen* (Festschrift Richard Schaeffler), Essen: Ludgerus, 1986, pp. 51–63.

- 1987: Das Leib-Seele-Problem: Dualismus, Monismus, Perspektivismus [The mind-body problem: Dualism, monism, perspectivism]. In: *Philosophia Naturalis* 24 (1987) 218–236.

- 1990: *Einführung in das sprachanalytische Philosophieren* [Introduction to doing philosophy in a linguistic key]. Darmstadt: Wissenschaftliche Buchgesellschaft.

- 1992: *Elemente einer Anatomie der Verpflichtung. Pragmatisch-wollenslogische Grundlegung einer Theorie des moralischen Argumentierens* [Elements of an anatomy of obligation. Groundwork of a theory of moral reasoning, based on pragmatics and a logic of willing]. Freiburg & Munich: Karl Alber.

- 1994: Zur Komplementarität von Freiheit und Notwendigkeit des menschlichen Handelns [On the complementarity of freedom and necessity in human action]. In: *Jahrbuch für Recht und Ethik / Annual Review of Law and Ethics* 2 (1994) 37–54.

- 1995a: Anthropologische Komplementarität und die 'Einheit der Sache'. Versuch einer skeptischen Lösung eines skeptischen Zweifels [Anthropological complementarity and the 'unity of the object'. An attempt to give a sceptical solution to a sceptical doubt]. In: L. Kreimendahl, ed., *Aufklärung und Skepsis. Studien zur Philosophie und Geistesgeschichte des 17. und 18. Jahrhunderts* (Festschrift Günter Gawlick), Stuttgart, frommann-holzboog 1995, pp. 107–129.

– 1995b: Verteilte Repräsentation, neurophysiologische Selbstversuche und Komplementarität [Distributed representation, neurophysiological self-experiments, and complementarity]. In: *Ethik und Sozialwissenschaften* 6 (1995) 93–96.

– 1995c: Do Illocutionary, or Neustic, Negations Exist? In: *Erkenntnis* 43 (1995) 127–136.

– 1995d: Universal Prescriptivism Revised; or: The Analyticity of the Golden Rule. In: *Revista Filosófica de Coimbra* 4 (N° 8, October 1995) 337–363.

– 1995e: Ein Problem des universellen Präskriptivismus: Implizieren Verpflichtungssätze Imperative logisch-semantisch oder "Ich-will"-Sätze pragmatisch? [A problem of universal prescriptivism: Do 'ought'-sentences entail imperatives, or do they imply 'I intend'-sentences pragmatically?] In: Christoph Fehige & Georg Meggle (eds.), *Zum moralischen Denken*. Frankfurt am Main: Suhrkamp, 1995, Vol. 1, pp. 229–253.

– 2001: Eine wollenslogische Weiterentwicklung des Universellen Präskriptivismus und die Begründung der Goldenen Regel [A further development of universal prescriptivism by means of a logic of willing, and a proof of the golden rule]. In: *Jahrbuch für Recht und Ethik / Annual Review of Law and Ethics* 9 (2001) 325–376.

– 2002: Philosophieren [Philosophising]. In: Thomas Spitzley/Ralf Stoecker (eds.), *Philosophie à la carte*, Paderborn: mentis, 2002, pp. 153–156.

– 2004: In Search of an Integrated Logic of Conviction and Intention. In: *Jahrbuch für Recht und Ethik / Annual Review of Law and Ethics* 12 (2004) 401–434.

– 2006: Some Remarks on Self-Identity and Identity Proper. (Circulated manuscript, discussed in the *Logisch-sprachanalytisches Kolloquium* [Logico-linguistic Colloquy] at the Institute of Philosophy, Ruhr-Universität Bochum, Germany, on February 2, 2007.)

– 2007: Reflexive monism versus complementarism: An analysis and criticism of the conceptual groundwork of Max Velmans's reflexive model of consciousness. In: *Phenomenology and the Cognitive Sciences* 6 (2007) 389–409.

– 2008: Peter Bieri über die Zukunft der "analytischen Philosophie". Eine unerlässliche Entgegnung [Peter Bieri on the future of 'analytic philosophy'. An inevitable retort]. Submitted to *Deutsche Zeitschrift für Philosophie* 56 (2008).

– & STRUBE, Werner 1985: *Analytische Philosophie* [Analytic philosophy]. Freiburg & Munich: Karl Alber (= *Handbuch Philosophie*, ed. by E. Stroeker & W. Wieland, Vol. 6).

HOLTON, Gerald 1981: Zur Genesis des Komplementaritätsgedankens [On the genesis of the conception of complementarity]. In: Gerald Holton, *Thematische Analyse der Wissenschaft. Die Physik Einsteins und seiner Zeit*, translated into German by Horst Huber, Frankfurt am Main: Suhrkamp, 1981, pp. 144–202.

HÖRMANN, Hans 1976: The Concept of Sense Constancy. In: *Lingua* 39 (1976) 269–280.

HRÓBJARTSSON, A. & GØTZSCHE, P. C. 2001: Is the placebo powerless? An analysis of clinical trials comparing placebo with no treatment. In: *New England Journal of Medicine* 344/21 (2001) 1594–1602.

HUGHES, G. E. & CRESSWELL, M. J. 1968: *An Introduction to Modal Logic*. London: Methuen. University Paperback 1972, reprinted 1977.

HUME, David 1739: *A Treatise of Human Nature*, London. New edition by L. A. Selby-Bigge, Oxford: Clarendon, 1888, reprinted 1967.

– 1748: *An Enquiry Concerning Human Understanding*, London. New edition by L. A. Selby-Bigge: *Enquiries concerning Human Understanding and concerning the Principles of Morals*, Oxford: Clarendon, 1888, 3rd ed. 1975.

HUSSERL, Edmund 1900: *Logische Untersuchungen* [Logical investigations]. Vol. I. 4th ed. Halle: Max Niemeyer, 1928.

- 1901a: *Logische Untersuchungen* [Logical investigations]. Vol. II, 1st Part (1st through 5th Investigation). 4th ed. Halle: Max Niemeyer, 1928.

- 1901b: *Logische Untersuchungen* [Logical investigations]. Vol. II, 2nd Part (6th Investigation). 4th ed. Tübingen: Max Niemeyer, 1968.

- 1907: *Die Idee der Phänomenologie* [The idea of phenomenology]. Ed. by Walter Biemel, The Hague: Nijhoff 1958 (HUSSERLIANA, Vol. II).

- 1913, tr. 1931: *Ideas. General Introduction to Pure Phenomenology*, tr. by W. R. Boyce Gibson. London, 1931. Collier Books, New York, 1962. – German original: *Ideen zu einer reinen Phänomenologie und phänomenologischen Philosophie*, Vol. I. Halle, 1913. Republished by Walter Biemel, The Hague: Nijhoff 1950 (HUSSERLIANA, Vol. III).

- 1923–1924: *Erste Philosophie (1923/24)*, II: *Theorie der phänomenologischen Reduktion* [First philosophy (1923/24), II: Theory of phenomenological reduction]. Ed. by Rudolf Boehm, The Hague: Nijhoff 1959 (HUSSERLIANA, Vol. VIII).

- 1925: *Phänomenologische Psychologie. Vorlesungen Sommersemester 1925* [Phenomenological psychology. Lectures, summer term 1925]. Ed. by Walter Biemel, The Hague: Nijhoff 1962 (HUSSERLIANA, Vol. IX).

- 1929a: *Formale und transzendentale Logik. Versuch einer Kritik der logischen Vernunft* [Formal and transcendental logics. An attempt at a critique of logical reason]. Republished by Paul Janssen, The Hague: Nijhoff 1974 (HUSSERLIANA, Vol. XVII).

- 1929b: *Cartesianische Meditationen und Pariser Vorträge* [Cartesian meditations and Paris lectures]. Ed. by S. Strasser, The Hague: Nijhoff 1950 (HUSSERLIANA, Vol. I).

- 1934–1937: *Die Krisis der europäischen Wissenschaften und die transzendentale Phänomenologie. Eine Einleitung in die phänomenologische Philosophie* [The crisis of the European sciences, and transcendental phenomenology. An introduction to phenomenological philosophy]. Ed. by Walter Biemel, The Hague; Nijhoff 1954 (HUSSERLIANA, Vol. VI).

- 1948: *Erfahrung und Urteil. Untersuchungen zur Genealogie der Logik* [Experience and judgement. Enquiries into the genealogy of logic]. Arranged and ed. by Ludwig Landgrebe. Hamburg: Claassen 1948.

KNEALE, William 1962: Modality *de dicto* and *de re*. In: Ernest Nagel, Patrick Suppes, Alfred Tarski (eds.), *Logic, Methodology and Philosophy of Science*, Stanford University Press 1962, pp. 622–633.

KNOOP, Michael 2001: Personal communication to the author, June 24, 2001.

- 2003: Präsupposition und logische Implikation bei Strawson [Strawson on Presupposition and Entailment]. (Circulated manuscript, discussed in the *Logisch-sprachanalytisches Kolloquium* [Logico-linguistic Colloquy] at the Institute of Philosophy, Ruhr-Universität Bochum, Germany, in 2003.)

KRETZMANN, Norman: Semantics, History of, in: Edwards 1967, Vol. 7, pp. 358–406.

KRIPKE, Saul A. 1971: Identity and Necessity. In: Munitz, Milton K. (ed.), *Identity and Individuation*, New York University Press, 1971, pp. 135–164.

- 1972: Naming and Necessity. In: Davidson, Donald & Harman, Gilbert (eds.), *Semantics of Natural Language*, Dordrecht 1972, pp. 253–355, 763–769.

- 1982: *Wittgenstein on Rules and Private Language. An Elementary Exposition.* Oxford: Basil Blackwell.

KÜNNE, Wolfgang 1983: *Abstrakte Gegenstände. Semantik und Ontologie* [Abstract objects. Semantics and ontology]. Frankfurt am Main: Suhrkamp.

LANDSCHEID, Ulf 1997: *Sätze über den Satz. Eine Theorie der Satzbedeutung und ihre Anwendung auf die Logik* [Sentences on the sentence. A theory of sentential meaning and its application to logic]. Frankfurt a. M.: Peter Lang.

- 2000: *Wittgenstein – Theorien und Tatsachen. Wittgensteins sprachanalytische Methode und die Lösung der Leib-Seele-Probleme* [Wittgenstein – theories and facts. Wittgenstein's linguistico-analytic method and the solution of the mind-body problems]. Freiburg & Munich: Karl Alber.

LANGFORD, Cooper Harold 1942: The Notion of Analysis in Moore's Philosophy. In: Schilpp 1942, pp. 321–342.

LEIBNIZ, Gottfried Wilhelm 1704: *Nouveaux essais sur l'entendement humain.* Reprinted in: Leibniz, *Philosophische Schriften*, ed. & tr. [into German] by Wolf von Engelhardt & Hans Heinz Holz, Vol. III.1 (1959) and III.2 (1961). Darmstadt: Wissenschaftliche Buchgesellschaft.

- 1714: Principes de la Nature et de la Grace, fondés en raison. Reprinted in: *Die philosophischen Schriften von Gottfried Wilhelm Leibniz*, ed. by C. J. Gerhardt, Vol. VI, pp. 598–606.

LEWIN, Kurt 1922: *Der Begriff der Genese in Physik, Biologie und Entwicklungsgeschichte. Eine Untersuchung zur vergleichenden Wissenschaftslehre* [The concept of genesis in physics, biology, and the history of development. An enquiry into the comparative theory of science]. Berlin.

- 1923: Die zeitliche Geneseordnung [The temporal order of genesis]. In: *Zeitschrift für Physik* 13 (1923) 62–81.

LINNEBO, Øystein 2005: To Be Is to Be an *F*. In: *dialectica* 59 (2005) 201–222.

LOCKE, John 1690: *An Essay Concerning Human Understanding.* New edition by P. H. Nidditch, Oxford 1975.

MACINTYRE, A. 1969: A Mistake about Causality in Social Science. In: P. Laslett & W. Runciman (eds.), *Philosophy, Politics, and Society*, 2nd Series, Oxford 1969, pp. 48–70.

MACKIE, J. L. 1965: Causes and Conditions. Reprinted in: Ernest Sosa (ed.), *Causation and Conditionals*, Oxford University Press (Oxford Readings in Philosophy), 1975, pp. 15–38.

MALCOLM, Norman 1958: Knowledge of Other Minds. Reprinted in: Malcolm 1963, pp. 130–140.

- 1959: *Dreaming.* London: Routledge & Kegan Paul. 4th impression, 1967.

- 1963: *Knowledge and Certainty. Essays and Lectures.* Englewood Cliffs: Prentice-Hall.

METZINGER, Thomas (ed.) 1995: *Bewusstsein* [Consciousness]. Paderborn, Munich, Vienna, & Zurich: Ferdinand Schöningh, 3rd ed. 1996.

- (ed.) 2006: *Grundkurs Philosophie des Geistes.* Band 1: *Phänomenales Bewusstsein* [Basic course Philosophy of Mind. Vol. 1: Phenomenal consciousness]. Paderborn: mentis.

MOORE, George Edward 1903: *Principia Ethica.* Cambridge University Press.

- 1913–1914: The Status of Sense-Data. Reprinted in: Moore 1922, pp. 168–196.

- 1918: Some Judgments of Perception. Reprinted in: Moore 1922, pp. 220–252.

- 1922: *Philosophical Studies*. London.
- 1925: A Defence of Common Sense. Reprinted in: Moore 1959, pp. 32–59.
- 1942: A Reply to My Critics: III. Philosophic Method: 11. Analysis. In: Schilpp 1942, pp. 660–667.
- 1944: Russell's 'Theory of Descriptions'. Reprinted in: Moore 1959, pp. 151–195.
- 1953: *Some Main Problems of Philosophy*. London: George Allen & Unwin.
- 1954–1955: Wittgenstein's Lectures in 1930–33. Reprinted in: Moore 1959, pp. 252–324.
- 1959: *Philosophical Papers*. London & New York: Allen & Unwin/Macmillan.

MORRIS, Charles William 1938: *Foundations of the Theory of Signs*. Chicago: The University of Chicago Press.

NAGEL, Thomas 1974: What is it like to be a bat? Reprinted in: Nagel 1979, pp. 165–180.
- 1978: Ethics without biology. Reprinted in: Nagel 1979, pp. 142–146.
- 1979: *Mortal Questions*. London, New York, Melbourne: Cambridge University Press.
- 1986: *The View From Nowhere*. New York: Oxford University Press.

NEFFE, Jürgen 2005: *Einstein. Eine Biographie* [Einstein. A biography]. Reinbek bei Hamburg: Rowohlt.

NÚÑEZ, Rafael & SWEETSER, Eve (2006): With the Future Behind Them. Convergent Evidence From Aymara Language and Gesture in the Crosslinguistic Comparison of Spatial Construals of Time. In: *Cognitive Science* 30 (2006) 1–50.

OBERSCHELP, Arnold 1992: *Logik für Philosophen* [Logic for philosophers]. Stuttgart & Weimar: J. B. Metzler, 2nd ed. 1997.

OPPENHEIMER, Julius Robert 1953: *Science and the Common Understanding*. New York.

PARDEY, Ulrich 1994: *Identität, Existenz und Reflexivität. Sprachanalytische Untersuchungen zur deskriptiven Metaphysik* [Identity, Existence, and Reflexivity. Linguistico-analytical investigations in the field of descriptive metaphysics]. Weinheim: Beltz Athenäum.
- 2004: *Freges Kritik an der Korrespondenztheorie der Wahrheit. Eine Verteidigung gegen die Einwände von Dummett, Künne, Soames and Stuhlmann-Laeisz.* [Frege's criticism of the correspondence theory of truth. A defence against the objections of Dummett, Künne, Soames, and Stuhlmann-Laeisz]. Paderborn: mentis.
- 2006: *Begriffskonflikte in Sprache, Logik, Metaphysik* [Conceptual dilemmas in language, logic, and metaphysics]. Paderborn: mentis.
- 2007: Freges Einwände gegen die Korrespondenztheorie der Wahrheit – eine Rehabilitation [Frege's objections against the correspondence theory of truth – a rehabilitation]. (Circulated manuscript, discussed in the *Logisch-sprachanalytisches Kolloquium* [Logico-linguistic Colloquy] at the Institute of Philosophy, Ruhr-Universität Bochum, Germany, on November 30 and December 7, 2007; intended for publication in an English version.)

PASCAL, Blaise 1669: *Pensées*. Édition de Ch.-M. des Granges. Paris: Garnier 1964.

PASSMORE, John 1961: Arguments to Meaninglessness: Excluded Opposites and Paradigm Cases. Reprinted in: Rorty 1967, pp. 183–200.

PATON, H. J. 1936: *Kant's Metaphysic of Experience. A Commentary on the First Half of the Kritik der reinen Vernunft*. Vol. I–II. London 1936, 2nd edition 1951.

PEIRCE, Charles Sanders 1931–1935: *Collected Papers*, Vol. 1–6, ed. by C. Hartshorne & P. Weiss. Cambridge, Mass. (Bibliographical data refer to volume and section.)

PITCHER, George (ed.) 1964: *Truth*. Englewood Cliffs, N. J.: Prentice-Hall.

PLANCK, Max 1946: Scheinprobleme der Wissenschaft [Pseudo-problems of science]. In: Planck, *Vorträge und Erinnerungen*, Darmstadt: Wissenschaftliche Buchgesellschaft, 1949, 11th ed. 1979, pp. 350–362.

POPPER, Karl R. 1934, tr. 1959: *The Logic of Scientific Discovery*. London, 1959. – German original: *Logik der Forschung*. Vienna, 1934 (allegedly, "1935"). 2nd, enlarged German edition: Tübingen: J. C. B. Mohr (Paul Siebeck), 1966.

– 1972: *Objective Knowledge. An Evolutionary Approach*. Oxford: Clarendon.

POSNER, Michael I. 1993: Seeing the Mind. In: *Science* 262 (29 October 1993) 673–674.

PRAUSS, Gerold 1971: *Erscheinung bei Kant. Ein Problem der "Kritik der reinen Vernunft"* [Kant on appearance(s). A problem of the 'Critique of pure reason']. Berlin: de Gruyter.

QUINE, Willard Van Orman 1950: *Methods of Logic*. London: Routledge & Kegan Paul, 3rd ed. 1974.

– 1960: *Word and Object*. Cambridge, Massachusetts: M.I.T. Press.

RORTY, Richard 1965: Mind-body identity, privacy and categories. Reprinted in: C. V. Borst1970: pp. 187–213.

– (ed.) 1967: *The Linguistic Turn. Recent Essays in Philosophical Method*. The University of Chicago Press.

ROTH, Gerhard 1992: Das konstruktive Gehirn: Neurobiologische Grundlagen von Wahrnehmung und Erkenntnis [The constructive brain: Neurobiological foundations of perception and cognition]. In: Siegfried J. Schmidt (ed.), *Kognition und Gesellschaft. Der Diskurs des Radikalen Konstruktivismus* 2, Frankfurt am Main: Suhrkamp, 1992, pp. 277–336.

– & SCHWEGLER, Helmut 1995: Das Geist-Gehirn-Problem aus der Sicht der Hirnforschung und eines nicht-reduktionistischen Physikalismus [The mind-brain problem seen from the point of view of brain research and a non-reductive physicalism]. In: *Ethik und Sozialwissenschaften* 6 (1995) No. 1, pp. 69–77.

RUSSELL, Bertrand 1905: On Denoting. Reprinted in: R. Russell, *Logic and Knowledge. Essays 1901–1950*, ed. by R. C. Marsh, London: Allen & Unwin, 1956, pp. 39–56.

– 1911: Knowledge by Acquaintance and Knowledge by Description. Reprinted in: *The Collected Papers of Bertrand Russell*, Vol. 6, London and New York, 1992, pp. 147–161.

RYLE, Gilbert 1932: Phenomenology. In: *Proceedings of the Aristotelian Society*, Suppl.Vol. 11 (1932) 68–83.

– 1938: Categories. Reprinted in: Ryle 1971, Vol II, pp. 170–184

– 1945: Philosophical Arguments. Reprinted in: Ryle 1971, Vol II, pp. 194–211.

– 1949: *The Concept of Mind*. London: Hutchinson. Peregrine Book (Harmondsworth) 1963.

– 1951: Ludwig Wittgenstein. Reprinted in: Ryle 1971, Vol. I, pp. 249–257.

– 1954: *Dilemmas*. Cambridge University Press.

– 1962: Phenomenology versus 'The Concept of Mind' [La phénoménologie contre *The Concept of Mind*]. Reprinted in: Ryle 1971, Vol. I, pp. 179–196.

– 1971: *Collected Papers*. Vol. I: Critical Essays; Vol. II: Collected Essays 1929–1968. London.

SARTRE, Jean-Paul 1936–1937: La transcendance de l'égo. Esquisse d'une description phénoménologique [The transcendence of the ego. Outline of a phenomenological description]. In: *Recherches philosophiques* 6 (1936–1937) 85–123.

– 1943: *L'être et le néant* [Being and nothingness]. Paris.

SCHILPP, Paul Arthur (ed.) 1942: *The Philosophy of G. E. Moore*. La Salle and London: Library of Living Philosophers, 3rd edition 1968.

SCHWENKE, Heiner 1992: *Autorität, Bewusstsein und Physikalisches. Systematische Studie zum Leib-Seele-Problem* [Authority, consciousness, and the physical. A systematic study concerning the mind-body problem]. Doctoral dissertation, University of Freiburg, Germany.

– 2005: Wissenschaftliche Methode und die Grenzen der Naturwissenschaften [Scientific method and the limits of natural science]. In: UNIVERSITASonline Archiv 3/2005 (http://www.hirzel.de/universitas/archiv/Schwenke1.pdf)

SEARLE, John R. 1969: *Speech Acts. An Essay in the Philosophy of Language*. Cambridge University Press.

– 1983: *Intentionality. An Essay in the Philosophy of Mind*. Cambridge University Press.

– 1990: Consciousness, explanatory inversion and cognitive science. In: *Behavioral and Brain Sciences* 13 (1990) 585–642.

– 1992: *The Rediscovery of the Mind*. Cambridge (Mass.) & London: MIT Press.

SEBEOK, Thomas A. & UMIKER-SEBEOK, Jean 1980: *You Know My Method. A Juxtaposition of Charles S. Peirce and Sherlock Holmes*. Bloomington, Indiana: Gaslight Publications.

SEIFERT, Josef 1973: *Leib und Seele. Ein Beitrag zur philosophischen Anthropologie* [Body and soul. A contribution to philosophical anthropology]. Salzburg & Munich: Anton Pustet.

SEPP, Hans Rainer (ed.) 1988: *Edmund Husserl und die Phänomenologische Bewegung. Zeugnisse in Text und Bild* [Edmund Husserl and the Phenomenological Movement. Testimonials in the form of texts and pictures]. Freiburg & Munich: Karl Alber.

SHOEMAKER, Sydney 1982: The Inverted Spectrum. In: *The Journal of Philosophy* 79 (1982), 357–381.

STEGMÜLLER, Wolfgang 1969: *Probleme und Resultate der Wissenschaftstheorie und Analytischen Philosophie, Band I: Wissenschaftliche Erklärung und Begründung* [Problems and results of the philosophy of science and analytic philosophy, Vol. I: Scientific explanation and justification]. Berlin, Heidelberg, New York: Springer.

STRAWSON, Peter Frederick 1950: On Referring. Reprinted in: Strawson 1971, pp. 1–27.

– 1952: *Introduction to Logical Theory*. London: Methuen. University Paperback 1963, reprinted 1967.

– 1959: *Individuals. An Essay in Descriptive Metaphysics*. London: Methuen. University Paperback 1964, reprinted 1969.

– 1971: *Logico-Linguistic Papers*. London & New York: Methuen, 1971. University Paperback, Reprint 1980.

STRUBE, Werner 1985: Analyse des Verstehensbegriffs [An analysis of the concept of understanding]. In: *Zeitschrift für allgemeine Wissenschaftstheorie / Journal for General Philosophy of Science* 16 (1985) 315–333.

UEXKÜLL, Jakob von 1909: *Umwelt und Innenwelt der Tiere* [Surrounding world and inner world of animals]. Berlin: J. Springer.

VELMANS, Max 1990: Consciousness, brain, and the physical world. In: *Philosophical Psychology* 3 (1990) 77–99.

– 1991: Is human information processing conscious? In: *Behavioral and Brain Sciences* 14 (1991) 651–726.

– 1996a: Consciousness and the 'causal paradox'. In: *Behavioral and Brain Sciences* 19 (1996) 537–542.

– 1996b (ed.): *The Science of Consciousness. Psychological, Neuropsychological and Clinical Reviews*. London & New York: Routledge.

– 2000: *Understanding Consciousness*. London and Philadelphia: Routledge.

– 2002: How Could Conscious Experiences Affect Brains? In: *Journal of Consciousness Studies* 9 (2002) 3–29.

– 2004: Personal communication to the author (e-mail of January 31, 2004).

– 2007: How experienced phenomena relate to things themselves: Kant, Husserl, Hoche, and reflexive monism. In: *Phenomenology and the Cognitive Sciences* 6 (2007) 411–423.

WALL, Patrick D. 1996: The placebo effect. In: Velmans 1996b, pp. 162–180.

WEBER, Max 1913: Über einige Kategorien der verstehenden Soziologie [On some categories of a sociology based on understanding]. In: Weber 1922, pp. 427–474.

– 1921: Soziologische Grundbegriffe [Some basic concepts of sociology]. Reprinted in: Weber 1922, pp. 541–581.

– 1922: Gesammelte Aufsätze zur Wissenschaftslehre [Collected papers on the theory of science]. 3rd, enlarged edition, ed. by Johannes Winkelmann, Tübingen: J. C. B. Mohr (Paul Siebeck), 1968.

WHITEHEAD, Alfred North & RUSSELL, Bertrand 1910: *Principia Mathematica*. Vol. I. Cambridge University Press: 2nd edition 1927. Paperback Edition to *56, Cambridge 1962.

WIGGINS, David 1965: Identity-Statements. In: R. J. Butler (ed.), *Analytical Philosophy*, Second Series, Oxford: Blackwell, 1965, pp. 40–71.

– 1980: *Sameness and Substance*. Oxford: Blackwell.

WINDMANN, Sabine & DURSTEWITZ, Daniel 2000: Phänomenales Erleben: Ein fundamentales Problem für die Psychologie und die Neurowissenschaften [Phenomenal experience: A fundamental problem for psychology and brain science]. In: *Psychologische Rundschau* 51 (2000) 75–82.

WITTGENSTEIN, Ludwig 1922: *Tractatus Logico-philosophicus*. London. Republished with a new translation by D. F. Pears and B. F. McGuinness. London, 1961.

– 1953: *Philosophische Untersuchungen / Philosophical Investigations*. Ed. by G. E. M. Anscombe, Rush Rhees, and G. H. von Wright, translated by G. E. M. Anscombe. Oxford: Basil Blackwell.

INDEX OF NAMES

INDEX OF SUBJECTS

dual-aspect theories 23f., 31, 119, 132f.,
    226–229, 231f., 256
'dualism, epistemological' (Velmans) 16
dualism, psychophysical 15f., 24, 31, 35, 64
    fn. 51, 101, 197f., 200 fn. 5

egocentricity, theoretical (methodical) 29
emotion (see also *phenomenon, noematic [cogi-
    tatum qua cogitatum], theoretical/emotional/
    practical [gerundive] features*) 130, 133, 210,
    217, 230, 237, 254
'empathy' 183
Empiricism, Logical 102
'enclave' 186f. with fn. 137, 221, 256
entailment 17, 35, 43 fn. 15, 47–50, 58, 74, 177
    fn. 118
– Hare's stronger definition of 39–41, 47–50
– Hare's weaker definition of 36–41, 46 fn. 22,
    47–50
– informal 36, 45f., 51, 86
– reflexivity of 50
– transitivity of 50
– transposability of 50
'entity' → *object in the purely formal sense*
equivalence, semantic 98, 105f., 140 with fn. 27,
    170
ESP 225 fn. 71
'esse est percipi' 21 fn. 14, 160, 200
essence(s) 28
ethics 135
– normative 27
event, neural [neurological, neuronal] → *brain
    activity*
evidence
– and criterion 118 fn. 34, 249
– empirical/non-empirical/quasi-empirical 61
    with fn. 46
– experiential 33
– experimental 61 with fn. 46
– linguistic 33, 61 with fn. 46
– linguistic forms of 187f.
– of the senses 223 fn. 67
– 'verifying' (see also *verification*) 32, 265
existence 64 fn. 50
– related to number 123 fn. 40, 190f.
experience, conscious → *consciousness, subjective*
experiments
– vs. thought-experiments 233–236

– psychophysical 233–236
explanation
– descriptive/normative 165 with fn. 80, 218
– 'mixed-perspective' (Velmans) (see also *'gap,
    explanatory'*) 226f.
– of linguistic findings 61–63
explication → *definition*
exteroception 134, 197, 201, 208 fn. 20, 226

'fact of the matter' (Quine) 29
falsehood and nonsense 94–96 with fn. 56,
    101–105, 107 fn. 11, 120 fn. 36, 120–122,
    127f. with fn. 50
falsification 183
feature → *phenomenon, noematic [cogitatum qua
    cogitatum]*
feeling → *sensation*
fiction 17, 180
'finding out' 166, 177–179, 187
force
– assertive 32 with fn. 48, 62 with fn. 47
– illocutionary 32 with fn. 48, 62 with fn. 47,
    180 fn. 122, 181
– prescriptive 78, 85
formalisation vs. generalisation 112, cf. 124
freedom (see also *action*)
– kinds of 252 with fn. 37

'gap, explanatory' (Velmans) 226f., 230f.,
    239
genidentity 128 fn. 53
genus and pseudo-genus 112, 124
'geometrical eye' (Wittgenstein) 246
geometry 48f., 73
gerundive → *phenomenon, noematic [cogitatum
    qua cogitatum]*
grammar 140f.
– 'universal' 89
– surface/depth 70, 83f., 131, 137, 188

hallucination 140 fn. 25, 176, 208
'hereby' (performative particle) and negation/
    possibilisation 84f., 126 fn. 46
Hesperus 108 fn. 12
Homo sapiens sapiens as a natural kind *sui
    generis* 131, 192–195, 242
hoping 41, 136
'horizon' (Husserl) 216f., 262